Thomas A. Mappes
Frostburg State College

Jane S. Zembaty
University of Dayton

SOCIAL ETHICS
Morality and Social Policy

McGraw-Hill Book Company
New York St. Louis San Francisco Auckland Bogotá Düsseldorf Johannesburg
London Madrid Mexico Montreal New Delhi Panama Paris São Paulo
Singapore Sydney Tokyo Toronto

Library of Congress Cataloging in Publication Data

Mappes, Thomas A
Social ethics: morality and social policy.

Includes bibliographical references.
1.   Social ethics—Addresses, essays, lectures.
2.   Ethics—Addresses, essays, lectures.   3.   Social
policy—Addresses, essays, lectures.   I.   Zembaty,
Jane S., joint author.   II.   Title.
HM216.M27   170   76-18753
ISBN 0-07-040120-9

SOCIAL ETHICS
Morality and Social Policy

567890   DODO   78321098

See Acknowledgments on pages 373–375.

Copyrights included on this page by reference.

This book was set in Melior by University Graphics, Inc.
The editors were Ellen B. Fuchs, Alice Felbinger, and James R. Belser;
the designer was Anne Canevari Green;
cover photograph by Al Green;
the production supervisor was Robert C. Pedersen.
R. R. Donnelley & Sons Company was printer and binder.

Contents

Preface   vii

iii

SEVEN / PORNOGRAPHY AND CENSORSHIP   226

EIGHT / VIOLENCE   259

NINE / ECONOMIC INJUSTICE   297

CONTENTS

Preface

Is the death penalty an ethically acceptable type of punishment? Is a society morally required to compensate members of previously discriminated-against groups by granting them preferential treatment with regard to hiring and school admissions? Is a society justified in restricting the access of consenting adults to pornographic materials? Does an affluent nation such as ours have a moral obligation to provide food for famine victims in underdeveloped nations?

The way we answer such moral questions and the social policies we adopt in keeping with our answers will directly affect our lives. It is not surprising, therefore, that in discussing these and other contemporary moral issues, rhetorical arguments are often used to elicit highly emotional responses. In order to provide a framework for an objective study of contemporary moral problems, we have attempted to bring the central issues into clear focus, while allowing the supporting arguments for widely diverse positions to be presented by those who embrace them.

Since we hope that *teachability* will prove to be the most salient characteristic of this book, each chapter includes several features calculated to enhance that quality. An introduction to each chapter both sets the ethical issues and scans the various positions together with their supporting argumentation. Every selection is prefaced by a headnote which provides both biographical data on the author and a short analysis of the underlying argument to be found in the selection. Every selection is followed by questions whose purpose is to elicit further critical analysis and discussion. Finally, each chapter concludes with a short annotated bibliography designed to guide the reader in further research.

We have tried to provide readings that are free of unnecessary technical jargon and yet introduce serious moral argumentation. Further, in order to emphasize the connection of contemporary moral problems with matters of social policy, we have introduced each set of readings with relevant legal opinions. We have taken substantial editorial license by deleting almost all the numerous citations that usually attend legal writing in order to render the legal opinions maximally readable to the nonlegal eye. Those interested in further legal research can check the acknowledgments page for the necessary bibliographical data to locate the cases in their original form.

We would be remiss not to express our indebtedness to all those whose work is reprinted in these pages. Also, we are indebted to others who in various ways have been helpful in the preparation of this book: Joy Kroeger Mappes, Jorn Bramann, Raymond M. Herbenick, John Salitrik, Alice Felbinger, Mabel Lancaster, and Sheryl Cox.

Thomas A. Mappes
Jane S. Zembaty

ONE

Abortion

As things now stand in the United States, restrictive abortion laws, except under narrowly defined conditions, have been ruled unconstitutional. Thus abortion is *legally* available, but the question of its ethical acceptability continues to be hotly debated.

SOME BACKGROUND CONSIDERATIONS

Discussions of the ethical acceptability of abortion often take for granted (1) an awareness of the various kinds of reasons that may be given for having an abortion and (2) a minimal sort of acquaintance with the biological development of a human fetus.

Reasons for Abortion. Why would a woman have an abortion? The following are among the many reasons given. (*a*) In certain extreme cases, if the fetus is allowed to develop normally and come to term, the mother herself will die. (*b*) In other cases it is not the mother's life but her health, physical or mental, that will be severely endangered if the pregnancy is allowed to continue. (*c*) There are also cases in which the pregnancy will probably, or surely, produce a severely deformed child, and (*d*) there are others in which the pregnancy is the result of rape or incest. (Abortions performed in the above four cases are commonly called *therapeutic abortions.*) (*e*) There are instances in which the mother is unmarried and there will be the social stigma of illegitimacy. (*f*) There are other instances in which having a child, or having another child, will be an unbearable financial burden. (*g*) Certainly common, and perhaps most common of all, are those instances in which having a child will interfere with the happiness of the woman, or the joint happiness of the parents, or even the joint happiness of a family unit that already includes children. Here there are almost endless possibilities: The woman may desire a professional career. A couple may be content and happy together and feel their relationship would be damaged by the intrusion of a child. Parents may have older children and not feel up to raising another child, etc.

The Biological Development of a Human Fetus. **During the course of a human pregnancy, in the nine-month period from conception to birth, the unborn entity undergoes a continual process of change and development.** *Conception* **takes place when a male germ cell (the spermatozoon) combines with a female germ cell (the ovum), resulting in a single cell (the single-cell zygote), which embodies the full genetic code, twenty-three pairs of chromosomes. The single-cell zygote soon begins a process of cellular division. The resultant multicell zygote, while continuing to grow and beginning to take shape, proceeds to move through the fallopian tube and then to undergo gradual** *implantation* **at the uterine wall. The unborn entity is formally designated a** *zygote* **up until the time that implantation is complete, almost two weeks after conception. Thereafter, until the end of the eighth week, roughly the point at which brain waves can be detected, the unborn entity is formally designated an** *embryo.* **It is in this embryonic period that organ systems and other human characteristics begin to undergo noticeable development. From the end of the eighth week until birth, the unborn entity is formally designated a** *fetus.* **(The term "fetus," however, is commonly used as a general term to designate the unborn entity, whatever its stage of development.) Two other points in the development of the fetus are especially noteworthy as relevant to discussions of abortion. Somewhere between the thirteenth and the twentieth weeks there occurs** *quickening,* **the point at which the mother begins to feel the movements of the fetus. And somewhere around the twenty-fourth week the fetus reaches** *viability,* **the point at which it is capable of surviving outside the womb.**

THE ETHICAL ISSUE

Up *to what point of fetal development,* if any, and *for what reasons,* if any, is abortion ethically acceptable? Some hold that abortion is *never* ethically acceptable, or at most is acceptable only where abortion is necessary to save the life of the mother. This view is frequently termed the *conservative* view on abortion. Others hold that abortion is *always* ethically acceptable—at any point of fetal development and for any reason. This view is frequently termed the *liberal* view on abortion. Still others are anxious to defend more *moderate* views, holding that abortion is ethically acceptable up to a certain point of fetal development *and/or* holding that *some* reasons provide a sufficient justification for abortion whereas others do not. There is one point of almost universal agreement: The answer that one gives to the issue of the ethical accepta-bility of abortion is largely dependent, though perhaps not exclusively so, on one's view of the *moral status* of the fetus.

THE MORAL STATUS OF THE FETUS

The concept of moral status is commonly explicated in terms of rights. On this construal, to say that a fetus has moral status is to say that the fetus has rights. What kind of rights, if any, does the fetus have? Does it have the same rights as more visible humans, and thus *full moral status,* as conservatives contend? Does it have some measure of rights, and thus a subsidiary or *partial moral status,* as some moderates contend? Or does it have no rights, and thus *no moral status,* as liberals contend? If the fetus has no rights, the liberal argument proceeds, then it does not have any more right to life than a piece of tissue such as an appendix, and an abortion is no more morally objectionable than an appendec-tomy. If the fetus has the same rights as any other human being, the conservative argument proceeds, then it has the same right to life as the latter and an abortion, except perhaps when the mother's life is in danger, is as morally objectionable as any other murder.

In contrast with the assignment of either full moral status or no moral status, if the fetus is assigned a subsidiary or *partial* moral status, then the issue of the ethical acceptability of abortion no longer appears so clear-cut. For example, if the fetus is thought to have some measure of a right to life, then there may well be a conflict with the mother's right to control her body. In such a case it is not immediately clear which right should take precedence. Does some measure of a right to life outweigh a full right to control one's body? The same set of difficulties is apparent when the question is raised in the following way: What reasons provide a sufficient justification for abortion? Is the mental health of the mother a strong enough reason? Is the stigma of illegitimacy a strong enough reason? Is the mere convenience of the mother a strong enough reason? It is the characteristic burden of a moderate view based on the concept of partial moral status to explicate the nature of such partial moral status and to show how the interest of one with partial moral status is to be weighed against the interest of those with full moral status.

"DRAWING THE LINE"

Discussions of the moral status of the fetus often refer directly to the biological development of the fetus and pose the question: At what point in the continuous development of the fetus do we have a human life? In the context of such discussions, "human" implies full moral status, "nonhuman" implies no moral status, and any notion of partial moral status is systematically excluded. To distinguish the human from the

3

nonhuman, to "draw the line," and to do so in a nonarbitrary way, is the central matter of concern. The *conservative* view on abortion holds that the line must be drawn at conception. Usually the conservative argues that conception is the only point at which the line can be nonarbitrarily drawn. Against attempts to draw the line at points such as implantation, quickening, viability, or birth, the conservative presses considerations of continuity in the development of the fetus. The conservative is sometimes said to employ "slippery slope arguments," that is, to argue that a line cannot be securely drawn anywhere along the path of fetal development. It is said that the line will inescapably slide back to the point of conception in order to find objective support. The conservative view as here outlined is defended in the selection by John T. Noonan.

The *liberal* view, on the other hand, is that the fetus remains nonhuman even in its most advanced stages of development. The liberal, of course, does not mean to deny that a fetus is biologically a human fetus. Rather the claim is that the fetus is not human in any morally significant sense, that is, that the fetus has no moral status. The essence of the liberal argument is that the moral community includes only *persons,* that a fetus is not a person, and thus that a fetus is not a member of the moral community. The liberal view as here outlined is defended in the selection by Mary Anne Warren.

In addition to these two extreme views on drawing the line, there is also the possibility of a more moderate view, in fact a whole continuum of moderate views. Whereas the conservative draws the line between human and nonhuman existence at conception and the liberal draws that same line at birth (or sometime thereafter), a moderate view may be generated by drawing the line somewhere between these two extremes. For example, one might draw the line where brain waves begin, or at quickening, etc. Viability is a point that seems especially attractive to many, though it is the burden of any such view to show that the point specified is a nonarbitrary one. Once such a point has been specified, however, it is then typically thought that abortion is ethically acceptable before that point, ethically unacceptable after that point.

T. A. M.

Justice Harry Blackmun

MAJORITY OPINION IN *ROE v. WADE*

Biographical Information. *Harry Blackmun (b. 1908), associate justice of the United States Supreme Court, is a graduate of Harvard Law School.*

After some fifteen years in private practice he became legal counsel to the Mayo Clinic (1950–1959). Justice Blackmun also served as United States circuit judge (1959–1970) before his appointment in 1970 to the Supreme Court.

Argument in the Selection. *In this case, a pregnant single woman, suing under the fictitious name of Jane Roe, challenged the constitutionality of the existing Texas criminal abortion law. According to the Texas Penal Code, the performance of an abortion, except to save the life of the mother, constituted a crime that was punishable by a prison sentence of two to five years. At the time this case was finally resolved by the Supreme Court, abortion legislation varied widely from state to state. Some states, principally New York, had already legalized abortion on demand. Most other states, however, had legalized various forms of therapeutic abortion but had retained some measure of restrictive abortion legislation.*

Justice Blackmun, writing an opinion concurred in by six other justices, argues that a woman's decision to terminate a pregnancy is encompassed by a right to privacy—but only up to a certain point in the development of the fetus. As the right to privacy is not an absolute right, it must yield at some point to the state's legitimate interests. Justice Blackmun contends that the state has a legitimate interest in protecting the health of the mother and that this interest becomes compelling at approximately the end of the first trimester in the development of the fetus. He also contends that the state has a legitimate interest in protecting potential life and that this interest becomes compelling at the point of viability.

It is . . . apparent that at common law, at the time of the adoption of our Constitution, and throughout the major portion of the 19th century, abortion was viewed with less disfavor than under most American statutes currently in effect. Phrasing it another way, a woman enjoyed a substantially broader right to terminate a pregnancy than she does in most States today. At least with respect to the early stage of pregnancy, and very possibly without such a limitation, the opportunity to make this choice was present in this country well into the 19th century. Even later, the law continued for some time to treat less punitively an abortion procured in early pregnancy. . . .

Three reasons have been advanced to explain historically the enactment of criminal abortion laws in the 19th century and to justify their continued existence.

It has been argued occasionally that these laws were the product of a Victorian social concern to discourage illicit sexual conduct. Texas, however, does not advance this justification in the present case, and it appears that no court or commentator has taken the argument seriously. . . .

A second reason is concerned with abortion as a medical procedure. When most criminal abortion laws were first enacted, the procedure was a hazardous one for the woman. This was particularly true prior to the development of antisepsis.

Antiseptic techniques, of course, were based on discoveries by Lister, Pasteur, and others first announced in 1867, but were not generally accepted and employed until about the turn of the century. Abortion mortality was high. Even after 1900, and perhaps until as late as the development of antibiotics in the 1940's, standard modern techniques such as dilation and curettage were not nearly so safe as they are today. Thus it has been argued that a State's real concern in enacting a criminal abortion law was to protect the pregnant woman, that is, to restrain her from submitting to a procedure that placed her life in serious jeopardy.

Modern medical techniques have altered this situation. Appellants and various *amici* refer to medical data indicating that abortion in early pregnancy, that is, prior to the end of first trimester, although not without its risk, is now relatively safe. Mortality rates for women undergoing early abortions, where the procedure is legal, appear to be as low as or lower than the rates for normal childbirth. Consequently, any interest of the State in protecting the woman from an inherently hazardous procedure, except when it would be equally dangerous for her to forgo it, has largely disappeared. Of course, important state interests in the area of health and medical standards do remain. The State has a legitimate interest in seeing to it that abortion, like any other medical procedure, is performed under circumstances that insure maximum safety for the patient. This interest obviously extends at least to the performing physician and his staff, to the facilities involved, to the availability of after-care, and to adequate provision for any complication or emergency that might arise. The prevalence of high mortality rates at illegal "abortion mills" strengthens, rather than weakens, the State's interest in regulating the conditions under which abortions are performed. Moreover, the risk to the woman increases as her pregnancy continues. Thus the State retains a definite interest in protecting the woman's own health and safety when an abortion is performed at a late stage of pregnancy.

The third reason is the State's interest—some phrase it in terms of duty—in protecting prenatal life. Some of the argument for this justification rests on the theory that a new human life is present from the moment of conception. The State's interest and general obligation to protect life then extends, it is argued, to prenatal life. Only when the life of the pregnant mother herself is at stake, balanced against the life she carries within her, should the interest of the embryo or fetus not prevail. Logically, of course, a legitimate state interest in this area need not stand or fall on acceptance of the belief that life begins at conception or at some other point prior to live birth. In assessing the State's interest, recognition may be given to the less rigid claim that as long as at least *potential* life is involved, the State may assert interests beyond the protection of the pregnant woman alone.

Parties challenging state abortion laws have sharply disputed in some courts the contention that a purpose of these laws, when enacted, was to protect prenatal life. Pointing to the absence of legislative history to support the contention, they claim that most state laws were designed solely to protect the woman. Because medical advances have lessened this concern, at least with respect to abortion in early pregnancy, they argue that with respect to such abortions the laws can no longer be justified by any state interest. There is some scholarly support for this view of original purpose. The few state courts called upon to interpret their laws in the late 19th and early 20th centuries did focus on the State's interest in protecting the woman's health rather than in preserving the embryo and fetus. . . .

The Constitution does not explicitly mention any right of privacy. In a line of decisions, however, going back perhaps as far as Union Pacific R. Co. v. Botsford (1891), the Court has recognized that a right of personal privacy, or a guarantee of certain areas or zones of privacy, does exist under the Constitution. In varying contexts the Court or individual Justices have indeed found at least the roots of that right in the First Amendment, . . . in the Fourth and Fifth Amendments . . . in the penumbras of the Bill of Rights . . . in the Ninth Amendment . . . or in the concept of liberty guaranteed by the first section of the Fourteenth Amendment. . . . These decisions make it clear that only personal rights that can be deemed "fundamental" or "implicit in the concept of ordered liberty," . . . are included in this guarantee of personal privacy. They also make it clear that the right has some extension to activities relating to marriage, . . . procreation, . . . contraception, . . . family relationships, . . . and child rearing and education, . . .

This right of privacy, whether it be founded in the Fourteenth Amendment's concept of personal liberty and restrictions upon state action, as we feel it is, or, as the District Court determined, in the Ninth Amendment's reservation of rights to the people, is broad enough to encompass a woman's decision whether or not to terminate her pregnancy. . . .

. . . [A]ppellants and some *amici* argue that the woman's right is absolute and that she is entitled to terminate her pregnancy at whatever time, in whatever way, and for whatever reason she alone chooses. With this we do not agree. Appellants' arguments that Texas either has no valid interest at all in regulating the abortion decision, or no interest strong enough to support any limitation upon the woman's sole determination, is unpersuasive. The Court's decisions recognizing a right of privacy also acknowledge that some state regulation in areas protected by that right is appropriate. As noted above, a state may properly assert important interests in safe-guarding health, in maintaining medical standards, and in protecting potential life. At some point in pregnancy, these respective interests become sufficiently compelling to sustain regulation of the factors that govern the abortion decision. The privacy right involved, therefore, cannot be said to be absolute. . . .

We therefore conclude that the right of personal privacy includes the abortion decision, but that this right is not unqualified and must be considered against important state interests in regulation.

We note that those federal and state courts that have recently considered abortion law challenges have reached the same conclusion. . . .

Although the results are divided, most of these courts have agreed that the right of privacy, however based, is broad enough to cover the abortion decision; that the right, nonetheless, is not absolute and is subject to some limitations; and that at some point the state interests as to protection of health, medical standards, and prenatal life, become dominant. We agree with this approach. . . .

The appellee and certain *amici* argue that the fetus is a "person" within the language and meaning of the Fourteenth Amendment. In support of this they outline at length and in detail the well-known facts of fetal development. If this suggestion of personhood is established, the appellant's case, of course, collapses, for the fetus' right to life is then guaranteed specifically by the Amendment. The appellant conceded as much on reargument. On the other hand, the appellee conceded on reargument that no case could be cited that holds that a fetus is a person within the meaning of the Fourteenth Amendment. . . .

All this, together with our observation, *supra,* that throughout the major portion of the 19th century prevailing legal abortion practices were far freer than they are today, persuades us that the word "person," as used in the Fourteenth Amendment, does not include the unborn. . . . Indeed, our decision in United States v. Vuitch (1971), inferentially is to the same effect, for we there would not have indulged in statutory interpretation favorable to abortion in specified circumstances if the necessary consequence was the termination of life entitled to Fourteenth Amendment protection.

. . . As we have intimated above, it is reasonable and appropriate for a State to decide that at some point in time another interest, that of health of the mother or that of potential human life, becomes significantly involved. The woman's privacy is no longer sole and any right of privacy she possesses must be measured accordingly.

Texas urges that, apart from the Fourteenth Amendment, life begins at conception and is present throughout pregnancy, and that, therefore, the State has a compelling interest in protecting that life from and after conception. We need not resolve the difficult question of when life begins. When those trained in the respective disciplines of medicine, philosophy, and theology are unable to arrive at any consensus, the judiciary, at this point in the development of man's knowledge, is not in a position to speculate as to the answer.

It should be sufficient to note briefly the wide divergence of thinking on this most sensitive and difficult question. There has always been strong support for the view that life does not begin until live birth. This was the belief of the Stoics. It appears to be the predominant, though not the unanimous, attitude of the Jewish faith. It may be taken to represent also the position of a large segment of the Protestant community, insofar as that can be ascertained; organized groups that have taken a formal position on the abortion issue have generally regarded abortion as a matter for the conscience of the individual and her family. As we have noted, the common law found greater significance in quickening. Physicians and their scientific colleagues have regarded that event with less interest and have tended to focus either upon conception or upon live birth or upon the interim point at which the fetus becomes "viable," that is, potentially able to live outside the mother's womb, albeit with artificial aid. Viability is usually placed at about seven months (28 weeks) but may occur earlier, even at 24 weeks. . . .

In areas other than criminal abortion the law has been reluctant to endorse any theory that life, as we recognize it, begins before live birth or to accord legal rights to the unborn except in narrowly defined situations and except when the rights are contingent upon live birth. . . . In short, the unborn have never been recognized in the law as persons in the whole sense.

In view of all this, we do not agree that, by adopting one theory of life, Texas may override the rights of the pregnant woman that are at stake. We repeat, however, that the State does have an important and legitimate interest in preserving and protecting the health of the pregnant woman, whether she be a resident of the State or a nonresident who seeks medical consultation and treatment there, and that it has still *another* important and legitimate interest in protecting the potentiality of human life. These interests are separate and distinct. Each grows in substantiality as the woman approaches term and, at a point during pregnancy, each becomes "compelling."

With respect to the State's important and legitimate interest in the health of

8

the mother, the "compelling" point, in the light of present medical knowledge, is at approximately the end of the first trimester. This is so because of the now established medical fact . . . that until the end of the first trimester mortality in abortion is less than mortality in normal childbirth. It follows that, from and after this point, a State may regulate the abortion procedure to the extent that the regulation reasonably relates to the preservation and protection of maternal health. Examples of permissible state regulation in this area are requirements as to the qualifications of the person who is to perform the abortion; as to the licensure of that person; as to the facility in which the procedure is to be performed, that is, whether it must be a hospital or may be a clinic or some other place of less-than-hospital status; as to the licensing of the facility; and the like.

This means, on the other hand, that, for the period of pregnancy prior to this "compelling" point, the attending physician, in consultation with his patient, is free to determine, without regulation by the State, that in his medical judgment the patient's pregnancy should be terminated. If that decision is reached, the judgment may be effectuated by an abortion free of interference by the State.

With respect to the State's important and legitimate interest in potential life, the "compelling" point is at viability. This is so because the fetus then presumably has the capability of meaningful life outside the mother's womb. State regulation protective of fetal life after viability thus has both logical and biological justifications. If the State is interested in protecting fetal life after viability, it may go so far as to proscribe abortion during that period except when it is necessary to preserve the life or health of the mother. . . .

To summarize and repeat:

1. A state criminal abortion statute of the current Texas type, that excepts from criminality only a *life saving* procedure on behalf of the mother, without regard to pregnancy stage and without recognition of the other interests involved, is violative of the Due Process Clause of the Fourteenth Amendment.

(a) For the stage prior to approximately the end of the first trimester, the abortion decision and its effectuation must be left to the medical judgment of the pregnant woman's attending physician.

(b) For the stage subsequent to approximately the end of the first trimester, the State, in promoting its interest in the health of the mother, may, if it chooses, regulate the abortion procedure in ways that are reasonably related to maternal health.

(c) For the stage subsequent to viability the State, in promoting its interest in the potentiality of human life, may, if it chooses, regulate, and even proscribe, abortion except where it is necessary, in appropriate medical judgment, for the preservation of the life or health of the mother.

2. The State may define the term "physician," as it has been employed in the preceding numbered paragraphs of this Part XI of this opinion, to mean only a physician currently licensed by the State, and may proscribe any abortion by a person who is not a physician as so defined.

. . . The decision leaves the State free to place increasing restrictions on abortion as the period of pregnancy lengthens, so long as those restrictions are tailored to the recognized state interests. The decision vindicates the right of the physician to administer medical treatment according to his professional judgment up to the points where important state interests provide compelling justifications for intervention. Up to those points the abortion decision in all its aspects is inherently, and primarily, a medical decision, and basic responsibility for it must rest with the physician. If an individual practitioner abuses the privilege of exercising proper medical judgment, the usual remedies, judicial and intraprofessional, are available. . . .

QUESTIONS

1. Justice Blackmun contends that the state's legitimate interest in protecting the health of the mother becomes *compelling* at the end of the first trimester. Does the Court's choice of this particular point as "compelling" have any substantial justification, or is the choice fundamentally arbitrary?

2. Justice Blackmun contends that the state's legitimate interest in protecting potential life becomes *compelling* at the point of viability. Does the Court's choice of this particular point as "compelling" have any substantial justification, or is the choice fundamentally arbitrary?

3. Justice Blackmun *explicitly* disavows entering into philosophical speculation on the problem of the beginning of human life. To what extent could it be said that he *implicitly* takes a philosophical position on this problem?

Justice Byron R. White

DISSENTING OPINION IN *ROE v. WADE*

Biographical Information. *Byron R. White (b. 1917), associate justice of the United States Supreme Court, first achieved national attention as an all-American football player at the University of Colorado. Thereupon he accepted a Rhodes scholarship for study at Oxford University (England). A graduate of Yale Law School, Justice White remained in private practice until 1960, served as United States deputy attorney general (1961–1962), and was appointed to the Supreme Court in 1962.*

Argument in the Selection. *Justice White, writing an opinion concurred in by Justice Rehnquist, contends that the Court, in sanctioning the abortion of a pre-viable fetus for any reason whatever, has overstepped its legitimate bounds and manufactured a "new constitutional right for pregnant mothers." He maintains that there is no constitutional warrant for denying to the legislatures of the states the power to weigh the interests of the mother versus the interests of the fetus and to legislate accordingly.*

At the heart of the controversy in these cases are those recurring pregnancies that pose no danger whatsoever to the life or health of the mother but are nevertheless unwanted for any one or more of a variety of reasons—convenience, family planning, economics, dislike of children, the embarrassment of illegitimacy, etc. The common claim before us is that for any one of such reasons, or for no reason at all, and without asserting or claiming any threat to life or health, any woman is entitled to an abortion at her request if she is able to find a medical advisor willing to undertake the procedure.

The Court for the most part sustains this position: During the period prior to the time the fetus becomes viable, the Constitution of the United States values the convenience, whim or caprice of the putative mother more than the life or potential life of the fetus; the Constitution, therefore, guarantees the right to an abortion as against any state law or policy seeking to protect the fetus from an abortion not prompted by more compelling reasons of the mother.

With all due respect, I dissent. I find nothing in the language or history of the Constitution to support the Court's judgment. The Court simply fashions and announces a new constitutional right for pregnant mothers and, with scarcely any reason or authority for its action, invests that right with sufficient substance to override most existing state abortion statutes. The upshot is that the people and the legislatures of the 50 States are constitutionally disentitled to weigh the relative importance of the continued existence and development of the fetus on the one hand against a spectrum of possible impacts on the mother on the other hand. As an exercise of raw judicial power, the Court perhaps has authority to do what it does today; but in my view its judgment is an improvident and extravagant exercise of the power of judicial review which the Constitution extends to this Court.

The Court apparently values the convenience of the pregnant mother more than the continued existence and development of the life or potential life which she carries. Whether or not I might agree with that marshalling of values, I can in no event join the Court's judgment because I find no constitutional warrant for imposing such an order of priorities on the people and legislatures of the States. In a sensitive area such as this, involving as it does issues over which reasonable men may easily and heatedly differ, I cannot accept the Court's exercise of its clear power of choice by interposing a constitutional barrier to state efforts to protect human life and by investing mothers and doctors with the constitutionally protected right to exterminate it. This issue, for the most part, should be left with the people and to the political processes the people have devised to govern their affairs.

It is my view, therefore, that the Texas statute is not constitutionally infirm because it denies abortions to those who seek to serve only their convenience rather than to protect their life or health. . . .

QUESTIONS

1. It has been suggested by some advocates of abortion on demand that the dissenting opinion of Justice White reveals an attitude of insensitivity to the personal significance of an unwanted pregnancy. Does Justice White's opinion manifest such an attitude?

2. If the Court as a whole had agreed with Justice White, then there would have been no constitutional impediment to restrictive abortion laws. Constitutional grounds aside, would you favor restrictive or permissive legislation? To what extent and on what grounds?

John T. Noonan, Jr.

AN ALMOST ABSOLUTE VALUE IN HISTORY

Biographical Information. *John T. Noonan, Jr. (b. 1926), is presently professor of law at the University of California at Berkeley. His academic interests extend beyond matters of law to philosophical and theological issues, and his intellectual allegiance in this regard is with the Roman Catholic tradition. Among his books are* Contraception: A History of Its Treatment by the Catholic Theologians and Canonists *(1965) and* The Morality of Abortion *(1970).*

Argument in the Selection. *Noonan, arguing the conservative view on abortion, immediately raises the question of how to determine the humanity of a being. In an updated version of the traditional theological view he contends that, if a being is conceived by human parents and thereby has a human genetic code, then that being is a human being. Conception is the point at which the nonhuman becomes the human. Noonan argues that other alleged criteria of humanity are inadequate. He also argues, primarily through an analysis of probabilities, that his own criterion of humanity is objectively based and nonarbitrary. Finally, Noonan contends, once the humanity of the fetus is recognized, we must judge abortion morally wrong, except in those rare cases where the mother's life is in danger.*

The most fundamental question involved in the long history of thought on abortion is: How do you determine the humanity of a being? To phrase the question that way is to put in comprehensive humanistic terms what the theologians either dealt with as an explicitly theological question under the heading of "ensoulment" or dealt with implicitly in their treatment of abortion. The Christian position as it originated did not depend on a narrow theological or philosophical concept. It had no relation to theories of infant baptism. It appealed to no special theory of instantaneous ensoulment. It took the world's view on ensoulment as that view changed from Aristotle to Zacchia. There was, indeed, theological influence affecting the theory of ensoulment finally adopted, and, of course, ensoulment itself was a theological concept, so that the position was always explained in theological terms. But the theological notion of ensoulment could easily be translated into humanistic language by substituting "human" for "rational soul''; the problem of knowing when a man is a man is common to theology and humanism.

If one steps outside the specific categories used by the theologians, the answer they gave can be analyzed as a refusal to discriminate among human beings on the basis of their varying potentialities. Once conceived, the being was recognized as man because he had man's potential. The criterion for humanity, thus, was simple and all-embracing: if you are conceived by human parents, you are human.

The strength of this position may be tested by a review of some of the other distinctions offered in the contemporary controversy over legalizing abortion. Perhaps the most popular distinction is in terms of viability. Before an age of so many months, the fetus is not viable, that is, it cannot be removed from the mother's womb and live apart from her. To that extent, the life of the fetus is absolutely dependent on the life of the mother. This dependence is made the basis of denying recognition to its humanity.

There are difficulties with this distinction. One is that the perfection of artificial incubation may make the fetus viable at any time: it may be removed and artificially sustained. Experiments with animals already show that such a procedure is possible. This hypothetical extreme case relates to an actual difficulty: there is considerable elasticity to the idea of viability. Mere length of life is not an exact measure. The viability of the fetus depends on the extent of its anatomical and functional development. The weight and length of the fetus are better guides to the state of its development than age, but weight and length vary. Moreover, different racial groups have different ages at which their fetuses are viable. Some evidence, for example, suggests that Negro fetuses mature more quickly than white fetuses. If viability is the norm, the standard would vary with race and with many individual circumstances.

The most important objection to this approach is that dependence is not ended by viability. The fetus is still absolutely dependent on someone's care in order to continue existence; indeed a child of one or three or even five years of age is absolutely dependent on another's care for existence; uncared for, the older fetus or the younger child will die as surely as the early fetus detached from the mother. The unsubstantial lessening in dependence at viability does not seem to signify any special acquisition of humanity.

A second distinction has been attempted in terms of experience. A being who has had experience, has lived and suffered, who possesses memories, is more human than one who has not. Humanity depends on formation by experience. The fetus is thus "unformed" in the most basic human sense.

This distinction is not serviceable for the embryo which is already experiencing and reacting. The embryo is responsive to touch after eight weeks and at least at that point is experiencing. At an earlier stage the zygote is certainly alive and responding to its environment. The distinction may also be challenged by the rare case where aphasia has erased adult memory: has it erased humanity? More fundamentally, this distinction leaves even the older fetus or the younger child to be treated as an unformed inhuman thing. Finally, it is not clear why experience as such confers humanity. It could be argued that certain central experiences such as loving or learning are necessary to make a man human. But then human beings who have failed to love or to learn might be excluded from the class called man.

A third distinction is made by appeal to the sentiments of adults. If a fetus dies, the grief of the parents is not the grief they would have for a living child. The fetus is an unnamed "it" till birth, and is not perceived as personality until at least the fourth month of existence when movements in the womb manifest a vigorous presence demanding joyful recognition by the parents.

Yet feeling is notoriously an unsure guide to the humanity of others. Many groups of humans have had difficulty in feeling that persons of another tongue, color, religion, sex, are as human as they. Apart from reactions to alien groups, we mourn the loss of a ten-year-old boy more than the loss of his one-day-old brother or his 90-year-old grandfather. The difference felt and the grief expressed vary with the potentialities extinguished, or the experience wiped out; they do not seem to point to any substantial difference in the humanity of baby, boy, or grandfather.

Distinctions are also made in terms of sensation by the parents. The embryo is felt within the womb only after about the fourth month. The embryo is seen only at birth. What can be neither seen nor felt is different from what is tangible. If the fetus cannot be seen or touched at all, it cannot be perceived as man.

Yet experience shows that sight is even more untrustworthy than feeling in determining humanity. By sight, color became an appropriate index for saying who was a man, and the evil of racial discrimination was given foundation. Nor can touch provide the test; a being confined by sickness, "out of touch" with others, does not thereby seem to lose his humanity. To the extent that touch still has appeal as a criterion, it appears to be a survival of the old English idea of "quickening"—a possible mistranslation of the Latin *animatus* used in the canon law. To that extent touch as a criterion seems to be dependent on the Aristotelian notion of ensoulment, and to fall when this notion is discarded.

Finally, a distinction is sought in social visibility. The fetus is not socially perceived as human. It cannot communicate with others. Thus, both subjectively and objectively, it is not a member of society. As moral rules are rules for the behavior of members of society to each other, they cannot be made for behavior toward what is not yet a member. Excluded from the society of men, the fetus is excluded from the humanity of men.

By force of the argument from the consequences, this distinction is to be rejected. It is more subtle than that founded on an appeal to physical sensation, but it is equally dangerous in its implications. If humanity depends on social recognition, individuals or whole groups may be dehumanized by being denied any status in their society. Such a fate is fictionally portrayed in 1984 and has actually been the lot of many men in many societies. In the Roman empire, for example, condemnation to slavery meant the practical denial of most human rights; in the Chinese Communist world, landlords have been classified as enemies of the people and so treated as nonpersons by the state. Humanity does not depend on social recognition, though often the failure of society to recognize the prisoner, the alien, the heterodox as human has led to the destruction of human beings. Anyone conceived by a man and a woman is human. Recognition of this condition by society follows a real event in the objective order, however imperfect and halting the recognition. Any attempt to limit humanity to exclude some group runs the risk of furnishing authority and precedent for excluding other groups in the name of the consciousness or perception of the controlling group in the society.

A philosopher may reject the appeal to the humanity of the fetus because he views "humanity" as a secular view of the soul and because he doubts the

14

existence of anything real and objective which can be identified as humanity. One answer to such a philosopher is to ask how he reasons about moral questions without supposing that there is a sense in which he and the others of whom he speaks are human. Whatever group is taken as the society which determines who may be killed is thereby taken as human. A second answer is to ask if he does not believe that there is a right and wrong way of deciding moral questions. If there is such a difference, experience may be appealed to: to decide who is human on the basis of the sentiment of a given society has led to consequences which rational men would characterize as monstrous.

The rejection of the attempted distinctions based on viability and visibility, experience and feeling, may be buttressed by the following considerations: Moral judgments often rest on distinctions, but if the distinctions are not to appear arbitrary fiat, they should relate to some real difference in probabilities. There is a kind of continuity in all life, but the earlier stages of the elements of human life possess tiny probabilities of development. Consider for example, the spermatozoa in any normal ejaculate: There are about 200,000,000 in any single ejaculate, of which one has a chance of developing into a zygote. Consider the oocytes which may become ova: there are 100,000 to 1,000,000 oocytes in a female infant, of which a maximum of 390 are ovulated. But once spermatozoon and ovum meet and the conceptus is formed, such studies as have been made show that roughly in only 20 percent of the cases will spontaneous abortion occur. In other words, the chances are about 4 out of 5 that this new being will develop. At this stage in the life of the being there is a sharp shift in probabilities, an immense jump in potentialities. To make a distinction between the rights of spermatozoa and the rights of the fertilized ovum is to respond to an enormous shift in possibilities. For about twenty days after conception the egg may split to form twins or combine with another egg to form a chimera, but the probability of either event happening is very small.

It may be asked, What does a change in biological probabilities have to do with establishing humanity? The argument from probabilities is not aimed at establishing humanity but at establishing an objective discontinuity which may be taken into account in moral discourse. As life itself is a matter of probabilities, as most moral reasoning is an estimate of probabilities, so it seems in accord with the structure of reality and the nature of moral thought to found a moral judgment on the change in probabilities at conception. The appeal to probabilities is the most commonsensical of arguments, to a greater or smaller degree all of us base our actions on probabilities, and in morals, as in law, prudence and negligence are often measured by the account one has taken of the probabilities. If the chance is 200,000,000 to 1 that the movement in the bushes into which you shoot is a man's, I doubt if many persons would hold you careless in shooting; but if the chances are 4 out of 5 that the movement is a human being's, few would acquit you of blame. Would the argument be different if only one out of ten children conceived came to term? Of course this argument would be different. This argument is an appeal to probabilities that actually exist, not to any and all states of affairs which may be imagined.

The probabilities as they do exist do not show the humanity of the embryo in the sense of a demonstration in logic any more than the probabilities of the movement in the bush being a man demonstrate beyond all doubt that the being is a man. The appeal is a "buttressing" consideration, showing the plausibility of the standard adopted. The argument focuses on the decisional factor in any moral judgment and assumes that part of the business of a moralist is drawing lines. One evidence of the nonarbitrary character of the line drawn is the difference of probabilities on either side of it. If a spermatozoon is destroyed, one destroys a being which had a chance of far less than 1 in 200 million of developing into a reasoning being, possessed of the genetic code, a heart and other organs, and capable of pain. If a fetus is destroyed, one destroys a being already possessed of the genetic code, organs, and sensitivity to pain, and one which had an 80 percent chance of developing further into a baby outside the womb who, in time, would reason.

The positive argument for conception as the decisive moment of humanization is that at conception the new being receives the genetic code. It is this genetic information which determines his characteristics, which is the biological carrier of the possibility of human wisdom, which makes him a self-evolving being. A being with a human genetic code is man.

This review of current controversy over the humanity of the fetus emphasizes what a fundamental question the theologians resolved in asserting the inviolability of the fetus. To regard the fetus as possessed of equal rights with other humans was not, however, to decide every case where abortion might be employed. It did decide the case where the argument was that the fetus should be aborted for its own good. To say a being was human was to say it had a destiny to decide for itself which could not be taken from it by another man's decision. But human beings with equal rights often come in conflict with each other, and some decision must be made as whose claims are to prevail. Cases of conflict involving the fetus are different only in two respects: the total inability of the fetus to speak for itself and the fact that the right of the fetus regularly at stake is the right to life itself.

The approach taken by the theologians to these conflicts was articulated in terms of "direct" and "indirect." Again, to look at what they were doing from outside their categories, they may be said to have been drawing lines or "balancing values." "Direct" and "indirect" are spatial metaphors; "line-drawing" is another. "To weigh" or "to balance" values is a metaphor of a more complicated mathematical sort hinting at the process which goes on in moral judgments. All the metaphors suggest that, in the moral judgments made, comparisons were necessary, that no value completely controlled. The principle of double effect was no doctrine fallen from heaven, but a method of analysis appropriate where two relative values were being compared. In Catholic moral theology, as it developed, life even of the innocent was not taken as an absolute. Judgments on acts affecting life issued from a process of weighing. In the weighing, the fetus was always given a value greater than zero, always a value separate and independent from its parents. This valuation was crucial and fundamental in all Christian thought on the subject and marked it off from any approach which considered that only the parents' interests needed to be considered.

Even with the fetus weighed as human, one interest could be weighed as equal or superior: that of the mother in her own life. The casuists between 1450 and 1895 were willing to weigh this interest as superior. Since 1895, that interest was given decisive weight only in the two special cases of the cancerous uterus and the ectopic pregnancy. In both of these cases the fetus itself had little chance of survival even if the abortion were not performed. As the balance was once struck in favor of the mother whenever her life was endangered, it could be so struck again. The balance reached between 1895 and 1930 attempted prudentially and pastorally to forestall a multitude of exceptions for interests less than life.

The perception of the humanity of the fetus and the weighing of fetal rights against other human rights constituted the work of the moral analysts. But what spirit animated their abstract judgments? For the Christian community it was the injunction of Scripture to love your neighbor as yourself. The fetus as human was a neighbor; his life had parity with one's own. The commandment gave life to what otherwise would have been only rational calculation.

The commandment could be put in humanistic as well as theological terms: Do not injure your fellow man without reason. In these terms, once the humanity of the fetus is perceived, abortion is never right except in self-defense. When life must be taken to save life, reason alone cannot say that a mother must prefer a child's life to her own. With this exception, now of great rarity, abortion violates the rational humanist tenet of the equality of human lives.

For Christians the commandment to love had received a special imprint in that the exemplar proposed of love was the love of the Lord for his disciples. In the light given by this example, self-sacrifice carried to the point of death seemed in the extreme situations not without meaning. In the less extreme cases, preference for one's own interests to the life of another seemed to express cruelty or selfishness irreconcilable with the demands of love.

QUESTIONS

1. Noonan discusses several alternative proposals for discriminating the human from the nonhuman, dismissing all of them in favor of his own proposal. If you think he may have dismissed any of the rejected proposals without sufficient reason, advance an argument in support of that proposal.

2. Argue for or against the following claim: Conception is an objectively based and nonarbitrary point at which to draw the line between the human and the nonhuman.

3. Evaluate the following argument: Let it be admitted that the fetus has full moral status from the moment of conception. Nevertheless, abortion in the case of rape is ethically acceptable because no person (i.e., the fetus) has the right to use another person's body, unless that right has been *freely* extended from the latter to the former.

Mary Anne Warren

ON THE MORAL AND LEGAL STATUS OF ABORTION

Biographical Information. *Mary Anne Warren is a philosopher who has taught at Sonoma State College (California) and now teaches at San Francisco State University. The article reprinted here first appeared in an issue of the Monist (January 1973) that was oriented around ethical, social, and political issues surrounding women's liberation.*

Argument in the Selection. Warren, defending the liberal view on abortion, promptly distinguishes two senses of the term "human": (1) One is human in the genetic sense when one is a member of the biological species Homo sapiens. (2) One is human in the moral sense when one is a full-fledged member of the moral community. Warren attacks the presupposition underlying Noonan's argument against abortion—that the fetus is human in the moral sense. She contends that the moral community, the set of beings with full and equal moral rights, consists of all and only people (persons). (Thus she takes the concept of personhood to be equivalent to the concept of humanity in the moral sense. After analyzing the concept of person, she concludes that a fetus is so unlike a person as to have no significant right to life. Nor, she argues, does the fetus's potential for being a person provide us any basis for ascribing to it any significant right to life. It follows, she contends, that a woman's right to obtain an abortion is absolute. Abortion is morally justified at any stage of fetal development. It also follows, she contends, that no legislation against abortion can be justified on the grounds of protecting the rights of the fetus.

The question which we must answer in order to produce a satisfactory solution to the problem of the moral status of abortion is this: How are we to define the moral community, the set of beings with full and equal moral rights, such that we can decide whether a human fetus is a member of this community or not? What sort of entity, exactly, has the inalienable rights to life, liberty, and the pursuit of happiness? Jefferson attributed these rights to all *men*, and it may or may not be fair to suggest that he intended to attribute them *only* to men. Perhaps he ought to have attributed them to all human beings. If so, then we arrive, first, at Noonan's problem of defining what makes a being human, and, second, at the equally vital question which Noonan does not consider, namely, What reason is there for identifying the moral community with the set of all human beings, in whatever way we have chosen to define that term?

1. ON THE DEFINITION OF 'HUMAN'

One reason why this vital second question is so frequently overlooked in the debate over the moral status of abortion is that the term 'human' has two distinct, but not often distinguished, senses. This fact results in a slide of meaning, which serves to conceal the fallaciousness of the traditional argument that since (1) it is wrong to kill innocent human beings, and (2) fetuses are innocent human beings, then (3) it is wrong to kill fetuses. For if 'human' is used in the same sense in both (1) and (2) then, whichever of the two senses is meant, one of these premises is question-begging. And if it is used in two different senses then of course the conclusion doesn't follow.

18

Thus, (1) is a self-evident moral truth,[1] and avoids begging the question about abortion, only if 'human being' is used to mean something like 'a full-fledged member of the moral community.' (It may or may not also be meant to refer exclusively to members of the species *Homo sapiens.*) We may call this the *moral* sense of 'human.' It is not to be confused with what we will call the *genetic* sense, i.e., the sense in which *any* member of the species is a human being, and no member of any other species could be. If (1) is acceptable only if the moral sense is intended, (2) is non-question-begging only if what is intended is the genetic sense.

In "Deciding Who is Human," Noonan argues for the classification of fetuses with human beings by pointing to the presence of the full genetic code, and the potential capacity for rational thought.[2] It is clear that what he needs to show, for his version of the traditional argument to be valid, is that fetuses are human in the moral sense, the sense in which it is analytically true that all human beings have full moral rights. But, in the absence of any argument showing that whatever is genetically human is also morally human, and he gives none, nothing more than genetic humanity can be demonstrated by the presence of the human genetic code. And, as we will see, the *potential* capacity for rational thought can at most show that an entity has the potential for *becoming* human in the moral sense.

2. DEFINING THE MORAL COMMUNITY

Can it be established that genetic humanity is sufficient for moral humanity? I think that there are very good reasons for not defining the moral community in this way. I would like to suggest an alternative way of defining the moral community, which I will argue for only to the extent of explaining why it is, or should be, self-evident. The suggestion is simply that the moral community consists of all and only *people,* rather than all and only human beings;[3] and probably the best way of demonstrating its self-evidence is by considering the concept of personhood, to see what sorts of entity are and are not persons, and what the decision that a being is or is not a person implies about its moral rights.

What characteristics entitle an entity to be considered a person? This is obviously not the place to attempt a complete analysis of the concept of personhood, but we do not need such a fully adequate analysis just to determine whether and why a fetus is or isn't a person. All we need is a rough and approximate list of the most basic criteria of personhood, and some idea of which, or how many, of these an entity must satisfy in order to properly be considered a person.

In searching for such criteria, it is useful to look beyond the set of people with

---

[1] Of course, the principle that it is (always) wrong to kill innocent human beings is in need of many other modifications, e.g., that it may be permissible to do so to save a greater number of other innocent human beings, but we may safely ignore these complications here.

[2] John Noonan, "Deciding Who is Human," *Natural Law Forum,* 13 (1968), 135.

[3] From here on, we will use 'human' to mean genetically human, since the moral sense seems closely connected to, and perhaps derived from, the assumption that genetic humanity is sufficient for membership in the moral community.

whom we are acquainted, and ask how we would decide whether a totally alien being was a person or not. (For we have no right to assume that genetic humanity is necessary for personhood.) Imagine a space traveler who lands on an unknown planet and encounters a race of beings utterly unlike any he has ever seen or heard of. If he wants to be sure of behaving morally toward these beings, he has to somehow decide whether they are people, and hence have full moral rights, or whether they are the sort of thing which he need not feel guilty about treating as, for example, a source of food.

How should he go about making this decision? If he has some anthropological background, he might look for such things as religion, art, and the manufacturing of tools, weapons, or shelters, since these factors have been used to distinguish our human from our prehuman ancestors, in what seems to be closer to the moral than the genetic sense of 'human.' And no doubt he would be right to consider the presence of such factors as good evidence that the alien beings were people, and morally human. It would, however, be overly anthropocentric of him to take the absence of these things as adequate evidence that they were not, since we can imagine people who have progressed beyond, or evolved without ever developing, these cultural characteristics.

I suggest that the traits which are most central to the concept of personhood, or humanity in the moral sense, are, very roughly, the following:

1. consciousness (of objects and events external and/or internal to the being), and in particular the capacity to feel pain;
2. reasoning (the *developed* capacity to solve new and relatively complex problems);
3. self-motivated activity (activity which is relatively independent of either genetic or direct external control);
4. the capacity to communicate, by whatever means, messages of an indefinite variety of types, that is, not just with an indefinite number of possible contents, but on indefinitely many possible topics;
5. the presence of self-concepts, and self-awareness, either individual or racial, or both.

Admittedly, there are apt to be a great many problems involved in formulating precise definitions of these criteria, let alone in developing universally valid behavioral criteria for deciding when they apply. But I will assume that both we and our explorer know approximately what (1)–(5) mean, and that he is also able to determine whether or not they apply. How, then, should he use his findings to decide whether or not the alien beings are people? We needn't suppose that an entity must have *all* of these attributes to be properly considered a person; (1) and (2) alone may well be sufficient for personhood, and quite probably (1)–(3) are sufficient. Neither do we need to insist that any one of these criteria is *necessary* for personhood, although once again (1) and (2) look like fairly good candidates for necessary conditions, as does (3), if 'activity' is construed so as to include the activity of reasoning.

All we need to claim, to demonstrate that a fetus is not a person, is that any being which satisfies none of (1)–(5) is certainly not a person. I consider this claim to be so obvious that I think anyone who denied it, and claimed that a being which satisfied none of (1)–(5) was a person all the same, would thereby demonstrate that he had no notion at all of what a person is—perhaps because he had confused the concept of a person with that of genetic humanity. If the opponents of abortion were to deny the appropriateness of these five criteria, I do not know what further arguments would convince them. We would probably have to admit that our conceptual schemes were indeed irreconcilably different, and that our dispute could not be settled objectively.

I do not expect this to happen, however, since I think that the concept of a person is one which is very nearly universal (to people), and that it is common to both proabortionists and antiabortionists, even though neither group has fully realized the relevance of this concept to the resolution of their dispute. Furthermore, I think that on reflection even the antiabortionists ought to agree not only that (1)–(5) are central to the concept of personhood, but also that it is a part of this concept that all and only people have full moral rights. The concept of a person is in part a moral concept; once we have admitted that x is a person we have recognized, even if we have not agreed to respect, x's right to be treated as a member of the moral community. It is true that the claim that x is a *human being* is more commonly voiced as part of an appeal to treat x decently than is the claim that x is a person, but this is either because 'human being' is here used in the sense which implies personhood, or because the genetic and moral senses of 'human' have been confused.

Now if (1)–(5) are indeed the primary criteria of personhood, then it is clear that genetic humanity is neither necessary nor sufficient for establishing that an entity is a person. Some human beings are not people, and there may well be people who are not human beings. A man or woman whose consciousness has been permanently obliterated but who remains alive is a human being which is no longer a person; defective human beings, with no appreciable mental capacity, are not and presumably never will be people; and a fetus is a human being which is not yet a person, and which therefore cannot coherently be said to have full moral rights. Citizens of the next century should be prepared to recognize highly advanced, self-aware robots or computers, should such be developed, and intelligent inhabitants of other worlds, should such be found, as people in the fullest sense, and to respect their moral rights. But to ascribe full moral rights to an entity which is not a person is as absurd as to ascribe moral obligations and responsibilities to such an entity.

3. FETAL DEVELOPMENT AND THE RIGHT TO LIFE

Two problems arise in the application of these suggestions for the definition of the moral community to the determination of the precise moral status of a human fetus. Given that the paradigm example of a person is a normal adult human being, then (1) How like this paradigm, in particular how far advanced since conception, does a human being need to be before it begins to have a right to life by virtue, not of being fully a person as of yet, but of being *like* a person? and (2) To what extent, if any, does the fact that a fetus has the *potential* for becoming a person endow it with some of the same rights? Each of these questions requires some comment.

In answering the first question, we need not attempt a detailed consideration of the moral rights of organisms which are not developed enough, aware enough, intelligent enough, etc., to be considered people, but which resemble people in some respects. It does seem reasonable to suggest that the more like a person, in the relevant respects, a being is, the stronger is the case for regarding it as having a right to life, and indeed the stronger its right to life is. Thus we ought to take seriously the suggestion that, insofar as "the human individual develops biologically in a continuous fashion . . . the rights of a human person might develop in the same way."[4] But we must keep in mind that the attributes which are relevant in determining whether or not an entity is enough like a person to be regarded as having some of the same moral rights are no different from those which are relevant to determining whether or not it is fully a person—i.e., are no different from (1)–(5)—and that being genetically human, or having recognizably human facial and other physical features, or detectable brain activity, or the capacity to survive outside the uterus, are simply not among these relevant attributes.

Thus it is clear that even though a seven- or eight-month fetus has features which make it apt to arouse in us almost the same powerful protective instinct as is commonly aroused by a small infant, nevertheless it is not significantly more personlike than is a very small embryo. It is *somewhat* more personlike; it can apparently feel and respond to pain, and it may even have a rudimentary form of consciousness, insofar as its brain is quite active. Nevertheless, it seems safe to say that it is not fully conscious, in the way that an infant of a few months is, and that it cannot reason, or communicate messages of indefinitely many sorts, does not engage in self-motivated activity, and has no self-awareness. Thus, in the relevant respects, a fetus, even a fully developed one, is considerably less personlike than is the average mature mammal, indeed the average fish. And I think that a rational person must conclude that if the right to life of a fetus is to be based upon its resemblance to a person, then it cannot be said to have any more right to life than, let us say, a newborn guppy (which also seems to be capable of feeling pain), and that a right of that magnitude could never override a woman's right to obtain an abortion, at any stage of her pregnancy.

There may, of course, be other arguments in favor of placing legal limits upon the stage of pregnancy in which an abortion may be performed. Given the relative safety of the new techniques of artificially inducing labor during the third trimester, the danger to the woman's life or health is no longer such an argument. Neither is the fact that people tend to respond to the thought of abortion in the later stages of pregnancy with emotional repulsion, since mere emotional responses cannot take the place of moral reasoning in determining what ought to be permitted. Nor, finally, is the frequently heard argument that legalizing abortion, especially late in the pregnancy, may erode the level of respect for human life, leading, perhaps, to an increase in unjustified euthanasia and other crimes. For this threat, if it is a threat, can be better met by educating people to the kinds of moral distinctions which we are making here than by limiting access to abortion (which limitation may, in its disregard for the rights of women, be just as damaging to the level of respect for human rights).

Thus, since the fact that even a fully developed fetus is not personlike enough

---

[4] Thomas L. Hayes, "A Biological View," *Commonweal,* 85 (March 17, 1967), 677–78; quoted by Daniel Callahan, in *Abortion: Law, Choice, and Morality* (London: Macmillan & Co., 1970).

to have any significant right to life on the basis of its personlikeness shows that no legal restrictions upon the stage of pregnancy in which an abortion may be performed can be justified on the grounds that we should protect the rights of the older fetus; and since there is no other apparent justification for such restrictions, we may conclude that they are entirely unjustified. Whether or not it would be indecent (whatever that means) for a woman in her seventh month to obtain an abortion just to avoid having to postpone a trip to Europe, it would not, in itself, be immoral, and therefore it ought to be permitted.

4. POTENTIAL PERSONHOOD AND THE RIGHT TO LIFE

We have seen that a fetus does not resemble a person in any way which can support the claim that it has even some of the same rights. But what about its *potential,* the fact that if nurtured and allowed to develop naturally it will very probably become a person? Doesn't that alone give it at least some right to life? It is hard to deny that the fact that an entity is a potential person is a strong prima facie reason for not destroying it; but we need not conclude from this that a potential person has a right to life, by virtue of that potential. It may be that our feeling that it is better, other things being equal, not to destroy a potential person is better explained by the fact that potential people are still (felt to be) an invaluable resource, not to be lightly squandered. Surely, if every speck of dust were a potential person, we would be much less apt to conclude that every potential person has a right to become actual.

Still, we do not need to insist that a potential person has no right to life whatever. There may well be something immoral, and not just imprudent, about wantonly destroying potential people, when doing so isn't necessary to protect anyone's rights. But even if a potential person does have some prima facie right to life, such a right could not possibly outweigh the right of a woman to obtain an abortion, since the rights of any actual person invariably outweigh those of any potential person, whenever the two conflict. Since this may not be immediately obvious in the case of a human fetus, let us look at another case.

Suppose that our space explorer falls into the hands of an alien culture, whose scientists decide to create a few hundred thousand or more human beings, by breaking his body into its component cells, and using these to create fully developed human beings, with, of course, his genetic code. We may imagine that each of these newly created men will have all of the original man's abilities, skills, knowledge, and so on, and also have an individual self-concept, in short that each of them will be a bona fide (though hardly unique) person. Imagine that the whole project will take only seconds, and that its chances of success are extremely high, and that our explorer knows all of this, and also knows that these people will be treated fairly. I maintain that in such a situation he would have every right to escape if he could, and thus to deprive all of these potential people of their potential lives; for his right to life outweighs all of theirs together, in spite of the fact that they are all genetically human, all innocent, and all have a very high probability of becoming people very soon, if only he refrains from acting.

Indeed, I think he would have a right to escape even if it were not his life which the alien scientists planned to take, but only a year of his freedom, or, indeed, only a day. Nor would he be obligated to stay if he had gotten captured (thus bringing all these people-potentials into existence) because of his own carelessness, or even if he had done so deliberately, knowing the consequences. Regardless of how he got captured, he is not morally obligated to remain in captivity for *any* period of time for the sake of permitting any number of potential people to come into actuality, so great is the margin by which one actual person's right to liberty outweighs whatever right to life even a hundred thousand potential people have. And it seems reasonable to conclude that the rights of a woman will outweigh by a similar margin whatever right to life a fetus may have by virtue of its potential personhood.

Thus, neither a fetus's resemblance to a person, nor its potential for becoming a person provides any basis whatever for the claim that it has any significant right to life. Consequently, a woman's right to protect her health, happiness, freedom, and even her life,[5] by terminating an unwanted pregnancy, will always override whatever right to life it may be appropriate to ascribe to a fetus, even a fully developed one. And thus, in the absence of any overwhelming social need for every possible child, the laws which restrict the right to obtain an abortion, or limit the period of pregnancy during which an abortion may be performed, are a wholly unjustified violation of a woman's most basic moral and constitutional rights.[6]

QUESTIONS

1. Argue for or against the following claim: Warren's analysis thoroughly undermines Noonan's conservative position on abortion.

2. It is sometimes objected to Warren that her views can logically be extended to morally justify infanticide as well as abortion. The objection takes the form of a reductio ad absurdum. That is, it is claimed that Warren's way of thinking must be wrong because it generates the "absurd" conclusion that infanticide is morally permissible. Does such a conclusion follow from Warren's views and, if so, is such a conclusion patently absurd?

Daniel Callahan

ABORTION DECISIONS: PERSONAL MORALITY

Biographical Information. *Daniel Callahan (born 1930), a philosopher, has been since 1969 the director of the Institute of Society, Ethics and the*

---

[5] That is, insofar as the death rate, for the woman, is higher for childbirth than for early abortion.

[6] My thanks to the following people, who were kind enough to read and criticize an earlier version of this paper: Herbert Gold, Gene Glass, Anne Lauterbach, Judith Thomson, Mary Mothersill, and Timothy Binkley.

Life Sciences. He has also been executive editor of The Commonweal
*(1961–1968), and his numerous publications reflect a wide range of
philosophical, theological, and religious concerns. Callahan's principal
work on the subject of abortion is* Abortion: Law, Choice and Morality
(1970), from which this selection is excerpted.

Argument in the Selection. *After declaring himself in support of permissive abortion legislation, Callahan proceeds to defend one kind of
moderate view on the problem of the ethical acceptability of abortion. On
the issue of the moral status of the fetus, he steers a middle course. He
rejects the "tissue" theory, the view that the fetus has negligible moral
status, on the grounds that such a theory is out of tune with both the
biological evidence and a respect for the sanctity of human life. On the
other hand, he contends that the fetus does not qualify as a person and
thus rejects the view that the fetus has full moral status. His contention
that the fetus is nevertheless an "important and valuable form of human
life" can be understood as implying that the fetus has some kind of
partial moral status.*

*In Callahan's view, a respect for the sanctity of human life should
incline every woman to a strong initial (moral) bias against abortion.
Yet, he argues, since a woman has duties to herself, her family, and her
society, there may be circumstances in which such duties would override
the prima facie duty not to abort. Callahan concludes by criticizing
various efforts to dissolve the "moral tension" involved in abortion
decisions.*

The strength of pluralistic societies lies in the personal freedom they afford
individuals. One is free to choose among religious, philosophical, ideological and
political creeds; or one can create one's own highly personal, idiosyncratic moral
code and view of the universe. Increasingly, the individual is free to ignore the
morals, manners and mores of society. The only limitations are upon those actions
which seem to present clear and present dangers to the common good, and even
there the range of prohibited actions is diminishing as more and more choices are
left to personal and private decisions. I have contended that, apart from some
regulatory laws, abortion decisions should be left, finally, up to the women
themselves. Whatever one may think of the morality of abortion, it cannot be
established that it poses a clear and present danger to the common good. Thus
society does not have the right decisively to interpose itself between a woman and
the abortion she wants. It can only intervene where it can be shown that some of
its own interests are at stake *qua* society. Regulatory laws of a minimal kind
therefore seem in order, since in a variety of ways already mentioned society will
be affected by the number, kind and quality of legal abortions. In short, with a few
important stipulations, what I have been urging is tantamount to saying that
abortion decisions should be private decisions. It is to accept, in principle, the
contention of those who believe that, in a free, pluralistic society, the woman

should be allowed to make her own moral choice on abortion and be allowed to implement that choice.

But pluralistic societies also lay a few traps for the unwary. It is not a large psychological step from saying that individuals should be left free to make up their own minds on some crucial moral issues (of which abortion is one) to an adoption of the view that one personal decision is as good as another, that any decision is a good one as long as it is honest or sincere, that a free decision equals a correct decision. However short the psychological step, the logical gap is very large. An absence of cant, hypocrisy and coercion may prepare the way for good personal decisions. But that is only to clean the room, and something must then be put in it. The hazard is that, once cleaned, it will be filled with capriciousness, sentimentality, a thinly disguised conformity to the reigning moral taste, or strongly felt but inadequately analyzed moral opinions. This is a particular danger in affluent pluralistic societies, heavily dominated by popular tastes, communication media and the absence of shared values. Philosophically, the view that all values are equally good and all private moral choices on a par is all but dead; but it still has a strong life at the popular level, where there is a tendency to act as if, once personal freedom is legally and socially achieved, moral questions cease to exist.

A considerable quantity of literature exists in the field of ethics concerned with such problems as subjective and objective values, the meaning and use of ethical principles and moral rules, the role of intentionality. That literature need not be reviewed here. But it is directly to the point to observe that a particular failing of the abortion-on-request literature is that it persistently scants the moral problem of how a woman, if granted the desired legal freedom to make her own decision about abortion, should go about making that decision. Up to a point, this deficiency is understandable. The immediate tactical problem has been to get the laws changed or repealed; that has been the burden of the public struggle, which has concentrated on statutes and legislators rather than on the moral contents and problems of personal decision-making. It is reasonable and legitimate to say that a woman should be left free to make the decision in the light of her own personal values; that is, I believe, the best legal solution. But it leaves totally untouched the question of how, once freedom is achieved, she ought to go about the personal business of forming a coherent, rational, sensitive moral perspective and opinion on abortion. After freedom, what then? Society may have no right to demand that a woman give it good reasons why she should have an abortion before permitting it. But this does not entail that the woman should not, as a morally responsible person, have good reasons to justify her desires or acts in her own eyes.

This is only to say that a solution of the legal problem is not the same as a solution to the moral problem. That the moral struggle is transferred from the public to the private sphere should not be taken to mean that the moral problem has been solved; only its public aspect, under a permissive law or a repeal of all laws, has been dealt with. The personal problem will remain.

Some women will be part of a religious group or ethical tradition which they freely choose and which can offer them something, possibly very much, in the way of helpful moral insight consistent with that tradition. The obvious course in that instance is for them to turn to their tradition to see what it has to offer them on the particular problem of abortion. But what of those who have no tradition to repair to or those who find their tradition wanting on this problem? One way or another, they will have to find some way of developing a set of ethical principles and moral rules to help them act responsibly, to justify their own conduct in their own eyes. To press the problem to a finer point, what ought they to think about as they try to work out their own views on abortion?

Only a few suggestions will be made here, taking the form of arguing for an ethic of personal responsibility which tries, in the process of decision-making, to make itself aware of a number of things. The biological evidence should be considered, just as the problem of methodology must be considered; the philo-sophical assumptions implicit in different uses of the word "human" need to be considered; a philosophical theory of biological analysis is required; the social consequences of different kinds of analyses and different meanings of the word "human" should be thought through; consistency of meaning and use should be sought to avoid *ad hoc* and arbitrary solutions.

It is my own conviction that the "developmental school" offers the most helpful and illuminating approach to the problem of the beginning of human life, avoiding, on the one hand, a too narrow genetic criterion of human life and, on the other, a too broad and socially dangerous social definition of the "human." Yet the kinds of problems which appear in any attempt to decide upon the beginning of life suggest that no one position can be either proved or disproved from biological evidence alone. It becomes a question of trying to do justice to the evidence while, at the same time, realizing that how the evidence is approached and used will be a function of one's way of looking at reality, one's moral policy, the values and rights one believes need balancing, and the type of questions one thinks need to be asked. At the very least, however, the genetic evidence for the uniqueness of zygotes and embryos (a uniqueness of a different kind than that of the uniqueness of sperm and ova), their potentiality for development into a human person, their early development of human characteristics, their genetic and organic distinct-ness from the organism of the mother, appear to rule out a treatment even of zygotes, much less the more developed stages of the conceptus, as mere pieces of "tissue," of no human significance or value. The "tissue" theory of the signifi-cance of the conceptus can only be made plausible by a systematic disregard of the biological evidence. Moreover, though one may conclude that a conceptus is only potential human life, in the process of continually actualizing its potential through growth and development, a respect for the sanctity of life, with its bias in favor even of undeveloped life, is enough to make the taking of such life a moral problem. There is a choice to be made and it is a moral choice. In the near future, it is likely that some kind of simple, safe abortifacient drug will be developed, which either prevents implantation or destroys the conceptus before it can develop. It will be tempting then to think that the moral dilemma has vanished, but I do not believe it will have.

It is possible to imagine a huge number of situations where a woman could, in good and sensitive conscience, choose abortion as a moral solution to her personal or social difficulties. But, at the very least, the bounds of morality are overstepped when either through a systematic intellectual negligence or a willful choosing of that moral solution most personally convenient, personal choice is deliberately made easy and problem-free. Yet it seems to me that a pressure in that direction is a growing part of the ethos of technological societies; it is easily possible to find people to reassure us that we need have no scruples about the way we act, whether the issue is war, the suppression of rebellion and revolution, discrimination against minorities or the use of technological advances. Pluralism makes possible the achieving of freer, more subtle moral thinking; but it is a possibility constantly endangered by cultural pressures which would simplify or dissolve moral doubts and anguish.

The question of abortion "indications" returns at the level of personal choice. I have contended that the advent of permissive laws should not mean a cessation of efforts to explore the problem of "indications." When a woman asks herself, as she ought, whether her reasons for wanting an abortion are sound reasons—which presumes abortion is a serious enough moral issue to warrant the need to provide oneself with good reasons for choosing it—she will be asking herself about justifiable indications. Thus, transposed from the legal to the personal level, the kinds of concerns adumbrated in the earlier chapters on indications remain fully pertinent. It was argued in those chapters that, with the possible exception of exceedingly rare instances of a direct threat to the physical life of the mother, one cannot speak of general categories of abortion indications as *necessitating* an abortion. In a number of circumstances, abortion may be a wise and justifiable solution to a distressed pregnancy. But when the language of necessity is used, the implication is that no other conceivable alternative is available. It may be granted, willingly enough, that some set of practical circumstances in some (possibly very many) concrete cases may indicate that abortion is the only feasible option open. But these cases cannot readily be determined in advance, and, for that reason, it is necessary to say that no formal indication as such (e.g., a psychiatric indication) entails a necessary, predetermined choice in favor of abortion.

The word "indication" remains the best word, suggesting that a number of given circumstances will bring the possibility or desirability of abortion to the fore. But to escalate the concept of an indication into that of a required procedure is to go too far. Abortion is one way to solve the problem of an unwanted or hazardous pregnancy (physically, psychologically, economically or socially), but it is rarely the only way, at least in affluent societies (I would be considerably less certain about making the same statement about poor societies). Even in the most extreme cases—rape, incest, psychosis, for instance—alternatives will usually be available and different choices, open. It is not necessarily the end of every woman's chance for a happy, meaningful life to bear an illegitimate child. It is not necessarily the automatic destruction of a family to have a seriously defective child born into it. It is not necessarily the ruination of every family living in overcrowded housing to have still another child. It is not inevitable that every immature woman would become even more so if she bore a child or another child. It is not inevitable that a gravely handicapped child can hope for nothing from life. It is not inevitable that every unwanted child is doomed to misery. It is not written in the essence of things, as a fixed law of human nature, that a woman cannot come to accept, love and be a good mother to a child who was initially unwanted. Nor is it a fixed law that she could not come to cherish a grossly deformed child. Naturally, these are only generalizations. The point is only that human beings are as a rule flexible, capable of doing more than they sometimes think they can, able to surmount serious dangers and challenges, able to grow and mature, able to transform inauspicious beginnings into satisfactory conclusions. Everything in life, even in procreative and family life, is not fixed in advance; the future is never wholly unalterable.

Yet the problem of personal question-asking must be pushed a step farther.

The way the questions are answered will be very much determined by a woman's way of looking at herself and at life. A woman who has decided, as a personal moral policy, that nothing should be allowed to stand in the way of her own happiness, goals and self-interest will have no trouble solving the moral problem. For her, an unwanted pregnancy will, by definition, be a pregnancy to be terminated. But only by a Pickwickian use of words could this form of reasoning be called moral. It would preclude any need to consult the opinion of others, any need to examine the validity of one's own viewpoint, any need to, for instance, ask when human life begins, any need to interrogate oneself in any way, intellectually or morally; will and desire would be king.

Assuming, however, that most women would seek a broader ethical horizon than that of their exclusively personal self-interest, what might they think about when faced with an abortion decision? A respect for the sanctity of human life should, I believe, incline them toward a general and strong bias against abortion. Abortion is an act of killing, the violent, direct destruction of potential human life, already in the process of development. That fact should not be disguised, or glossed over by euphemism and circumlocution. It is not the destruction of a human person—for at no stage of its development does the conceptus fulfill the definition of a person, which implies a developed capacity for reasoning, willing, desiring and relating to others—but it is the destruction of an important and valuable form of human life. Its value and its potentiality are not dependent upon the attitude of the woman toward it; it grows by its own biological dynamism and has a genetic and morphological potential distinct from that of the woman. It has its own distinctive and individual future. If contraception and abortion are both seen as forms of birth limitation, they are distinctly different acts; the former precludes the possibility of a conceptus being formed, while the latter stops a conceptus already in existence from developing. The bias implied by the principle of the sanctity of human life is toward the protection of all forms of human life, especially, in ordinary circumstances, the protection of the right to life. That right should be accorded even to doubtful life; its existence should not be wholly dependent upon the personal self-interest of the woman.

Yet she has her own rights as well, and her own set of responsibilities to those around her; that is why she may have to choose abortion. In extreme situations of overpopulation, she may also have a responsibility for the survival of the species or of a people. In many circumstances, then, a decision in favor of abortion—one which overrides the right to life of that potential human being she carries within—can be a responsible moral decision, worthy neither of the condemnation of others nor of self-condemnation. But the bias of the principle of the sanctity of life is against a routine, unthinking employment of abortion; it bends over backwards not to take life and gives the benefit of the doubt to life. It does not seek to diminish the range of responsibility toward life—potential or actual—but to extend it. It does not seek the narrowest definition of life, but the widest and the richest. It is mindful of individual possibility, on the one hand, and of a destructive human tendency, on the other, to exclude from the category of "the human" or deny rights to those beings whose existence is or could prove burdensome to others.

The language used to describe abortion will have an important bearing on the sensitivities and imagination of those women who must make abortion decisions. Abortion can be talked about in the language of medical technology and technique—as, say, "a therapeutic procedure involving the emptying of the uterine contents." That language is neutral, clinical, unemotional. Or abortion can be talked about in the emotive language of relieving woman from suffering, or meeting the need for freedom among women, or saving a nation from a devastating overpopulation. Both kinds of language have their place, for abortion has more than one result and meaning and abortion can legitimately be talked about in more than one way. What is objectionable is a conscious manipulation of language to incite an irrational emotional response, to allay doubts or to mislead the imagination. Particularly misleading is one commonly employed mixture of rhetorical modes by advocates of abortion on request. That is the use of a detached, clinical language to describe the actual operation itself combined with an emotive rhetoric to evoke the personal and social goods which an abortion can bring about. Thus, when every effort is made to suggest that emotion and feeling are perfectly appropriate to describe the social and personal goals of abortion, but that a clinical language only is appropriate when the actual technique and medical objective of an abortion is described, then the moral imagination is being misled.

Any human act can be described in impersonal, technological language, just as any act can be described in emotive language. What is wanted is an equity in the language. It is fair enough and to the point to say that in many circumstances abortion will save a woman's health or her family. It only becomes misleading when the act itself, as distinguished from its therapeutic goal, is talked about in an entirely different way. For, abortion is not just an "emptying of the uterine contents." It is also an act of killing; there will be no abortion unless the conceptus is killed (or its further existence made impossible, which amounts to the same thing). If it is appropriate to evoke the imagination and elicit sympathy for those women in a distressed pregnancy who could be helped by abortion, it is no less appropriate to evoke the imagination about what actually occurs in an abortion "procedure."

Imagination should also come into play at another point. It is often argued by proponents of abortion that there is no need for a woman ever to take any chances in a distressed pregnancy, particularly in the instance of an otherwise healthy woman who, if she has an abortion on one occasion, could simply get pregnant again on another, more auspicious occasion. This might be termed the "replacement theory" of abortion indications: since fetus "x" can be replaced by fetus "y," then there is no reason why a woman should have any scruples about such a replacement. This way of conceiving the choices effectively dissolves them; it becomes important only to know whether a woman can get pregnant again when she wants to. But this strategy can be employed only at the price of convincing oneself that there is no difference whatever among embryos or fetuses, that they all have exactly the same potentiality. But even the sketchiest knowledge of the genetic uniqueness of each conceptus (save in the instance of monozygotic twins), and thus the different genetic potentialities of each, should raise doubts on that point. Yet, having said that, I would not want to deny that the possibility of a further pregnancy could have an important bearing on the moral reasoning of a woman whose present pregnancy was threatening. If, out of a sense of responsibility toward her present children or her present life situation, a woman decided that an abortion was the wisest, most moral course, then the possibility that she could become pregnant later, when these responsibilities would be less pressing, would be a pertinent consideration.

The goal of these remarks is to keep alive in the consciences of women who have an abortion choice a moral tension; and it is to hope that they will be willing to bear the pain and the uncertainty of having to make a moral choice. It is the automatic, unthinking and unimaginative personal solution of abortion questions which women themselves should be extremely wary of, either for or against an abortion. A woman can, with little trouble, find both people and books to reassure her that there is no problem about abortion at all; or people and books to convince her that she would be a moral monster if she chose abortion. A woman can choose in advance the views she will listen to and thus have her predispositions confirmed. Yet a willingness to keep alive a moral tension, and to be wary of precipitous solutions, presupposes two things. First, that the woman herself wants to do what is right, realizing that what is right may not always be that which is most convenient, most easy or most immediately apt to solve a pressing problem. It is simply not the case that what one wants to do, or would like to do, or is predisposed to do is necessarily the right thing to do. A willingness seriously to entertain that moral perception—which, of course, does not in itself imply a decision for or against an abortion—is one sign of moral seriousness.

Second, moral seriousness presupposes one is concerned with the protection and furthering of life. This means that, out of respect for human life, one bends over backwards not to eliminate human life, not to desensitize oneself to the meaning and value of potential life, not to seek definitions of the "human" which serve one's self-interest only. A desire to respect human life in all of its forms means, therefore, that one voluntarily imposes upon oneself a pressure against the taking of life; that one demands of oneself serious reasons for doing so, even in the case of a very early embryo; that one use not only the mind but also the imagination when a decision is being made; that one seeks not to evade the moral issues but to face them; that one searches out the alternatives and conscientiously entertains them before turning to abortion. A bias in favor of the sanctity of human life in all of its forms would include a bias against abortion on the part of women; it would be the last rather than the first choice when unwanted pregnancies occurred. It would be an act to be avoided if at all possible.

A bias of this kind, voluntarily imposed by a woman upon herself, would not trap her; for it is also part of a respect for the dignity of life to leave the way open for an abortion when other reasonable choices are not available. For she also has duties toward herself, her family and her society. There can be good reasons for taking the life even of a very late fetus; once that also is seen and seen as a counterpoise in particular cases to the general bias against the taking of potential life, the way is open to choose abortion. The bias of the moral policy implies the need for moral rules which seek to preserve life. But, as a policy which leaves room for choice—rather than entailing a fixed set of rules—it is open to flexible interpretation when the circumstances point to the wisdom of taking exception to the normal ordering of the rules in particular cases. Yet, in that case, one is not genuinely taking exception to the rules. More accurately, one would be deciding that, for the preservation or furtherance of other values or rights—species-rights, person-rights—a choice in favor of abortion would be serving the sanctity of life. That there would be, in that case, conflict between rights, with one set of rights set aside (reluctantly) to serve another set, goes without saying. A subversion of the principle occurs when it is made out that there is no conflict and thus nothing to decide.

QUESTIONS

1. Argue for or against the following claim: Callahan has advanced considerations that thoroughly undermine Warren's view of the moral status of the fetus.

2. According to Callahan, the fetus is neither a "person" nor a "piece of tissue." Reasoning from this moderate point of view, assess the ethical acceptability of an abortion desired for each of the following reasons: (1) the physical health of the mother, (2) the mental health of the mother, (3) a high probability of a severely deformed child, (4) rape, (5) illegitimacy, (6) the personal happiness of the mother.

SUGGESTED ADDITIONAL READINGS

Beauchamp, Tom L., ed. *Ethics and Public Policy*. Chapter 6. Englewood Cliffs, N.J.: Prentice-Hall, Inc., 1975. This chapter on abortion consists of a set of rather difficult articles, heavily emphasizing the distinction between *killing* and *letting die*.

Callahan, Daniel. *Abortion: Law, Choice and Morality*. New York: Macmillan, 1970. Callahan provides a wealth of useful data relevant to deciding various medical, social, and legal questions about abortion. Against this background, he discusses the ethical acceptability of abortion, ultimately defending a moderate position.

Feinberg, Joel, ed. *The Problem of Abortion*. Belmont, Calif.: Wadsworth Publishing Company, Inc., 1973. This excellent anthology features a wide range of articles on both the moral and legal aspects of abortion.

Hare, R. M. "Abortion and the Golden Rule." *Philosophy and Public Affairs*, vol. 4, no. 3, 1975. In this important but difficult article, Hare develops a novel line of argument in support of a moderate stance on the ethical acceptability of abortion.

Noonan, John T., Jr., ed. *The Morality of Abortion: Legal and Historical Perspectives*. Cambridge, Mass.: Harvard University Press, 1970. This book contains a series of readings representing various theological perspectives on abortion. The conservative view is prominent.

Perkins, Robert L., ed. *Abortion: Pro and Con*. Cambridge, Mass.: Schenkman Publishing Company, 1974. This anthology contains a spectrum of articles defending various positions on the morality of abortion. All the articles were written specifically or altered specifically for this volume.

Thomson, Judith Jarvis. "A Defense of Abortion." *Philosophy and Public Affairs*, vol. 1, no. 1, 1971. In this widely discussed article, Thomson develops an interesting line of attack against the conservative view. For the sake of argument, she grants the premise that the fetus (from conception) is a person. Still, she argues, under certain conditions abortion remains morally permissible.

Tooley, Michael. "Abortion and Infanticide." *Philosophy and Public Affairs*, vol. 2, no. 1, 1972. Tooley investigates the question of what properties an organism must possess in order to qualify as having a serious right to life. On his analysis, neither a fetus nor an infant can be said to have a serious right to life, and thus both infanticide and abortion are ethically acceptable.

TWO
Euthanasia

Recently the question of euthanasia has emerged as a crucial ethical issue. As biomedical technology has advanced, new techniques have been developed to prolong life. Life-sustaining devices such as respirators, artificial kidneys, and intravenous feeding have made it possible to sustain the life of an individual artificially long after that individual has lost the capacity to sustain life independently. It is not unusual to find a person who has lived a long and useful life now permanently incapable of functioning in any recognizably human fashion. Biological life continues; but some find it tempting to say that human life, in any meaningful sense, has ceased. In one case the patient is in an irreversible coma, reduced to a vegetative existence. In another case the patient's personality has completely deteriorated. In still another case the patient alternates inescapably between excruciating pain and drug-induced stupor. In each of these cases, the quality of human life has deteriorated. There is no longer any capacity for creative employment, intellectual pursuit, or the cultivation of interpersonal relationships. In short, in each of these three cases life seems to have been rendered meaningless in the sense that the individual has lost all capacity for normal human satisfactions. In the first case there is simply no consciousness, which is a necessary condition of deriving satisfaction. In the second case consciousness has been dulled to such an extent that there is no longer any capacity for satisfaction. In the third case excruciating pain and sedation combine to undercut the possibility of satisfaction.

When a person in such circumstances voluntarily requests that his or her life be ended, or when such a person is incapable of making the request but had previously formally declared that he or she would not wish a meaningless existence to be prolonged, we are confronted with the issue of voluntary euthanasia. If the person in such circumstances had never made such a formal declaration and yet is incapable of making the request, as, for example, the comatose patient, the issue of involuntary euthanasia arises when the immediate family or attending physician decides that the patient's life should be terminated. Ethical arguments concerning euthanasia center on two major questions: (1) Is euthanasia ever morally justified; and if it is, under what conditions is it morally justified? (2) Should there be a legal right to euthanasia?

IS EUTHANASIA EVER MORALLY JUSTIFIED?

Some people argue that euthanasia can never be morally justified. On their view, the freedom to end any human life, including one's own, should never be included among human freedoms. From a religious perspective it is argued that God alone has the right to end a life since only God can create life. Or the claim is made that euthanasia is never permissible because according to God's law the "killing" of innocents is never permissible and euthanasia involves the "killing" of innocents. From a nonreligious perspective it is argued that a respect for the sanctity of human life precludes the deliberate taking of that life. Or the claim is made that a respect for the sanctity of human life is necessary to the maintenance of a social order. Any action or moral rule which lessens this respect endangers the social order. Since the acceptance of euthanasia will serve to lessen such respect, euthanasia should be prohibited.

Other people argue that some cases of euthanasia can be morally justified. Those holding this position often make two distinctions: (1) The distinction noted earlier between voluntary and involuntary euthanasia and (2) a distinction between active and passive euthanasia. Passive euthanasia involves the withholding or withdrawal of some extraordinary means to prolong life. In some of the cases, the patient is terminally ill and will soon die without the use of the respirator or kidney machine or without the heart or kidney transplant. Many of those considered as candidates for passive euthanasia have suffered irreversible brain damage so that they are incapable of any cognitive activity and without the use of respirators even incapable of sustaining biological life. If passive euthanasia is practiced, such patients are not "killed" but simply allowed to die a natural death. In contrast, active euthanasia involves the direct taking of a life, as, for example, by injecting a patient with a lethal dose of a pain-killing drug.

Those who support the moral acceptability of euthanasia usually stress the moral desirability of voluntary euthanasia, granting that involuntary euthanasia requires other, perhaps more difficult, arguments.[1] The primary case for the moral acceptability of voluntary

---

[1] Those who argue in support of voluntary euthanasia do not usually concern themselves with the practical difficulty of determining when consent is truly voluntary. That problem is usually discussed in the context of discussions about the dangers of legalizing euthanasia.

euthanasia is based on an appeal to humanitarian feelings. Is it not cruel and inhumane to force the patients described earlier to stay alive "at all costs" when they are comatose or in constant pain or deteriorating and aware of their own deterioration? When the patients in question will die shortly anyway, such an appeal is especially cogent. This humanitarian appeal is often conjoined with an appeal to the primacy of individual liberty. (Individuals should be free to do as they choose as long as their actions do not result in any harm to others.) Since those suffering individuals who decide to hasten their deaths harm no one, their freedom to end their lives should not be infringed.

On the basis of such arguments some maintain that only passive voluntary euthanasia is morally acceptable while others argue that voluntary euthanasia is always morally acceptable. The latter see no morally significant difference between active and passive euthanasia— between withholding treatment from a terminally ill patient and actively taking the life of the patient. Furthermore, they maintain, it is often more humane to end the patient's life quickly (e.g., through the injection of a lethal dose of some drug) than to simply withhold treatment and wait for the patient to die.

The moral significance of the distinction between active and passive euthanasia is often the subject of debate among some who do not concern themselves primarily with the distinction between voluntary and involuntary euthanasia. In their arguments, the focus is not on whether the decision to end life is made by the patient or the patient's family or physician but on whether there is a morally significant difference between active and passive euthanasia such that even if the latter is morally acceptable, the former is not. This issue is debated by two writers in this chapter, James Rachels and Tom L. Beauchamp. They examine a recent AMA statement which condemns the "intentional termination of the life of one human being by another—mercy killing" but accepts the patient's or the patient's immediate family's right to decide to end the use of extraordinary means to prolong life. This AMA policy statement would appear to support the moral acceptability of the practice of passive euthanasia, voluntary or involuntary, while rejecting the moral acceptability of active euthanasia.

SHOULD THERE BE A LEGAL RIGHT TO EUTHANASIA?

Suppose we decide that some form of euthanasia is morally acceptable. A further question must still be considered: Should there be a legal right to euthanasia? In the last decade, attempts have been made to legalize euthanasia both in the United States and in Great Britain. In 1969, a proposed euthanasia bill received the support of forty members of the British House of Lords; sixty-one members voted against it. If the bill had been enacted into law, doctors would have had the authority to grant euthanasia to those who at least thirty days previously had made a declaration requesting the administration of euthanasia in certain specified circumstances. Before euthanasia would be administered, however, two doctors would have to certify that the patient was suffering from an "irremediable physical condition of a distressing character."[2] In the United States, various states have tried to pass bills legalizing euthanasia. Kentucky actually enacted a voluntary euthanasia bill, but it was declared unconstitutional by the United States Circuit Court of Appeals in October 1975. The Sackett bill, reprinted in this chapter, was defeated in Florida despite strong support. This bill would have included the right to be permitted to die with dignity among our "inalienable" rights. As the situation now stands, we have no such legal right to death with dignity whether the exercise of that right requires simply the deliberate withdrawal of some life-sustaining equipment or some more direct action. Some attempts have been made by families of comatose patients to obtain court permission to have life-sustaining equipment disconnected from patients with irreversible brain damage. One such attempt was made in the famous Quinlan case (see the first reading in this chapter) when the parents of the comatose Karen Quinlan requested that her physicians be ordered to disconnect the mechanical respirator which was artificially sustaining her vital life processes. In ruling against the Quinlans, the judge ruled that "there is no constitutional right to die that can be asserted by a parent for his incompetent adult child."[3]

Attempts to establish such a right by legalizing even voluntary euthanasia are often resisted by those who agree that some cases of voluntary euthanasia are morally acceptable. Although they see nothing morally wrong with individual acts of voluntary euthanasia, they argue against any systematic social policy permitting voluntary euthanasia, either active or passive. Their arguments are usually based on the ground that such a policy would result in undesirable consequences. Like Yale Kamisar in our selections, they make the following claims: (1) Any law legalizing voluntary euthanasia will lead to abuses by physicians, families, and others having an interest in the matter. Patients may feel pressured to give consent or their consent may be given under the influence of drugs which affect their capacity to reason clearly. Here the emphasis is on the difficulty of deciding when genuine

---

[2]"Voluntary Euthanasia Bill 1969," reprinted in Marvin Kohl, ed., *Beneficent Euthanasia* (Buffalo, N.Y.: Prometheus Books, 1975), pp. 241–244.

[3] Justice Robert Muir, Jr., J.S.C., "Opinion in the Matter of Karen Quinlan," Superior Court of New Jersey, Chancery Division, Morris County, New Jersey, Nov. 10, 1975, an excerpt from which is reprinted in this chapter.

consent has been given. (2) Doctors are fallible. Since there will be medical mistakes in judging a patient to be incurable, such a law will result in needless deaths. (3) The legalization of voluntary euthanasia will lead to the legalization of involuntary euthanasia and the subsequent "mercy killing" not only of irreversibly comatose patients but also of the senile, deformed, and perhaps eventually the politically undesirable.

Those who like Glanville Williams in this chapter support the legalization of voluntary euthanasia argue for such legalization on the ground that prohibitive laws are cruel and inhumane. The argument here parallels the one for the moral acceptability of euthanasia. The claim that laws which forbid euthanasia are cruel and inhumane is conjoined with an appeal to personal liberty: The freedom of the patient and the doctor should not be infringed when their actions do not harm others. Since persons who choose to hasten their own deaths are not harming others, the state has no right to pass laws which limit their liberty by denying them the right to choose to die with dignity. The supporters of legalized euthanasia recognize that some bad consequences may result from such legislation. However, they tend to minimize the potential dangers.

J. S. Z.

Justice Robert Muir, Jr.

OPINION IN THE MATTER OF KAREN QUINLAN

Biographical Information. *Robert Muir, Jr. (b. 1932), justice of the Superior Court of New Jersey, is a graduate of the New York University Law School. After graduating from law school, Justice Muir went into private practice for a short time, specializing in municipal law. Before being appointed to the Superior Court of New Jersey in 1973, Justice Muir served as a justice of the Morris County Court.*

Argument in the Selection. *Joseph Quinlan, the father of comatose, twenty-one-year-old Karen Quinlan, asked to be appointed guardian of the person and property of his daughter on grounds of mental incompetency. At that time Karen's vital life processes were being sustained by a mechanical respirator. Quinlan asked the court to authorize the discontinuance of all extraordinary means of sustaining Karen's life processes.*

37

*Justice Muir refused to grant Quinlan's requests. Among the reasons
given by Justice Muir for his refusal are the following. (1) Karen Quinlan
is alive by legal and medical definition. (2) If the treating physician
believes that the use of life-sustaining apparatus should continue, there
is a duty to continue using it. (3) The state has an interest in preserving
life. There is no constitutional right to die which a parent of an incompetent adult child can assert on that child's behalf. It is also worth noting
that Justice Muir dismisses the significance of the active-passive
distinction.* [1]

[Dr. Morse, the neurologist in charge of Karen Quinlan's case] asserted with
medical certainty that Karen Quinlan is not brain dead. He identified the Ad Hoc
Committee of Harvard Medical School Criteria as the ordinary medical standard
for determining brain death and that Karen satisfied none of the criteria. These
criteria are set forth in a 1968 report entitled "Report of the Ad Hoc Committee of
Harvard Medical School to Examine the Definition of Brain Death": A Definition
of "Irreversible Coma," 205. J.A.M.A. 85 (1968).

The report reflects that it is concerned "only with those comatose individuals
who have discernible central nervous system activity" and the problem of determining the characteristics of a permanently non-functioning brain. The criteria as
established are:

"1. Unreceptivity and Unresponsitivity—There is a total unawareness to
externally applied stimuli and inner need and complete unresponsiveness . . .
Even the most intensely painful stimuli evoke no vocal or other response, not
even a groan, withdrawal of a limb, or quickening of respiration.
"2. No Movements or Breathing—Observations covering a period of at
least one hour by physicians is adequate to satisfy the criteria of no spontaneous muscular movement or spontaneous respiration or response to stimuli
such as a pain, touch, sound or light. After the patient is on a mechanical
respirator, the total absence of spontaneous breathing may be established by
turning off the respirator for three minutes and observing whether there is any
effort on the part of the subject to breathe spontaneously. . . .

---

[1]In a later decision by the Supreme Court of New Jersey, Justice Muir's decision was
overturned. Justice C. J. Hughes granted Joseph Quinlan's request to be appointed guardian
of the person of Karen Quinlan with full authority to choose her presiding physicians. In
overturning Justice Muir's decision, Justice Hughes states that in cases such as Karen
Quinlan's "the focal point of decision should be the prognosis as to the reasonable possibility of return to cognitive and sapient life, as distinguished from the forced continuance of
that biological existence to which Karen seems to be doomed." In contrast to Justice Muir,
Justice Hughes contends that there is a significant difference between an act of homicide and
the removal of life-sustaining equipment from someone in Karen Quinlan's condition.
Here we reprint Justice Muir's rather than Justice Hughes' decision for reasons of chapter
balance. Justice Muir's contention that removing Karen Quinlan from the respirator would
be an act of homicide and his claim that there is no constitutional right to die provide an
excellent contrast to the claims made in the "Sackett Bill," the second reading in this
chapter.

"3. No Reflexes—Irreversible coma with abolition of central nervous system activity is evidenced in part by the absence of elicitable reflexes. The pupil will be fixed and dilated and will not respond to a direct source of bright light. Since the establishment of a fixed, dilated pupil is clear-cut in clinical practice, there would be no uncertainty as to its presence. Ocular movement (to head turning and to irrigation of ears with ice water) and blinking are absent. There is no evidence of postural activity (deliberate or other). Swallowing, yawning, vocalization are in abeyance. Corneal and pharyngeal reflexes are absent.

As a rule the stretch of tendon reflexes cannot be elicited; i.e., tapping the tendons of the biceps, triceps, and pronator muscles, quadriceps and gastrocnemius muscles with reflex hammer elicits no contraction of the respective muscles. Plantar or noxious stimulation gives no response.

"4. Flat Electroencephalogram—of great confirmatory value is the flat or isoelectric EEG. . . .

All tests must be repeated at least 24 hours later with no change.

The validity of such data as indications of irreversible cerebral damage depends on the exclusion of two conditions: hypothermia (temperature below 90°F.) or central nervous system depressants, such as barbiturates."

Dr. Morse reflected carefully in his testimony on Karen's prognosis. He described her condition as a chronic or "persistent vegetative state". Dr. Fred Plum, a creator of the phrase, describes its significance by indicating the brain as working in two ways. "We have an internal vegetative regulation which controls body temperature, which controls breathing, which controls to a considerable degree blood pressure, which controls to some degree heart rate, which controls chewing, swallowing and which controls sleeping and waking. We have a more highly developed brain, which is uniquely human, which controls our relation to the outside world, our capacity to talk, to see, to feel, to sing, to think. . . . Brain death necessarily must mean the death of both of these functions of the brain, vegetative and the sapient. Therefore, the presence of any function which is regulated or governed or controlled by the deeper parts of the brain which in layman's terms might be considered purely vegetative would mean that the brain is not biologically dead." . . .

Dr. Morse states Karen Quinlan will not return to a level of cognitive function (i.e., that she will be able to say "Mr. Coburn I'm glad you are my guardian.") What level or plateau she will reach is unknown. He does not know of any course of treatment that can be given and cannot see how her condition can be reversed but is unwilling to say she is in an irreversible state or condition. He indicated there is a possibility of recovery but that level is unknown particularly due to the absence of pre-hospital history. . . .

Mrs. Quinlan and the children were the first to conclude Karen should be removed from the respirator. Mrs. Quinlan, working at the local parish church, had ongoing talks with Father Trapasso, who supported her conclusion and indicated that it was a permissible practice within the tenets of Roman Catholic teachings.

Mr. Quinlan was slower in making his decision. His hope for recovery continued despite the disheartening medical reports. Neither his wife nor Father Trapasso made any attempt to influence him. A conflict existed between letting her natural body functioning control her life and the hope for recovery. . . .

Once having made the determination, the Quinlans approached hospital officials to effectuate their decision. . . .

The Quinlans on July 31, 1975, signed the following:

"We authorize and direct Doctor Morse to discontinue all extraordinary measures, including the use of a respirator for our daughter Karen Quinlan.

"We acknowledge that the above named physician has thoroughly discussed the above with us and that the consequences have been fully explained to us. Therefore, we hereby RELEASE from any and all liability the above named physician, associates and assistants of his choice, Saint Clare's Hospital and its agents and employees."

The Quinlans, upon signing the release, considered the matter decided. Dr. Morse, however, felt he could not and would not agree to the cessation of the respirator assistance. . . . After checking on other medical case histories, he concluded to terminate the respirator would be a substantial deviation from medical tradition, that it involved ascertaining "quality of life", and that he would not do so.

Karen Quinlan is quoted as saying she never wanted to be kept alive by extraordinary means. The statements attributed to her by her mother, sister and a friend are indicated to have been made essentially in relation to instances where close friends or relatives were terminally ill. In one instance, an aunt, in great pain, was terminally ill from cancer. In another instance, the father of a girl friend was dying under like circumstances. In a third circumstance, a close family friend was dying of a brain tumor. Mrs. Quinlan testified her daughter was very full of life, that she loved life and did not want to be kept alive in any way she would not enjoy life to the fullest. . . .

All defendants rely on *John F. Kennedy Memorial Hospital v. Heston*, 58 N.J. 576 (1971) to challenge the constitutional claims asserting no constitutional right to die exists and arguing a compelling State interest in favor of preserving human life.

They all, essentially, contend, since Karen Quinlan is medically and legally alive, the Court should not authorize termination of the respirator, that to do so would be homicide and an act of euthanasia.

The doctors suggest the decision is one more appropriately made by doctors than by a court of law and that under the circumstances of this case a decision in favor of the plaintiff would require ascertainment of quality of life standards to serve as future guide lines.

The Prosecutor, if plaintiff is granted the relief sought, requests a declaratory judgment "with regard to the effect of the homicide statutes and his duty of enforcement."

The hospital also seeks a declaratory judgment that the criteria outlined by the Ad Hoc Committee of the Harvard Medical School to Examine the Definition of Brain Death be sanctioned as the ordinary medical standards for determination of brain death. . . .

Karen Quinlan is by legal and medical definition alive. She is not dead by the Ad Hoc Committee of Harvard Medical School standards nor by the traditional definition, the stoppage of blood circulation and related vital functions. The quality of her living is described as a persistent vegetative state, a description that engenders total sorrow and despair in an emotional sense. She does not exhibit

40

cognitive behavior (i.e., the process of knowing or perceiving). Those qualities unique to man, the higher mental functions, are absent. Her condition is categorized as irreversible and the chance of returning to discriminate functioning remote. Nevertheless, while her condition is neurologically activated, due to the absence of a pre-hospital history, and in light of medical histories showing other comatose patients surviving longer coma periods, there is some medical qualification on the issue of her returning to discriminative functioning and on whether she should be removed from the respirator. There is a serious question whether she can live off the respirator and survive (at least two physicians indicated she could not). It is also apparent that extensive efforts to wean her from the respirator created a danger of more extensive brain injury. There is no treatment suggested. . . .

None of the doctors testified there was *no* hope. The hope for recovery is remote but no doctor talks in the absolute. Certainly he cannot and be credible in light of the advancements medical science has known and the inexactitudes of medical science.

There *is* a duty to continue the life assisting apparatus, if within the treating physician's opinion, it should be done. Here Dr. Morse has refused to concur in the removal of Karen from the respirator. It is his considered position that medical tradition does not justify that act. There is no mention in the doctor's refusal of concern over criminal liability and the Court concludes that such is not the basis for his determination. It is significant that Dr. Morse, a man who demonstrated strong empathy and compassion, a man who has directed care that impressed all the experts, is unwilling to direct Karen's removal from the respirator.

The assertion that Karen would elect, if competent, to terminate the respirator requires careful examination.

She made these statements at the age of twenty. In the words of her mother, she was full of life. She made them under circumstances where another person was suffering, suffering in at least one instance from severe pain. While perhaps it is not too significant, there is no evidence she is now in pain. . . .

The conversations with her mother and friends were theoretical ones. She was not personally involved. It was not under the solemn and sobering fact that death is a distinct choice, *see In re Estate of Brooks,* 32 Ill. 2d. 361,205 N.E.2d. 435(1965). Karen Quinlan while she was in complete control of her mental faculties to reason out the staggering magnitude of the decision not to be "kept alive" did not make a decision. This is not the situation of a Living Will which is based upon a concept of informed consent.

While the repetition of the conversations indicates an awareness of the problems of terminal illness, the elements involved—the vigor of youth that espouses the theoretical good and righteousness, the absence of being presented the question as it applied to her—are not persuasive to establish a probative weight sufficient to persuade this Court that Karen Quinlan would elect her own removal from the respirator. . .

It is also noted the concept of the Court's power over a person suffering under a disability is to *protect* and aid the best interests. . . . Here the authorization sought, if granted, would result in Karen's death. The natural processes of her body are not shown to be sufficiently strong to sustain her by themselves. The authorization, therefore, would be to permit Karen Quinlan to die. This is not protection. It is not something in her best interests, in a temporal sense, and it is in a temporal sense that I must operate whether I believe in life after death or not. The single most important temporal quality Karen Ann Quinlan has is life. This Court will not authorize that life to be taken from her. . . .

The Common Law concept of homicide, the unlawful killing of one person by another, is reflected in our codified law. *N.J.S.A.* 2A:113-1, 2 and 5. The intentional taking of another's life, regardless of motive, is sufficient grounds for conviction. *State v. Ehlers*, 98 *N.J.L.* 236, 240-241 (E. & A. 1922); *See People v. Conley*, 64 *Cal.* 2d. 310, 411 *P.* 2d. 911, 49 *Cal. Rptr.* 815 (Sup. Ct. 1966). Humanitarian motives cannot justify the taking of a human life. *See State v. Ehlers, supra,* at 240-241. The fact that the victim is on the threshold of death or in terminal condition is no defense to a homicide charge. *State v. Mally,* 139 *Mont.* 599, 366 *P.* 2d. 868, 873 (Sup. Ct. 1961).

New Jersey has adopted the principles of the Common Law against homicide. While some of the aforecited decisions are from other jurisdictions, they are reflections of the Common Law and therefore dispositive of the manner this State would treat like circumstances. It is a reasonable construction that the law of this State would preclude the removal of Karen Quinlan from the respirator. As such, a Court of Equity must follow the positive statutory law; it cannot supersede it.

A significant amount of the legal presentation to the court has involved whether the act of removing Karen from the respirator constitutes an affirmative act, or could be considered an act of omission. An intricate discussion on semantics and form is not required since the substance of the sought for authorization would result in the taking of the life of Karen Quinlan when the law of the State indicates that such an authorization would be a homicide. . . .

There is no constitutional right to die that can be asserted by a parent for his incompetent adult child. . . .

In *John F. Kennedy Memorial Hospital v. Heston,* 58 *N.J.* 576 (1971), Justice Weintraub indicated "it seems correct to say there is no constitutional right to die". [at 580] In doing so, the Court recognized the State's interest in preserving life. Equally, this Court recognizes the State's interest in preserving life, particularly in this instance where the Court sits in the capacity of *parens patriae*. There is a presumption that one chooses to go on living. The presumption is not overcome by the prior statements of Karen Quinlan. As previously noted, she did not make the statements as a personal confrontation. Additionally, it is not Karen who asserts her religious belief but her parents. In those instances where the parental standing to assert the religious belief has been upheld, it dealt with future life conduct of their children, not the ending of life. *Wisconsin v. Yoder* (1972); *Pierce v. Society of Sisters* (1925).

The right to life and the preservation of it are "interests of the highest order" and this Court deems it constitutionally correct to deny Plaintiff's request.

QUESTIONS

1. What kinds of considerations should be taken into account when the decision is made to discontinue the use of respirators and other life-sustaining apparatus? (a) The age of the patient? (b) The social responsibilities of the patient? (c) Others' need for the equipment? (d) The length of time the patient will live without the machine? (e) The

quality of the life the patient is living with the use of the equipment? (e.g., Has the patient suffered such irreversible brain damage that even with the equipment the patient is incapable of any cognitive activity whatever?) (f) Any other considerations you can suggest?

2. Who should decide when the use of life-sustaining apparatus should be discontinued? The physicians? A hospital ethics committee? The patients? The immediate family? The courts?

3. In overturning Justice Muir's decision, Justice Hughes states, "There would be no criminal homicide in the circumstances of this case. . . . The ensuing death would not be a homicide but rather expiration from existing natural causes. . . . There is a real and in this case a determinative distinction between the unlawful taking of the life of another and the ending of artificial life-support systems as a matter of self-determination." Argue *against* Justice Hughes and in support of Justice Muir that removing Karen from the respirator would be an act of homicide—the unlawful killing of one person by another.

Walter Sackett

AN ACT RELATING TO THE RIGHT TO DIE WITH DIGNITY (FLORIDA LEGISLATURE)

Biographical Information. Walter Sackett (b. 1905), a physician and surgeon, has maintained his medical practice since 1941 in Miami, Florida. He also has been since 1966 a member of the Florida House of Representatives and has become a spokesman for the movement to legalize voluntary euthanasia.

Argument in the Selection. Sackett's bill was introduced to the Florida Legislature in 1971 and defeated (despite strong support). It provides a good example of potential legislation to legalize voluntary euthanasia. (As the language of the bill is somewhat ambiguous, it also perhaps dramatizes the difficulties involved in drafting such legislation.) The bill would permit anyone to execute and record a document (often called a "living will") specifying that his or her life shall not be meaninglessly prolonged. The bill also provides, seemingly, in the case of a person who is mentally or physically incapacitated, that the decision of a meaningless existence can be made by a spouse or persons of first-degree kinship, or if there are no such people by a panel of physicians.

Be It Enacted by the Legislature of the State of Florida:

Section 1. All natural persons are equal before the law and have inalienable rights, among them the right to enjoy and defend life and liberty, to be permitted to die with dignity, to pursue happiness, to be rewarded for industry, and to

43

acquire, possess, and protect property. No person shall be deprived of any right because of race, religion, or national origin.

Section 2. Any person, with the same formalities as required by law for the execution of a last will and testament, may execute a document directing that he shall have the right to death with dignity, and that his life shall not be prolonged beyond the point of a meaningful existence.

Section 3. In the event any person is unable to make such a decision because of mental or physical incapacity, a spouse or person or persons of first degree kinship shall be allowed to make such a decision, provided written consent is obtained from:

(1) The spouse or person of first degree kinship, or

(2) In the event of two (2) persons of first degree kinship, both such persons, or

(3) In the event of three (3) or more persons of first degree kinship, the majority of those persons.

Section 4. If any person is disabled and there is no kinship as provided in section 3, death with dignity shall be granted any person if in the opinion of three (3) physicians the prolongation of life is meaningless.

Section 5. Any document executed hereunder must be recorded with the clerk of the circuit court in order to be effective.

Section 6. This act shall take effect upon becoming law.

QUESTIONS

1. If you were a legislator would you vote for or against Sackett's bill? What moral justification would you give for your decision?
2. Write a draft of a bill that would be, in your view, an improvement over Sackett's.

Yale Kamisar

EUTHANASIA LEGISLATION: SOME NONRELIGIOUS OBJECTIONS

Biographical Information. Yale Kamisar (b. 1929) is a graduate of Columbia Law School and is presently professor of law at the University of Michigan. He has served on several national commissions and has coauthored such books as Criminal Justice in Our Time *(1963) and* Constitutional Law: Cases, Comments and Questions *(3d ed., 1970).*

Argument in the Selection. Kamisar, in a debate with Glanville Williams, argues against the legalization of voluntary euthanasia, especially against the specific proposal advanced by Williams for its legalization.

Kamisar holds that voluntary euthanasia may be acceptable on pure philosophical (ethical) grounds, yet he argues that it ought not to be legalized. He advances three major lines of argument, all focusing on alleged bad effects that will attend the legalization of voluntary euthanasia. (1) It is difficult to ascertain whether consent is voluntary. Thus there is substantial danger that the law will be abused. (2) The judgment that a person is incurably ill may be wrong on two counts: (a) The diagnostic judgment may be in error. (b) The judgment that no cure will be available within the life expectancy of the patient may be in error. Thus there is substantial risk that some will die unnecessarily. (3) To legalize voluntary euthanasia is to accept the "thin edge of the wedge," thus preparing the way for the legalization of involuntary euthanasia.

A book by Glanville Williams, *The Sanctity of Life and the Criminal Law*,[1] once again brought to the fore the controversial topic of euthanasia, more popularly known as 'mercy-killing'. In keeping with the trend of the euthanasia movement over the past generation, Williams concentrates his efforts for reform on the *voluntary* type of euthanasia, for example the cancer victim begging for death, as opposed to the *involuntary* variety—that is, the case of the congenital idiot, the permanently insane or the senile. . . .

The existing law on euthanasia is hardly perfect. But if it is not too good, neither, as I have suggested, is it much worse than the rest of the criminal law. At any rate, the imperfections of existing law are not cured by Williams's proposal. Indeed, I believe adoption of his views would add more difficulties than it would remove.

Williams strongly suggests that 'euthanasia can be condemned only according to a religious opinion'.[2] He tends to view the opposing camps as Roman Catholics versus Liberals. Although this has a certain initial appeal to me, a non-Catholic and self-styled liberal, I deny that this is the only way the battle lines can, or should, be drawn. I leave the religious arguments to the theologians. I share the view that 'those who hold the faith may follow its precepts without requiring those who do not hold it to act as if they did'.[3] But I do find substantial utilitarian obstacles on the high road to euthanasia. I am not enamoured of the *status quo* on mercy-killing. But while I am not prepared to defend it against all comers, I am prepared to defend it against the proposals for change which have come forth to date.

As an ultimate philosophical proposition, the case for voluntary euthanasia is strong. Whatever may be said for and against suicide generally, the appeal of death is immeasurably greater when it is sought not for a poor reason or just any

[1] First published in the U.S. in 1957, by arrangement with the Columbia Law School. Page references in the notes following relate to the British edition (Faber & Faber, 1958).

[2] Williams, p. 278.

[3] Wechsler and Michael, 'A Rationale of the Law of Homicide', *Columbia Law Review*, 37 (1937).

reason, but for 'good cause', so to speak; when it is invoked not on behalf of a 'socially useful' person, but on behalf of, for example, the pain-racked 'hopelessly incurable' cancer victim. *If* a person is *in fact* (1) presently incurable, (2) beyond the aid of any respite which may come along in his life expectancy, suffering (3) intolerable and (4) unmitigable pain and of a (5) fixed and (6) rational desire to die, I would hate to have to argue that the hand of death should be stayed. But abstract propositions and carefully formed hypotheticals are one thing; specific proposals designed to cover everyday situations are something else again.

In essence, Williams's specific proposal is that death be authorized for a person in the above situation 'by giving the medical practitioner a wide discretion and trusting to his good sense'.[4] This, I submit, raises too great a risk of abuse and mistake to warrant a change in the existing law. That a proposal entails risk of mistake is hardly a conclusive reason against it. But neither is it irrelevant. Under any euthanasia programme the consequences of mistake, of course, are always fatal. As I shall endeavour to show, the incidence of mistake of one kind or another is likely to be quite appreciable. If this indeed be the case, unless the need for the authorized conduct is compelling enough to override it, I take it the risk of mistake *is* a conclusive reason against such authorization. I submit, too, that the possible radiations from the proposed legislation—for example, involuntary euthanasia of idiots and imbeciles (the typical 'mercy-killings' reported by the press)—and the emergence of the legal precedent that there are lives not 'worth living'—give additional cause for reflection.

I see the issue, then, as the need for voluntary euthanasia versus (1) the incidence of mistake and abuse; and (2) the danger that legal machinery initially designed to kill those who are a nuisance to themselves may some day engulf those who are a nuisance to others. . . .

THE 'CHOICE'

Under current proposals to establish legal machinery, elaborate or otherwise, for the administration of a quick and easy death, it is not enough that those authorized to pass on the question decide that the patient, in effect, is 'better off dead'. The patient must concur in this opinion. Much of the appeal in the current proposal lies in this so-called 'voluntary' attribute.

But is the adult patient really in a position to concur? Is he truly able to make euthanasia a 'voluntary' act? There is a good deal to be said, is there not, for Dr Frohman's pithy comment that the 'voluntary' plan is supposed to be carried out 'only if the victim is both sane and crazed by pain'.[5]

By hypothesis, voluntary euthanasia is not to be resorted to until narcotics have long since been administered and the patient has developed a tolerance to them. *When*, then, does the patient make the choice? While heavily drugged? Or

---

[4] Williams, p. 302.

[5] Frohman, 'Vexing Problems in Forensic Medicine: A Physician's View', *New York Univ. Law Review*, 31 (1956), 1215, 1222.

is narcotic relief to be withdrawn for the time of decision? But if heavy dosage no longer deadens pain, indeed, no longer makes it bearable, how overwhelming is it when whatever relief narcotics offer is taken away too?

'Hypersensitivity to pain after analgesia has worn off is nearly always noted'.[6] Moreover, 'the mental side-effects of narcotics, unfortunately for anyone wishing to suspend them temporarily without unduly tormenting the patient, appear to outlast the analgesic effect' and 'by many hours'.[7] The situation is further complicated by the fact that 'a person in terminal stages of cancer who had been given morphine steadily for a matter of weeks would certainly be dependent upon it physically and would probably be addicted to it and react with the addict's response'.[8]

The narcotics problem aside, Dr Benjamin Miller, who probably has personally experienced more pain than any other commentator on the euthanasia scene, observes:

> Anyone who has been severely ill knows how distorted his judgment became during the worst moments of the illness. Pain and the toxic effect of disease, or the violent reaction to certain surgical procedures may change our capacity for rational and courageous thought.[9]

Undoubtedly, some euthanasia candidates will have their lucid moments. How they are to be distinguished from fellow-sufferers who do not, or how these instances are to be distinguished from others when the patient is exercising an irrational judgment, is not an easy matter. Particularly is this so under Williams's proposal, where no specially qualified persons, psychiatrically trained or otherwise, are to assist in the process.

Assuming, for purposes of argument, that the occasion when a euthanasia candidate possesses a sufficiently clear mind can be ascertained and that a request for euthanasia is then made, there remain other problems. The mind of the pain-racked may occasionally be clear, but is it not also likely to be uncertain and variable? This point was pressed hard by the great physician, Lord Horder, in the House of Lords debates:

> During the morning depression he [the patient] will be found to favour the application under this Bill, later in the day he will think quite differently, or will have forgotten all about it. The mental clarity with which noble Lords who present this Bill are able to think and to speak must not be thought to have any counterpart in the alternating moods and confused judgments of the sick man.[10]

The concept of 'voluntary' in voluntary euthanasia would have a great deal more substance to it if, as is the case with voluntary admission statutes for the mentally ill, the patient retained the right to reverse the process within a specified

---

[6] Goodman and Gilman, *The Pharmacological Basis of Therapeutics* (2nd edn, 1955), p. 235.

[7] Sharpe, 'Medication as a Threat to Testamentary Capacity', *N. Carolina Law Review*, 35 (1957), 380, 392, and medical authorities cited therein.

[8] Sharpe, op. cit., 384.

[9] 'Why I Oppose Mercy Killings', *Woman's Home Companion* (June 1950), pp. 38, 103.

[10] *House of Lords Debates*, 103, 5th series (1936), cols 466, 492–3.

number of days after he gives written notice of his desire to do so—but unfortunately this cannot be. The choice here, of course, is an irrevocable one.

The likelihood of confusion, distortion or vacillation would appear to be serious drawbacks to any voluntary plan. Moreoever, Williams's proposal is particularly vulnerable in this regard, since as he admits, by eliminating the fairly elaborate procedure of the American and British Societies' plans, he also eliminates a time period which would furnish substantial evidence of the patient's settled intention to avail himself of euthanasia.[11] But if Williams does not always choose to slug it out, he can box neatly and parry gingerly:

> [T]he problem can be exaggerated. Every law has to face difficulties in application, and these difficulties are not a conclusive argument against a law if it has a beneficial operation. The measure here proposed is designed to meet the situation where the patient's consent to euthanasia is clear and incontrovertible. The physician, conscious of the need to protect himself against malicious accusations, can devise his own safeguards appropriate to the circumstances; he would normally be well advised to get the patient's consent in writing, just as is now the practice before operations. Sometimes the patient's consent will be particularly clear because he will have expressed a desire for ultimate euthanasia while he is still clear-headed and before he comes to be racked by pain; if the expression of desire is never revoked, but rather is reaffirmed under the pain, there is the best possible proof of full consent. If, on the other hand, there is no such settled frame of mind, and if the physician chooses to administer euthanasia when the patient's mind is in a variable state, he will be walking in the margin of the law and may find himself unprotected.[12]

If consent is given at a time when the patient's condition has so degenerated that he has become a fit candidate for euthanasia, when, if ever, will it be 'clear and incontrovertible'? Is the suggested alternative of consent in advance a satisfactory solution? Can such a consent be deemed an informed one? Is this much different from holding a man to a prior statement of intent that if such and such an employment opportunity would present itself he would accept it, or if such and such a young woman were to come along he would marry her? Need one marshal authority for the proposition that many an 'iffy' inclination is disregarded when the actual facts are at hand?

Professor Williams states that where a pre-pain desire for 'ultimate euthanasia' is 'reaffirmed' under pain, 'there is the best possible proof of full consent'. Perhaps. But what if it is alternately renounced and reaffirmed under pain? What if it is neither affirmed or renounced? What if it is only renounced? Will a physician be free to go ahead on the ground that the prior desire was 'rational', but the present desire 'irrational'? Under Williams's plan, will not the physician frequently 'be walking in the margin of the law'—just as he is now? Do we really accomplish much more under this proposal than to put the euthanasia principle on the books?

Even if the patient's choice could be said to be 'clear and incontrovertible', do not other difficulties remain? Is this the kind of choice, assuming that it can be

[11] Williams, pp. 306–7.
[12] Id., p. 307.

made in a fixed and rational manner, that we want to offer a gravely ill person? Will we not sweep up, in the process, some who are not really tired of life, but think others are tired of them; some who do not really want to die, but who feel they should not live on, because to do so when there looms the legal alternative of euthanasia is to do a selfish or a cowardly act? Will not some feel an obligation to have themselves 'eliminated' in order that funds allocated for their terminal care might be better used by their families or, financial worries aside, in order to relieve their families of the emotional strain involved?

It would not be surprising for the gravely ill person to seek to inquire of those close to him whether he should avail himself of the legal alternative of euthanasia. Certainly, he is likely to wonder about their attitude in the matter. It is quite possible, is it not, that he will not exactly be gratified by any inclination on their part—however noble their motives may be in fact—that he resort to the new procedure? At this stage, the patient-family relationship may well be a good deal less than it ought to be.

And what of the relatives? If their views will not always influence the patient, will they not at least influence the attending physician? Will a physician assume the risks to his reputation, if not his pocketbook, by administering the *coup de grâce* over the objection—however irrational—of a close relative. Do not the relatives, then, also have a 'choice'? Is not the decision on their part to do nothing and say nothing *itself* a 'choice'? In many families there will be some, will there not, who will consider a stand against euthanasia the only proof of love, devotion and gratitude for past events? What of the stress and strife if close relatives differ over the desirability of euthanatizing the patient?

At such a time, members of the family are not likely to be in the best state of mind, either, to make this kind of decision. Financial stress and conscious or unconscious competition for the family's estate aside,

> The chronic illness and persistent pain in terminal carcinoma may place strong and excessive stresses upon the family's emotional ties with the patient. The family members who have strong emotional attachment to start with are most likely to take the patient's fears, pains and fate personally. Panic often strikes them. Whatever guilt feelings they may have toward the patient emerge to plague them.
>
> If the patient is maintained at home, many frustrations and physical demands may be imposed on the family by the advanced illness. There may develop extreme weakness, incontinence and bad odors. The pressure of caring for the individual under these circumstances is likely to arouse a resentment and, in turn, guilt feelings on the part of those who have to do the nursing.[13]

Nor should it be overlooked that while Professor Williams would remove the various procedural steps and personnel contemplated in the British and American Bills and bank his all on the 'good sense' of the general practitioner, no man is immune to the fear, anxieties and frustrations engendered by the apparently helpless, hopeless patient. Not even the general practitioner. . .

---

[13] Zarling, 'Psychological Aspects of Pain in Terminal Malignancies', *Management of Pain in Cancer* (Schiffrin edn, 1956), pp. 211–12.

THE 'HOPELESSLY INCURABLE' PATIENT AND THE FALLIBLE DOCTOR

Professor Williams notes as 'standard argument' the plea that 'no sufferer from an apparently fatal illness should be deprived of his life because there is always the possibility that the diagnosis is wrong, or else that some remarkable cure will be discovered in time'.[14] . . .

Until the Euthanasia Societies of Great Britain and America had been organized and a party decision reached, shall we say, to advocate euthanasia only for incurables on their request, Dr Abraham L. Wolbarst, one of the most ardent supporters of the movement, was less troubled about putting away 'insane or defective people [who] have suffered mental incapacity and tortures of the mind for many years' than he was about the 'incurables'.[15] He recognized the 'difficulty involved in the decision as to incurability' as one of the 'doubtful aspects of euthanasia': 'Doctors are only human beings, with few if any supermen among them. They make honest mistakes, like other men, because of the limitations of the human mind.'[16]

He noted further that 'it goes without saying that, in recently developed cases with a possibility of cure, euthanasia should not even be considered', that 'the law might establish a limit of, say, ten years in which there is a chance of the patient's recovery'.[17]

Dr Benjamin Miller is another who is unlikely to harbour an ulterior theological motive. His interest is more personal. He himself was left to die the death of a 'hopeless' tuberculosis victim, only to discover that he was suffering from a rare malady which affects the lungs in much the same manner but seldom kills. Five years and sixteen hospitalizations later, Dr Miller dramatized his point by recalling the last diagnostic clinic of the brilliant Richard Cabot, on the occasion of his official retirement:

> He was given the case records [complete medical histories and results of careful examinations] of two patients and asked to diagnose their illnesses. . . . The patients had died and only the hospital pathologist knew the exact diagnosis beyond doubt, for he had seen the descriptions of the postmortem findings. Dr Cabot, usually very accurate in his diagnosis, that day missed both.
>
> The chief pathologist who had selected the cases was a wise person. He had purposely chosen two of the most deceptive to remind the medical students and young physicians that even at the end of a long and rich experience one of the greatest diagnosticians of our time was still not infallible.[18]

Richard Cabot was the John W. Davis, the John Lord O'Brian, of his profession. When one reads the account of his last clinic, one cannot help but think how fallible the *average* general practitioner must be, how fallible the *young doctor*

---

[14] Williams, p. 283.

[15] Wolbarst, 'Legalize Euthanasia!', *The Forum,* 94 (1935), 330, 332. But see Wolbarst, 'The Doctor Looks at Euthanasia,' *Medical Record,* 149 (1939), 354.

[16] Wolbarst, 'Legalize Euthanasia!', loc. cit.

[17] Ibid., 332.

[18]Op. cit. (n. 9 above), p. 39.

just starting practice must be—and this, of course, is all that some small communities have in the way of medical care—how fallible the *worst* practitioner, young or old, must be. If the range of skill and judgment among licensed physicians approaches the wide gap between the very best and the very worst members of the bar—and I have no reason to think it does not—then the minimally competent physician is hardly the man to be given the responsibility for ending another's life. Yet, under Williams's proposal at least, the marginal physician, as well as his more distinguished brethren, would have legal authorization to make just such decisions. Under Williams's proposal, euthanatizing a patient or two would all be part of the routine day's work. . . .

Faulty diagnosis is only one ground for error. Even if the diagnosis is correct, a second ground for error lies in the possibility that some measure of relief, if not a full cure, may come to the fore within the life expectancy of the patient. Since Glanville Williams does not deign this objection to euthanasia worth more than a passing reference,[19] it is necessary to turn elsewhere to ascertain how it has been met. One answer is: 'It must be little comfort to a man slowly coming apart from multiple sclerosis to think that fifteen years from now, death might not be his only hope.'[20]

To state the problem this way is of course, to avoid it entirely. How do we know that fifteen *days* or fifteen *hours* from now, 'death might not be [the incurable's] only hope'?

A second answer is: '[N]o cure for cancer which might be found "tomorrow" would be of any value to a man or woman "so far advanced in cancerous toxemia as to be an applicant for euthanasia".'[21]

As I shall endeavour to show, this approach is a good deal easier to formulate than it is to apply. For one thing, it presumes that we know today *what* cures will be found tomorrow. For another, it overlooks that if such cases can be said to exist, the patient is likely to be *so far* advanced in cancerous toxemia as to be no longer capable of understanding the step he is taking and hence *beyond* the stage when euthanasia ought to be administered.

Thirty-six years ago, Dr Haven Emerson, then President of the American Public Health Association, made the point that 'no one can say today what will be incurable tomorrow. No one can predict what disease will be fatal or permanently incurable until medicine becomes stationary and sterile'.[22] . . .

VOLUNTARY VERSUS INVOLUNTARY EUTHANASIA

Ever since the 1870s, when what was probably the first euthanasia debate of the modern era took place, most proponents of the movement—at least when they are

---

[19] See Williams, p. 283.

[20] 'Pro & Con: Shall We Legalize "Mercy Killing"?', *Reader's Digest* (Nov. 1938), pp. 94, 96.

[21] James, 'Euthanasia—Right or Wrong?', *Survey Graphic* (May 1948), pp. 241, 243; Wolbarst, 'The Doctor Looks at Euthanasia', *Medical Record*, 149 (1939), 354, 355.

[22] Emerson, 'Who Is Incurable? A Query and a Reply', *New York Times* (Oct. 22, 1933), § 8, p. 5 col. 1.

pressed—have taken considerable pains to restrict the question to the plight of the unbearably suffering incurable who *voluntarily seeks* death, while most of their opponents have striven equally hard to frame the issue in terms which would encompass certain involuntary situations as well, e.g. the 'congenital idiots', the 'permanently insane', and the senile.

Glanville Williams reflects the outward mood of many euthanasiasts when he scores those who insist on considering the question from a broader angle:

> The [British Society's] bill [debated in the House of Lords in 1936 and 1950] excluded any question of compulsory euthanasia, even for hopelessly defective infants. Unfortunately, a legislative proposal is not assured of success merely because it is worded in a studiously moderate and restrictive form. The method of attack, by those who dislike the proposal, is to use the 'thin end of the wedge' argument. . . . There is no proposal for reform on any topic, however conciliatory and moderate, that cannot be opposed by this dialectic.[23]

Why was the bill 'worded in a studiously moderate and restrictive form'? If it were done as a matter of principle, if it were done in recognition of the ethico-moral-legal 'wall of separation' which stands between voluntary and compulsory 'mercy-killings', much can be said for the euthanasiasts' lament about the methods employed by the opposition. But if it were done as a matter of political expediency—with great hopes and expectations of pushing through a second and somewhat less restrictive bill as soon as the first one had sufficiently 'educated' public opinion and next a third, still less restrictive bill—what standing do the euthanasiasts then have to attack the methods of the opposition? No cry of righteous indignation could ring more hollow, I would think, than the protest from those utilizing the 'wedge' principle themselves that their opponents are making the wedge objection. . . .

The boldness and daring which characterize most of Glanville Williams's book dim perceptibly when he comes to involuntary euthanasia proposals. As to the senile, he states:

> At present the problem has certainly not reached the degree of seriousness that would warrant an effort being made to change traditional attitudes towards the sanctity of life of the aged. Only the grimmest necessity could bring about a change that, however cautious in its approach, would probably cause apprehension and deep distress to many people, and inflict a traumatic injury upon the accepted code of behaviour built up by two thousand years of the Christian religion. It may be, however, that as the problem becomes more acute it will itself cause a reversal of generally accepted values.[24]

To me, this passage is the most startling one in the book. On page 310 Williams invokes 'traditional attitudes towards the sanctity of life' and 'the accepted code of behaviour built up by two thousand years of the Christian religion' to check the extension of euthanasia to the senile, but for 309 pages he had been merrily rolling along debunking both. Substitute 'cancer victim' for 'the

---

[23] Williams, pp. 297–8.
[24] Williams, p. 310.

aged' and Williams's passage is essentially the argument of many of his *opponents* on the voluntary euthanasia question.

The unsupported comment that 'the problem [of senility] has certainly not reached the degree of seriousness' to warrant euthanasia is also rather puzzling, particularly coming as it does after an observation by Williams on the immediately preceding page that 'it is increasingly common for men and women to reach an age of "second childishness and mere oblivion", with a loss of almost all adult faculties except that of digestion'.[25]

How 'serious' does a problem have to be to warrant a change in these 'traditional attitudes'? If, as the statement seems to indicate, 'seriousness' of the problem is to be determined numerically, the problem of the cancer victim does not appear to be as substantial as the problem of the senile. For example, taking just the 95,837 first admissions to 'public prolonged-care hospitals' for mental diseases in the United States in 1955, 23,561—or one-fourth—were cerebral arteriosclerosis or senile brain disease cases. I am not at all sure that there are twenty thousand cancer victims per year who die *unbearably painful* deaths. Even if there were, I cannot believe that among their ranks are some twenty thousand per year who, when still in a rational state, so long for a quick and easy death that they would avail themselves of legal machinery for euthanasia.

If the problem of the incurable cancer victim has reached 'the degree of seriousness that would warrant an effort being made to change traditional attitudes towards the sanctity of life', as Williams obviously thinks it has, then so has the problem of senility. In any event, the senility problem will undoubtedly soon reach even Williams's requisite degree of seriousness:

> A decision concerning the senile may have to be taken within the next twenty years. The number of old people are increasing by leaps and bounds. Pneumonia, 'the old man's friend', is now checked by antibiotics. The effects of hardship, exposure, starvation and accident are now minimized. Where is this leading us? . . . What of the drooling, helpless, disorientated old man or the doubly incontinent old woman lying log-like in bed? Is it here that the real need for euthanasia exists?[26]

If, as Williams indicates, 'seriousness' of the problem is a major criterion for euthanatizing a category of unfortunates, the sum total of mentally deficient persons would appear to warrant high priority, indeed.

When Williams turns to the plight of the 'hopelessly defective infants', his characteristic vim and vigour are, as in the senility discussion, conspicuously absent:

> While the Euthanasia Society of England has never advocated this, the Euthanasia Society of America did include it in its original programme. The proposal certainly escapes the chief objection to the similar proposal for senile dementia: it does not create a sense of insecurity in society, because infants cannot, like adults, feel anticipatory dread of being done to death if

[25] Ibid.

[26] Banks, 'Euthanasia', *Bulletin of the New York Academy of Medicine,* 26 (1950), 297, 305.

their condition should worsen. Moreover, the proposal receives some support on eugenic grounds, and more importantly on humanitarian grounds—both on account of the parents, to whom the child will be a burden all their lives, and on account of the handicapped child itself. (It is not, however, proposed that any child should be destroyed against the wishes of its parents.) Finally, the legalization of euthanasia for handicapped children would bring the law into closer relation to its practical administration, because juries do not regard parental mercy-killing as murder. For these various reasons the proposal to legalize humanitarian infanticide is put forward from time to time by individuals. They remain in a very small minority, and the proposal may at present be dismissed as politically insignificant.[27]

It is understandable for a reformer to limit his present proposals for change to those with a real prospect of success. But it is hardly reassuring for Williams to cite the fact that only 'a very small minority' has urged euthanasia for 'hopelessly defective infants' as the *only* reason for not pressing for such legislation now. If, as Williams sees it, the only advantage voluntary euthanasia has over the involuntary variety lies in the organized movements on its behalf, that advantage can readily be wiped out.

In any event, I do not think that such 'a very small minority' has advocated 'humanitarian infanticide'. Until the organization of the British and American societies led to a concentration on the voluntary type, and until the by-products of the Nazi euthanasia programme somewhat embarrassed, if only temporarily, most proponents of involuntary euthanasia, about as many writers urged one type as another. Indeed, some euthanasiasts have taken considerable pains to demonstrate the superiority of defective infant euthanasia over incurably ill euthanasia.

As for dismissing euthanasia of defective infants as 'politically insignificant', the only poll that I know of which measured the public response to both types of euthanasia revealed that *45 per cent favoured euthanasia for defective infants under certain conditions while only 37.3 per cent approved euthanasia for the incurably and painfully ill under any conditions.*[28] Furthermore, of those who favoured the mercy-killing cure for incurable adults, some 40 per cent would require only family permission or medical board approval, but not the patient's permission.

Nor do I think it irrelevant that while public resistance caused Hitler to yield on the adult euthanasia front, the killing of malformed and idiot children continued unhindered to the end of the war, the definition of 'children' expanding all the while. Is it the embarrassing experience of the Nazi euthanasia programme which has rendered destruction of defective infants presently 'politically insignificant'? If so, is it any more of a jump from the incurably and painfully ill to the unorthodox political thinker than it is from the hopelessly defective infant to the same 'unsavoury character'? Or is it not so much that the euthanasiasts are troubled by the Nazi experience as it is that they are troubled that the public is troubled by the Nazi experience?

I read Williams's comments on defective infants for the proposition that there are some very good reasons for euthanatizing defective infants, but the time is not

---

[27] Williams, pp. 311–12.
[28] The Fortune Quarterly Survey: IX, *Fortune Magazine* (July 1937), pp. 96, 106.

yet ripe. When will it be? When will the proposal become politically significant? After a voluntary euthanasia law is on the books and public opinion is sufficiently 'educated'?

Williams's reasons for not extending euthanasia—once we legalize it in the narrow 'voluntary' area—to the senile and the defective are much less forceful and much less persuasive than his arguments for legalizing voluntary euthanasia in the first place. I regard this as another reason for not legalizing voluntary euthanasia in the first place.

QUESTIONS

1. On your view, does Kamisar discuss all the undesirable consequences of legalizing voluntary euthanasia? If you think there may be others, specify them.

2. Is Kamisar's wedge argument a substantial argument or, as it is sometimes alleged, a rhetorical scare tactic?

Glanville Williams

EUTHANASIA LEGISLATION: A REJOINDER TO THE NONRELIGIOUS OBJECTIONS

Biographical Information. *Glanville Williams (b. 1911) is a fellow of Jesus College and Rouse Ball Professor of the Laws of England at the University of Cambridge. Since 1959 he has been a member of the Standing Committee on Criminal Law Revision. Williams is a prominent spokesman for the movement to legalize voluntary euthanasia, and his primary work in this regard is* The Sanctity of Life and the Criminal Law *(U.S. ed., 1957; British ed., 1958). Among his other works are* The Proof of Guilt *(1955; 3d ed., 1963) and* The Mental Element in Crime *(1965).*

Argument in the Selection. *Before beginning his direct reply to the arguments raised by Kamisar in the previous selection, Williams reiterates the basic case for the legalization of voluntary euthanasia. On his view there are two principal arguments (1) it is simply cruel to refuse an agonized and incurably ill person's request for "merciful release." (2) There is no demonstrable social interest sufficient to warrant the infringement of liberty (the patient's and the doctor's) that accompanies the legal prohibition of voluntary euthanasia.*

In response to Kamisar's arguments against the legalization of voluntary euthanasia, Williams acknowledges that there is the possibility of abuse (concerning the ascertaining of consent), the possibility of mistaken diagnoses, and the possibility of dramatic medical discoveries. But he plays down the force of such factors and argues that they do not warrant the continued legal prohibition of voluntary euthanasia. In response to Kamisar's claim that the legalization of euthanasia is the thin edge of the wedge that will open the door to legalized involuntary euthanasia, Williams argues that this claim is without foundation.

I welcome Professor Kamisar's reply to my argument for voluntary euthanasia, because it is on the whole a careful, scholarly work, keeping to knowable facts and accepted human values. It is, therefore, the sort of reply that can be rationally considered and dealt with. In this short rejoinder I shall accept most of Professor Kamisar's valuable notes, and merely submit that they do not bear out his conclusion.

The argument in favour of voluntary euthanasia in the terminal stages of painful diseases is a quite simple one, and is an application of two values that are widely recognized. The first value is the prevention of cruelty. Much as men differ in their ethical assessments, all agree that cruelty is an evil—the only difference of opinion residing in what is meant by cruelty. Those who plead for the legalization of euthanasia think that it is cruel to allow a human being to linger for months in the last stages of agony, weakness and decay, and to refuse him his demand for merciful release. There is also a second cruelty involved—not perhaps quite so compelling, but still worth consideration: the agony of the relatives in seeing their loved one in his desperate plight. Opponents of euthanasia are apt to take a cynical view of the desires of relatives, and this may sometimes be justified. But it cannot be denied that a wife who has to nurse her husband through the last stages of some terrible disease may herself be so deeply affected by the experience that her health is ruined, either mentally or physically. Whether the situation can be eased for such a person by voluntary euthanasia I do not know; probably it depends very much upon the individuals concerned, which is as much as to say that no solution in terms of a general regulatory law can be satisfactory. The conclusion should be in favour of individual discretion.

The second value involved is that of liberty. The criminal law should not be invoked to repress conduct unless this is demonstrably necessary on social grounds. What social interest is there in preventing the sufferer from choosing to accelerate his death by a few months? What positive value does his life still possess for society, that he is to be retained in it by the terrors of the criminal law?

And, of course, the liberty involved is that of the doctor as well as that of the patient. It is the doctor's responsibility to do all he can to prolong worth-while life, or, in the last resort, to ease his patient's passage. If the doctor honestly and sincerely believes that the best service he can perform for his suffering patient is to accede to his request for euthanasia, it is a grave thing that the law should forbid him to do so.

This is the short and simple case for voluntary euthanasia, and, as Kamisar admits, it cannot be attacked directly on utilitarian grounds. Such an attack can only be by finding possible evils of an indirect nature. These evils, in the view of Professor Kamisar, are (1) the difficulty of ascertaining consent, and arising out of that the danger of abuse; (2) the risk of an incorrect diagnosis; (3) the risk of administering euthanasia to a person who could later have been cured by developments in medical knowledge; (4) the 'wedge' argument. . . .

Kamisar's first objection, under the heading 'The Choice', is that there can be no such thing as truly voluntary euthanasia in painful and killing diseases. He seeks to impale the advocates of euthanasia on an old dilemma. Either the victim is not yet suffering pain, in which case his consent is merely an uninformed and anticipatory one—and he cannot bind himself by contract to be killed in the future—or he is crazed by pain and stupefied by drugs, in which case he is not of sound mind. I have dealt with this problem in my book; Kamisar has quoted generously from it, and I leave the reader to decide. As I understand Kamisar's position, he does not really persist in the objection. With the laconic 'perhaps', he seems to grant me, though unwillingly, that there are cases where one can be sure of the patient's consent. But having thus abandoned his own point, he then goes off to a different horror, that the patient may give his consent only in order to relieve his relatives of the trouble of looking after him.

On this new issue, I will return Kamisar the compliment and say: 'Perhaps'. We are certainly in an area where no solution is going to make things quite easy and happy for everybody, and all sorts of embarrassments may be conjectured. But these embarrassments are not avoided by keeping to the present law: we suffer from them already. If a patient, suffering pain in a terminal illness, wishes for euthanasia partly because of his pain and partly because he sees his beloved ones breaking under the strain of caring for him, I do not see how this decision on his part, agonizing though it may be, is necessarily a matter of discredit either to the patient himself or to his relatives. The fact is that, whether we are considering the patient or his relatives, there are limits to human endurance.

Kamisar's next objection rests on the possibility of mistaken diagnosis. . . . I agree with him that, before deciding on euthanasia in any particular case, the risk of mistaken diagnosis would have to be considered. Everything that is said in the essay would, therefore, be most relevant when the two doctors whom I propose in my suggested measure come to consult on the question of euthanasia; and the possibility of mistake might most forcefully be brought before the patient himself. But have these medical questions any true relevance to the legal discussion?

Kamisar, I take it, notwithstanding his wide reading in medical literature, is by training a lawyer. He has consulted much medical opinion in order to find arguments against changing the law. I ought not to object to this, since I have consulted the same opinion for the opposite purpose. But what we may well ask ourselves is this: is it not a trifle bizarre that we should be doing so at all? Our profession is the law, not medicine. How does it come about that lawyers have to examine medical literature to assess the advantages and disadvantages of a medical practice?

If the import of this question is not immediately clear, let me return to my imaginary state of Ruritania. Many years ago, in Ruritania as elsewhere, surgical operations were attended with great risk. Lister had not discovered antisepsis, and surgeons killed as often as they cured. In this state of things, the legislature of Ruritania passed a law declaring all surgical operations to be unlawful in principle, but providing that each specific type of operation might be legalized by a statute specially passed for the purpose. The result is that, in Ruritania, as expert medical opinion sees the possibility of some new medical advance, a pressure group has to be formed in order to obtain legislative approval for it. Since there is little public interest in these technical questions, and since, moreover, surgical operations are thought in general to be inimical to the established religion, the pressure group has to work for many years before it gets a hearing. When at last a proposal for legalization is seriously mooted, the lawyers and politicians get to work upon it, considering what possible dangers are inherent in the new operation. Lawyers and politicians are careful people, and they are perhaps more prone to see the dangers than the advantages in a new departure. Naturally they find allies among some of the more timid or traditional or less knowledgeable members of the medical profession, as well as among the priesthood and the faithful. Thus it is small wonder that whereas appendicectomy has been practised in civilized countries since the beginning of the present century, a proposal to legalize it has still not passed the legislative assembly of Ruritania.

It must be confessed that on this particular matter the legal prohibition has not been an unmixed evil for the Ruritanians. During the great popularity of the appendix operation in much of the civilized world during the 'twenties and 'thirties of this century, large numbers of these organs were removed without adequate cause, and the citizens of Ruritania have been spared this inconvenience. On the other hand, many citizens of that country have died of appendicitis, who would have been saved if they had lived elsewhere. And whereas in other countries the medical profession has now learned enough to be able to perform this operation with wisdom and restraint, in Ruritania it is still not being performed at all. Moreover, the law has destroyed scientific inventiveness in that country in the forbidden fields.

Now, in the United States and England we have no such absurd general law on the subject of surgical operations as they have in Ruritania. In principle, medical men are left free to exercise their best judgment, and the result has been a brilliant advance in knowledge and technique. But there are just two—or possibly three—'operations' which are subject to the Ruritanian principle. These are abortion, euthanasia, and possibly sterilization of convenience. In these fields we, too, must have pressure groups, with lawyers and politicians warning us of the possibility of inexpert practitioners and mistaken diagnosis, and canvassing medical opinion on the risk of an operation not yielding the expected results in terms of human happiness and the health of the body politic. In these fields we, too, are forbidden to experiment to see if the foretold dangers actually come to pass. Instead of that, we are required to make a social judgment on the probabilities of good and evil before the medical profession is allowed to start on its empirical tests.

This anomaly is perhaps more obvious with abortion than it is with euthanasia. Indeed, I am prepared for ridicule when I describe euthanasia as a medical operation. Regarded as surgery it is unique, since its object is not to save or prolong life but the reverse. But euthanasia has another object which it shares with many surgical operations—the saving of pain. And it is now widely recognized, as Lord Dawson said in the debate in the House of Lords, that the saving of pain is a legitimate aim of medical practice. The question whether euthanasia will effect a net saving of pain and distress is, perhaps, one that we can attempt to answer only by trying it. But it is obscurantist to forbid the experiment on the ground that until it is performed we cannot certainly know its results. Such an attitude, in any other field of medical endeavour, would have inhibited progress.

The argument based on mistaken diagnosis leads into the argument based on the possibility of dramatic medical discoveries. Of course, a new medical discovery which gives the opportunity of remission or cure will almost at once put an end to mercy-killings in the particular group of cases for which the discovery is made. On the other hand, the discovery cannot affect patients who have already died from their disease. The argument based on mistaken diagnosis is therefore concerned only with those patients who have been mercifully killed just before the discovery becomes available for use. The argument is that such persons may turn out to have been 'mercy-killed' unnecessarily, because if the physician had waited a bit longer they would have been cured. Because of this risk for this tiny fraction of the total number of patients, patients who are dying in pain must be left to do so, year after year, against their entreaty to have it ended.

Just how real is the risk? When a new medical discovery is claimed, some time commonly elapses before it becomes tested sufficiently to justify large-scale production of the drug, or training in the techniques involved. This is a warning period when euthanasia in the particular class of case would probably be halted anyway. Thus it is quite probable that when the new discovery becomes available, the euthanasia process would not in fact show any mistakes in this regard.

Kamisar says that in my book I 'did not deign this objection to euthanasia more than a passing reference'. I still do not think it is worth any more than that.

He advances the familiar but hardly convincing arguments that the quantitative need for euthanasia is not large. As one reason for this argument, he suggests that not many patients would wish to benefit from euthanasia, even if it were allowed. I am not impressed by the argument. It may be true, but it is irrelevant. So long as there are *any* persons dying in weakness and grief who are refused their request for a speeding of their end, the argument for legalizing euthanasia remains. Next, he suggests that there is no great need for euthanasia because of the advances made with pain-killing drugs. He has made so many quotations from my book that I cannot complain that he has not made more, but there is one relevant point that he does not mention. In my book, recognizing that medical science does manage to save many dying patients from the extreme of physical pain, I pointed out that it often fails to save them from an artificial, twilight existence, with nausea, giddiness, and extreme restlessness, as well as the long hours of consciousness of a hopeless condition. A dear friend of mine, who died of cancer of the bowel, spent his last months in just this state, under the influence of morphine, which deadened pain, but vomiting incessantly, day in and day out. The question that we have to face is whether the unintelligent brutality of such an existence is to be imposed on one who wishes to end it. . . .

The last part of the essay is devoted to the ancient 'wedge' argument which I have already examined in my book: It is the trump card of the traditionalist, because no proposal for reform, however strong the arguments in its favour, is immune from the wedge objection. In fact, the stronger the arguments in favour of a reform, the more likely it is that the traditionalist will take the wedge objection—it is then the only one he has. C. M. Cornford put the argument in its proper place when he said that the wedge objection means this: that you should not act justly today, for fear that you may be asked to act still more justly tomorrow.

We heard a great deal of this type of argument in England in the nineteenth century, when it was used to resist almost every social and economic change. In the present century we have had less of it, but it is still accorded an exaggerated importance in some contexts. When lecturing on the law of torts in an American university a few years ago, I suggested that just as compulsory liability insurance for automobiles had spread practically throughout the civilized world, so we should in time see the law of tort superseded in this field by a system of state insurance for traffic accidents, administered independently of proof of fault. The suggestion was immediately met by one student with a horrified reference to 'creeping socialism'. That is the standard objection made by many people to any proposal for a new department of state activity. The implication is that you must resist every proposal, however admirable in itself, because otherwise you will never be able to draw the line. On the particular question of socialism, the fear is belied by the experience of a number of countries which have extended state control of the economy without going the whole way to socialistic state regimentation.

Kamisar's particular bogey, the racial laws of Nazi Germany, is an effective one in the democratic countries. Any reference to the Nazis is a powerful weapon to prevent change in the traditional taboo on sterilization as well as euthanasia. The case of sterilization is particularly interesting on this; I dealt with it at length in my book, though Kamisar does not mention its bearing on the argument. When proposals are made for promoting voluntary sterilization on eugenic and other grounds, they are immediately condemned by most people as the thin end of a wedge leading to involuntary sterilization; and then they point to the practices of the Nazis. Yet a more persuasive argument pointing in the other direction can easily be found. Several American states have sterilization laws, which for the most part were originally drafted in very wide terms to cover desexualization as well as sterilization, and authorizing involuntary as well as voluntary operations. This legislation goes back long before the Nazis; the earliest statute was in Indiana in 1907. What has been its practical effect? In several American states it has hardly been used. A few have used it, but in practice they have progressively restricted it until now it is virtually confined to voluntary sterilization. This is so, at least, in North Carolina, as Mrs Woodside's study strikingly shows. In my book I summed up the position as follows:

> The American experience is of great interest because it shows how remote from reality in a democratic community is the fear—frequently voiced by Americans themselves—that voluntary sterilization may be the 'thin end of the wedge', leading to a large-scale violation of human rights as happened in Nazi Germany. In fact, the American experience is the precise opposite— starting with compulsory sterilization, administrative practice has come to put the operation on a voluntary footing.

But it is insufficient to answer the 'wedge' objection in general terms; we must consider the particular fears to which it gives rise. Kamisar professes to fear certain other measures that the Euthanasia Societies may bring up if their present measure is conceded to them. Surely these other measures, if any, will be debated on their merits? Does he seriously fear that anyone in the United States or in Great

Britain is going to propose the extermination of people of a minority race or religion? Let us put aside such ridiculous fancies and discuss practical politics.

Kamisar is quite right in thinking that a body of opinion would favour the legalization of the involuntary euthanasia of hopelessly defective infants, and some day a proposal of this kind may be put forward. The proposal would have distinct limits, just as the proposal for voluntary euthanasia of incurable sufferers has limits. I do not think that any responsible body of opinion would now propose the euthanasia of insane adults, for the perfectly clear reason that any such practice would greatly increase the sense of insecurity felt by the borderline insane and by the large number of insane persons who have sufficient understanding on this particular matter.

Kamisar expresses distress at a concluding remark in my book in which I advert to the possibility of old people becoming an overwhelming burden on mankind. I share his feeling that there are profoundly disturbing possibilities here; and if I had been merely a propagandist, intent upon securing agreement for a specific measure of law reform, I should have done wisely to have omitted all reference to this subject. Since, however, I am merely an academic writer, trying to bring such intelligence as I have to bear on moral and social issues, I deemed the topic too important and threatening to leave without a word. I think I have made it clear, in the passages cited, that I am not for one moment proposing any euthanasia of the aged in present society; such an idea would shock me as much as it shocks Kamisar and would shock everybody else. Still, the fact that we may one day have to face is that medical science is more successful in preserving the body than in preserving the mind. It is not impossible that, in the foreseeable future, medical men will be able to preserve the mindless body until the age, say, of a thousand, while the mind itself will have lasted only a tenth of that time. What will mankind do then? It is hardly possible to imagine that we shall establish huge hospital-mausolea where the aged are kept in a kind of living death. Even if it is desired to do this, the cost of the undertaking may make it impossible.

This is not an immediately practical problem, and we need not yet face it. The problem of maintaining persons afflicted with senile dementia is well within our economic resources as the matter stands at present. Perhaps some barrier will be found to medical advance which will prevent the problem becoming more acute. Perhaps, as time goes on, and as the alternatives become more clearly realized, men will become more resigned to human control over the mode of termination of life. Or the solution may be that after the individual has reached a certain age, or a certain degree of decay, medical science will hold its hand, and allow him to be carried off by natural causes. But what if these natural causes are themselves painful? Would it not then be kinder to substitute human agency?

In general, it is enough to say that we do not have to know the solutions to these problems. The only doubtful moral question upon which we have to make an immediate decision in relation to involuntary euthanasia is whether we owe a moral duty to terminate the life of an insane person who is suffering from a painful and incurable disease. Such a person is left unprovided for under the legislative proposal formulated in my book. The objection to any system of involuntary euthanasia of the insane is that it may cause a sense of insecurity. It is because I think that the risk of this fear is a serious one that a proposal for the reform of the law must exclude its application to the insane.

61

QUESTIONS

1. Williams alleges that there is no legitimate social interest sufficient to warrant the infringement of personal liberty that accompanies the legal prohibition of voluntary euthanasia. How do you think Kamisar would answer this argument?

2. Should there be a legal right to euthanasia?

James Rachels

ACTIVE AND PASSIVE EUTHANASIA

Biographical Information. *James Rachels teaches in the Philosophy Department at the University of Miami. His interest in ethical issues is reflected in the article reprinted here as well as in other articles such as "Two Arguments against Ethical Egoism," Philosophia (1974). Rachels is also the editor of* Moral Problems: A Collection of Philosophical Essays *(1971, 2d ed. 1975).*

Argument in the Selection. *Rachels argues that "the traditional distinction" between active and passive euthanasia requires critical analysis. The conventional doctrine is that there is such an important moral difference between the two that, although the latter is sometimes permissible, the former is always forbidden. This doctrine may be challenged for several reasons. First of all, active euthanasia is in many cases more humane than passive euthanasia. Second, the conventional doctrine leads to decisions concerning life and death on irrelevant grounds. Third, the doctrine rests on a distinction between killing and letting die that itself has no moral importance. Fourth, the most common arguments in favor of the doctrine are invalid.*

The distinction between active and passive euthanasia is thought to be crucial for medical ethics. The idea is that it is permissible, at least in some cases, to withhold treatment and allow a patient to die, but it is never permissible to take any direct action designed to kill the patient. This doctrine seems to be accepted by most doctors, and it is endorsed in a statement adopted by the House of Delegates of the American Medical Association on December 4, 1973:

> The intentional termination of the life of one human being by another—mercy killing—is contrary to that for which the medical profession stands and is contrary to the policy of the American Medical Association.
> The cessation of the employment of extraordinary means to prolong the life of the body when there is irrefutable evidence that biological death is

62

imminent is the decision of the patient and/or his immediate family. The advice and judgment of the physician should be freely available to the patient and/or his immediate family.

However, a strong case can be made against this doctrine. In what follows I will set out some of the relevant arguments, and urge doctors to reconsider their views on this matter.

To begin with a familiar type of situation, a patient who is dying of incurable cancer of the throat is in terrible pain, which can no longer be satisfactorily alleviated. He is certain to die within a few days, even if present treatment is continued, but he does not want to go on living for those days since the pain is unbearable. So he asks the doctor for an end to it, and his family joins in the request.

Suppose the doctor agrees to withhold treatment, as the conventional doctrine says he may. The justification for his doing so is that the patient is in terrible agony, and since he is going to die anyway, it would be wrong to prolong his suffering needlessly. But now notice this. If one simply withholds treatment, it may take the patient longer to die, and so he may suffer more than he would if more direct action were taken and a lethal injection given. This fact provides strong reason for thinking that, once the initial decision not to prolong his agony has been made, active euthanasia is actually preferable to passive euthanasia, rather than the reverse. To say otherwise is to endorse the option that leads to more suffering rather than less, and is contrary to the humanitarian impulse that prompts the decision not to prolong his life in the first place.

Part of my point is that the process of being "allowed to die" can be relatively slow and painful, whereas being given a lethal injection is relatively quick and painless. Let me give a different sort of example. In the United States about one in 600 babies is born with Down's syndrome. Most of these babies are otherwise healthy—that is, with only the usual pediatric care, they will proceed to an otherwise normal infancy. Some, however, are born with congenital defects such as intestinal obstructions that require operations if they are to live. Sometimes, the parents and the doctor will decide not to operate, and let the infant die. Anthony Shaw describes what happens then:

> . . . When surgery is denied [the doctor] must try to keep the infant from suffering while natural forces sap the baby's life away. As a surgeon whose natural inclination is to use the scalpel to fight off death, standing by and watching a salvageable baby die is the most emotionally exhausting experience I know. It is easy at a conference, in a theoretical discussion, to decide that such infants should be allowed to die. It is altogether different to stand by in the nursery and watch as dehydration and infection wither a tiny being over hours and days. This is a terrible ordeal for me and the hospital staff—much more so than for the parents who never set foot in the nursery.[1]

I can understand why some people are opposed to all euthanasia, and insist that such infants must be allowed to live. I think I can also understand why other people favor destroying these babies quickly and painlessly. But why should

[1] Shaw A: 'Doctor, Do We Have a Choice?' The New York Times Magazine, January 30, 1972, p 54.

anyone favor letting "dehydration and infection wither a tiny being over hours and days?" The doctrine that says that a baby may be allowed to dehydrate and wither, but may not be given an injection that would end its life without suffering, seems so patently cruel as to require no further refutation. The strong language is not intended to offend, but only to put the point in the clearest possible way.

My second argument is that the conventional doctrine leads to decisions concerning life and death made on irrelevant grounds.

Consider again the case of the infants with Down's syndrome who need operations for congenital defects unrelated to the syndrome to live. Sometimes, there is no operation, and the baby dies, but when there is no such defect, the baby lives on. Now, an operation such as that to remove an intestinal obstruction is not prohibitively difficult. The reason why such operations are not performed in these cases is, clearly, that the child has Down's syndrome and the parents and doctor judge that because of that fact it is better for the child to die.

But notice that this situation is absurd, no matter what view one takes of the lives and potentials of such babies. If the life of such an infant is worth preserving, what does it matter if it needs a simple operation? Or, if one thinks it better that such a baby should not live on, what difference does it make that it happens to have an unobstructed intestinal tract? In either case, the matter of life and death is being decided on irrelevant grounds. It is the Down's syndrome, and not the intestines, that is the issue. The matter should be decided, if at all, on that basis, and not be allowed to depend on the essentially irrelevant question of whether the intestinal tract is blocked.

What makes this situation possible, of course, is the idea that when there is an intestinal blockage, one can "let the baby die," but when there is no such defect there is nothing that can be done, for one must not "kill" it. The fact that this idea leads to such results as deciding life or death on irrelevant grounds is another good reason why the doctrine should be rejected.

One reason why so many people think that there is an important moral difference between active and passive euthanasia is that they think killing someone is morally worse than letting someone die. But is it? Is killing, in itself, worse than letting die? To investigate this issue, two cases may be considered that are exactly alike except that one involves killing whereas the other involves letting someone die. Then, it can be asked whether this difference makes any difference to the moral assessments. It is important that the cases be exactly alike, except for this one difference, since otherwise one cannot be confident that it is this difference and not some other that accounts for any variation in the assessments of the two cases. So, let us consider this pair of cases:

In the first, Smith stands to gain a large inheritance if anything should happen to his six-year-old cousin. One evening while the child is taking his bath, Smith sneaks into the bathroom and drowns the child, and then arranges things so that it will look like an accident.

In the second, Jones also stands to gain if anything should happen to his six-year-old cousin. Like Smith, Jones sneaks in planning to drown the child in his bath. However, just as he enters the bathroom Jones sees the child slip and hit his head, and fall face down in the water. Jones is delighted; he stands by, ready to push the child's head back under if it is necessary, but it is not necessary. With only a little thrashing about, the child drowns all by himself, "accidentally," as Jones watches and does nothing.

Now Smith killed the child, whereas Jones "merely" let the child die. That is the only difference between them. Did either man behave better, from a moral point of view? If the difference between killing and letting die were in itself a morally important matter, one should say that Jones's behavior was less reprehensible than Smith's. But does one really want to say that? I think not. In the first place, both men acted from the same motive, personal gain, and both had exactly the same end in view when they acted. It may be inferred from Smith's conduct that he is a bad man, although that judgment may be withdrawn or modified if certain further facts are learned about him—for example, that he is mentally deranged. But would not the very same thing be inferred about Jones from his conduct? And would not the same further considerations also be relevant to any modification of this judgment? Moreover, suppose Jones pleaded, in his own defense, "After all, I didn't do anything except just stand there and watch the child drown. I didn't kill him; I only let him die." Again, if letting die were in itself less bad than killing, this defense should have at least some weight. But it does not. Such a "defense" can only be regarded as a grotesque perversion of moral reasoning. Morally speaking, it is no defense at all.

Now, it may be pointed out, quite properly, that the cases of euthanasia with which doctors are concerned are not like this at all. They do not involve personal gain or the destruction of normal healthy children. Doctors are concerned only with cases in which the patient's life is of no further use to him, or in which the patient's life has become or will soon become a terrible burden. However, the point is the same in these cases: the bare difference between killing and letting die does not, in itself, make a moral difference. If a doctor lets a patient die, for humane reasons, he is in the same moral position as if he had given the patient a lethal injection for humane reasons. If his decision was wrong—if, for example, the patient's illness was in fact curable—the decision would be equally regrettable no matter which method was used to carry it out. And if the doctor's decision was the right one, the method used is not in itself important.

The AMA policy statement isolates the crucial issue very well; the crucial issue is "the intentional termination of the life of one human being by another." But after identifying this issue, and forbidding "mercy killing," the statement goes on to deny that the cessation of treatment is the intentional termination of a life. This is where the mistake comes in, for what is the cessation of treatment, in these circumstances, if it is not "the intentional termination of the life of one human being by another?" Of course it is exactly that, and if it were not, there would be no point to it.

Many people will find this judgment hard to accept. One reason, I think, is that it is very easy to conflate the question of whether killing is, in itself, worse than letting die, with the very different question of whether most actual cases of killing are more reprehensible than most actual cases of letting die. Most actual cases of killing are clearly terrible (think, for example, of all the murders reported in the newspapers), and one hears of such cases every day. On the other hand, one hardly ever hears of a case of letting die, except for the actions of doctors who are motivated by humanitarian reasons. So one learns to think of killing in a much worse light than of letting die. But this does not mean that there is something about killing that makes it in itself worse than letting die, for it is not the bare difference between killing and letting die that makes the difference in these cases. Rather, the other factors—the murderer's motive of personal gain, for example,

65

contrasted with the doctor's humanitarian motivation—account for different reactions to the different cases.

I have argued that killing is not in itself any worse than letting die; if my contention is right, it follows that active euthanasia is not any worse than passive euthanasia. What arguments can be given on the other side? The most common, I believe, is the following:

"The important difference between active and passive euthanasia is that, in passive euthanasia, the doctor does not do anything to bring about the patient's death. The doctor does nothing, and the patient dies of whatever ills already afflict him. In active euthanasia, however, the doctor does something to bring about the patient's death: he kills him. The doctor who gives the patient with cancer a lethal injection has himself caused his patient's death; whereas if he merely ceases treatment, the cancer is the cause of the death."

A number of points need to be made here. The first is that it is not exactly correct to say that in passive euthanasia the doctor does nothing, for he does do one thing that is very important: he lets the patient die. "Letting someone die" is certainly different, in some respects, from other types of action—mainly in that it is a kind of action that one may perform by way of not performing certain other actions. For example, one may let a patient die by way of not giving medication, just as one may insult someone by way of not shaking his hand. But for any purpose of moral assessment, it is a type of action nonetheless. The decision to let a patient die is subject to moral appraisal in the same way that a decision to kill him would be subject to moral appraisal: it may be assessed as wise or unwise, compassionate or sadistic, right or wrong. If a doctor deliberately let a patient die who was suffering from a routinely curable illness, the doctor would certainly be to blame for what he had done, just as he would be to blame if he had needlessly killed the patient. Charges against him would then be appropriate. If so, it would be no defense at all for him to insist that he didn't "do anything." He would have done something very serious indeed, for he let his patient die.

Fixing the cause of death may be very important from a legal point of view, for it may determine whether criminal charges are brought against the doctor. But I do not think that this notion can be used to show a moral difference between active and passive euthanasia. The reason why it is considered bad to be the cause of someone's death is that death is regarded as a great evil—and so it is. However, if it has been decided that euthanasia—even passive euthanasia—is desirable in a given case, it has also been decided that in this instance death is no greater an evil than the patient's continued existence. And if this is true, the usual reason for not wanting to be the cause of someone's death simply does not apply.

Finally, doctors may think that all of this is only of academic interest—the sort of thing that philosophers may worry about but that has no practical bearing on their own work. After all, doctors must be concerned about the legal consequences of what they do, and active euthanasia is clearly forbidden by the law. But even so, doctors should also be concerned with the fact that the law is forcing upon them a moral doctrine that may well be indefensible, and has a considerable effect on their practices. Of course, most doctors are not now in the position of being coerced in this matter, for they do not regard themselves as merely going along with what the law requires. Rather, in statements such as the AMA policy statement that I have quoted, they are endorsing this doctrine as a central point of medical ethics. In that statement, active euthanasia is condemned not merely as illegal but as "contrary to that for which the medical profession stands," whereas passive euthanasia is approved. However, the preceding considerations suggest that there is really no moral difference between the two, considered in themselves (there may be important moral differences in some cases in their *consequences*, but, as I pointed out, these differences may make active euthanasia, and not passive euthanasia, the morally preferable option). So, whereas doctors may have to discriminate between active and passive euthanasia to satisfy the law, they should not do any more than that. In particular, they should not give the distinction any added authority and weight by writing it into official statements of medical ethics.

QUESTIONS

1. If you were a physician, what would you do when the parents of a baby with Down's syndrome decided against surgery? Would you let the baby slowly die from dehydration and starvation, or would you take some active step to end the baby's life? Would you take the case to court to force the surgery? How would you justify your decision?

2. Rewrite the two paragraphs Rachels cites from the AMA statement so that your version of the statement avoids Rachels's criticisms.

Tom L. Beauchamp

A REPLY TO RACHELS ON ACTIVE AND PASSIVE EUTHANASIA

Biographical Information. Tom L. Beauchamp teaches philosophy at Georgetown University and is a senior research scholar at the Kennedy Institute for the Study of Human Reproduction and Bioethics. He is the editor of Ethics and Public Policy *and of* Philosophical Problems of Causation, *as well as a coeditor with Joel Feinberg and William T. Blackstone of* Contemporary Introduction to Philosophy *and, with LeRoy Walters, of* Contemporary Issues in Bioethics. *His interest in social and ethical issues is reflected in this article, in the article on reverse discrimination printed on page 183 of this book, and in his paper "Paternalism and Biobehavioral Control" in* The Monist *(January 1976).*

Argument in the Selection. Against Rachels, Beauchamp defends the moral relevance of the distinction between active and passive euthanasia used by the American Medical Association. Beauchamp grants that the distinction is sometimes morally irrelevant, but he argues that it does not follow that it is always so. He first points out the dissimilarities between the two cases which Rachels presents to show the nonrelevance of the active-passive distinction and the kinds of cases with which the AMA statement is concerned. He then gives two arguments for the moral relevance of the distinction. The first invokes the concept of responsibility. The second combines the wedge argument with considerations of social utility.

James Rachels has recently argued that the distinction between active and passive euthanasia is neither appropriately used by the American Medical Association nor generally useful for the resolution of moral problems of euthanasia.[1] Indeed he believes this distinction—which he equates with the killing/letting die distinction—does not in itself have any moral importance. The chief object of his attack is the following statement adopted by the House of Delegates of the American Medical Association in 1973:

> The intentional termination of the life of one human being by another—mercy killing—is contrary to that for which the medical profession stands and is contrary to the policy of the American Medical Association.
>
> The cessation of the employment of extraordinary means to prolong the life of the body when there is irrefutable evidence that biological death is imminent is the decision of the patient and/or his immediate family. The advice and judgment of the physician should be freely available to the patient and/or his immediate family. (62–63)

Rachels constructs a powerful and interesting set of arguments against this statement. In this paper I both (1) challenge his contentions on the grounds that he does not appreciate the moral reasons which give weight to the active/passive distinction and (2) provide a constructive account of the moral relevance of the active/passive distinction.

I

I would concede that the active/passive distinction is *sometimes* morally irrelevant. Of this Rachels convinces me. But it does not follow that it is *always* morally irrelevant. What we need, then, is a case where the distinction is a morally relevant one and an explanation why it is so. Rachels himself uses the method of examining two cases which are exactly alike except that "one involves killing whereas the other involves letting die" (64). We may profitably begin by comparing the kinds of cases governed by the AMA's doctrine with the kinds of cases adduced by Rachels in order to assess the adequacy and fairness of his cases.

The second paragraph of the AMA statement is confined to a narrowly restricted range of passive euthanasia cases, viz., those (a) where the patients are

---

[1] "Active and Passive Euthanasia," *New England Journal of Medicine* 292, pp. 78–80 (January 9, 1975). [All page references in parentheses refer to Rachels's article as reprinted in this chapter.]

on extraordinary means, (b) where irrefutable evidence of imminent death is available, and (c) where patient or family consent is available. Rachels' two cases involve conditions notably different from these:

> In the first, Smith stands to gain a large inheritance if anything should happen to his six-year-old cousin. One evening while the child is taking his bath, Smith sneaks into the bathroom and drowns the child, and then arranges things so that it will look like an accident.
>
> In the second, Jones also stands to gain if anything should happen to his six-year-old cousin. Like Smith, Jones sneaks in planning to drown the child in his bath. However, just as he enters the bathroom Jones sees the child slip and hit his head, and fall face down in the water. Jones is delighted; he stands by, ready to push the child's head back under if it is necessary, but it is not necessary. With only a little thrashing about, the child drowns all by himself, "accidentally," as Jones watches and does nothing.
>
> Now Smith killed the child, whereas Jones "merely" let the child die. That is the only difference between them (64–65).

Rachels says there is no moral difference between the cases in terms of our moral assessments of Smith and Jones' behavior. This seems fair enough, but what can Rachels' cases be said to prove, as they are so markedly disanalogous to the sorts of cases envisioned by the AMA proposal? Rachels concedes important disanalogies, but thinks them irrelevant:

> The point is the same in these cases: the bare difference between killing and letting die does not, in itself, make a moral difference. If a doctor lets a patient die, for humane reasons, he is in the same moral position as if he had given the patient a lethal injection for humane reasons (65).

Three observations are immediately in order. First, Rachels seems to infer that from such cases we can conclude that the distinction between killing and letting die is *always* morally irrelevant. This conclusion is fallaciously derived. What the argument in fact shows, being an analogical argument, is only that in all *relevantly similar* cases the distinction does not in itself make a moral difference. Since Rachels concedes that other cases are disanalogous, he seems thereby to concede that his argument is as weak as the analogy itself. (We shall see in the next section how weak the analogy is.) Second, Rachels' cases involve two unjustified actions, one of killing and the other of letting die. The AMA statement distinguishes one set of cases of unjustified killing and another of *justified* cases of allowing to die. Nowhere is it claimed by the AMA that what *makes* the difference in these cases is the active/passive distinction itself. It is only implied that one set of cases, the justified set, *involves* (passive) letting die while the unjustified set *involves* (active) killing. While it is said that justified euthanasia cases are passive ones and unjustified ones active, it is not said either that what *makes* some acts justified is the fact of their being passive or that what *makes* others unjustified is the fact of their being active. This fact will prove to be of vital importance.

The third and most important point is that in both of Rachels' cases the respective moral agents—Smith and Jones—are morally responsible for the death of the child and are morally blameworthy—even though Jones is not *causally* responsible. In the first case death is caused by the agent, while in the second it is not; yet the second agent is no less morally responsible. While the law might find only the first homicidal, morality condemns the motives in each case as equally wrong, and it holds that the duty to save life in such cases is as compelling as the duty not to take life. I suggest that it is largely because of this equal degree of moral responsibility that there is no morally relevant difference in Rachels' cases. In the cases envisioned by the AMA, however, an agent is held to be responsible for taking life by actively killing but is not held to be morally required to preserve life, and so not responsible for death, when removing the patient from extraordinary means (under conditions a–c above). I shall elaborate this latter point as a defense of the AMA position momentarily. My only conclusion thus far is the negative one that Rachels' arguments rest on weak foundations. His cases are not relevantly similar to euthanasia cases and do not support his apparent conclusion that the active/passive distinction is *always* morally irrelevant.

II

I wish now to provide a positive account of the moral relevance of the active/ passive distinction. I shall adduce two arguments in justification of a limited use of the distinction. The first elaborates the theme of responsibility, and the second a rather more speculative reason for invoking the distinction. I begin with an actual case, the celebrated Quinlan case.[2] Karen Quinlan was in a coma, and was on a mechanical respirator which artificially sustained her vital processes and which her parents wished to cease. At least some physicians believed there was irrefutable evidence that biological death was imminent and the coma irreversible. This case, under this description, closely conforms to the passive cases envisioned by the AMA. During an interview the father, Mr. Quinlan, asserted that he did not wish to kill his daughter, but only to remove her from the machines in order to see whether she would live or would die a natural death.[3] Suppose he had said—to envision now a second and hypothetical, but parallel case—that he wished only to see her die painlessly and therefore wished that the doctor could induce death by an overdose of morphine. Most of us would think the second act, which involves active killing, morally unjustified in these circumstances, while many of us would think the first act morally justified. (This is not the place to consider whether in fact it is justified, and if so under what conditions.) What accounts for the apparent morally relevant difference?

I have considered these two cases in order to follow Rachels' method of entertaining parallel cases where the only difference is that the one case involves killing and the other letting die. However, there is a further difference, and an important one which crops up in the euthanasia context. The difference rests in our judgments of medical fallibility and moral responsibility. Mr. Quinlan seems to think that, after all, the doctors might be wrong. There is a remote possibility that she might live without the aid of a machine. But whether or not the medical prediction of death turns out to be accurate, if she dies then no one is morally

---

[2] As recorded in the Opinion of Judge Robert Muir, Jr., Docket No. C-201-75 of the Superior Court of New Jersey, Chancery Division, Morris County (November 10, 1975).

[3] See Judge Muir's Opinion, p. 18—a slightly different statement but on the subject.

responsible for directly bringing about or causing her death, as they would be if they caused her death by killing her. Rachels finds explanations which appeal to causal conditions unsatisfactory (66); but this is perhaps only because he fails to see the nature of the causal link. To bring about her death is by that act to preempt the possibility of life. To "allow her to die" by removing artificial equipment is to allow for the possibility of wrong diagnosis or incorrect prediction and hence to absolve oneself of moral responsibility for the taking of life under false assumptions. There may, of course, be utterly no empirical possibility of recovery in some cases since recovery would violate a law of nature. However, judgments of empirical impossibility in medicine are notoriously problematic—my reason for emphasizing medical fallibility. And in all the hard cases I think we do not *know* that recovery is empirically impossible, even if *good evidence* is available.

The above reason for invoking the active/passive distinction can now be generalized: Active termination of life removes all possibility of life for the patient, while passively ceasing extraordinary means may not. This is not trivial since patients have survived in several celebrated cases where, in knowledgeable physicians' judgments, there was "irrefutable" evidence that death was imminent.[4]

One may, of course, be entirely responsible and culpable for another's death *either* by killing him *or* by letting him die. In such cases, of which Rachels' are examples, there is no morally significant difference between killing and letting die precisely because whatever one does, omits, or refrains from doing does not absolve one of responsibility. Either active or passive involvement renders one responsible for the death of another, and both involvements are equally wrong for the same principled moral reason: it is (prima facie) morally wrong to bring about the death of an innocent person capable of living whenever the causal intervention or negligence is intentional. (I use causal terms here because causal involvement need not be active, as when by one's negligence one is nonetheless causally responsible.) But not all cases of killing and letting die fall under this same moral principle. One is sometimes culpable for killing, because morally responsible as agent for death, as when one pulls the plug on a respirator sustaining a recovering patient (a murder). But one is sometimes not culpable for letting die because not morally responsible as agent, as when one pulls the plug on a respirator sustaining an irreversibly comatose and unrecoverable patient (a routine procedure, where one is *merely* causally responsible).[5] Different degrees and means of involvement assess different degrees of responsibility, and our assessments of culpability can become intricately complex. The only point which now concerns us, however, is that because different moral principles may govern very similar circumstances, we are sometimes morally culpable for killing but not for letting die.

---

[4] This problem of the strength of evidence also emerged in the Quinlan trial, as physicians disagreed whether the evidence was "irrefutable." Such disagreement, when added to the problems of medical fallibility and causal responsibility just outlined, provides one important argument against the *legalization* of active euthanasia, as perhaps the AMA would agree.

[5] Among the moral reasons why one is held to be responsible in the first sort of case and not responsible in the second sort are, I believe, the two grounds for the active/passive distinction under discussion in this section.

A second argument may now be adduced in defense of the active/passive distinction. I shall develop this argument by combining (1) so-called wedge or slippery slope arguments with (2) recent arguments in defense of rule utilitarianism. I shall explain each in turn and show how in combination they may be used to defend the active/passive distinction.

(1) *Wedge arguments* proceed as follows: if killing were allowed, even under the guise of a merciful extinction of life, a dangerous wedge would be introduced which places all "undesirable" or "unworthy" human life in a precarious condition. Proponents of wedge arguments believe the initial wedge places us on a slippery slope for at least one of two reasons: (i) It is said that our justifying principles leave us with no principled way to avoid the slide into saying that all sorts of killings would be justified under similar conditions. Here it is thought that once killing is allowed, a firm line between justified and unjustified killings cannot be securely drawn. It is thought best not to redraw the line in the first place, for redrawing it will inevitably lead to a downhill slide. It is then often pointed out that as a matter of historical record this is precisely what has occurred in the darker regions of human history, including the Nazi era, where euthanasia began with the best of intentions for horribly ill, non-Jewish Germans and gradually spread to anyone deemed an enemy of the people. (ii) Second, it is said that our basic principles against killing will be gradually eroded once some form of killing is legitimated. For example, it is said that permitting voluntary euthanasia will lead to permitting involuntary euthanasia, which will in turn lead to permitting euthanasia for those who are a nuisance to society (idiots, recidivist criminals, defective newborns, and the insane, e.g.). Gradually other principles which instill respect for human life will be eroded or abandoned in the process.

I am not inclined to accept the first reason.[6] If our justifying principles are themselves justified, then any action they warrant would be justified. Accordingly, I shall only be concerned with the second approach.

(2) *Rule utilitarianism* is the position that a society ought to adopt a rule if its acceptance would have better consequences for the common good (greater social utility) than any comparable rule could have in that society. Any action is right if it conforms to a valid rule and wrong if it violates the rule. Sometimes it is said that alternative *rules* should be measured against one another, while it has also been suggested that whole moral *codes* (complete sets of rules) rather than individual rules should be compared. While I prefer the latter formulation (Brandt's), this internal dispute need not detain us here. The important point is that a particular rule or a particular code of rules is morally justified if and only if there is no other competing rule or moral code whose acceptance would have a higher utility value for society, and where a rule's acceptability is contingent upon the consequences which would result if the rule were made current.

Wedge arguments, when conjoined with rule utilitarian arguments, may be applied to euthanasia issues in the following way. We presently subscribe to a no-active-euthanasia rule (which the AMA suggests we retain). Imagine now that in

---

[6] An intelligent argument of this form, but one I find unacceptable for reasons given below, is Arthur Dyck, "Beneficent Euthanasia and Benemortasia: Alternative Views of Mercy," in M. Kohl, ed., *Beneficent Euthanasia* (Buffalo: Prometheus Books, 1975), pp. 120f.

our society we make current a restricted-active-euthanasia rule (as Rachels seems to urge). Which of these two moral rules would, if enacted, have the consequence of maximizing social utility? Clearly a restricted-active-euthanasia rule would have *some* utility value, as Rachels notes, since some intense and uncontrollable suffering would be eliminated. However, it may not have the highest utility value in the structure of our present code or in any imaginable code which could be made current, and therefore may not be a component in the ideal code for our society. If wedge arguments raise any serious questions at all, as I think they do, they rest in this area of whether a code would be weakened or strengthened by the addition of active euthanasia principles. For the disutility of introducing legitimate killing into one's moral code (in the form of active euthanasia rules) may, in the long run, outweigh the utility of doing so, as a result of the eroding effect such a relaxation would have on rules in the code which demand respect for human life. If, for example, rules permitting active killing were introduced, it is not implausible to suppose that destroying defective newborns (a form of involuntary euthanasia) would become an accepted and common practice, that as population increases occur the aged will be even more neglectable and neglected than they now are, that capital punishment for a wide variety of crimes would be increasingly tempting, that some doctors would have appreciably reduced fears of actively injecting fatal doses whenever it seemed to them propitious to do so, and that laws of war against killing would erode in efficacy even beyond their already abysmal level. A hundred such possible consequences might easily be imagined. But these are sufficient to make the larger point that such rules permitting killing could lead to a general reduction of respect for human life. Rules against killing in a moral code are not *isolated* moral principles; they are pieces of a web of rules against killing which forms a moral code. The more threads one removes, the weaker the fabric becomes. And if, as I believe, moral principles against active killing have the deep and continuously civilizing effect of promoting respect for life, and if principles which allow passively letting die (as envisioned in the AMA statement) do not themselves cut against this effect, then this seems an important reason for the maintenance of the active/passive distinction. (By the logic of the above argument passively letting die would also have to be prohibited if a rule permitting it had the serious adverse consequence of eroding acceptance of rules protective of respect for life. While this prospect seems to me highly improbable, I can hardly claim to have refuted those conservatives who would claim that even rules which sanction letting die place us on a precarious slippery slope.)

A troublesome problem, however, confronts my use of utilitarian and wedge arguments. Most all of us would agree that both killing and letting die are justified under some conditions. Killings in self-defense and in "just" wars are widely accepted as justified because the conditions excuse the killing. If society can withstand these exceptions to moral rules prohibiting killing, then why is it not plausible to suppose society can accept another excusing exception in the form of justified active euthanasia? This is an important and worthy objection, but not a decisive one. The defenseless and the dying are significantly different classes of persons from aggressors who attack individuals and/or nations. In the case of aggressors, one does not confront the question whether their lives are no longer *worth living*. Rather, we reach the judgment that the aggressors' morally blameworthy actions justify counteractions. But in the case of the dying and the otherwise ill, there is no morally blameworthy action to justify our own. Here we are required to accept the judgment that their lives are no longer *worth living* in order to believe that the termination of their lives is justified. It is the latter sort of judgment which is feared by those who take the wedge argument seriously. We do not now permit and never have permitted the taking of morally blameless lives. I think this is the key to understanding why recent cases of intentionally allowing the death of defective newborns (as in the famous case at Johns Hopkins Hospital) have generated such protracted controversy. Even if such newborns could not have led meaningful lives (a matter of some controversy), it is the wedged foot in the door which creates the most intense worries. For if we once take a decision to allow a restricted infanticide justification or any justification at all on grounds that a life is not meaningful or not worth living, we have qualified our moral rules against killing. That this qualification is a matter of the utmost seriousness needs no argument. I mention it here only to show why the wedge argument has moral force even though we *already* allow some very different conditions to justify intentional killing.

I reach only a guarded conclusion. While I am unsure about the predictions made in wedge arguments, I find it equally impossible to ignore them. They point to a fearful and not unlikely danger inherent in the legalization of active euthanasia. It is hard to say where the burden of proof rests. The evidence is everywhere imperfect, yet sufficient to generate controversy. Those who would endorse limited euthanasia rules, however, have given scant attention to the problems of legalizing active euthanasia which are pointed to by wedge arguments. Yet the matter is sufficiently momentous that I think we ought to be most cautious in embracing even highly restricted active euthanasia rules, which involve a rather fundamental change in our moral code, until some further assurance on this score is received. And this provides a second reason for insisting upon the moral relevance of the active/passive distinction.

III

It may still be insisted that my case has not touched Rachels' leading claim, for I have not shown, as Rachels puts it, that it is "the bare difference between killing and letting die that makes the difference in these cases" (65). True, I have not shown this, and in my judgment it cannot be shown. But this concession does not require capitulation to Rachels' argument. I adduced a case which is at the center of our moral intuition that killing is morally different (in at least some cases) from letting die; and I then attempted to account for at least part of the grounds for this belief. The grounds turn out to be other than the *bare* difference, but nevertheless *make* the distinction morally relevant.

It is also worth noticing that there is nothing in the AMA statement which says that the bare difference between killing and letting die itself and alone makes the difference in our differing moral assessments of rightness and wrongness. Rachels forces this interpretation on the statement. Some philosophers may have thought bare difference makes the difference, but there is scant evidence that the

AMA or any thoughtful ethicist *must* believe it in order to defend the relevance and importance of the active/passive distinction. When this conclusion is coupled with my earlier argument that from Rachels' paradigm cases it follows only that the active/passive distinction is sometimes, but not always, morally irrelevant, it would seem that his case against the AMA is decisively impaired.

QUESTIONS

1. Defend Rachels against Beauchamp by improving Rachels's arguments wherever necessary.

2. Beauchamp argues that the distinction between killing and letting die is *sometimes* morally relevant. One of his arguments involves the notion of responsibility: "We are sometimes morally culpable for killing but not for letting die." Support Beauchamp's argument by suggesting cases of "letting die" which do not involve moral culpability.

SUGGESTED ADDITIONAL READINGS

Downing, A. B., ed. *Euthanasia and the Right to Death: The Case for Voluntary Euthanasia.* New York: Humanities Press; London: Peter Owen, 1969. This collection of euthanasia articles is written from many perspectives—philosophical, humanitarian, sociological, legal, and medical.

Gould, Jonathan, and Lord Craigmyle, eds. *Your Death Warrant?* New York: Arlington House, 1971. This is a collection of arguments *against* the legalization of euthanasia. It includes an investigation of the euthanasia movement as well as an examination of proposals which have been made to legalize euthanasia and the implications of these proposals. In these writings, the authors try to bring out the medical, social, legal, and ethical grounds against both the claim that euthanasia is morally acceptable and the claim that it ought to be legalized.

Kohl, Marvin, ed. *Beneficent Euthanasia.* Buffalo, N.Y.: Prometheus Books, 1975. This book contains arguments both for and against euthanasia. It includes clear statements of traditional religious positions (Roman Catholic, Jewish) and also nonreligious ones. The articles deal with the distinction between passive and active euthanasia as well as with the medical and legal questions involved in the issue. There is also an excellent annotated bibliography on euthanasia.

Mannes, Marya. "The Right to Die: Should There Be a Law?" *Medical Opinion*, vol. 3, pp. 35–39, May 1974. This is a selection from Mannes's book *Last Rights* (New York: William Morrow & Company, 1973). Mannes argues that we have no more moral right to legislate styles of dying than we have to legislate styles of living as long as those lifestyles have no detrimental effect on anyone else. She views restrictive euthanasia laws as an attempt to legislate morality and argues against the morality and practicality of such legislation. Although arguing for euthanasia, she stresses the need for clear guidelines designed to prevent abuses by ill-intentioned persons.

Williams, Glanville. *The Sanctity of Life and the Criminal Law.* New York: Alfred A. Knopf, 1957. This book discusses both abortion and euthanasia, among other topics, under the general rubric of the sanctity of human life and with special emphasis on decriminalization.

Winter, Arthur, ed. *The Moment of Death: A Symposium.* Springfield, Ill.: C. C. Thomas, 1969. The essays in this collection investigate the criteria for determining that death has occurred. Medical experts such as neuroscientists, cardiac surgeons, and medical examiners attempt to clarify those biological principles which are relevant to death and to the basic characteristics of humanity.

THREE

The Death Penalty

Since 1967 all convicted criminals who have been sentenced to death in the United States have received stays of execution. Their fate continues to depend upon further decisions of the Supreme Court in regard to the constitutionality of the death penalty. But beyond the constitutional issue there is the more general issue of the ethical acceptability of the death penalty. Many, especially those in law enforcement and government positions, continually reassert that society cannot do without it. They say, for example, "Without the death penalty to deter potential criminals, serious crime will run rampant." Many others say, with equal conviction, that the death penalty is a cruel and barbarous practice, effectively serving no purpose that could not be equally well served by a more humane punishment. "How long," they ask, "must we indulge this uncivilized and pointless lust for revenge?" A central ethical question, then, is whether the death penalty should continue to be a feature of our legal system.

THE CONSTITUTIONAL ISSUE

The Eighth Amendment to the Constitution of the United States explicitly prohibits the infliction of "cruel and unusual" punishment. Is the death penalty *by its very nature* a cruel and unusual punishment and thus unconstitutional? The Supreme Court of the United States has not comprehensively ruled on this precise point, but it has ruled in the case of *Furman v. Georgia* (1972) that the death penalty *as currently administered* is a cruel and unusual punishment, thus unconstitutional. In *Furman v. Georgia* the Supreme Court considered three cases together, one case in which the death penalty was imposed for murder and two in which the death penalty was imposed for rape. The death penalty, as imposed in all three cases, was found to be unconstitutional. An important question, however, is whether there was any particular irregularity in these cases. Was there perhaps anything about the general proceedings or the sentencing that would render them atypical of the general run of cases in which the death penalty is imposed? It does not seem so. True, in each of the three cases the sentence of death was rendered at the discretion of the jury, which decided between death and life imprisonment; but such discretionary powers have long been a standard part of sentencing procedures. Thus, the Supreme Court's action in *Furman v. Georgia* is normally taken to mean that the death penalty *as currently administered* is unconstitutional, because it violates the Eighth Amendment.

Numerous perplexities surround the constitutionality of the death penalty. The existence of such perplexities is evidenced not only by the fact that the decision reached in *Furman v. Georgia* was by a mere five-to-four majority, but also by the fact that nine divergent opinions were delivered. There was substantial disagreement not only on the basic issue, but also in the supporting rationale. Very few Supreme Court cases generate such a basic division, and even fewer generate such a diversity of viewpoints. Both Justice Marshall and Justice Brennan argued straightforwardly that the death penalty *by its very nature* is a cruel and unusual punishment. From this perspective it would not matter how much the procedures of its administration might be modified. It would still remain a cruel and unusual punishment. Among the reasons advanced to support this contention, two are especially noteworthy. (1) The death penalty is excessive in the sense of being unnecessary; lesser penalties are capable of serving the desired legislative purpose. (2) The death penalty is abhorrent to currently existing moral values.

The other three justices (Douglas, White, and Stewart) who voted with the majority did not commit themselves to the position that the death penalty *by its very nature* is unconstitutional. Rather they argued the aforementioned contention that the death penalty *as currently administered* is unconstitutional. Two arguments in support of this more guarded contention were especially prominent. (1) The death penalty in its contemporary setting is administered with such infrequency and with such reluctance that the threat of execution has lost any deterrent effect it might have. Thus, since the circumstances of the death penalty's present administration effectively undercut its presumed purpose, it must be held to be a "cruel and unusual" punishment and accordingly to be in violation of the Eighth Amendment. (2) The death penalty in its contemporary setting is, as a common matter of course, inflicted at the discretion of a jury (or sometimes a judge). The absence of explicit standards to govern the decision between life and death allows a wide range of unchecked prejudice to operate freely under the heading of "discretion." For example, "discretion" seems to render blacks more prone than whites to the death penalty. Such standardless discretion violates not only the Eighth Amendment but also the Fourteenth Amendment, which guarantees "due process of law."

As matters have developed in the wake of *Furman v. Georgia,* it is especially the Court's objection to *standardless discretion* that provides an opening for the many individual states still anxious to retain the death penalty as a viable component of their legal systems. Many believe that certain procedures for inflicting the death penalty might be devised so as to avoid the charge of standardless discretion. Two such approaches have become prominent. (1) Some states have moved to dissolve the objection of standardless discretion by simply making the death penalty *mandatory* for certain crimes. At this writing, the Maryland Legislature has just enacted a law making the death penalty mandatory in the cases of certain first-degree murders, such as the murder of a police officer and the murder of a kidnap victim. (2) States such as Texas and Georgia have taken an equally obvious approach to avoid the objection of standardless discretion. It consists in the effort to establish standards that would definitively govern the decision of the jury (or the judge) in choosing between life and death. If either or both of these two approaches are ultimately found constitutionally satisfactory by the Supreme Court, the death penalty may well continue to play a role in the legal systems of those states that desire its retention.

It is possible that the death penalty could be ruled constitutionally acceptable and yet remain ethically unacceptable. Or, for that matter, it might in the end be ruled unconstitutional and yet be found ethically quite acceptable. Simply put, the constitutional issue is one thing, the ethical issue quite another. We must now approach the death penalty in its ethical dimensions. Of course, in one respect the constitutional issue is dependent on the ethical issue, for it is clear that at least some members of the Supreme Court consider current moral opinion to be a relevant factor in assessing whether or not the death penalty is to qualify as a cruel and unusual punishment. But what moral opinion *ought* we to hold?

THE ETHICAL ISSUE

In any discussion of the ethical acceptability of the death penalty, it is important to remember that the death penalty is a kind of punishment. In fact, it is commonly viewed as the most serious kind of punishment, hence the term "*capital* punishment." Philosophers have generally agreed that punishment as a general social practice is ethically acceptable. Indeed, however uneasy we might feel about inflicting harm on another person, it is hard to visualize a complex society managing to survive without an established legal system of punishment. However, to say that philosophers are *generally* agreed on the ethical acceptability of punishment is not to say that there are no dissenters from this view. Some have argued that society could be structured in ways that would not demand commitment to a legal system of punishment as we know it. For example, might it not be that undesirable social behavior could be adequately kept in check by therapeutic treatment rather than by traditional kinds of punishment? Such a system would certainly have the advantage of being more humane, but it seems doubtful that present therapeutic techniques are adequate to the task. Perhaps future scientific advance will render such an alternative more plausible. If so, it may be that one day the whole practice of (nontherapeutic) punishment will have to be rejected on ethical grounds. But for now it is generally agreed that punishment, as a general social practice, is ethically acceptable. What remains an open and hotly debated ethical issue is whether or not the death penalty, as a distinctive kind of punishment, ought to play a role in our legal system of punishment.

Those in favor of retaining the death penalty are commonly called *retentionists*. Retentionists differ among themselves as to the extent to which they support the employment of the death penalty, as well as in regard to the supporting arguments they find acceptable. But anyone who supports the retention of the death penalty—to whatever extent and for whatever reason—is by definition a retentionist. Those in favor of abolishing the death penalty are commonly called *abolitionists*. Abolitionists, by definition, refuse to support any employment whatever of the death penalty. Like the retentionists, however, they differ among themselves concerning the supporting arguments they find acceptable.

There is one extreme, and not widely embraced, abolitionist line of thought. It is based on the belief that the sanctity of human life demands absolute nonviolence. On this view, it is thought that killing of any kind, for any reason, is always and everywhere morally wrong. No one has the right to take a human life, not in self-defense, not in war, not in any circumstance. Thus, since the death penalty obviously involves a kind of killing, it is an ethically unacceptable form of punishment and must be abolished. This general view, which is associated with the Quakers and other pacifists, has struck most moral philosophers as implausible. Can we really think that killing, when it is the only course that will save oneself from an unprovoked violent assault, is morally wrong? Can we really think, if circumstances were such that killing a madman was the *only* possible way of stopping him from exploding a bomb in the midst of a kindergarten class, that such killing would be morally wrong? The defender of absolute nonviolence is sometimes inclined at this point to argue that violence will only breed violence, and there may indeed be much truth in this claim. Still, most do not agree that such a claim supports the contention that *all* killing is morally wrong, and if *some* killing is ethically acceptable, perhaps the death penalty itself is ethically acceptable. What arguments can be made on its behalf?

RETENTIONIST ARGUMENTS

Broadly speaking, arguments for the retention of the death penalty usually emphasize either (1) considerations of *justice* or (2) considerations of *social utility*. Those who emphasize considerations of justice develop their case along the following line: When the moral order is upset by the commission of some offense, it is only right that the disorder be rectified by punishment equal in intensity to the seriousness of the offense. This view is reflected in remarks such as "The scales of justice demand retribution" and "The offender must pay for the crime." Along this line, the philosopher Immanuel Kant (1724–1804) is famous for his unequivocal defense of the principle of retaliation. According to this principle, punishment is to be inflicted in a measure that will equalize the offense. And when the offense is murder, *only* capital punishment is sufficient to equalize it.

Although the plea for retribution continues to be heard frequently, many retentionists (and obviously abolitionists as well) have come to feel quite uneasy with the Kantian line of thought just mentioned. Perhaps this uneasiness has been provoked by our growing awareness of the way in which social conditions, such as ghetto living, seem to spawn criminal activity. At any rate, many contemporary observers find it increasingly difficult to say simply, with Kant, "Yes, kill him; he *deserves* it."

Considerations of social utility have long played a role in discussions of the justification of punishment in general. So it is not surprising that such considerations are used in defense of retaining the death penalty. Utilitarianism, as a distinct school of moral philosophy, locates the primary justification of punishment in its social utility. Utilitarians acknowledge that punishment consists in the infliction of evil upon another person, but they hold that such evil is far outweighed by the future benefits that accrue to society. Imprisonment, for example, might lead to such socially desirable effects as (1) *rehabilitation* of the criminal, (2) temporary or permanent *protection* from the imprisoned criminal, and (3) the *deterrence* of other potential criminals. When utilitarian considerations are recruited in support of the retention of the *death* penalty, it is clear that rehabilitation of the criminal can play no part in the case. But retentionists do frequently promote considerations of protection and deterrence.

Accordingly, retentionists often appeal to considerations of protection and argue that the death penalty is the only effective way to protect society from certain *violence-prone and irreformable* criminals. (Notice that an important difficulty here would be finding effective criteria for the recognition of those criminals who are truly "violence-prone and irreformable.") Life imprisonment, it is said, cannot assure society of the needed protection, because criminals such as these pose an imminent threat even to their prison guards and fellow inmates. Furthermore, escape is always possible.

But many retentionists think that the strongest case for the death penalty is not to be made on grounds of protecting society from convicted criminals but rather on grounds of deterring potential criminals. Because of the intense fear that most people have of death, it is argued, the death penalty functions as a uniquely effective deterrent to serious crime. With the appearance of this argument the debate between retentionists and abolitionists focuses totally on a factual issue. Is the death penalty indeed a more substantial deterrent than life imprisonment? Facts and figures often seem to dominate this particular aspect of the debate, and it is by no means easy to discern the true state of affairs.

ABOLITIONIST ARGUMENTS

What now can be said of the abolitionist case against the death penalty? Most abolitionists do not care to argue the extreme position, already discussed, of absolute nonviolence, yet they often do want to commit themselves seriously to the "sanctity of human life." They argue that the taking of a human life, while perhaps sometimes morally permissible, is a very serious matter, not to be permitted in the absence of weighty overriding reasons. At face value, they argue, the death penalty is cruel and inhumane. And since retentionists have not succeeded in advancing substantial reasons in its defense, it must be judged an ethically unacceptable practice. Against retentionist arguments based on retribution as a demand of justice, abolitionists frequently argue that the "demand of justice" is nothing but a mask for a barbarous vengeance. Against retentionist arguments based on considerations of social utility, they simply argue that other more humane punishments will serve equally well. Besides these direct arguments against retentionist arguments, abolitionists also prominently incorporate into their overall case the following consideration: It is impossible to guarantee that mistakes will not be made in the administration of punishment. But this factor is especially important in regard to the death penalty, because only *capital* punishment is irrevocable.

T. A. M.

Justice Thurgood Marshall

CONCURRING OPINION IN *FURMAN v. GEORGIA*

Biographical Information. *Thurgood Marshall (b. 1908), associate justice of the United States Supreme Court, is the first black ever to be appointed to the Supreme Court. Much of his distinguished private career has been given over to providing legal counsel for groups dedicated to the advancement of civil rights. Justice Marshall also served as United States circuit judge (1961–1965) and United States solicitor general (1965– 1967), before his appointment in 1967 to the Supreme Court.*

Argument in the Selection. *Justice Marshall argues that the death penalty by its very nature is a cruel and unusual punishment, thus in violation of the Eighth Amendment. He begins by analyzing the meaning of "cruel and unusual" punishment as established by previous decisions of the Supreme Court. Then he argues that the death penalty falls within the scope of "cruel and unusual" punishment for two individually sufficient reasons: (1) It is excessive and unnecessary. (2) It is abhorrent to currently existing moral values.*

These three cases present the question whether the death penalty is a cruel and unusual punishment prohibited by the Eighth Amendment to the United States Constitution.

In No. 69-5003, Furman was convicted of murder for shooting the father of five children when he discovered that Furman had broken into his home early one morning. Nos. 69-5030 and 69-5031 involve state convictions for forcible rape. Jackson was found guilty of rape during the course of a robbery in the victim's home. The rape was accomplished as he held the pointed ends of scissors at the victim's throat. Branch also was convicted of a rape committed in the victim's home. No weapon was utilized, but physical force and threats of physical force were employed.

The criminal acts with which we are confronted are ugly, vicious, reprehensible acts. Their sheer brutality cannot and should not be minimized. But, we are not called upon to condone the penalized conduct; we are asked only to examine the penalty imposed on each of the petitioners and to determine whether or not it violates the Eighth Amendment. The question then is not whether we condone rape or murder, for surely we do not; it is whether capital punishment is "a punishment no longer consistent with our own self-respect" and, therefore, violative of the Eighth Amendment.

The elasticity of the constitutional provision under consideration presents dangers of too little or too much self-restraint. Hence, we must proceed with caution to answer the question presented. . . .

Thus, the history of the clause clearly establishes that it was intended to

83

prohibit cruel punishments. We must now turn to the case law to discover the manner in which courts have given meaning to the term "cruel." . . .

In *Howard v. Fleming* (1903), the Court, in essence, followed the approach advocated by the dissenters in *O'Neil*. In rejecting the claim that 10-year sentences for conspiracy to defraud were cruel and unusual, the Court (per Mr. Justice Brewer) considered the nature of the crime, the purpose of the law, and the length of the sentence imposed.

The Court used the same approach seven years later in the landmark case of *Weems v. United States* (1910). Weems, an officer of the Bureau of Coast Guard and Transportation of the United States Government of the Philippine Islands, was convicted of falsifying a "public and official document." He was sentenced to 15 years' incarceration at hard labor with chains on his ankles, to an unusual loss of his civil rights, and to perpetual surveillance. Called upon to determine whether this was a cruel and unusual punishment, the Court found that it was. . . .

The Court made it plain beyond any reasonable doubt that excessive punishments were as objectionable as those that were inherently cruel. . . .

Perhaps the most important principle in analyzing "cruel and unusual" punishment questions is one that is reiterated again and again in the prior opinions of the Court: i.e., the cruel and unusual language "must draw its meaning from the evolving standards of decency that mark the progress of a maturing society." Thus, a penalty that was permissible at one time in our Nation's history is not necessarily permissible today. . . .

Faced with an open question, we must establish our standards for decision. The decisions discussed in the previous section imply that a punishment may be deemed cruel and unusual for any one of four distinct reasons.

First, there are certain punishments that inherently involve so much physical pain and suffering that civilized people cannot tolerate them—e.g., use of the rack, the thumbscrew, or other modes of torture. . . .

Second, there are punishments that are unusual, signifying that they were previously unknown as penalties for a given offense. . . . Prior decisions leave open the question of just how much the word "unusual" adds to the word "cruel." . . .

Third, a penalty may be cruel and unusual because it is excessive and serves no valid legislative purpose. . . . Both the Chief Justice and Mr. Justice Powell seek to ignore or to minimize this aspect of the Court's prior decisions. But, . . . this Court has steadfastly maintained that a penalty is unconstitutional whenever it is unnecessarily harsh or cruel. This is what the Founders of this country intended; this is what their fellow citizens believed the Eighth Amendment provided; . . .

Fourth, where a punishment is not excessive and serves a valid legislative purpose, it still may be invalid if popular sentiment abhors it. . . .

It is immediately obvious, then, that since capital punishment is not a recent phenomenon, if it violates the Constitution, it does so because it is excessive or unnecessary, or because it is abhorrent to currently existing moral values. . . .

There are six purposes conceivably served by capital punishment: retribution, deterrence, prevention of repetitive criminal acts, encouragement of guilty pleas and confessions, eugenics and economy. . . .

The most hotly contested issue regarding capital punishment is whether it is better than life imprisonment as a deterrent to crime. . . .

It must be kept in mind that the question to be considered is not simply whether capital punishment is a deterrent, but whether it is a better deterrent than life imprisonment.

There is no more complex problem than determining the deterrent efficacy of the death penalty. "Capital punishment has obviously failed as a deterrent when a murder is committed. We can number its failures. But we cannot number its successes. No one can ever know how many people have refrained from murder because of the fear of being hanged." This is the nub of the problem and it is exacerbated by the paucity of useful data. . . .

Despite the fact that abolitionists have not proved non-deterrence beyond a reasonable doubt, they have succeeded in showing by clear and convincing evidence that capital punishment is not necessary as a deterrent to crime in our society. This is all that they must do. . . .

There is but one conclusion that can be drawn from all of this—i.e., the death penalty is an excessive and unnecessary punishment that violates the Eighth Amendment. The statistical evidence is not convincing beyond all doubt, but, it is persuasive. . . .

In addition, even if capital punishment is not excessive, it nonetheless violates the Eighth Amendment because it is morally unacceptable to the people of the United States at this time in their history.

In judging whether or not a given penalty is morally acceptable, most courts have said that the punishment is valid unless "it shocks the conscience and sense of justice of the people." . . .

While a public opinion poll obviously is of some assistance in indicating public acceptance or rejection of a specific penalty, its utility cannot be very great. This is because whether or not a punishment is cruel and unusual depends, not on whether its mere mention "shocks the conscience and sense of justice of the people," but on whether people who were fully informed as to the purposes of the penalty and its liabilities would find the penalty shocking, unjust, and unacceptable. . . .

It has often been noted that American citizens know almost nothing about capital punishment. Some of the conclusions arrived at in the preceding section and the supporting evidence would be critical to an informed judgment on the morality of the death penalty: e.g., that the death penalty is no more effective a deterrent than life imprisonment, that convicted murderers are rarely executed, but are usually sentenced to a term in prison; that convicted murderers usually are model prisoners, and that they almost always become law-abiding citizens upon their release from prison; that the costs of executing a capital offender exceed the costs of imprisoning him for life; that while in prison, a convict under sentence of death performs none of the useful functions that life prisoners perform; that no attempt is made in the sentencing process to ferret out likely recidivists for execution; and that the death penalty may actually stimulate criminal activity.

This information would almost surely convince the average citizen that the death penalty was unwise, but a problem arises as to whether, it would convince him that the penalty was morally reprehensible. This problem arises from the fact that the public's desire for retribution even though this is a goal that the legislature cannot constitutionally pursue as its sole justification for capital punishment, might influence the citizenry's view of the morality of capital punishment. The solution to the problem lies in the fact that no one has ever seriously advanced retribution as a legitimate goal of our society. Defenses of capital punishment are always mounted on deterrent or other similar theories. This should not be surprising. It is the people of this country who have urged in the past that prisons rehabilitate as well as isolate offenders, and it is the people who have injected a sense of purpose into our penology. I cannot believe that at this stage in our history, the American people would ever knowingly support purposeless vengeance. Thus, I believe that the great mass of citizens would conclude on the basis of the material already considered that the death penalty is immoral and therefore unconstitutional.

But, if this information needs supplementing, I believe that the following facts would serve to convince even the most hesitant of citizens to condemn death as sanction: capital punishment is imposed discriminatorily against certain identifiable classes of people; there is evidence that innocent people have been executed before their innocence can be proved; . . .

Regarding discrimination, it has been said that "[i]t is usually the poor, the illiterate, the underprivileged, the member of the minority group—the man who, because he is without means, and is defended by a court-appointed attorney— who becomes society's sacrificial lamb. . . ."

There is also overwhelming evidence that the death penalty is employed against men and not women. Only 32 women have been executed since 1930, while 3,827 men have met a similar fate. . . .

Just as Americans know little about who is executed and why, they are unaware of the potential dangers of executing an innocent man. . . .

No matter how careful courts are, the possibility of perjured testimony, mistaken honest testimony, and human error remain all too real. . . .

Assuming knowledge of all the facts presently available regarding capital punishment, the average citizen would, in my opinion, find it shocking to his conscience and sense of justice. For this reason alone capital punishment cannot stand. . . .

In striking down capital punishment, this Court does not malign our system of government. On the contrary, it pays homage to it. Only in a free society could right triumph in difficult times, and could civilization record its magnificent advancement. In recognizing the humanity of our fellow beings, we pay ourselves the highest tribute. We achieve "a major milestone in the long road up from barbarism" and join the approximately 70 other jurisdictions in the world which celebrate their regard for civilization and humanity by shunning capital punishment.

I concur in the judgments of the Court.

QUESTIONS

1. Justice Marshall, denying that the death penalty is a more effective deterrent than life imprisonment, finds the death penalty an "excessive and unnecessary punishment." Argue for or against the claim that the death penalty is a more effective deterrent than life imprisonment.

2. Justice Marshall contends that the death penalty is "morally unacceptable to the people of the United States at this time in their history." Argue for or against this claim.

Chief Justice Warren Burger

DISSENTING OPINION IN *FURMAN v. GEORGIA*

Biographical Information. Warren Burger (b. 1907) is chief justice of the United States Supreme Court. Admitted to the Minnesota bar in 1931, he then spent a number of years in private practice, while simultaneously serving on the faculty of the Mitchell College of Law in St. Paul. Chief Justice Burger also served as assistant attorney general (1953–1956) and as judge of the U.S. Court of Appeals, Washington (1956–1969). In 1969 he was appointed to the Supreme Court.

Argument in the Selection. Chief Justice Burger contends against Justice Marshall that the death penalty does not violate the Eighth Amendment. First, he argues against Justice Marshall's contention that the death penalty is abhorrent to currently existing moral values. Second, he argues against Justice Marshall's construing the Eighth Amendment to exclude "unnecessary" punishment.

At the onset it is important to note that only two members of the Court, Mr. Justice Brennan and Mr. Justice Marshall, have concluded that the Eighth Amendment prohibits capital punishment for all crimes and under all circumstances. Mr. Justice Douglas has also determined that the death penalty contravenes the Eighth Amendment, although I do not read his opinion as necessarily requiring final abolition of the penalty. . . .

Mr. Justice Stewart and Mr. Justice White have concluded that petitioners' death sentences must be set aside because prevailing sentencing practices do not comply with the Eighth Amendment. . . .

If we were possessed of legislative power, I would either join with Mr. Justice Brennan and Mr. Justice Marshall or, at the very least, restrict the use of capital punishment to a small category of the most heinous crimes. Our constitutional inquiry, however, must be divorced from personal feelings as to the morality and efficacy of the death penalty, and be confined to the meaning and applicability of the uncertain language of the Eighth Amendment. There is no novelty in being called upon to interpret a constitutional provision that is less than self-defining, but, of all our fundamental guarantees, the ban on "cruel and unusual punishments" is one of the most difficult to translate into judicially manageable terms. . . .

The critical fact is that this Court has never had to hold that a mode of punishment authorized by a domestic legislature was so cruel as to be fundamentally at odds with our basic notions of decency. Judicial findings of impermissible cruelty have been limited, for the most part, to offensive punishments devised without specific authority by prison officials, not by legislatures. . . .

There are no obvious indications that capital punishment offends the conscience of society to such a degree that our traditional deference to the legislative

87

judgment must be abandoned. It is not a punishment such as burning at the stake that everyone would ineffably find to be repugnant to all civilized standards. Nor is it a punishment so roundly condemned that only a few aberrant legislatures have retained it on the statute books. Capital punishment is authorized by statute in 40 States. . . .

Capital punishment has also been attacked as violative of the Eighth Amendment on the ground that it is not needed to achieve legitimate penal aims and is thus "unnecessarily cruel." As a pure policy matter, this approach has much to recommend it, but it seeks to give a dimension to the Eighth Amendment that it was never intended to have and promotes a line of inquiry that this Court has never before pursued. . . .

The legislatures can and should make an assessment of the deterrent influence of capital punishment, both generally and as affecting the commission of specific types of crimes. If legislatures come to doubt the efficacy of capital punishment, they can abolish it, either completely or on a selective basis. If new evidence persuades them that they have acted unwisely, they can reverse their field and reinstate the penalty to the extent it is thought warranted. An Eighth Amendment ruling by judges cannot be made with such flexibility or discriminating precision. . . .

QUESTIONS

1. Chief Justice Burger contends that "there are no obvious indications that capital punishment offends the conscience of society." Construct a reply to this point in the spirit of Justice Marshall.

2. On Chief Justice Burger's minority view, the employment of the death penalty is a matter that should be left to legislative judgment. If you were possessed of legislative power, to which crimes would you append the death penalty?

Jacques Barzun

IN FAVOR OF CAPITAL PUNISHMENT

Biographical Information. *Jacques Barzun (b. 1907 in France) continues today a long and most distinguished academic career at Columbia University in New York City. His years there have been divided between teaching in the Department of History and serving in various high-level administrative posts. Barzun's numerous published works span a great range of historical and educational topics, and they also reveal a continuing concern with contemporary social problems. A Catalogue of Crime (1971) especially evidences his concern with problems of criminal punishment.*

Argument in the Selection. Barzun, a retentionist, is anxious to disso-
ciate the grounds of his retentionist position from considerations of
retribution and deterrence. On his view, the case for the retention of the
death penalty can be built only on considerations of societal protection.
Barzun contends that in certain cases the death penalty is warranted,
indeed demanded, on the grounds of societal protection. His central
thesis is that the death penalty is warranted in the case of any person
who "has not been endowed with adequate controls against irrationally
taking the life of another."

Barzun is also concerned to attack two arguments that are often
employed by the abolitionist. Surely, it is said, the death penalty violates
the sanctity of human life. But, replies Barzun, here we find largely a
rhetorical slogan, "the sanctity of human life," which functions to mask
inconsistencies and narrowness of vision in the abolitionist stance. Do
not most abolitionists support wars and other kinds of killing? And do
they not speak of the sanctity of life at the same time that they manifest
no concern whatsoever for the quality of life? Further, against the aboli-
tionist argument that capital punishment is irrevocable, leaving no room
to correct mistakes, Barzun argues that capital punishment is not alone
in this regard. All punishment is irrevocable.

I readily concede at the outset that present ways of dealing out capital punishment
are as revolting as Mr. Koestler says in his harrowing volume, *Hanged by the
Neck*. Like many of our prisons, our modes of execution should change. But this
objection to barbarity does not mean that capital punishment—or rather, judicial
homicide—should not go on. The illicit jump we find here, on the threshold of the
inquiry, is characteristic of the abolitionist and must be disallowed at every point.
Let us bear in mind the possibility of devising a painless, sudden and dignified
death, and see whether its administration is justifiable.

The four main arguments advanced against the death penalty are: 1. punishment for crime is a primitive idea rooted in revenge; 2. capital punishment does
not deter; 3. judicial error being possible, taking life is an appalling risk; 4. a
civilized state, to deserve its name, must uphold, not violate, the sanctity of
human life.

I entirely agree with the first pair of propositions, which is why, a moment
ago, I replaced the term capital punishment with "judicial homicide." The uncontrollable brute whom I want put out of the way is not to be punished for his
misdeeds, nor used as an example or a warning; he is to be killed for the protection
of others, like the wolf that escaped not long ago in a Connecticut suburb. No
anger, vindictiveness or moral conceit need preside over the removal of such
dangers. But a man's inability to control his violent impulses or to imagine the
fatal consequences of his acts should be a presumptive reason for his elimination
from society. This generality covers drunken driving and teen-age racing on
public highways, as well as incurable obsessive violence; it might be extended (as
I shall suggest later) to other acts that destroy, precisely, the moral basis of
civilization.

89

But why kill? I am ready to believe the statistics tending to show that the prospect of his own death does not stop the murderer. For one thing he is often a blind egotist, who cannot conceive the possibility of his own death. For another, detection would have to be infallible to deter the more imaginative who, although afraid, think they can escape discovery. Lastly, as Shaw long ago pointed out, hanging the wrong man will deter as effectively as hanging the right one. So, once again, why kill? If I agree that moral progress means an increasing respect for human life, how can I oppose abolition?

I do so because on this subject of human life, which is to me the heart of the controversy, I find the abolitionist inconsistent, narrow or blind. The propaganda for abolition speaks in hushed tones of the sanctity of human life, as if the mere statement of it as an absolute should silence all opponents who have any moral sense. But most of the abolitionists belong to nations that spend half their annual income on weapons of war and that honor research to perfect means of killing. These good people vote without a qualm for the political parties that quite sensibly arm their country to the teeth. The West today does not seem to be the time or place to invoke the absolute sanctity of human life. As for the clergymen in the movement, we may be sure from the experience of two previous world wars that they will bless our arms and pray for victory when called upon, the sixth commandment notwithstanding.

"Oh, but we mean the sanctity of life *within* the nation!" Very well: is the movement then campaigning also against the principle of self-defense? Absolute sanctity means letting the cutthroat have his sweet will of you, even if you have a poker handy to bash him with, for you might kill. And again, do we hear any protest against the police firing at criminals on the street—mere bank robbers usually—and doing this, often enough, with an excited marksmanship that misses the artist and hits the bystander? The absolute sanctity of human life is, for the abolitionist, a slogan rather than a considered proposition.

Yet it deserves examination, for upon our acceptance or rejection of it depend such other highly civilized possibilities as euthanasia and seemly suicide. The inquiring mind also wants to know, why the sanctity of *human* life alone? My tastes do not run to household pets, but I find something less than admirable in the uses to which we put animals—in zoos, laboratories and space machines—without the excuse of the ancient law, "Eat or be eaten."

It should moreover be borne in mind that this argument about sanctity applies—or would apply—to about ten persons a year in Great Britain and to between fifty and seventy-five in the United States. These are the average numbers of those executed in recent years. The count by itself should not, of course, affect our judgment of the principle: one life spared or forfeited is as important, morally, as a hundred thousand. But it should inspire a comparative judgment: there are hundreds and indeed thousands whom, in our concern with the horrors of execution, we forget: on the one hand, the victims of violence; on the other, the prisoners in our jails. . . .

As in all great questions, the moralist must choose, and choosing has a price. I happen to think that if a person of adult body has not been endowed with adequate controls against irrationally taking the life of another, that person must be judicially, painlessly, regretfully killed before that mindless body's horrible automation repeats.

I say "irrationally" taking life, because it is often possible to feel great sympathy with a murderer. Certain *crimes passionnels* can be forgiven without being condoned. Blackmailers invite direct retribution. Long provocation can be an excuse, as in that engaging case of some years ago, in which a respectable carpenter of seventy found he could no longer stand the incessant nagging of his wife. While she excoriated him from her throne in the kitchen—a daily exercise for fifty years—the husband went to his bench and came back with a hammer in each hand to settle the score. The testimony to his character, coupled with the sincerity implied by the two hammers, was enough to have him sent into quiet and brief seclusion.

But what are we to say of the type of motive disclosed in a journal published by the inmates of one of our Federal penitentiaries? The author is a bank robber who confesses that money is not his object:

> My mania for power, socially, sexually, and otherwise can feel no degree of satisfaction until I feel sure I have struck the ultimate of submission and terror in the minds and bodies of my victims. . . . It's very difficult to explain all the queer fascinating sensations pounding and surging through me while I'm holding a gun on a victim, watching his body tremble and sweat. . . . This is the moment when all the rationalized hypocrisies of civilization are suddenly swept away and two men stand there facing each other morally and ethically naked, and right and wrong are the absolute commands of the man behind the gun.

This confused echo of modern literature and modern science defines the choice before us. Anything deserving the name of cure for such a man presupposes not only a laborious individual psychoanalysis, with the means to conduct and to sustain it, socially and economically, but also a re-education of the mind, so as to throw into correct perspective the garbled ideas of Freud and Nietzsche, Gide and Dostoevski, which this power-seeker and his fellows have derived from the culture and temper of our times. Ideas are tenacious and give continuity to emotion. Failing a second birth of heart and mind, we must ask: How soon will this sufferer sacrifice a bank clerk in the interests of making civilization less hypocritical? And we must certainly question the wisdom of affording him more than one chance. The abolitionists' advocacy of an unconditional "let live" is in truth part of the same cultural tendency that animates the killer. The Western peoples' revulsion from power in domestic and foreign policy has made of the state a sort of counterpart of the bank robber: both having power and neither knowing how to use it. Both waste lives because hypnotized by irrelevant ideas and crippled by contradictory emotions. If psychiatry were sure of its ground in diagnosing the individual case, a philosopher might consider whether such dangerous obsessions should not be guarded against by judicial homicide *before* the shooting starts.

I raise the question not indeed to recommend the prophylactic execution of potential murderers, but to introduce the last two perplexities that the abolitionists dwarf or obscure by their concentration on changing an isolated penalty. One of these is the scale by which to judge the offenses society wants to repress. I can for example imagine a truly democratic state in which it would be deemed a form of treason punishable by death to create a disturbance in any court or deliberative assembly. The aim would be to recognize the sanctity of orderly discourse in arriving at justice, assessing criticism and defining policy. Under such a law, a natural selection would operate to remove permanently from the scene persons who, let us say, neglect argument in favor of banging on the desk with their shoe. Similarly, a bullying minority in a diet, parliament or skupshtina would be prosecuted for treason to the most sacred institutions when fists or flying inkwells replace rhetoric. That the mere suggestion of such a law sounds ludicrous shows how remote we are from civilized institutions, and hence how gradual should be our departure from the severity of judicial homicide.

I say gradual and I do not mean standing still. For there is one form of barbarity in our law that I want to see mitigated before any other. I mean imprisonment. The enemies of capital punishment—and liberals generally— seem to be satisfied with any legal outcome so long as they themselves avoid the vicarious guilt of shedding blood. They speak of the sanctity of life, but have no concern with its quality. They give no impression of ever having read what it is certain they have read, from Wilde's *De Profundis* to the latest account of prison life by a convicted homosexual. Despite the infamy of concentration camps, despite Mr. Charles Burney's remarkable work, *Solitary Confinement*, despite riots in prisons, despite the round of escape, recapture and return in chains, the abolitionists' imagination tells them nothing about the reality of being caged. They read without a qualm, indeed they read with rejoicing, the hideous irony of "Killer Gets Life"; they sigh with relief instead of horror. They do not see and suffer the cell, the drill, the clothes, the stench, the food; they do not feel the sexual racking of young and old bodies, the hateful promiscuity, the insane monotony, the mass degradation, the impotent hatred. They do not remember from Silvio Pellico that only a strong political faith, with a hope of final victory, can steel a man to endure long detention. They forget that Joan of Arc, when offered "life," preferred burning at the stake. Quite of another mind, the abolitionists point with pride to the "model prisoners" that murderers often turn out to be. As if a model prisoner were not, first, a contradiction in terms, and second, an exemplar of what a free society should not want.

I said a moment ago that the happy advocates of the life sentence appear not to have understood what we know they have read. No more do they appear to read what they themselves write. In the preface to his useful volume of cases, *Hanged in Error*, Mr. Leslie Hale, M.P., refers to the tardy recognition of a minor miscar- riage of justice—one year in jail: "The prisoner emerged to find that his wife had died and that his children and his aged parents had been removed to the work- house. By the time a small payment had been assessed as 'compensation' the victim was incurably insane." So far we are as indignant with the law as Mr. Hale. But what comes next? He cites the famous Evans case, in which it is very probable that the wrong man was hanged, and he exclaims: "While such mistakes are possible, should society impose an irrevocable sentence?" Does Mr. Hale really ask us to believe that the sentence passed on the first man, whose wife died and who went insane, was in any sense *revocable*? Would not any man rather be Evans dead than that other wretch "emerging" with his small compensation and his reasons for living gone?

Nothing is revocable here below, imprisonment least of all. The agony of a trial itself is punishment, and acquittal wipes out nothing. Read the heart-rending diary of William Wallace, accused quite implausibly of having murdered his wife and "saved" by the Court of Criminal Appeals—but saved for what? Brutish ostracism by everyone and a few years of solitary despair. The cases of Adolf Beck, of Oscar Slater, of the unhappy Brooklyn bank teller who vaguely resembled a forger and spent eight years in Sing Sing only to "emerge" a broken, friendless, useless, "compensated" man—all these, if the dignity of the individual has any meaning, had better have been dead before the prison door ever opened for them. This is what counsel always says to the jury in the course of a murder trial and counsel is right: far better hang this man than "give him life." For my part, I would choose death without hesitation. If that option is abolished, a demand will one day be heard to claim it as a privilege in the name of human dignity. I shall believe in the abolitionist's present views only after he has emerged from twelve months in a convict cell.

The detached observer may want to interrupt here and say that the argument has now passed from reasoning to emotional preference. Whereas the objector to capital punishment *feels* that death is the greatest of evils, I *feel* that imprisonment is worse than death. A moment's thought will show that feeling is the appropriate arbiter. All reasoning about what is right, civilized and moral rests upon sentiment, like mathematics. Only, in trying to persuade others, it is important to single out the fundamental feeling, the prime intuition, and from it to reason justly. In my view, to profess respect for human life and be willing to see it spent in a penitentiary is to entertain liberal feelings frivolously. To oppose the death penalty because, unlike a prison term, it is irrevocable is to argue fallaciously.

In the propaganda for abolishing the death sentence the recital of numerous miscarriages of justice commits the same error and implies the same callousness: what is at fault in our present system is not the sentence but the fallible procedure. Capital cases being one in a thousand or more, who can be cheerful at the thought of all the "revocable" errors? What the miscarriages point to is the need for reforming the jury system, the rules of evidence, the customs of prosecution, the machinery of appeal. The failure to see that this is the great task reflects the sentimentality I spoke of earlier, that which responds chiefly to the excitement of the unusual. A writer on Death and the Supreme Court is at pains to point out that when that tribunal reviews a capital case, the judges are particularly anxious and careful. What a left-handed compliment to the highest judicial conscience of the country! Fortunately, some of the champions of the misjudged see the issue more clearly. Many of those who are thought wrongly convicted now languish in jail because the jury was uncertain or because a doubting governor commuted the death sentence. Thus Dr. Samuel H. Sheppard, Jr., convicted of his wife's murder in the second degree is serving a sentence that is supposed to run for the term of his natural life. The story of his numerous trials, as told by Mr. Paul Holmes, suggests that police incompetence, newspaper demagogy, public envy of affluence and the mischances of legal procedure fashioned the result. But Dr. Sheppard's vindicator is under no illusion as to the conditions that this "lucky" evader of the electric chair will face if he is granted parole after ten years: "It will carry with it no right to resume his life as a physician. His privilege to practice medicine was blotted out with his conviction. He must all his life bear the stigma of a

93

parolee, subject to unceremonious return to confinement for life for the slightest misstep. More than this, he must live out his life as a convicted murderer."

What does the moral conscience of today think it is doing? If such a man is a dangerous repeater of violent acts, what right has the state to let him loose after ten years? What is, in fact, the meaning of a "life sentence" that peters out long before life? Paroling looks suspiciously like an expression of social remorse for the pain of incarceration, coupled with a wish to avoid "unfavorable publicity" by freeing a suspect. The man is let out when the fuss has died down; which would mean that he was not under lock and key for our protection at all. He *was* being punished, just a little—for so prison seems in the abolitionist's distorted view, and in the jury's and the prosecutor's, whose "second degree" murder suggests killing someone "just a little."

If, on the other hand, execution and life imprisonment are judged too severe and the accused is expected to be harmless hereafter—punishment being ruled out as illiberal—what has society gained by wrecking his life and damaging that of his family?

What we accept, and what the abolitionist will clamp upon us all the more firmly if he succeeds, is an incoherence which is not remedied by the belief that second degree murder merits a kind of second degree death; that a doubt as to the identity of a killer is resolved by commuting real death into intolerable life; and that our ignorance whether a maniac will strike again can be hedged against by measuring "good behavior" within the gates and then releasing the subject upon the public in the true spirit of experimentation.

These are some of the thoughts I find I cannot escape when I read and reflect upon this grave subject. If, as I think, they are relevant to any discussion of change and reform, resting as they do on the direct and concrete perception of what happens, then the simple meliorists who expect to breathe a purer air by abolishing the death penalty are deceiving themselves and us. The issue is for the public to judge; but I for one shall not sleep easier for knowing that in England and America and the West generally a hundred more human beings are kept alive in degrading conditions to face a hopeless future; while others—possibly less conscious, certainly less controlled—benefit from a premature freedom dangerous alike to themselves and society. In short, I derive no comfort from the illusion that in giving up one manifest protection of the law-abiding, we who might well be in any of these three roles—victim, prisoner, licensed killer—have struck a blow for the sanctity of human life.

QUESTIONS

1. Barzun thinks that the death penalty is warranted in the case of any person who "has not been endowed with adequate controls against irrationally taking the life of another." Do you think it is possible to specify criteria for identifying such people? If so, spell out and defend your criteria. If not, advance an argument to show why it is impossible to specify such criteria.

2. Construct an abolitionist response to Barzun's claim that *all* punishment is irrevocable.

3. Does Barzun treat the abolitionist fairly in his attack upon the abolitionist commitment to "the sanctity of human life"?

Sidney Hook

THE DEATH SENTENCE

Biographical Information. Sidney Hook (b. 1902) is now, after some forty years of teaching philosophy at New York University, professor emeritus. Much of his philosophical analysis has centered on various aspects of human freedom, often as related to social, political, and legal issues. His numerous publications include Political Power and Personal Freedom *(1959).* The Paradoxes of Freedom *(1962), and* The Place of Religion in a Free Society *(1968).*

Argument in the Selection. Hook supports the retention of the death penalty for employment in two diverse cases. (1) Some criminal defendants, when sentenced to life imprisonment, may in fact prefer death. Their preference should be honored. (2) Some convicted murderers, having served one prison sentence, murder again. When such twice-guilty murderers are found to be sane, and when there is a reasonable probability that they will attempt to murder again, the death penalty should be imposed. In arguing for both (1) and (2), Hook attempts to turn humanitarian considerations, usually part of the abolitionist case, against the abolitionist. To resist (1), he argues, is to treat the convicted criminal in an inhumane way. Similarly, to resist (2) involves a posture of inhumanity. Do we not care about the lives of the murderer's future victims?

Since I am not a fanatic or absolutist, I do not wish to go on record as being categorically opposed to the death sentence in all circumstances. I should like to recognize two exceptions. A defendant convicted of murder and sentenced to life should be permitted to choose the death sentence instead. Not so long ago a defendant sentenced to life imprisonment made this request and was rebuked by the judge for his impertinence. I can see no valid grounds for denying such a request out of hand. It may sometimes be denied, particularly if a way can be found to make the defendant labor for the benefit of the dependents of his victim as is done in some European countries. Unless such considerations are present, I do not see on what reasonable ground the request can be denied, particularly by those who believe in capital punishment. Once they argue that life imprisonment

95

is either a more effective deterrent or more justly punitive, they have abandoned their position.

In passing, I should state that I am in favor of permitting *any* criminal defendant, sentenced to life imprisonment, the right to choose death. I can understand why certain jurists, who believe that the defendant wants thereby to cheat the state out of its mode of punishment, should be indignant at the idea. They are usually the ones who believe that even the attempt at suicide should be deemed a crime—in effect saying to the unfortunate person that if he doesn't succeed in his act of suicide, the state will punish him for it. But I am baffled to understand why the absolute abolitionist, dripping with treacly humanitarianism, should oppose this proposal. I have heard some people actually oppose capital punishment in certain cases on the ground that: "Death is too good for the vile wretch! Let him live and suffer to the end of his days." But the absolute abolition-ist should be the last person in the world to oppose the wish of the lifer, who regards this form of punishment as torture worse than death, to leave our world.

My second class of exceptions consists of those who having been sentenced once to prison for premeditated murder, murder again. In these particular cases we have evidence that imprisonment is not a sufficient deterrent for the individual in question. If the evidence shows that the prisoner is so psychologically consti-tuted that, without being insane, the fact that he can kill again with impunity may lead to further murderous behavior, the court should have the discretionary power to pass the death sentence if the criminal is found guilty of a second murder.

In saying that the death sentence should be *discretionary* in cases where a man has killed more than once, I am *not* saying that a murderer who murders again is more deserving of death than the murderer who murders once. Bluebeard was not twelve times more deserving of death when he was finally caught. I am saying simply this: that in a sub-class of murderers, i.e., those who murder several times, there may be a special group of sane murderers who, knowing that they will not be executed, will not hesitate to kill again and again. For *them* the argument from deterrence is obviously valid. Those who say that there must be no exceptions to the abolition of capital punishment cannot rule out the existence of such cases on *a priori* grounds. If they admit that there is a reasonable probability that such murderers will murder again or attempt to murder again, a probability which usually grows with the number of repeated murders, and still insist they would *never* approve of capital punishment, I would conclude that they are indifferent to the lives of the human beings doomed, on their position, to be victims. What fancies itself as a humanitarian attitude is sometimes an expression of sentimen-talism. The reverse coin of sentimentalism is often cruelty.

Our charity for all human beings must not deprive us of our common sense. Nor should our charity be less for the future or potential victims of the murderer than for the murderer himself. There are crimes in this world which are, like acts of nature, beyond the power of men to anticipate or control. But not all or most crimes are of this character. So long as human beings are responsible and educa-ble, they will respond to praise and blame and punishment. It is hard to imagine it but even Hitler and Stalin were once infants. Once you *can* imagine them as infants, however, it is hard to believe that they were already monsters in their cradles. Every confirmed criminal was once an amateur. The existence of con-firmed criminals testifies to the defects of our education—where they can be reformed—and of our penology—where they cannot. That is why we are under the moral obligation to be intelligent about crime and punishment. Intelligence should teach us that the best educational and penological system is the one which prevents crimes rather than punishes them; the next best is one which punishes crime in such a way as to prevent it from happening again.

QUESTIONS

1. Evaluate the success of Hook's effort to turn humanitarian considerations against the abolitionist.
2. Argue for or against the following claim: The death penalty is not justified on grounds of societal protection because life imprisonment can equally well serve this purpose.

Hugo Adam Bedau

DEATH AS A PUNISHMENT

Biographical Information. Hugo Adam Bedau (b. 1926) is professor of philosophy at Tufts University in Medford, Massachusetts. Social philosophy, political philosophy, and legal philosophy are his primary philosophical interests. Bedau is certainly one of the most prominent spokesmen for the abolitionist movement in the United States. He is president of the American League to Abolish Capital Punishment and is editor of The Death Penalty in America *(rev. ed., 1967). His concern for other contemporary ethical issues is reflected in his editorship of* Civil Disobedience *(1969) and* Justice and Equality *(1971).*

Argument in the Selection. Bedau, representing the abolitionist perspective, attempts to refute the various arguments constructed by Barzun and Hook in the two previous selections. Against Barzun, Bedau contends that the abolitionist can sanction killing in self-defense without being guilty of inconsistency. Also against Barzun, Bedau argues that there is indeed a special kind of irrevocability associated with the death penalty. With regard to Hook's contention that a criminal sentenced to life imprisonment ought to be able to choose the death penalty instead, Bedau argues that Hook overlooks the distinction between choosing death for someone else and choosing it for oneself. As a result, Bedau contends, Hook winds up defending not the institution of capital punishment but a different institution, a sophisticated form of "supervised suicide."

For Bedau, the principal argument raised by both Hook and Barzun is that the death penalty is the only solution for the hardened and violent criminal. Hook would have the death penalty available as punishment for the "sane unreformable twice-guilty murderer," but Bedau raises

97

several difficulties about the concept of sanity. Moreover, he argues that Hook cannot specify any clear criterion for establishing when there would be "a reasonable probability" that a two-time murderer will once again attempt to murder. Against Barzun's version of the principal argument under discussion, Bedau contends that it is not at all a defense of capital punishment, but rather a defense of a distinct societal institution, a policy of eugenic killing.

Let me now turn to the case for the death penalty that Professors Barzun and Hook have made out, for it deserves the closest attention. (I should say from the onset that I am quite aware of the several differences between Hook's and Barzun's arguments; and I know there is some risk of misrepresenting their views by allying them as closely as I have at several points. The reader will have to judge whether I have been unfair to one in the course of objecting to the other.)

It will not go unnoticed that, unlike many retentionists, they concede a great deal to the opposition. They understand that the question is not one of capital punishment or no punishment. They share our doubts about the social utility of the motives that usually animate the defenders of the death penalty. They admit that the doctrine of general deterrence cannot any longer be the lynch-pin of a reasonable man's defense of capital punishment in America. They implicitly recognize that the burden of proof is on them as advocates of killing certain types of persons, not on those who would let even the worst convicts live. As Professor Barzun rather wistfully comments, his concessions almost make him happier with the abolitionist than against him.[1] Almost, but not quite. What remains of the case for the death penalty that he and Professor Hook are able to construct would crumble if several crucial distinctions were drawn, distinctions that would clarify their arguments and enable us to see the full consequences of the principles they espouse.

For example, one distinction of importance, neglected by Professor Barzun, is between a man's killing someone else when there is a clear and present danger that he will otherwise be the victim of some violent act, and the state's killing a man as a punishment, i.e., between a man's right to defend himself and society's right to punish criminals. It is because Barzun fails to make this distinction that he thinks abolitionists are inconsistent in appealing to the sanctity of human life. So far as law and the prevailing morality of Western civilization have been concerned, respect for human life has never been an obstacle to the use of force in self-defense; indeed, it has always been thought to be its justification. It has, however, obligated anyone who pleads self-defense in justification of a killing to satisfy society that the force he used really was necessary in the circumstances and was motivated solely by a desire to ward off imminent harm to himself. But to kill a person who in fact is not at the time dangerous (because he is in prison), on the

---

[1] Likewise Professor Hook; at least, his remarks in reply to Judge Samuel Leibowitz, in *New York Law Forum* (August 1961), pp. 296–300, strongly suggest this.

possibility that he might at some later date be dangerous, would be to use unjustifiable force and thus to flout the respect human life is due. Were it to be shown that there is a threat to society, or to any of its members, in allowing a criminal in prison to remain there, comparable to the danger a man invites in a dark alley if he turns his back on a thug who has a weapon in his hand and violence on his mind, then—but *only* then—would it be inconsistent for the abolitionist to tolerate force sufficient to kill the thug in the alley but to refuse to kill the prisoner. It may be that the pacifist, with his commitment to the absolute sanctity of human life, would in theory and in practice have to tolerate the slaughter of innocent lives (including his own). But if such a disaster were a likely consequence of abolishing the death penalty, or of extending parole at least in principle to all capital offenders, few of us who favor both would advocate either. The facts here, in terms of which the degree of risk can alone be measured, happen to be on our side.[2]

On the issue of whether abolition of the death penalty would improve the lot of persons unjustly convicted, I think both Professor Hook and Professor Barzun are misled and confusing. Barzun is unquestionably right when he points to cases where men have been exonerated after years in prison, only to find that their lives have been destroyed. Of course, abolishing the death penalty is no remedy for the injustice of convicting and punishing an innocent man. It is obviously as *wrong* to imprison an innocent man as it is to kill him. But I should have thought it is just as obviously *worse* for him to be killed than for him to be imprisoned. This point must not be blurred by speculating whether it is worse from the convict's point of view to be dead than to be imprisoned and perhaps never vindicated or released. If an innocent convict thinks he is better off dead than alive, this is for *him* to determine, not us. What we must decide is the less metaphysical question of what general penal policy the state should adopt, on the understanding that the policy will in practice be applied not only to the numerous guilty but also to a few who are innocent. No one can deny, even if Hook and Barzun neglect to stress it, that the *only* way the state is in a position to do something for the victim of a miscarriage of justice is if it has refused as a matter of principle to kill *any* of its convicts. Executing an innocent man is not impossible,[3] and it is a great risk to run for the questionable advantage of executing a few guilty ones.

Nor am I impressed by the "humanitarian" concern for the agony of a man erroneously convicted which, in claiming to deliver him from the greater evil, would take not only his freedom but his life as well. I cannot believe in point of fact that Tom Mooney would have been better off had he been hanged in 1917 for a crime he did not commit, rather than pardoned as he was more than twenty years later. I know of no evidence that he came to the opposite conclusion. I leave it for anyone acquainted with the case of James Fulton Foster to judge whether he would have been better off dead than as he is: alive, exonerated, and free.[4] Are these cases as exceptional as Professor Barzun evidently believes? Even if they

[2] See Chapter Seven, "Parole of Capital Offenders, Recidivism, and Life Imprisonment," *The Death Penalty in America.*

[3] See Chapter Eight, "Murder, Errors of Justice, and Capital Punishment," *The Death Penalty in America.*

[4] See Chapter Nine, "The Question of Identity," *The Death Penalty in America.*

were, how could putting a Mooney or a Foster to death ever be justified on *humanitarian* grounds?

These reflections suggest a general point. There is a fundamental distinction to be made between choosing the death penalty for yourself and choosing it for someone else. Both Hook and Barzun seem to believe that imprisonment, even for a guilty man (and certainly for themselves, were *they* in prison, innocent or guilty), may be a far worse punishment than execution, and that abolitionists deceive themselves in believing that they advocate the lesser penalty. I doubt that this is so: but even if it were, I am certain that their argument is a deception.

Just as most abolitionists would agree that if the death penalty must be kept then less gruesome modes of execution ought to be adopted than those currently in use, many of us would also agree that we ought to consider allowing our penal authorities, under proper judicial and medical supervision, to cooperate with any long-term prisoner who is too dangerous to be released and who would honestly and soberly prefer to be dead rather than endure further imprisonment. That there are such convicts I am willing to concede. The question here is this: is it wisest for the state to allow a convict to take his own life if he decides that it would be better for him to be dead than to suffer any more imprisonment? Can a person in good physical health, in a tolerable prison environment, and who professes to want to die be of sound mind? (or isn't that important?) Does not civilized society always have a fundamental interest, if not an obligation, to try to provide even for its most incompetent members in that most oppressive of environments, a prison, some opportunity to make their lives worth living? Wouldn't a policy that amounts to euthanasia for certain convicts run counter to this interest and sap the motive to satisfy it?

These questions are not new, for they arise whenever "mercy killing" as a social policy is advocated. But they are instructive, for they indicate how the issue under discussion has subtly changed. No longer are we considering how we ought to punish crimes. Instead, we are asking whether we ought to allow a convict, if he so wishes, to be painlessly put to death for no other reason than so that his imprisonment and his despair may come to an end—as if there were no better alternatives! This question, and the other questions above, has little to do with the one posed by capital punishment: is it wisest for the state to impose death or imprisonment as the punishment for certain crimes, irrespective of what the convicts in question may prefer? To give an affirmative answer to the former is not to decide the latter at all. In arguing, as Hook and Barzun do, that convicts should have the right to obtain from their custodians the means for a decent suicide, they have not argued for capital punishment. They have not even shown that any convict who chooses death rather than imprisonment has made the wiser choice. It is a great misfortune, and shows the confusion I have imputed to him, that Professor Hook raises this whole issue as (in his words) one of several "exceptions" to his general disapproval of capital punishment. Supervised suicide for those convicts who want it, irrespective of their crime, is not an "exception" in which capital punishment would remain as part of a penal system; supervised suicide is an entirely different matter, as we have seen, with questions all its own. . . .

Quite independently of the foregoing considerations Hook and Barzun advance what is by far their strongest argument for the death penalty, namely, that there is no other solution for the very worst criminals, those whose sole instinct is

Kill, Kill, Kill. Having agreed on this, they disagree on everything else. Professor Hook plainly thinks these criminals are the *sane* unreformable twice-guilty murderers, for this is the class of criminals he expressly and repeatedly specifies. But it is just as clear that it is the "escaped lunatic," the "sudden maniac," the criminally *insane* killer (or rapist, or mugger), whether reformable or not, whom Professor Barzun is anxious to see executed. Moreover, whereas Hook insists that *mandatory* death penalties are unjustifiable, Barzun's preference must run the other way. For if our insistence on parole looks to him too much like "an expression of social remorse for the pain of incarceration," what must he think of a life sentence in the first place but that it is an expression of the jury's remorse for convicting the man at all? And it is just such sentimental nonsense, whether in a Parole Board or a jury, that is out of place when your safety and mine is at stake. Finally, whereas Professor Hook's argument presupposes that he regards the execution of a sane murderer as a *punishment,* it is very doubtful whether this is how Professor Barzun views the executions of those whom he would have put to death. Whether or not it was his intention, he makes it clear that it is "judicial homicide" he favors, and so far as he defends the death penalty it is mainly because it accomplishes much the same thing, namely, eugenic executions.[5] I think Professor Hook has come to the defense of the death penalty on behalf of a small if not non-existent class of criminals. Whether or not we make the "exception" he advises, it appears that in practice it will make little difference (though, if my argument below is correct, this may not be so). Professor Barzun, however, has altogether ceased to defend the death penalty, and a great deal both in theory and practice depends on understanding why this is so.

What conception of insanity Professor Hook would accept, he does not indicate. Yet any defense of the death penalty for *sane* unreformable murderers turns on this point. He contends that there is no "*a priori* ground" to rule out the possibility of sane murderers murdering again after a term of imprisonment. He infers that the death penalty is necessary to prevent such criminals from repeating their crimes. But is there really no such *a priori* ground? Any murderer who murders again, after a term of imprisonment and under at least somewhat different circumstances—ought he not by definition to be classified as criminally irresponsible? Must he not be suffering from some mental or emotional defect, whether or not it has been identified by psychiatrists, which warrants the label, "insanity"? It is more than a mere possibility.

Of course, the classic Anglo-American definition of "insanity," in terms of the M'Naghten Rules of 1843, would never yield any such result. But these Rules are slowly giving way to others that might provide this.[6] For all that Professor Hook or I know, it may be that a careful study of the psychopathology of unreformed murderers would show a set of symptoms that would entitle them without exception to be treated as insane. If no such set of symptoms were located, or even

[5] Not only a critic is bound to understand Barzun's position in this way, as is proved by the noted scholar who found himself in "complete agreement" with Barzun and construed his views exactly as I have; see *The American Scholar* (Summer 1962), pp. 446 f.

[6] See the essays collected by Richard Nice (ed.), *Crime and Insanity* (1958); and also the bibliography prepared by Dorothy Campbell Tompkins, *Insanity and the Criminal Law* (1960).

hypothesized, I admit it would be arbitrary to stretch "insane" so as to describe every such murderer for no other reason than that he repeated his offense. But arbitrariness and the *a priori* with it lie all around us in this area. It must not be forgotten that the term, "insane," unlike "paranoid," has never been a description of any set of symptoms. It has never been related to forms of mental illness via empirical hypotheses contributed by psychopathology. It is simply the term employed by the law when a court wishes to hold an accused not accountable for his criminal acts by reason of his "unsoundness of mind." The kinds and causes of his "unsoundness of mind" are not legal but medical questions. The legal questions concern how to frame and to apply a general rule that will specify as insane all and only those persons whose acts are traceable to their mental ill-health and who, on that account, are to be excused from criminal responsibility and its consequences.

Professor Hook's confidence that in theory at least there may be sane multiple murderers must derive from *his* definition of "insane"; and such a definition is itself an "*a priori* ground." Depending on where we want to come out, we can make assumptions in the form of a definition of "insane" which will have the result that all, or some, or no unreformed murderers are insane. The trouble is not, as Hook asserts, that there is no "*a priori* ground" for ruling out the possibility of such criminals, but that such a ground, being only an *a priori* one, in the sense that it consists of a definition, has other alternatives equally *a priori* but with very different consequences.

What this shows is that if one's purpose is really to execute unreformable murderers, it is best to ignore the incidental facts of their sanity. Otherwise, one's purpose may be frustrated by nothing more than a change in the legal definition of "insanity." Professor Barzun, who does not scruple on this question, has all the advantages, and hard-core retentionists would be well advised to ally themselves with his position rather than Hook's.

It is also necessary to argue with Professor Hook on empirical grounds. What is the probability that there are any "sane" persons knowledgeable and imaginative enough to know what might be in store for them if they commit another murder, vicious enough to kill with cool deliberation, and still stupid enough to risk years of imprisonment after having already experienced it (for we are hypothesizing that our murderers are repeaters)? The probability is apparently so slight that competent authorities agree it is negligible.[7] But we do not need to settle for the educated guesses of the authorities. Five states (Michigan, Minnesota, Wisconsin, Rhode Island, Maine) have long been without capital punishment for murder. If they have suffered from the problem of the sane unreformable murderer (as their courts define "sanity"), there has been plenty of time to remedy it by adopting just such a statute as Professor Hook recommends. Is their failure merely proof of public apathy? Or is it perhaps proof that in these states, the most vindictive have become abolitionists, and that their vindictiveness has gone to their heads: they relish the knowledge, shared with Professor Barzun, that in their jurisdictions the murderer suffers the ultimate punishment, literal life imprisonment; and public satisfaction in this knowledge more than compensates for the risk that one of the unreformables might sometime be paroled?

---

[7] See the Introduction to Chapter Six, *The Death Penalty in America.*

I have yet to mention my strongest objection to Professor Hook's argument. It arises from what may be only a casual comment. Professor Barzun, it will be recalled, asks why society must wait until a man has killed several times before he may be executed, given that we are willing to have murderers executed at all. Elsewhere, Hook has said what amounts to his reply: because "the first time a man murders we are not sure that he is a mad dog."[8] (Let us merely note the curious turn of phrase which has him eventually defending the execution of sane "mad dogs.") This is reasonable enough. But Hook now expresses the doctrine, in his essay in Chapter Three, that second-time murderers ought to be executed where there is "a reasonable probability" they "will murder again or attempt to murder again." This is a somewhat unsettling idea, and a revealing one as well. Would Hook consider allowing a court to sentence a person to death even if he had not yet committed a second murder, and had not even attempted one, so long as it was "reasonably probable" that he would? Suppose we had a delinquency diagnostic test which would tell us with "reasonable probability" that a given person would attempt to commit his *first* murder and that he would not respond to subsequent imprisonment. What would Professor Hook allow us to do with such knowledge? If he would allow us to execute a man after he has twice murdered, or after one murder and an attempted second murder, on the ground that there is no "reasonable probability" of rehabilitating him in prison, why should he not allow us to execute the man when he has killed but once? Or, indeed, before he has killed or attempted to kill at all? Is it the risk that even "reasonable probabilities" may in fact not lead to valid predictions? Then by the same token, executing a man no matter how many murders he has committed and no matter how often he has failed to respond to rehabilitation must also be rejected. Thus, the line Professor Hook attempts to draw between murderers deserving execution and those deserving imprisonment, which began by appearing firm and clear, turns out, thanks to the way one can manipulate the notion of "reasonable probabilities," to be no line at all.

Professor Barzun, unlike Professor Hook, directs his putative defense of the death penalty toward the class of criminals that, because of its number and danger, is of somewhat greater significance: the class inclined to violent and brutal acts, whether or not they are insane, whether or not they are reformable, and whether or not they have already committed any crimes. Barzun seems willing to embrace the "prophylactic execution of potential murderers," though only on the admittedly speculative assumption that the courts had a reliable test to predict future violence. Except for reservations about the sanity of those to be executed, Professor Hook's position, if I am right, leads to a similar conclusion. So this is the end of their line of argument purportedly advanced on behalf of the death penalty. The only way we can regard the desirability of such executions as relevant to the issue is if we ignore the fact that a system of capital punishment is, after all, a system of *punishment,* and that in such a system death can be inflicted on a person only for what he has done. A system of judicially sanctioned homicide, in which people are executed (at least in theory) *before* they have committed any crime at all, and thus are "punished" for what they will do and for the sort of person they will become, is not a system of punishment at all.

[8] See *New York Law Forum* (August 1961), p. 297.

It is not a novel idea, either. In 1922, George Bernard Shaw, inspired both by genuine distress over the plight of men imprisoned for life and by pseudo-Darwinian eugenics, defended just such a system in his provocative essay, "The Crime of Imprisonment." But at least he recognized that in taking the position he did, he was *not* advancing an argument in favor of capital punishment or any other sort of punishment. Shaw defended the remarkable position that "we have no right to punish anybody." His conclusion that "persons who give more trouble than they are worth will run the risk of being . . . returned to the dust from which they sprung,"[9] was expressly offered as a reasonable man's alternative to every known system of punishment. On such a view the actual commission of a crime would be nothing but an incontrovertible symptom of a social disease which, whether or not it might be curable or might have been avoided, can be controlled only by exterminating the sick man. Were there some sure way of identifying the crime-prone before they break out with the fatal (to us) symptoms, there is every reason to put them out of the way. The medical analogy, to be sure, is not very apt. We are in effect advised to exterminate the sick and, if possible, the disease-prone, whereas analogy to public health measures suggests that we should bend every effort to immunize everyone with a suitable vaccine. Be that as it may, as Shaw well understood, to adopt such a system would certainly result in executions. But they would not be punishments, and the system would not be a system of capital punishment.

To take the line I have is not merely to quibble evasively. I do not want it thought that whereas I object to Barzun's defense of eugenic killings because he implies they are capital punishments, I would welcome them as readily as he and Shaw do if only they were called what they are. For I have serious reservations about the Shaw-Barzun position even when properly described and candidly defended for what it is. But each social question in its own time and place. One ought to be prepared to debate the merits of "judicial homicide" as a eugenic policy, for the very same reason one ought to be prepared to discuss euthanasia and abortion.[10] These practices, like capital punishment itself, consist essentially in ending or preventing someone else's life, presumably for good reasons, and thus they pose variations on a theme of incomparable moral importance. But these issues are clearly independent of each other. Just as nothing has prevented us in the past from having capital punishment without also having euthanasia or eugenic killings, there is nothing to prevent us in the future from abolishing the death penalty and introducing executions in the name of mercy and social hygiene. It will be time enough to discuss these proposals when they are up for serious debate. Meanwhile, it does not take a philosopher to see that the death penalty can no more be defended by an argument for eugenic killings than it can be defended by an argument for suicide.

Yet the problem of the "incurables" does exist, and Professors Barzun and Hook have performed a service in forcing everyone to face this terrible fact. There is little doubt that some who have been executed fall into this category. One thinks

[9] *The Crime of Imprisonment* (1946), pp. 97–98.

[10] In this connection, one might read Joseph Fletcher, *Man, Morals and Medicine* (1954), and Glanville Williams, *The Sanctity of Life and the Criminal Law* (1957).

of Albert Fish in New York,[11] Gordon Northcott in California,[12] and Charles Starkweather in Nebraska,[13] to name only a few. In the light of our present knowledge about psychopathology and the actual methods of therapy and the personnel at our disposal, it would have been unreasonable to have hoped to cure and eventually release these men. But what does this prove? Not that it was theoretically impossible to cure them. Not that other men just as sick have never been known to get well. Not that such men cannot be safely incarcerated, for life if necessary. Apparently Professor Barzun is convinced that it is not worth our trouble to imprison such criminals possibly for life and that (as Professor Hook also believes) it is worse for them to be *made* to stay alive in prison rather than to be put to death; and that, regrettable as it may be, capital punishment ought to be preserved in America because it is a system that even now fairly well achieves the result he desires.

On the other hand, I am convinced that anyone who takes this view has thoroughly confused the possible merits of a utopian society, in which a hypothetically infallible system of "social defense" operates to eradicate all and only the unpreventable and incurable killers, with the very real evils of every known system of criminal justice which uses the death penalty. There is no doubt that a large number of the more than 7,000 persons capitally punished since 1900 in this nation were far from incurable. Fish, Northcott, and Starkweather are the much-publicized exceptions, not the rule. At the present time, no one has any idea how to work out a system of capital punishment that would be applied only to such persons, assuming for the sake of the argument that it would be desirable to execute them. In the end, there seems to me to be an enormous distance between Barzun's and Hook's implicit factual assumptions about society, crime, and the administration of justice, in terms of which they find their conclusions persuasive, and the actual circumstances in which the death penalty exists in this country. While they cannot be held responsible for what they have not defended, it is regrettable that the present system of capital punishment will reap the benefit of their argument.

QUESTIONS

1. How do you think Barzun would respond to the criticisms advanced by Bedau against his position?

2. How do you think Hook would respond to the criticisms advanced by Bedau against his position?

3. Bedau argues that both Barzun and Hook, while allegedly advancing justifications for the practice of capital punishment, in fact advance justifications for distinct societal institutions. In each case, does Bedau's argument make a substantial point or merely a trivial point about terminology? Explain your answer.

---

[11] See Francis Wertham, *The Show of Violence* (1949).
[12] See Clinton Duffy, *88 Men and 2 Women* (1962).
[13] See James Reinhardt, *The Murderous Trail of Charles Starkweather* (1960).

David A. Conway

CAPITAL PUNISHMENT AND DETERRENCE: SOME CONSIDERATIONS IN DIALOGUE FORM

Biographical Information. David A. Conway is a philosopher who teaches at the University of Missouri at St. Louis. He has published articles, on various philosophical topics, in such journals as Philosophical Studies and the International Journal for Philosophy of Religion.

Argument in the Selection. Conway provides a lively dialogue between a retentionist, a proponent (P) of capital punishment, and an abolitionist, an opponent (O) of capital punishment. Presumably the opponent is Conway himself. P supports the retention of the death penalty on grounds of deterrence. As the dialogue progresses, P advances three retentionist arguments and O answers them. (1) According to the "preference argument" capital punishment must be a uniquely effective deterrent, precisely because people do in fact much prefer life imprisonment to death. Against this argument Conway advances reasons to show that "what we fear the most" may not yet in practice be a more effective deterrent. (2) According to the "rational-person-deterrent argument" the fact that rational people seldom murder shows that capital punishment is an effective deterrent, i.e., that it deters rational people. Conway argues that the alleged causal connection here has not been shown but only presumed. (3) According to the "best-bet argument," in the absence of definitive knowledge as to whether it is true or false that capital punishment is a uniquely effective deterrent, our best bet is to go with capital punishment. Conway investigates the various perplexities of this argument. He concludes that, without evidence showing that there is at least a strong possibility that capital punishment is a uniquely effective deterrent, opting for capital punishment is a very bad bet indeed.

P: I am happy to learn that our state legislature is trying to restore C.P.[1] Many of the legislators think they can pass a bill prescribing C.P. that the Supreme Court would not find unconstitutional.

O: Yes, that is true in many legislatures.[2] But it is hardly something I am happy about. Not only do I think C.P. is wrong, but I see a great danger in the present situation. The prime question in the minds of too many legislators seems to be, How do we draft laws that the court would not object to? The more basic question, Is C.P. ethically justifiable? may be lost sight of altogether.

[1] I shall use "C.P." for "capital punishment" throughout this paper.

[2] In addition, President Nixon in March of 1973 called for restoration of C.P., saying that he is convinced that it deters the commission of some types of crimes.

P: Perhaps, but if necessary, I think C.P. can be justified easily enough.

O: Are you some sort of retributivist?

P: Not at all. I hold that deterrence is the aim of punishment and that it is the central issue in the minds of legislators. They, as I am, are worried about the sheer lack of personal safety in our society.

O: .I didn't know that you had any strong feelings on this subject.

P: I didn't until recently. Then I read an interview in a newspaper. Ernest van den Haag, in response to questions from Philip Nobile, gives some arguments for C.P. that I find very convincing.[3] And I would bet that legislators do too.

I. THE PREFERENCE ARGUMENT

O: How can you think that C.P. is an effective deterrent? What about all of the statistical studies that have failed to show that this is true?[4]

P: I admit that such studies are inconclusive. But I am not relying on them to show the deterrent value of C.P. A simpler fact will do the job. Consider this exchange in the van den Haag interview:

Nobile: Is it true that capital punishment is a better deterrent than irrevocable life imprisonment?

van den Haag: Yes, and that I can prove. I noticed a story in the paper the other day about a French heroin smuggler who pleaded guilty in a New York court because, as his lawyer admitted, he preferred irrevocable life imprisonment here to the guillotine in France.
In fact, all prisoners prefer life. For even if the sentence is irrevocable, as long as there's life, psychologically, there's hope.

O: That argument is pretty popular among policemen and some editorial writers. In fact, Hugo Bedau in *The Death Penalty in America* includes a passage from Police Chief Allen which gives this argument. Bedau also mentions it in one of his essays in that volume, but he does not argue against it, although he does argue against some pro-C.P. views of Sidney Hook and Jacques Barzun.[5]

P: What does that mean? That serious philosophers do not bother to argue against policemen and editorial writers? or that this particular argument is too stupid to bother with?

O: I'm not sure what it means. But I do think this argument is worth taking seriously. For it is intuitively plausible, and it rests on an empirical premise which seems to me to be almost indisputably true. That is, almost all of us would, at least consciously, given the present choice between being subjected to life imprisonment and to C.P., choose the former. Still, the argument is not convincing.

---

[3] *St. Louis Globe-Democrat*, 6–7 January 1973. The arguments that van den Haag puts forth in this interview are currently quite popular among "intellectual conservatives" (e.g. writers for the *National Review* and conservative newspapers). The importance of his views is much greater than would be indicated just by the fact that one person happened to express them in a newspaper interview.

[4] See, for instance, Hugo Bedau, *The Death Penalty in America* (Garden City: Double-day, 1967), especially chapters 6 and 7.

[5] Ibid., pp. 135–136, 220.

107

P: Why not?

O: There are a couple of reasons. First, you are saying that if, given that I must choose between some punishment x and another punishment y, I would strongly prefer y, then it follows that knowing that x will be inflicted on me if I perform some action will more effectively deter me from performing that action than will knowing that y will be inflicted. But consider that, given the choice, I would strongly prefer one thousand years in hell to eternity there. Nonetheless, if one thousand years in hell were the penalty for some action, it would be quite sufficient to deter me from performing that action. The additional years would do nothing to discourage me further.

Similarly, the prospect of the death penalty, while worse, may not have any greater deterrent effect than does that of life imprisonment. In fact, I would imagine that either prospect would normally deter the rational man, while the man irrational enough not to be deterred by life imprisonment wouldn't be deterred by anything.[6] So, the deterrent value of the two may be indistinguishable in practice even though one penalty may be definitely preferable to the other, if one is forced to choose between them.

P: I see. Still there could be potential killers who are deterred by one and not by the other.

O: Of course there *could be*. But have you forgotten what this discussion is about? You were supposed to have a proof that there are such people.

P: OK. What is your other argument?

O: Well, before, I argued that C.P. may not be an additional deterrent even if we assume that the criminal expects to be caught. But surely most do not expect to be caught or they hold no expectations at all, i.e. they are acting in "blind passion." In these cases, the punishment is irrelevant. If, however, we assume at least minimal rationality on the part of the criminal, he knows that there is some chance that he will be caught. Let us say that he believes that there is a one in ten chance that he will be, and also that the actuality of punishment x is sufficient to deter him from performing some actions from which punishment y would not deter him. It does not follow from this that a one in ten chance of x would deter him from performing any actions that a one in ten chance of y would not. To put it abstractly, we can assign to the death penalty 100 "disutility units" and to life imprisonment 50 "disutility units" to represent a significant difference between their undesirability. If the chance of either punishment actually being inflicted, however, is only one in ten, the difference becomes much less significant (i.e. $1/10 \cdot 100$ vs. $1/10 \cdot 50$, or 10 vs. 5 disutility units). We do not, of course, actually think in such precise terms of probability and utility units, but we do often approximate such reasoning. For instance, if it is important that I get to my destination quickly, I may be willing to (actually) be fined for speeding while I am not willing to (actually) smash up my car and possibly myself. The difference between the two "penalties," if actually inflicted, is very great, great enough that one deters and the other does not. If, however, I know that there is only a slight chance of

[6] For a similar supposition, see Bedau, p. 272. There, however, the point is not made specifically in relation to the "Preference Argument."

108

either occurring, the deterrent effect of the threats may be virtually indistinguishable, and I may speed on my way.

There are, then, at least two reasons for not equating "what we fear the
most" with "what will most effectively deter us." Both of these are overlooked by those of you who give the "preference argument."

II. THE RATIONAL PERSON–DETERRENT ARGUMENT

O: What else did you find in the van den Haag interview?
P: Well, there is this.
   Nobile: Most capital crimes are crimes of passion in which family members or
      friends kill each other. You can't stop this sort of thing with the threat of
      execution.
   van den Haag: It's perfectly true that the irrational person won't be deterred
      by any penalty. But to the extent that murder is an act of passion, the
      death penalty has already deterred all rational persons.
O: And you agree with that?
P: I suppose not. It does seem to be a pretty clear case of *post hoc, ergo propter
   hoc* reasoning.[7] Still, there is a smaller point to be made here. Van den Haag
   says that C.P. has deterred rational persons. We do not know that it has. But,
   we also don't know that it hasn't. You opponents of C.P. are always saying
   something like, "Virtually all capital crimes are committed by persons in an
   irrational frame of mind. Therefore, C.P. (or any other punishment) cannot be
   regarded as a deterrent." So, you say, rational persons just do not (often)
   murder; I say, maybe they do not because of the threat of C.P. And so you
   cannot simply cite the fact that they do not as an argument against C.P.
O: I have to grant you that point. What you say has been often enough said before,
   and, yet, without attempting to answer the point, my fellow opponents of C.P.
   too often just go on saying "rational people seldom murder." We must
   seriously try to show that rational people seldom murder even in the absence
   of C.P., rather than just continuing to recite "rational people seldom murder."

III. THE BEST-BET ARGUMENT

O: Do you have any more arguments to trot out?
P: There is another in the van den Haag interview, and I have been saving the best
   for last.
O: Let's hear it.
P: All right.
   Nobile: You're pretty cavalier about executions, aren't you?
   van den Haag: If we have capital punishment, our risk is that it is unnecessary
      and no additional deterrence is achieved. But if we do not have it, our

---

[7] For a more complete critique of the same argument, see Bedau, pp. 268–269.

risk is that it might have deterred future murderers and spared future victims. Then it's a matter of which risk you prefer and I prefer to protect the victims.

Nobile: But you're gambling with the lives of condemned men who might otherwise live.

van den Haag: You're right. But we're both gambling. I'm gambling by executing and you're gambling by not executing.

We can see the force of this more clearly if we specify all of the possible outcomes. ("C.P. works" means "C.P. is a uniquely effective deterrent.")

	C.P. Works	C.P. Does Not Work
We bet C.P. works	(a) We win: Some murderers die, but innocents, who would otherwise die, are spared.	(b) We lose: Some murderers die for no purpose. The lives of others are unaffected.
We bet C.P. does not work	(c) We lose: Murderers live, but some innocents needlessly die.	(d) We win: Murderers live and the lives of others are unaffected.

To make it more clear, suppose that we assign utility values in this way:

Each murderer saved (not executed)	$+5$
Each murderer executed	-5
Each innocent person saved (not murdered)	$+10$
Each innocent person murdered	-10

And assume also that, if C.P. works, each execution saves five innocents (a conservative estimate, surely). Potential gains and losses can be represented as:

$$(a) \quad \begin{array}{r} -5 \\ +50 \\ \hline +45 \end{array} \qquad\qquad (b) \; -5$$

$$(c) \quad \begin{array}{r} +5 \\ -50 \\ \hline -45 \end{array} \qquad\qquad (d) \; +5$$

Now we can clearly see that not only do we have less to lose by betting on C.P., but we also have more to gain. It would be quite irrational not to bet on it.

O: Pascal lives.

P: What's that?

O: Nothing. But look, you have to admit that there is an unsavory air about the argument. Nobile is right; the very notion of gambling with human lives seems morally repugnant.

P: Maybe. But the fact is, as van den Haag says, we are also gambling if we do not execute, so you would do so as much as I.

110

O: If so, then what your argument does is make very apparent the sort of point retributivists have always made. In Kantian terms, this sort of gambling with human lives is a particularly crude form of treating human beings as means rather than ends.

P: You are willing to take a retributivist position in order to avoid the force of the argument?

O: No. I will leave vengeance to the Lord, if he wants it. Anyway, I am not convinced there are not other reasons for rejecting your argument. I cannot get over the feeling that, in some sense, you are gambling with lives in a way that I am not.

P: Maybe that is a feeling that requires therapy to get over. Let me say it once more: If either of us loses our wager, human lives are needlessly lost. Granted, if you win yours, no life is lost at all, while if I win mine, the criminal loses his; but since he loses it and others gain theirs, that cannot be what is disturbing you. There is nothing disturbing about the prospect of saving many innocents.

O: Wait now. I think that I am beginning to see what is going on here. . . . Van den Haag says, "It's a matter of which risk you prefer and I prefer to protect the victims." This immediately makes us think of the situation in a misleading way, for it seems to imply that while I would risk the lives of potential victims, he would risk the lives of convicted criminals. Or, minimally, it implies that there are risks of a like kind on both sides. But he isn't risking the lives of criminals; he is taking their lives and risking that some further good will come of this.

Put the same thing a slightly different way. It has been said in our discussion that on either bet, the result could be the needless loss of life. This makes the bets look more parallel than they are. If we bet your way, lives *have been lost,* and the risk is that this is needless. If we bet my way, it is *possible* that *lives may be lost,* needlessly. The difference between *lives lost,* perhaps needlessly, and *perhaps lives lost,* strikes me as a very significant one.

Now it should be clear that there is a sense in which you are gambling and I am not. It is exactly the sense in which I would be gambling if I used my last ten dollars to buy a lottery ticket but would not be if I used the money for groceries. Opting for a certain good, rather than risking it on a chance of a greater future good, is exactly what we mean when we say we refuse to gamble. Not gambling is taking the sure thing.

On the plausible moral principle, gambling with human lives is wrong, I can, then, reject the "Best-bet Argument."

P: But if you understand "gambling" as not taking the sure thing, that moral principle is much too strong. Unless you have infallible knowledge that C.P. deters, on that principle it could never be justified, even under conditions in which you would want to adopt it. For even if it were ninety *percent* certain that it deters, you would still be gambling. And there are other circumstances in which we must gamble with lives in this way. Suppose you were almost, but not quite, certain a madman was about to set off all the bombs in the Western hemisphere. On that principle, you would not be justified in shooting him, even if it were the only possible way to stop him.

O: Yes, I suppose that I must grant you that. But perhaps my suppositions that gambling is taking the risk and that gambling with human lives is wrong, taken together, at least partially account for my intuitive revulsion with van den Haag's argument.

P: That may be. But so far, your intuitions have come to nothing in producing a genuine objection to the argument. I might add that I cannot even agree with your intuition that not gambling is taking the sure thing. Don't we sometimes disapprove of the person who refuses to take out life insurance or automobile liability insurance on the grounds that he is unwisely gambling that he will not die prematurely or be responsible for a highway accident? And he is taking the sure thing, keeping the premium money in his pocket. So, in common sense terms, failure to take a wise bet is sometimes "gambling."

O: You are right again. And I thank you.

P: For what?

O: For saying just what I needed to hear in order to get straight on this whole business. As I indicated before, once we properly set out the betting situation, it does not appear that you proponents *have* such a good bet. But in addition, I have (along with Nobile) been plagued by the feeling that there is something *in principle* wrong with the argument, that you would gamble with human lives while I would not. Now I understand that these two objections are actually only one objection.

P: How so?

O: Your insurance examples make the point. They show that what we intuitively think of as "gambling" is simply taking the more risky course of action, i.e. making a bad bet. So, my intuitive worry resulted simply from my conviction that your bet on C.P. is "gambling," i.e. that it is the riskier course of action; or, and this comes to the same thing, it is a *bad* bet.

P: So you admit that there is nothing in principle wrong with my argument. That it all depends on whether the bet on C.P. is a good bet.

O: I think I must. But that does not change my views about C.P. Once the bet is clarified, it should be clear that you are asking us to risk too much, to actually take a human life on far too small a chance of saving others. It is just a rotten bet.

P: But it is not. As I have said, the life of each murderer is clearly worth much less than the life of an innocent, and, besides, each criminal life lost may save many innocents.

O: This business about how much lives are "worth" seems pretty suspicious to me. According to some, human life qua human life is sacred and so all lives have the same value. According to others, the continued life of an innocent child is of much less importance than that of a criminal, since it is the criminal, qua criminal, who needs a chance to cleanse his soul. Or we could consider the potential social usefulness of the individual. If we do this, it is by no means obvious that the average murderer has less potential than the average person (consider Chessman or Leopold).

P: How can you talk like that? Have you ever seen the battered, maimed body of an innocent child, raped and brutally murdered? Compare the value of that life against that of the beast who performed the deed, and then can you doubt that the child is worth 10,000 times the criminal?

O: That seems to me to be based on a desire for revenge against "the beast," rather than on any evaluation of the "value of different lives." I admit to sharing such feelings, in some moods, at least, but it is not at all clear how they are relevant. Anyway, let's drop this. I am willing to rely on my feelings and grant, for argument purposes, that the life of a murderer is worth somewhat less than that of an innocent.

The basic problem with your wager is simply that we have no reason to think C.P. does work, and in the absence of such reason, the probability that it does is virtually zero. In general, you proponents seem confused about evidence. First, you say C.P. deters. Then you are confronted with evidence such as: State A and State B have virtually identical capital crime rates but State A hasn't had C.P. for one hundred years. You reply, for instance, that this could be because State A has more Quakers, who are peace-loving folk and so help to keep the crime rate down. And, you say, with C.P. and all those Quakers, State A, perhaps, could have had an even lower crime rate.[8] Since we do not know about all such variables, the evidence is "inconclusive."[9] Here, "inconclusive" can only mean that while the evidence does not indicate that C.P. deters, it also does not demonstrate that it does not.

The next thing we see is you proponents saying that we just do not know whether C.P. deters or not, since the evidence is "inconclusive." But for this to follow, "inconclusive" must mean something like "tends to point both ways." The only studies available, on your own account, fail to supply any evidence at all that it *does* deter. From this, we cannot get "inconclusive" in the latter sense; we can't say that "we just don't know" whether it deters; we can only conclude, "we have no reason to think it does." Its status as a deterrent is no different from, e.g. prolonged tickling of murderers' feet. It could deter, but why think it does?

P: That's an absurd comparison that only a professional philosopher could think of. Common sense tells us that C.P. is a likely deterrent and foot-tickling is not.

O: I don't see how we can rely very heavily on the common sense of a law-abiding man to tell us how murderers think and why they act. Common sense also tells us that pornography should inflame the passions and therefore increase sex crimes, but Denmark's recent experience indicates quite the opposite.

P: So you demand that we have definite, unequivocal evidence and very high probability that C.P. deters before it could be said to be justifiable.

O: No, I never said that. That is what most of my fellow opponents of C.P. seem to demand. In fact, even though this would probably horrify most opponents, I think the "Best-bet Argument" shows that that demand is too strong. Given the possible gains and losses, if there is even a strong possibility that it works, I do not think it would be irrational to give it another try. But we should do so in full cognizance of the betting situation. We would be taking lives on the chance that there will be more than compensating saving of lives. And, I also think that it is damned difficult to show that there is even a strong possibility that C.P. deters.

P: Not really. Consider the fact that, given a choice between life imprisonment and C.P., prisoners always prefer . . .

O: Good night.

---

[8] Neglecting the fact that, with C.P., the crime rate also could have been higher (cf. Sidney Hook, "The Death Sentence," in Bedau, pp. 147–148).

[9] For such a use of "inconclusive," see J. Edgar Hoover, in Bedau, p. 134.

QUESTIONS

1. In Conway's dialogue, O seems to get the best of P. Is there any line of argument that you think P should have pressed against O? If so, develop that line of argument.
2. Argue for or against the following claim: We have no reason to think that the death penalty is a uniquely effective deterrent.

SUGGESTED ADDITIONAL READINGS

Bedau, Hugo Adam, ed. *The Death Penalty in America* (rev. ed.). Garden City, N.Y.: Doubleday, 1967. This classic work is a general reader, reflecting all aspects of the contemporary discussion of the death penalty. It is especially noteworthy in providing a wealth of factual data which, even if now somewhat outdated, retains its reference value.

———. "The Death Penalty as a Deterrent: Argument and Evidence" and "A Concluding Note." *Ethics,* 80, 81 (1970). These two articles constitute the abolitionist side in an important controversy between Bedau and Ernest van den Haag (cf. below).

Black, Charles L., Jr. *Capital Punishment: The Inevitability of Caprice and Mistake.* New York: W. W. Norton & Company, Inc., 1974. Black, in this short and most readable book, argues for abolition on the grounds that it is virtually impossible to eliminate arbitrariness and mistake from the numerous decisions that lead to the imposition of the death penalty.

Camus, Albert. *Reflections on the Guillotine: An Essay on Capital Punishment.* Translated by Richard Howard. Michigan City, Ind.: Fridtjof-Karla Press, 1959. In this lengthy article, Camus provides a strong, partially literary indictment of the practice of capital punishment.

Ezorsky, Gertrude, ed. *Philosophical Perspectives on Punishment.* Albany: State University of New York Press, 1972. This book is an excellent anthology on a wide range of general philosophical questions concerning punishment. There is a small section on capital punishment.

Goldberg, Steven. "On Capital Punishment." *Ethics,* 85 (1974). Goldberg, ultimately sympathetic to retentionism, focuses on the difficulties involved in the factual question of whether or not the death penalty is a uniquely effective deterrent.

McCafferty, James A., ed. *Capital Punishment.* New York: Lieber-Atherton, 1972. This general anthology is especially useful because it includes several position papers that reflect the views (both retentionist and abolitionist) taken by people who are directly involved in the administration of criminal justice.

Van den Haag, Ernest. "On Deterrence and the Death Penalty" and "Deterrence and the Death Penalty: A Rejoinder." *Ethics,* 78, 81 (1968, 1970). These two articles constitute the retentionist side in an important controversy between van den Haag and Hugo Adam Bedau (cf. above).

FOUR
Sexual Equality

In 1848 a demand for sexual equality was issued by the Seneca Falls Woman's Convention:

> We hold these truths to be self-evident: that all men and women are created equal; . . .
> The history of mankind is a history of repeated injuries and usurpations on the part of man toward woman, having in direct object the establishment of an absolute tyranny over her.[1]

At that time the right to vote, to own property, to serve on juries, to be accepted in most professions, and to receive equal pay for equal work were all denied to women. Today there are women in most professions. Women have the right to vote, the right to own property, and the right to jury duty. Why then should it be thought that there is a need for continued manifestos such as the following recent echo of the one made in 1848?

> Radical feminism recognizes the oppression of women as a fundamental political oppression wherein women are categorized as an inferior class based upon their sex. . . .
> Radical feminism is political because it recognizes that a group of individuals (men) have organized together for power over women, and that they have set up institutions throughout society to maintain this power. . . .
> The oppression of women is manifested in particular institutions, constructed and maintained to keep women in their place.

[1] Judith Hole and Ellen Levine, "The First Feminists," in *Radical Feminism*, ed. by Anne Koedt, Ellen Levine, and Anita Rapone (New York: Quadrangle Books, 1973), p. 7.

Among these are the institutions of marriage, motherhood, love and sexual intercourse.[2]

Such manifestos continue, despite the gain in rights mentioned above, because the status of women, as perceived by radical feminists, is that of an oppressed group. One such feminist, Kate Millett, succinctly expresses this view in "Sexual Politics: A Manifesto for Revolution":

> Oppressed groups are denied education, economic independence, the power of office, representation, an image of dignity and self-respect, equality of status, and recognition as human beings. Throughout history women have been consistently denied all this, and their denial today, while attenuated and partial is nevertheless consistent.[3]

In answer to those who claim that the political oppression of women is a thing of the past, Millett and other feminists, both radical and moderate ones, point to an existent general cultural pattern of discriminatory treatment based on sex. In support of the charge of continued sexual discrimination, feminists cite the kind of evidence presented at the Congressional Hearings on Equal Rights in Education and Employment: (1) Vocational counseling which directs girls into nursing and education, boys into engineering, space science, and computer technology; (2) gross differences between the median earnings of full-time employed males and females—men, $7,664; women, $4,457; (3) reports on the percentages of women in the highest and lowest grades in civil service—in the lowest grades, women make up 86 percent of the grades; in the highest grade, they make up less than one-tenth of 1 percent; (4) the small percentages of women in the most prestigious professions—women in the United States constitute 9 percent of all full professors, 3.5 percent of all lawyers, 7 percent of all physicians, and 1 percent of all engineers.

For reasons such as these, feminists argue that women are an oppressed and discriminated-against group and issue demands for sexual equality. They demand an egalitarian society—one in which the members of one sex are not in an economically, educationally, and socially advantageous position in relation to the other sex—and criticize as sexist any society in which women are systematically accorded unequal treatment by the educational, political, business, and social institutions of that society. That our society is a nonegalitarian one in which women are often accorded unequal treatment is an undeniable fact. What concerns us in this chapter is whether any moral justification can ever be given for society's unequal treatment of the sexes.

---

[2] "Politics of the Ego: A Manifesto for N.Y. Radical Feminists," ibid., pp. 379, 381.

[3] Kate Millett, "Sexual Politics: A Manifesto for Revolution," ibid., p. 365.

THE PRINCIPLE OF EQUALITY

One way to determine whether or not a social practice is morally correct is to see if it is either permitted or required by the *principle of equality.*[4] According to that principle, equals *must* be treated as equals while unequals should be treated unequally, in proportion to their differences. This is a formal principle of justice attributed to Aristotle. But what constitutes equality or inequality? In what ways must two individuals be alike before we can claim that they must receive the same treatment? In what ways must two individuals differ before we can claim that they should be accorded unequal treatment?

The usual way of answering these questions is to say that the differences between individuals must be relevant to the treatment in question. If Joe Smith and John Doe both apply for a job as a lifeguard, a difference in the color of their hair obviously has nothing to do with which one of them should get the job. But if Joe is a nonswimmer and John an Olympic swimming champion, that difference between them is *relevant* to the treatment they receive in this case. So we can say that people are entitled to the same treatment when there are no differences between them which are relevant to the treatment in question. Sex may be relevant when a wet nurse is being hired. But it is not relevant when a choice is being made between competing accountants, though mathematical ability is here relevant.

Note what has just been claimed: Sex is *not* a relevant characteristic when an accountant is being hired. If a qualified woman accountant is told that she cannot apply for an accounting position simply because of her sex, she is not receiving the same treatment as male accountants whose applications are accepted. When this happens, the principle of equality is clearly violated.

The discussion so far has focused on that part of the principle of equality which states that equals must be treated equally. But the principle also states that unequals should be treated unequally. Children, for example, are not always accorded the same treatment by society as adults. They cannot sign binding contracts until of legal age, for example. That they are sometimes treated unequally in comparison with adults is in keeping with the principle of equality since children generally are incapable of exercising the same rational capacities as adults.

Thus, both institutional practices which treat equals equally and those which treat unequals unequally are morally correct according to the principle of equality. It is only when equals are treated unequally that the principle is violated. Yet some persons who accept the principle

---

[4] To say a social practice is *required* by a moral principle is to say that we must institute such a practice if we are to act in a morally correct way. To say it is *permitted* is to say that its institution will not violate the moral principle.

of equality have sometimes used sex as a relevant criterion for denying women equal treatment in social, political, and economic areas. Why do they think that such treatment is permitted by the principle of equality? In Aristotle's own case the answer is simple. He claims that there are *inherent differences* between men and women. Men by nature have the capacity to rule, but women do not. For Aristotle, such differences are just as relevant in determining women's political status as mathematical ability is in determining who should be hired as an accountant in the example discussed above. Since women, according to Aristotle's theory of human nature, are not the equals of men in the relevant respects, unequal economic and political treatment of women is required by the principle of equality.

SEXUAL DIFFERENCES AND THE PRINCIPLE OF EQUALITY

Is it plausible to make such an Aristotelian claim today? Consider the kinds of things you often hear people say: "No woman should ever be president of the United States. Women are too emotional for the job." "Women can't manage other women." Or consider this statement made to a woman student recently: "We expect women who come here to be competent, good students, but we don't expect them to be brilliant or original."[5] Note what all these examples have in common. The sex of an individual is seen as a relevant factor when the capacity of that individual to perform certain tasks is being judged. Sex is here considered a relevant factor because differences in sex are believed to be correlated with psychological differences—differences in cognitive capacity or emotional makeup. These psychological differences are assumed to be relevant to the roles in question. As a result of such beliefs about female psychological characteristics, women are often treated unequally by the institutions of society. Is such inequality of treatment consistent with the principle of equality? Some who claim it is argue in an Aristotelian way: Sexual psychological differences relevant to job performance do exist. Furthermore, these differences are natural ones; that is, they are genetically caused. Thus some of the unequal treatment accorded women is in

---

[5] Quoted in a statement made by Ann Sutherland Harris to the Congressional Hearings on Equal Rights in Education and Employment. This statement is quoted in Catharine R. Stimpson, ed., *Discrimination against Women: Congressional Hearings on Equal Rights in Education and Employment* (New York: R. R. Bowker Company, 1973), p. 399.

keeping with the principle of equality because women are *by their very nature* unequal to men in relevant ways.

Much that is written by those who, like Mill and Millett in this chapter, argue *for* the *equal* economic, political, and social treatment of the sexes focuses on the factual claims used to support the above argument. Sometimes the existence of sexually related psychological differences is denied. The claim here is that even though we believe, for example, that most women are passive and most men aggressive, these beliefs are incorrect. Beliefs about male and female psychological differences acquired through cultural training lead us to dismiss the counterevidence (the many atypical cases we encounter) as "mere" exceptions to the rule. At other times, the following argument is made: Even if it is the case that on the average women are more passive and men more aggressive, or men on the average more mathematically inclined than women, this does not prove that there are *natural* differences between the sexes relevant to society-assigned role differences. Rather, it is because society differentiates between male and female roles and trains individuals to conform to these roles that the sexes tend to develop different psychological characteristics. If there is such a difference between the sexes, then the difference is artificial and not natural. It is the unjustified unequal treatment accorded to the sexes by educational and other socializing institutions that causes any psychological differences between them which might be relevant in denying women access to the most authoritative and prestigious positions in society. Thus, such unequal treatment is not based on any natural inequality between the sexes. Rather, it is society's unequal treatment of the sexes which produces the artificial psychological differences which society then uses to attempt to justify the further unequal economic, social, and educational treatment of the sexes.

Some philosophers prescind from the whole discussion of the *causes* of the assumed psychological differences between the sexes and focus on a different question: Even if there are psychological differences between the sexes (natural or socially induced), such that women *on the average* are more emotional and more passive than men as well as less capable on the average of abstract thought, does society have the right to deny systematically some roles to *all* women simply because many women are incapable of filling them? According to the principle of equality, social practices resulting in such systematic exclusion are not justified when the psychological differences are not universal. According to that principle, each individual is entitled to be judged simply on the basis of individual merit and not on the basis of the "average" psychological makeup of that individual's sexual group. Thus the practices criticized by the feminists *are* morally incorrect according to the principle of equality if the relevant psychological differences between the sexes are statistical and not universal.

OTHER ARGUMENTS FOR SEXUAL DISCRIMINATION

Regardless of whether the unequal treatment of the sexes is morally correct according to the principle of equality, some nonegalitarians such as J. R. Lucas and Steven Goldberg in this chapter still maintain that such treatment is morally acceptable. Such proponents of the moral acceptability of discriminatory treatment usually argue that there are natural psychological differences between the sexes which make most women incapable of competing with men on an equal basis. On the basis of this claim, further claims are made. Goldberg, for example, who maintains that there are differences in the hormonal makeup of the sexes which are responsible for the differences in their aggression level, argues that a nonegalitarian society is inevitable given this difference in aggressiveness. Even if some women are capable of competing with men, women on the whole will be better off in the long run if direct competition between the sexes is minimized. Others, like Lucas, argue in a similar way that it is in the best interest of women or in the best interest of society as a whole to establish social institutions which will enforce and perpetuate sexual roles. Joyce Trebilcot in this chapter analyzes and evaluates all such claims while Susan Haack focuses specifically on Lucas's version of the argument.

J. S. Z.

Justice Joseph P. Bradley

CONCURRING OPINION IN *BRADWELL v. ILLINOIS*

Biographical Information. *Justice Joseph P. Bradley (1813–1892) was appointed associate justice of the United States Supreme Court in 1868 by President Grant. While serving as an associate justice (1868–1892) he wrote opinions which are influential in United States constitutional law.*

Argument in the Selection. *This case (1873) furnishes an example of the overt and, at one time, widely accepted unequal treatment of women. Myra Bradwell's application for a license to practice law was denied by the Illinois Supreme Court simply on the basis of sex. Her appeal to the Supreme Court of the United States was made and denied on constitutional grounds. In a concurring opinion which goes beyond the Constitution, Justice Bradley expresses the following opinion: There are natural differences between the sexes. These natural differences are recognized*

120

by civil law. The legislator has the prerogative to take such natural differences into consideration when he prescribes regulations governing the admission of persons to professions and fields requiring special skill and confidence.

I concur in the judgment of the court in this case, by which the judgment of the Supreme Court of Illinois is affirmed, but not for the reasons specified in the opinion just read. . . .

The claim that, under the fourteenth amendment of the Constitution, which declares that no State shall make or enforce any law which shall abridge the privileges and immunities of citizens of the United States, the statute law of Illinois, or the common law prevailing in that State, can no longer be set up as a barrier against the right of females to pursue any lawful employment for a livelihood (the practice of law included), assumes that it is one of the privileges and immunities of women as citizens to engage in any and every profession, occupation, or employment in civil life.

It certainly cannot be affirmed, as an historical fact, that this has ever been established as one of the fundamental privileges and immunities of the sex. On the contrary, the civil law, as well as nature herself, has always recognized a wide difference in the respective spheres and destinies of man and woman. Man is, or should be, woman's protector and defender. The natural and proper timidity and delicacy which belongs to the female sex evidently unfits it for many of the occupations of civil life. The constitution of the family organization, which is founded in the divine ordinance, as well as in the nature of things, indicates the domestic sphere as that which properly belongs to the domain and functions of womanhood. The harmony, not to say identity, of interests and views which belong, or should belong, to the family institution is repugnant to the idea of a woman adopting a distinct and independent career from that of her husband. So firmly fixed was this sentiment in the founders of the common law that it became a maxim of that system of jurisprudence that a woman had no legal existence separate from her husband, who was regarded as her head and representative in the social state and, notwithstanding some recent modifications of this civil status, many of the special rules of law flowing from and dependent upon this cardinal principle still exist in full force in most States. One of these is, that a married woman is incapable, without her husband's consent, of making contracts which shall be binding on her or him. This very incapacity was one circumstance which the Supreme Court of Illinois deemed important in rendering a married woman incompetent fully to perform the duties and trusts that belong to the office of an attorney and counsellor.

It is true that many women are unmarried and not affected by any of the duties, complications, and incapacities arising out of the married state, but these are exceptions to the general rule. The paramount destiny and mission of woman are to fulfil the noble and benign offices of wife and mother. This is the law of the Creator. And the rules of civil society must be adapted to the general constitution of things, and cannot be based upon exceptional cases.

The humane movements of modern society, which have for their object the

121

multiplication of avenues for woman's advancement, and of occupations adapted to her condition and sex, have my heartiest concurrence. But I am not prepared to say that it is one of her fundamental rights and privileges to be admitted into every office and position, including those which require highly special qualifications and demanding special responsibilities. In the nature of things it is not every citizen of every age, sex, and condition that is qualified for every calling and position. It is the prerogative of the legislator to prescribe regulations founded on nature, reason, and experience for the due admission of qualified persons to professions and callings demanding special skill and confidence. This fairly belongs to the police power of the State; and, in my opinion, in view of the peculiar characteristics, destiny, and mission of woman, it is within the province of the legislature to ordain what offices, positions, and callings shall be filled and discharged by men, and shall receive the benefit of those energies and responsibilities, and that decision and firmness which are presumed to predominate in the sterner sex.

QUESTIONS

1. Are there any sound reasons for believing in inherent differences between the sexes?
2. If there are such differences, are they relevant in assessing candidates for law school or for admission to the bar?

John Stuart Mill

THE SUBJECTION OF WOMEN

Biographical Information. John Stuart Mill (1806–1873) is known primarily as an advocate of utilitarianism. Unlike most contemporary philosophers, Mill was not an academician. He had a successful career with the British East India Company and served one term as a member of Parliament. While a member of Parliament, Mill submitted the first bill on the enfranchisement of women to the House of Commons. Mill's classic feminist work, The Subjection of Women, *from which this selection is excerpted, was written late in his career. Among his related works are* On Liberty *and* Utilitarianism.

Argument in the Selection. Mill is one of the proponents of sexual equality. He argues that sex is not a relevant occupational criterion. In Mill we see one of the earliest arguments against the following set of claims:

122

1. *There are crucial natural differences between the sexes.*
2. *Because of these differences women lack the capacity to do some of the things that men can do.*
3. *Since they lack these capacities, they will fail in the attempt and be unhappy as a result.*
4. *Therefore, it is for their own good that some occupations be forbidden to women.*

Mill's argument against this set of claims is classic: He agrees with his opponents that women in his society possess some characteristics such as submissiveness and meekness which would seem to make them inferior to men. But, he argues, these characteristics are the result of the training process by which the interests of society (that is, the interests of men) are maintained. If you want to see what women can do, Mill says, look at the things they have done when they have been given the opportunity to do them.

The generality of the male sex cannot yet tolerate the idea of living with an equal. Were it not for that, I think that almost everyone, in the existing state of opinion in politics and political economy, would admit the injustice of excluding half the human race from the greater number of lucrative occupations, and from almost all high social functions; ordaining from their birth either that they are not, and cannot by any possibility become, fit for employments which are legally open to the stupidest and basest of the other sex, or else that however fit they may be, those employments shall be interdicted to them, in order to be preserved for the exclusive benefit of males. In the last two centuries, when (which was seldom the case) any reason beyond the mere existence of the fact was thought to be required to justify the disabilities of women, people seldom assigned as a reason their inferior mental capacity; which, in times when there was a real trial of personal faculties (from which all women were not excluded) in the struggles of public life, no one really believed in. The reason given in those days was not women's unfitness, but the interest of society, by which was meant the interest of men, just as the *raison d'état,* meaning the convenience of the government, and the support of existing authority, was deemed a sufficient explanation and excuse for the most flagitious crimes. In the present day, power holds a smoother language, and whomsoever it oppresses, always pretends to do so for their own good: accordingly, when anything is forbidden to women, it is thought necessary to say, and desirable to believe, that they are incapable of doing it, and that they depart from their real path of success and happiness when they aspire to it. But to make this reason plausible (I do not say valid), those by whom it is urged must be prepared to carry it to a much greater length than anyone ventures to do in the face of present experience. It is not sufficient to maintain that women on the average are less gifted than men on the average, with certain of the higher mental faculties, or that a smaller number of women than of men are fit for occupations and functions of the highest intellectual character. It is necessary to maintain that no women at all are fit for them, and that the most eminent women are inferior in mental faculties to the most mediocre of the men on whom those functions at present devolve. For if the performance of the function is decided either by competition, or by any mode of choice which secures regard to the public interest, there needs be no apprehension that any important employments will fall into the hands of women inferior to average men, or to the average of their male competitors. The only result would be that there would be fewer women than men in such employments; a result certain to happen in any case, if only from the preference always likely to be felt by the majority of women for the one vocation in which there is nobody to compete with them. Now, the most determined depreciator of women will not venture to deny, that when we add the experience of recent times to that of ages past, women, and not a few merely, but many women, have proved themselves capable of everything, perhaps without a single exception, which is done by men, and of doing it successfully and creditably. The utmost that can be said is, that there are many things which none of them have succeeded in doing as well as they have been done by some men—many in which they have not reached the very highest rank. But there are extremely few, dependent only on mental faculties, in which they have not attained the rank next to the highest. Is not this enough, and much more than enough, to make it a tyranny to them, and a detriment to society, that they should not be allowed to compete with men for the exercise of these functions? Is it not a mere truism to say, that such functions are often filled by men far less fit for them than numbers of women, and who would be beaten by women in any fair field of competition? What difference does it make that there may be men somewhere, fully employed about other things, who may be still better qualified for the things in question than these women? Does not this take place in all competitions? Is there so great a superfluity of men fit for high duties, that society can afford to reject the service of any competent person? Are we so certain of always finding a man made to our hands for any duty or function of social importance which falls vacant, that we lose nothing by putting a ban upon one half of mankind, and refusing beforehand to make their faculties available, however distinguished they may be? And even if we could do without them, would it be consistent with justice to refuse to them their fair share of honour and distinction, or to deny to them the equal moral right of all human beings to choose their occupation (short of injury to others) according to their own preferences, at their own risk? Nor is the injustice confined to them; it is shared by those who are in a position to benefit by their services. To ordain that any kind of persons shall not be physicians, or shall not be advocates, or shall not be Members of Parliament, is to injure not them only, but all who employ physicians or advocates, or elect Members of Parliament, and who are deprived of the stimulating effect of greater competition on the exertions of the competitors, as well as restricted to a narrower range of individual choice.

It will perhaps be sufficient if I confine myself, in the details of my argument, to functions of a public nature: since, if I am successful as to those, it probably will be readily granted that women should be admissible to all other occupations to which it is at all material whether they are admitted or not. . . .

Any woman, who succeeds in an open profession, proves by that very fact that she is qualified for it. And in the case of public offices, if the political system of the country is such as to exclude unfit men, it will equally exclude unfit women: while if it is not, there is no additional evil in the fact that the unfit persons whom it admits may be either women or men. As long therefore as it is acknowledged that even a few women may be fit for these duties, the laws which shut the door on those exceptions cannot be justified by any opinion which can be held respecting the capacities of women in general. But, though this last consideration is not essential, it is far from being irrelevant. An unprejudiced view of it gives additional strength to the arguments against the disabilities of women, and reinforces them by high considerations of practical utility.

Let us first make entire abstraction of all psychological considerations tending to show, that any of the mental differences supposed to exist between women and men are but the natural effect of the differences in their education and circumstances, and indicate no radical difference, far less radical inferiority, of nature. Let us consider women only as they already are, or as they are known to have been; and the capacities which they have already practically shown. What they have done, that at least, if nothing else, it is proved that they can do. When we consider how sedulously they are all trained away from, instead of being trained towards, any of the occupations or objects reserved for men, it is evident that I am taking a very humble ground for them, when I rest their case on what they have actually achieved. For, in this case, negative evidence is worth little, while any positive evidence is conclusive. It cannot be inferred to be impossible that a woman should be a Homer, or an Aristotle, or a Michael Angelo, or a Beethoven, because no woman has yet actually produced works comparable to theirs in any of those lines of excellence. This negative fact at most leaves the question uncertain, and open to psychological discussion. But it is quite certain that a woman can be a Queen Elizabeth, or a Deborah, or a Joan of Arc, since this is not inference, but fact. Now it is a curious consideration, that the only things which the existing law excludes women from doing, are the things which they have proved that they are able to do. There is no law to prevent a women from having written all the plays of Shakespeare, or composed all the operas of Mozart. But Queen Elizabeth or Queen Victoria, had they not inherited the throne, could not have been entrusted with the smallest of the political duties, of which the former showed herself equal to the greatest. . . .

Is it reasonable to think that those who are fit for the greater functions of politics, are incapable of qualifying themselves for the less? Is there any reason in the nature of things, that the wives and sisters of princes should, whenever called on, be found as competent as the princes themselves to *their* business, but that the wives and sisters of statesmen, and administrators, and directors of companies, and managers of public institutions, should be unable to do what is done by their brothers and husbands? The real reason is plain enough; it is that princesses, being more raised above the generality of men by their rank than placed below them by their sex, have never been taught that it was improper for them to concern themselves with politics; but have been allowed to feel the liberal interest natural to any cultivated human being, in the great transactions which took place around them, and in which they might be called on to take a part. The ladies of reigning families are the only women who are allowed the same range of interests and freedom of development as men; and it is precisely in their case that there is not found to be any inferiority. Exactly where and in proportion as women's capacities for government have been tried, in that proportion have they been found adequate. . . .

Let us now consider [one] of the admitted superiorities of clever women, greater quickness of apprehension. Is not this pre-eminently a quality which fits a person for practice? In action, everything continually depends upon deciding promptly. In speculation, nothing does. A mere thinker can wait, can take time to consider, can collect additional evidence; he is not obliged to complete his philosophy at once, lest the opportunity should go by. The power of drawing the best conclusion possible from insufficient data is not indeed useless in philosophy; the construction of a provisional hypothesis consistent with all known facts is often the needful basis for further inquiry. But this faculty is rather serviceable in philosophy, than the main qualification for it: and, for the auxiliary as well as for the main operation, the philosopher can allow himself any time he pleases. He is in no need of the capacity of doing rapidly what he does; what he rather needs is patience, to work on slowly until imperfect lights have become perfect, and a conjecture has ripened into a theorem. For those, on the contrary, whose business is with the fugitive and perishable—with individual facts, not kinds of facts— rapidity of thought is a qualification next only in importance to the power of thought itself. He who has not his faculties under immediate command, in the contingencies of action, might as well not have them at all. He may be fit to criticise, but he is not fit to act. Now it is in this that women, and the men who are most like women, confessedly excel. The other sort of man, however pre-eminent may be his faculties, arrives slowly at complete command of them: rapidity of judgment and promptitude of judicious action, even in the things he knows best, are the gradual and late result of strenuous effort grown into habit.

It will be said, perhaps, that the greater nervous susceptibility of women is a disqualification for practice, in anything but domestic life, by rendering them mobile, changeable, too vehemently under the influence of the moment, incapable of dogged perseverance, unequal and uncertain in the power of using their faculties. I think that these phrases sum up the greater part of the objections commonly made to the fitness of women for the higher class of serious business. Much of all this is the mere overflow of nervous energy run to waste, and would cease when the energy was directed to a definite end. Much is also the result of conscious or unconscious cultivation; as we see by the almost total disappearance of "hysterics" and fainting-fits, since they have gone out of fashion. Moreover, when people are brought up, like many women of the higher classes (though less so in our own country than in any other), a kind of hot-house plants, shielded from the wholesome vicissitudes of air and temperature, and untrained in any of the occupations and exercises which give stimulus and development to the circulatory and muscular system, while their nervous system, especially in its emotional department, is kept in unnaturally active play; it is no wonder if those of them who do not die of consumption, grow up with constitutions liable to derangement from slight causes, both internal and external, and without stamina to support any task, physical or mental, requiring continuity of effort. But women brought up to work for their livelihood show none of these morbid characteristics, unless indeed they are chained to an excess of sedentary work in confined and unhealthy rooms. Women who in their early years have shared in the healthful physical education and bodily freedom of their brothers, and who obtain a sufficiency of pure air and exercise in after-life, very rarely have any excessive susceptibility of nerves which can disqualify them for active pursuits. . . .

No production in philosophy, science, or art, entitled to the first rank, has been the work of a woman. Is there any mode of accounting for this, without supposing that women are naturally incapable of producing them?

In the first place, we may fairly question whether experience has afforded sufficient grounds for an induction. It is scarcely three generations since women, saving very rare exceptions, have begun to try their capacity in philosophy, science, or art. It is only in the present generation that their attempts have been at all numerous; and they are even now extremely few, everywhere but in England and France. It is a relevant question, whether a mind possessing the requisites of first-rate eminence in speculation or creative art could have been expected, on the mere calculation of chances, to turn up during that lapse of time, among the women whose tastes and personal position admitted of their devoting themselves to these pursuits. In all things which there has yet been time for—in all but the very highest grades in the scale of excellence, especially in the department in which they have been longest engaged, literature (both prose and poetry)— women have done quite as much, have obtained fully as high prizes and as many of them, as could be expected from the length of time and the number of competitors. If we go back to the earlier period when very few women made the attempt, yet some of those few made it with distinguished success. The Greeks always accounted Sappho among their great poets; and we may well suppose that Myrtis, said to have been the teacher of Pindar, and Corinna, who five times bore away from him the prize of poetry, must at least have had sufficient merit to admit of being compared with that great name. Aspasia did not leave any philosophical writings; but it is an admitted fact that Socrates resorted to her for instruction, and avowed himself to have obtained it.

If we consider the works of women in modern times, and contrast them with those of men, either in the literary or the artistic department, such inferiority as may be observed resolves itself essentially into one thing: but that is a most material one; deficiency of originality. Not total deficiency; for every production of mind which is of any substantive value, has an originality of its own—is a conception of the mind itself, not a copy of something else. Thoughts original, in the sense of being unborrowed—of being derived from the thinker's own observations or intellectual processes—are abundant in the writings of women. But they have not yet produced any of those great and luminous new ideas which form an era in thought, nor those fundamentally new conceptions in art, which open a vista of possible effects not before thought of, and found a new school. Their compositions are mostly grounded on the existing fund of thought, and their creations do not deviate widely from existing types. This is the sort of inferiority which their works manifest: for in point of execution, in the detailed application of thought, and the perfection of style, there is no inferiority. Our best novelists in point of composition, and of the management of detail, have mostly been women; and there is not in all modern literature a more eloquent vehicle of thought than the style of Madame de Staël, nor, as a specimen of purely artistic excellence, anything superior to the prose of Madame Sand, whose style acts upon the nervous system like a symphony of Haydn or Mozart. High originality of conception is, as I have said, what is chiefly wanting. And now to examine if there is any manner in which this deficiency can be accounted for.

Let us remember, then, so far as regards mere thought, that during all that period in the world's existence, and in the progress of cultivation, in which great and fruitful new truths could be arrived at by mere force of genius, with little previous study and accumulation of knowledge—during all that time women did not concern themselves with speculation at all. From the days of Hypatia to those of the Reformation, the illustrious Heloisa is almost the only woman to whom any such achievement might have been possible; and we know not how great a capacity of speculation in her may have been lost to mankind by the misfortunes of her life. Never since any considerable number of women have begun to cultivate serious thought, has originality been possible on easy terms. Nearly all the thoughts which can be reached by mere strength of original faculties, have long since been arrived at, and originality, in any high sense of the word, is now scarcely ever attained but by minds which have undergone elaborate discipline, and are deeply versed in the results of previous thinking. It is Mr. Maurice, I think, who has remarked on the present age, that its most original thinkers are those who have known most thoroughly what had been thought by their predecessors: and this will always henceforth be the case. Every fresh stone in the edifice has now to be placed on the top of so many others, that a long process of climbing, and of carrying up materials, has to be gone through by whoever aspires to take a share in the present stage of the work. How many women are there who have gone through any such process? Mrs. Somerville, alone perhaps of women, knows as much of mathematics as is now needful for making any considerable mathematical discovery: is it any proof of inferiority in women, that she has not happened to be one of the two or three persons who in her lifetime have associated their names with some striking advancement of the science? Two women, since political economy has been made a science, have known enough of it to write usefully on the subject: of how many of the innumerable men who have written on it during the same time, is it possible with truth to say more? If no woman has hitherto been a great historian, what woman has had the necessary erudition? If no woman is a great philologist, what woman has studied Sanscrit and Slavonic, the Gothic of Ulphila and the Persic of the Zendavesta? Even in practical matters we all know what is the value of the originality of untaught geniuses. It means, inventing over again in its rudimentary form something already invented and improved upon by many successive inventors. When women have had the preparation which all men now require to be eminently original, it will be time enough to begin judging by experience of their capacity for originality.

It no doubt often happens that a person, who has not widely and accurately studied the thoughts of others on a subject, has by natural sagacity a happy intuition, which he can suggest, but cannot prove, which yet when matured may be an important addition to knowledge: but even then, no justice can be done to it until some other person, who does possess the previous acquirements, takes it in hand, tests it, gives it a scientific or practical form, and fits it into its place among the existing truths of philosophy or science. Is it supposed that such felicitous thoughts do not occur to women? They occur by hundreds to every woman of intellect. But they are mostly lost, for want of a husband or friend who has the other knowledge which can enable him to estimate them properly and bring them before the world: and even when they are brought before it, they generally appear as his ideas, not their real author's. Who can tell how many of the most original thoughts put forth by male writers, belong to a woman by suggestion, to themselves only by verifying and working out? If I may judge by my own case, a very large proportion indeed. . . .

(There are other reasons, besides those which we have now given, that help to explain why women remain behind men, even in the pursuits which are open to both. For one thing, very few women have time for them. This may seem a paradox; it is an undoubted social fact. The time and thoughts of every woman have to satisfy great previous demands on them for things practical. There is, first, the superintendence of the family and the domestic expenditure, which occupies at least one woman in every family, generally the one of mature years and acquired experience; unless the family is so rich as to admit of delegating that task to hired agency, and submitting to all the waste and malversation inseparable from that mode of conducting it. The superintendence of a household, even when not in other respects laborious, is extremely onerous to the thoughts; it requires incessant vigilance, an eye which no detail escapes, and presents questions for consideration and solution, foreseen and unforeseen, at every hour of the day, from which the person responsible for them can hardly ever shake herself free. If a woman is of a rank and circumstances which relieve her in a measure from these cares, she has still devolving on her the management for the whole family of its intercourse with others—of what is called society, and the less the call made on her by the former duty, the greater is always the development of the latter: the dinner parties, concerts, evening parties, morning visits, letter-writing, and all that goes with them. All this is over and above the engrossing duty which society imposes exclusively on women, of making themselves charming. A clever women of the higher ranks finds nearly a sufficient employment of her talents in cultivating the graces of manner and the arts of conversation. To look only at the outward side of the subject: the great and continual exercise of thought which all women who attach any value to dressing well (I do not mean expensively, but with taste, and perception of natural and of artificial *convenance*) must bestow upon their own dress, perhaps also upon that of their daughters, would alone go a great way towards achieving respectable results in art, or science, or literature, and does actually exhaust much of the time and mental power they might have to spare for either. If it were possible that all this number of little practical interests (which are made great to them) should leave them either much leisure, or much energy and freedom of mind, to be devoted to art or speculation, they must have a much greater original supply of active faculty than the vast majority of men. But this is not all. Independently of the regular offices of life which devolve upon a woman, she is expected to have her time and faculties always at the disposal of everybody. If a man has not a profession to exempt him from such demands, still, if he has a pursuit, he offends nobody by devoting his time to it; occupation is received as a valid excuse for his not answering to every casual demand which may be made on him. Are a woman's occupations, especially her chosen and voluntary ones, ever regarded as excusing her from any of what are termed the calls of society? Scarcely are her most necessary and recognised duties allowed as an exemption. It requires an illness in the family, or something else out of the common way, to entitle her to give her own business the precedence over other people's amusement. She must always be at the beck and call of somebody, generally of everybody. If she has a study or a pursuit, she must snatch any short interval which accidentally occurs to be employed in it. A celebrated woman, in a work which I hope will some day be published, remarks truly that everything a woman does is done at odd times. Is it wonderful then, if she does not attain the highest eminence in things which require consecutive attention, and the concentration on them of the chief interest of life? Such is philosophy, and such, above all, is art, in which, besides the devotion of the thoughts and feelings, the hand also must be kept in constant exercises to attain high skill.

QUESTIONS

1. Using Mill's arguments, write a rebuttal to Justice Bradley's opinion.
2. You are a member of an all-male legislative branch of government in a nation where women do not have the right to vote. Do you have the moral right to determine what is in the best interest of women?

Kate Millett

A CRITIQUE OF PATRIARCHY

Biographical Information. *Katherine Murray (Kate) Millett is an active feminist and the author of* Sexual Politics, *from which this excerpt is taken. She is also the author of* The Prostitution Papers *and of a brief radical feminist manifesto, "Sexual Politics: A Manifesto for Revolution." The latter was written in connection with an organizational meeting of the first women's liberation group at Columbia University in 1968. Millett has taught at the University of North Carolina at Chapel Hill, Barnard College, and Sacramento (California) State College.*

Argument in the Selection. *Like Mill, Millett argues for sexual equality and criticizes the male-dominated system which she claims perpetuates sexual inequality. What is novel in Millett's analysis is her description of the relation between the sexes as a political one. "Political" is used in a broad sense. It refers to a relation in which the members of one group are dominant over the members of another one. For Millett the relation between the sexes is analogous to the relation between the races in America. Both are examples of the control of "one collectivity, defined by birth, over another collectivity, also defined by birth." Millett maintains that the political inequality between the sexes is both universal and arbitrary. Sexual political inequality is universal since it transcends particular political and economic systems such as those based on capitalism and communism. It is arbitrary because it is not based on nature.*

In introducing the term "sexual politics," one must first answer the inevitable question "Can the relationship between the sexes be viewed in a political light at all?'' The answer depends on how one defines politics.[1] This essay does not define the political as that relatively narrow and exclusive world of meetings, chairmen, and parties. The term "politics" shall refer to power-structured relationships, arrangements whereby one group of persons is controlled by another. By way of parenthesis one might add that although an ideal politics might simply be conceived of as the arrangement of human life on agreeable and rational principles from whence the entire notion of power *over* others should be banished, one must confess that this is not what constitutes the political as we know it, and it is to this that we must address ourselves.

The following sketch, which might be described as "notes toward a theory of patriarchy," will attempt to prove that sex is a status category with political implications. Something of a pioneering effort, it must perforce be both tentative and imperfect. Because the intention is to provide an overall description, statements must be generalized, exceptions neglected, and subheadings overlapping and, to some degree, arbitrary as well.

The word "politics" is enlisted here when speaking of the sexes primarily because such a word is eminently useful in outlining the real nature of their relative status, historically and at the present. It is opportune, perhaps today even mandatory, that we develop a more relevant psychology and philosophy of power relationships beyond the simple conceptual framework provided by our traditional formal politics. Indeed, it may be imperative that we give some attention to defining a theory of politics which treats of power relationships on grounds less conventional than those to which we are accustomed.[2] I have therefore found it pertinent to define them on grounds of personal contact and interaction between members of well-defined and coherent groups: races, castes, classes, and sexes. For it is precisely because certain groups have no representation in a number of recognized political structures that their position tends to be so stable, their oppression so continuous.

In America, recent events have forced us to acknowledge at last that the relationship between the races is indeed a political one which involves the general control of one collectivity, defined by birth, over another collectivity, also defined by birth. Groups who rule by birthright are fast disappearing, yet there remains one ancient and universal scheme for the domination of one birth group by another—the scheme that prevails in the area of sex. The study of racism has convinced us that a truly political state of affairs operates between the races to perpetuate a series of oppressive circumstances. The subordinated group has inadequate redress through existing political institutions, and is deterred thereby from organizing into conventional political struggle and opposition.

[1] The American Heritage Dictionary's fourth definition is fairly approximate: "methods or tactics involved in managing a state or government." *American Heritage Dictionary* (New York: American Heritage and Houghton Mifflin, 1969). One might expand this to a set of strategems designed to maintain a system. If one understands patriarchy to be an institution perpetuated by such techniques of control, one has a working definition of how politics is conceived in this essay.

[2] I am indebted here to Ronald V. Samson's *The Psychology of Power* (New York: Random House, 1968) for his intelligent investigation of the connection between formal power structures and the family and for his analysis of how power corrupts basic human relationships.

131

Quite in the same manner, a disinterested examination of our system of sexual relationship must point out that the situation between the sexes now, and throughout history, is a case of that phenomenon Max Weber defined as herrschaft, a relationship of dominance and subordinance.[3] What goes largely unexamined, often even unacknowledged (yet is institutionalized nonetheless) in our social order, is the birthright priority whereby males rule females. Through this system a most ingenious form of "interior colonization" has been achieved. It is one which tends moreover to be sturdier than any form of segregation, and more rigorous than class stratification, more uniform, certainly more enduring. However muted its present appearance may be, sexual dominion obtains nevertheless as perhaps the most pervasive ideology of our culture and provides its most fundamental concept of power.

This is so because our society, like all other historical civilizations, is a patriarchy.[4] The fact is evident at once if one recalls that the military, industry, technology, universities, science, political office, and finance—in short, every avenue of power within the society, including the coercive force of the police, is entirely in male hands. As the essence of politics is power, such realization cannot fail to carry impact. What lingers of supernatural authority, the Deity, "His" ministry, together with the ethics and values, the philosophy and art of our culture—its very civilization—as T. S. Eliot once observed, is of male manufacture.

If one takes patriarchal government to be the institution whereby that half of the populace which is female is controlled by that half which is male, the principles of patriarchy appear to be two fold: male shall dominate female, elder male shall dominate younger. However, just as with any human institution, there is frequently a distance between the real and the ideal; contradictions and exceptions do exist within the system. While patriarchy as an institution is a social constant so deeply entrenched as to run through all other political, social, or economic forms, whether of caste or class, feudality or bureaucracy, just as it pervades all major religions, it also exhibits great variety in history and locale. In democracies,[5] for example, females have often held no office or do so (as now) in such minuscule numbers as to be below even token representation. Aristocracy,

---

[3] "Domination in the quite general sense of power, i.e. the possibility of imposing one's will upon the behavior of other persons, can emerge in the most diverse forms." In this central passage of *Wirtschaft und Gesellschaft* Weber is particularly interested in two such forms: control through social authority ("patriarchal, magisterial, or princely") and control through economic force. In patriarchy as in other forms of domination "that control over economic goods, i.e. economic power, is a frequent, often purposively willed, consequence of domination as well as one of its most important instruments." Quoted from Max Rheinstein's and Edward Shil's translation of portions of *Wirtschaft und Gesellschaft* entitled *Max Weber on Law in Economy and Society* (New York: Simon and Schuster, 1967), pp. 323–24.

[4] No matriarchal societies are known to exist at present. Matrilineality, which may be, as some anthropologists have held, a residue or a transitional stage of matriarchy, does not constitute an exception to patriarchal rule, it simply channels the power held by males through female descent—, e.g. the Avunculate.

[5] Radical democracy would, of course, preclude patriarchy. One might find evidence of a general satisfaction with a less than perfect democracy in the fact that women have so rarely held power within modern "democracies."

on the other hand, with its emphasis upon the magic and dynastic properties of blood, may at times permit women to hold power. The principle of rule by elder males is violated even more frequently. Bearing in mind the variation and degree in patriarchy—as say between Saudi Arabia and Sweden, Indonesia and Red China—we also recognize our own form in the U.S. and Europe to be much altered and attenuated by the reforms described in the next chapter.

I IDEOLOGICAL

Hannah Arendt[6] has observed that government is upheld by power supported either through consent or imposed through violence. Conditioning to an ideology amounts to the former. Sexual politics obtains consent through the "socialization" of both sexes to basic patriarchal polities with regard to temperament, role, and status. As to status, a pervasive assent to the prejudice of male superiority guarantees superior status in the male, inferior in the female. The first item, temperament, involves the formation of human personality along stereotyped lines of sex category ("masculine" and "feminine"), based on the needs and values of the dominant group and dictated by what its members cherish in themselves and find convenient in subordinates: aggression, intelligence, force, and efficacy in the male; passivity, ignorance, docility, "virtue," and ineffectuality in the female. This is complemented by a second factor, sex role, which decrees a consonant and highly elaborate code of conduct, gesture and attitude for each sex. In terms of activity, sex role assigns domestic service and attendance upon infants to the female, the rest of human achievement, interest, and ambition to the male. The limited role allotted the female tends to arrest her at the level of biological experience. Therefore, nearly all that can be described as distinctly human rather than animal activity (in their own way animals also give birth and care for their young) is largely reserved for the male. Of course, status again follows from such an assignment. Were one to analyze the three categories one might designate status as the political component, role as the sociological, and temperament as the psychological—yet their interdependence is unquestionable and they form a chain. Those awarded higher status tend to adopt roles of mastery, largely because they are first encouraged to develop temperaments of dominance. That this is true of caste and class as well is self-evident.

II BIOLOGICAL

Patriarchal religion, popular attitude, and to some degree, science as well[7] assumes these psycho-social distinctions to rest upon biological differences

---

[6] Hannah Arendt, "Speculations on Violence," *The New York Review of Books,* Vol. XII No. 4, February 27, 1969, p. 24.

[7] The social, rather than the physical sciences are referred to here. Traditionally, medical science had often subscribed to such beliefs. This is no longer the case today, when the best medical research points to the conclusion that sexual stereotypes have no bases in biology.

between the sexes, so that where culture is acknowledged as shaping behavior, it is said to do no more than cooperate with nature. Yet the temperamental distinctions created in patriarchy ("masculine" and "feminine" personality traits) do not appear to originate in human nature, those of role and status still less.

The heavier musculature of the male, a secondary sexual characteristic and common among mammals, is biological in origin but is also culturally encouraged through breeding, diet and exercise. Yet it is hardly an adequate category on which to base political relations *within civilization*.[8] Male supremacy, like other political creeds, does not finally reside in physical strength but in the acceptance of a value system which is not biological. Superior physical strength is not a factor in political relations—vide those of race and class. Civilization has always been able to substitute other methods (technic, weaponry, knowledge) for those of physical strength, and contemporary civilization has no further need of it. At present, as in the past, physical exertion is very generally a class factor, those at the bottom performing the most strenuous tasks, whether they be strong or not.

It is often assumed that patriarchy is endemic in human social life, explicable or even inevitable on the grounds of human physiology. Such a theory grants patriarchy logical as well as historical origin. . . .

The question of the historical origins of patriarchy—whether patriarchy originated primordially in the male's superior strength, or upon a later mobilization of such strength under certain circumstances—appears at the moment to be unanswerable. It is also probably irrelevant to contemporary patriarchy, where we are left with the realities of sexual politics, still grounded, we are often assured, on nature. Unfortunately, as the psycho-social distinctions made between the two sex groups which are said to justify their present political relationship are not the clear, specific, measurable and neutral ones of the physical sciences, but are instead of an entirely different character—vague, amorphous, often even quasi-religious in phrasing—it must be admitted that many of the generally understood distinctions between the sexes in the more significant areas of role and temperament, not to mention status, have in fact, essentially cultural, rather than biological, bases. Attempts to prove that temperamental dominance is inherent in the male (which for its advocates, would be tantamount to validating, logically as well as historically, the patriarchal situation regarding role and status) have been notably unsuccessful. Sources in the field are in hopeless disagreement about the

---

[8] "The historians of Roman laws, having very justly remarked that neither birth nor affection was the foundation of the Roman family, have concluded that this foundation must be found in the power of the father or husband. They make a sort of primordial institution of this power; but they do not explain how this power was established, unless it was by the superiority of strength of the husband over the wife, and of the father over the children. Now, we deceive ourselves sadly when we thus place force as the origin of law. We shall see farther on that the authority of the father or husband, far from having been the first cause, was itself an effect; it was derived from religion, and was established by religion. Superior strength, therefore, was not the principle that established the family." Numa Denis Fustel de Coulanges, *The Ancient City* (1864). English translation by Willard Small (1873), Doubleday Anchor Reprint, pp. 41–42. Unfortunately Fustel de Coulanges neglects to mention how religion came to uphold patriarchal authority, since patriarchal religion is also an effect, rather than an original cause.

nature of sexual differences, but the most reasonable among them have despaired of the ambition of any definite equation between temperament and biological nature. It appears that we are not soon to be enlightened as to the existence of any significant inherent differences between male and female beyond the bio-genital ones we already know. Endocrinology and genetics afford no definite evidence of determining mental-emotional differences.

Not only is there insufficient evidence for the thesis that the present social distinctions of patriarchy (status, role, temperament) are physical in origin, but we are hardly in a position to assess the existing differentiations, since distinctions which we know to be culturally induced at present so outweigh them. Whatever the "real" differences between the sexes may be, we are not likely to know them until the sexes are treated differently, that is alike. And this is very far from being the case at present. Important new research not only suggests that the possibilities of innate temperamental differences seem more remote than ever, but even raises questions as to the validity and permanence of psycho-sexual identity. In doing so it gives fairly concrete positive evidence of the overwhelmingly *cultural* character of gender, i.e. personality structure in terms of sexual category. . .

Although there is no biological reason why the two central functions of the family (socialization and reproduction) need be inseparable from or even take place within it, revolutionary or utopian efforts to remove these functions from the family have been so frustrated, so beset by difficulties, that most experiments so far have involved a gradual return to tradition. This is strong evidence of how basic a form patriarchy is within all societies, and of how pervasive its effects upon family members. It is perhaps also an admonition that change undertaken without a thorough understanding of the sociopolitical institution to be changed is hardly productive. And yet radical social change cannot take place without having an effect upon patriarchy. And not simply because it is the political form which subordinates such a large percentage of the population (women and youth) but because it serves as a citadel of property and traditional interests. Marriages are financial alliances, and each household operates as an economic entity much like a corporation. As one student of the family states it, "the family is the keystone of the stratification system, the social mechanism by which it is maintained." . . .

[III] EDUCATIONAL AND ECONOMIC

. . . As patriarchy enforces a temperamental imbalance of personality traits between the sexes, its educational institutions, segregated or co-educational, accept a cultural programing toward the generally operative division between "masculine" and "feminine" subject matter, assigning the humanities and certain social sciences (at least in their lower or marginal branches) to the female—and science and technology, the professions, business and engineering to the male. Of course the balance of employment, prestige and reward at present lie with the latter. Control of these fields is very eminently a matter of political power. One might also point out how the exclusive dominance of males in the more prestigious fields directly serves the interests of patriarchal power in industry, government, and the military. And since patriarchy encourages an imbalance in human temperament along sex lines, both divisions of learning (science and the humanities) reflect this imbalance. The humanities, because not exclusively male, suffer in prestige: the sciences, technology, and business, because they are nearly exclusively male reflect the deformation of the "masculine" personality, e.g., a certain predatory or aggressive character. . .).

[IV] PSYCHOLOGICAL

The aspects of patriarchy already described have each an effect upon the psychology of both sexes. Their principal result is the interiorization of patriarchal ideology. Status, temperament, and role are all value systems with endless psychological ramifications for each sex. Patriarchal marriage and the family with its ranks and division of labor play a large part in enforcing them. The male's superior economic position, the female's inferior one have also grave implications. The large quantity of guilt attached to sexuality in patriarchy is overwhelmingly placed upon the female, who is, culturally speaking, held to be the culpable or the more culpable party in nearly any sexual liaison, whatever the extenuating circumstances. A tendency toward the reification of the female makes her more often a sexual object than a person. This is particularly so when she is denied human rights through chattel status. Even where this has been partly amended the cumulative effect of religion and custom is still very powerful and has enormous psychological consequences. Woman is still denied sexual freedom and the biological control over her body through the cult of virginity, the double standard, the prescription against abortion, and in many places because contraception is physically or psychically unavailable to her.
   The continual surveillance in which she is held tends to perpetuate the infantilization of women even in situations such as those of higher education. . . .
   When in any group of persons, the ego is subjected to such invidious versions of itself through social beliefs, ideology, and tradition, the effect is bound to be pernicious. This coupled with the persistent though frequently subtle denigration women encounter daily through personal contacts, the impressions gathered from the images and media about them, and the discrimination in matters of behavior, employment, and education which they endure, should make it no very special cause for surprise that women develop group characteristics common to those who suffer minority status and a marginal existence. A witty experiment by Philip Goldberg proves what everyone knows, that having internalized the disesteem in which they are held, women despise both themselves and each other. This simple test consisted of asking women undergraduates to respond to the scholarship in an essay signed alternately by one John McKay and one Joan McKay. In making their assessments the students generally agreed that John was a remarkable thinker, Joan an unimpressive mind. Yet the articles were identical: the reaction was dependent on the sex of the supposed author. . . .
   Perhaps patriarchy's greatest psychological weapon is simply its universality and longevity. A referent scarcely exists with which it might be contrasted or by which it might be confuted. While the same might be said of class, patriarchy has a still more tenacious or powerful hold through its successful habit of passing itself off as nature. Religion is also universal in human society and slavery was

once nearly so; advocates of each were fond of arguing in terms of fatality, or irrevocable human "instinct"— "biological origins." When a system of power is thoroughly in command, it has scarcely need to speak itself aloud; when its workings are exposed and questioned, it becomes not only subject to discussion, but even to change.

QUESTIONS

1. Is the position of women in our society really analogous to that of minority groups such as blacks, chicanos, and native Americans?
2. Compare Millett's claims with Mill's. In what respects are their positions similar?

Steven Goldberg

THE INEVITABILITY OF PATRIARCHY

Biographical Information. *Steven Goldberg teaches in the Department of Sociology at the City College of New York. He is the author of a book,* The Inevitability of Patriarchy *(from which this selection is excerpted), and of* "On Capital Punishment" *(Ethics, vol. 85, 1974).*

Argument in the Selection. *Goldberg is the first writer in this section to argue against sexual equality and in support of the nonegalitarianism found in a patriarchy. He attacks the following basic assumption of Mill and Millett: There is no natural difference between the sexes which makes the male-dominated society inevitable. Goldberg claims that there is such a difference—a hormonal one. Owing to hormonal differences, males are inherently more aggressive than females. This greater aggressiveness assures male domination of the high-status roles in society.*

Moreover, Goldberg argues, if society does not socialize women away from competing with men, then most women will be condemned to failure and unhappiness. Given the innate aggression advantage of men over women, consider what would happen if society did not socialize women against competing with men for society's high-status positions. Some women would be aggressive enough to succeed. The vast majority would be failures, however, socialized to desire high-status positions but incapable of attaining them.

The view of man and woman in society that implicitly underlies all of the arguments of the feminists is this: there is nothing inherent in the nature of human beings or of society that necessitates that any role or task (save those requiring great strength or the ability to give birth) be associated with one sex or the other;[1] there is no natural order of things decreeing that dyadic and social authority must be associated with men, nor is there any reason why it must be men who rule in every society. Patriarchy, matriarchy, and "equiarchy" are all equally possible and—while every society may invoke "the natural order of things" to justify its particular system—all the expectations we have of men and women are culturally determined and have nothing to do with any sort of basic male or female nature.[2]

There is nothing internally contradictory in such a hypothesis; indeed, it is an ideal place from which to begin an empirical investigation into the nature of man, woman, and society. However, the feminist does not use this as a heuristic first step but unquestioningly accepts it as true. . . .

I believe that in the past we have been looking in the wrong direction for the answer to the question of why every society rewards male roles with higher status than it does female roles (even when the male tasks in one society are the female tasks in another). While it is true that men are always in the positions of authority from which status tends to be defined, male roles are not given high status primarily *because* men fill these roles; men fill these roles because their biological aggression "advantage"* can be manifested *in any non-child related area rewarded by high status in any society.* (Again: the line of reasoning used in this book demonstrates only that the biological factors we discuss would make the

---

[1] "*It is time that we realized that the whole structure of male and female personality is entirely imposed by social conditioning.* All the possible traits of human personality have in this conditioning been *arbitrarily* assigned into two categories; thus aggression is masculine, passivity feminine. . . .*" [Emphasis added]. (Kate Millett, *Barnard Alumnae*, Spring, 1970, p. 28.) This statement expresses the assumption which underpins all of Dr. Millett's *Sexual Politics* (New York: Doubleday, 1970).

[2] The best presentation of the feminist assumption is unquestionably John Stuart Mill's *The Subjection of Women*. As an impassioned plea for women's rights Mill's essay is both moving and illuminating. As an attempt to explain the etiology of sexually differentiated behavior and institutions it is indefensible. One is tempted, given the fact that the author of the essay was Mill, to ascribe its inadequacies to the fact that little of the relevant anthropological evidence, and none of the relevant hormonal evidence, was available at the time. But the weakness of Mill's analysis is attributable even more to the fallacious reasoning that his preconceived conclusions demanded. For example, Mill argues that we can have no conception of the limits of possibility imposed by innate sexual differences, or even of whether such limits exist, because no society has been composed of one sex; thus he does not even attempt to explain why the conceptions of male and female held by his society are not reversed in any other society. Similarly Mill attempts to dismiss the possibility of the determinativeness of innate sexual differences by invoking the irrelevant fact that slave owners defended slavery with the invocation of physiological racial differences that do not exist; this fact is correct, of course, but it casts no more doubt on the likelihood that innate sexual differences are determinative to sexual differences in behavior and institutions than it does on the certainty that physiology is determinative to the ability to give birth. Mill's reasoning has been accepted without question by modern feminist writers.

* Ed. note: Goldberg claims that because of hormonal differences between the sexes, the male has a greater capacity for aggression "or a lower threshold at which aggression is released" (p. 82). It is this greater capacity for aggression which gives males the advantage over females in competitive situations.

social institutions we discuss inevitable and does not preclude the existence of other forces also leading in the same direction; there may be a biologically based tendency for women to prefer male leadership, but there need not be for male attainment of leadership and high-status roles to be inevitable.) . . . This aggression "advantage" can be most manifested and can most enable men to reap status rewards *not* in those relatively homogeneous, collectivist primitive societies in which both male and female must play similar economic roles if the society is to survive or in the monarchy (which guarantees an occasional female leader); this biological factor will be given freest play in the complex, relatively individualistic, bureaucratic, democratic society which, of necessity, must emphasize organizational authority and in which social mobility is relatively free of traditional barriers to advancement. There were more female heads of state in the first two-thirds of the sixteenth century than in the first two-thirds of the twentieth.

The mechanisms involved here are easily seen if we examine any roles that males have attained by channeling their aggression toward such attainment. We will assume for now that equivalent women could *perform* the tasks of roles as well as men if they could attain the roles.[3] Here we can speak of the corporation president, the union leader, the governor, the chairman of an association, or any other role or position for which aggression is a precondition for attainment. Now the environmentalist and the feminist will say that the fact that all such roles are nearly always filled by men is attributable not to male aggression but to the fact that women have not been allowed to enter the competitive race to attain these positions, that they have been told that these positions are in male areas, and that girls are socialized away from competing with boys in general. Women are socialized in this way, but again we must ask why. If innate male aggression has nothing to do with male attainment of positions of authority and status in the political, academic, scientific, or financial spheres, if aggression has nothing to do with the reasons why *every* society socializes girls away from those areas which are given high status and away from competition in general, then why is it never the *girls* in any society who are socialized toward these areas, why is it never the nonbiological roles played by women that have high status, why is it always boys who are told to compete, and why do women never "force" men into the low-status, nonmaternal roles that women play in every society?

These questions pose no problem if we acknowledge a male aggression that enables men to attain any nonbiological role given high status by any society. For one need merely consider the result of society's *not* socializing women away from

---

[3] I assume this for the present in order to demonstrate that these will be male roles even if women can *perform* these roles as well as men when they can attain them. It should be pointed out, however, that the line between attainment and performance is not always clear in a bureaucratic society or in leadership in any society; much of the performance of an executive or leader concerns his ability to maintain the authority which his position gives him. Therefore, it is possible that the greater innate male aggression, particularly when opposed to the lesser innate female aggression, leads to *performance* by the male which is superior to that of the female. This does not, of course, mean that the male at any level of the hierarchy has an advantage over the exceptional woman who was aggressive enough to attain a comparable position, but it might indicate that men in general have an innate advantage over women in general which is relevant to the *performance* of bureaucratic and leadership roles.

competitions with men, from its *not* directing girls toward roles women are more capable of playing than are men or roles with status low enough that men will not strive for them. No doubt some women would be aggressive enough to succeed in competitions with men and there would be considerably more women in high-status positions than there are now. But most women would lose in such competitive struggles with men (because men have the aggression advantage) and so most women would be forced to live adult lives as failures in areas in which the society had *wanted them to succeed.* It is women, far more than men, who would never allow a situation in which girls were socialized in such a way that the vast majority of them were doomed to adult lifetimes of failure to live up to their own expectations. Now I have no doubt that there is a biological factor that gives women the desire to emphasize maternal and nurturance roles, but the point here is that we can accept the feminist assumption that there is no female propensity of this sort and still see that a society must socialize women away from roles that men will attain through their aggression. For if women did not develop an alternative set of criteria for success their sense of their own competence would suffer intolerably. It is undeniable that the resulting different values and expectations that are attached to men and women will tend to work against the aggressive woman while they work for the man who is no more aggressive. But this is the unavoidable result of the fact that most men are more aggressive than most women so that this woman, who is as aggressive as the average man, but more aggressive than most women, is an exception. Furthermore, even if the sense of competence of each sex did not necessitate society's attaching to each sex values and expectations based on those qualities possessed by each sex, observation of the majority of each sex by the population would "automatically" lead to these values and expectations being attached to men and women.

SOCIALIZATION'S CONFORMATION TO BIOLOGICAL REALITY

Socialization is the process by which society prepares children for adulthood. The way in which its goals conform to the reality of biology is seen quite clearly when we consider the method in which testosterone generates male aggression (testosterone's serially developing nature). Preadolescent boys and girls have roughly equal testosterone levels, yet young boys are far more aggressive than young girls. Eva Figes has used this observation to dismiss incorrectly the possibility of a hormone-aggression association.[4] Now it is quite probable that the boy is more aggressive than the girl for a purely biological reason. . . . There is evidence of male-female differences in the behavior of infants shortly after birth (when differential socialization is not a plausible explanation of such differences). The fetal alteration of the boy's brain by the testosterone that was generated by his testes has probably left him far more sensitive to the aggression-related properties of the testosterone that is present during boyhood than the girl, who did not receive such alteration. But let us for the moment assume that this is not the case. This does not

[4] Eva Figes, *Patriarchal Attitudes* (Greenwich, Conn.: Fawcett World, 1971), p. 8.

at all reduce the importance of the hormonal factor. For even if the boy is more aggressive than the girl only because the society allows him to be, the boy's socialization still flows from society's acknowledging biological reality. Let us consider what would happen if girls have the same innate aggression as boys and if a society did not socialize girls away from aggressive competitions. Perhaps half of the third-grade baseball team would be female. As many girls as boys would frame their expectations in masculine values and girls would develop not their feminine abilities but their masculine ones. During adolescence, however, the same assertion of the male chromosomal program that causes the boys to grow beards raises their testosterone level, and their potential for aggression, to a level far above that of the adolescent woman. If society did not teach young girls that beating boys at competitions was unfeminine (behavior inappropriate for a woman), if it did not socialize them away from the political and economic areas in which aggression leads to attainment, these girls would grow into adulthood with self-images based not on succeeding in areas for which biology has left them better prepared than men, but on competitions that most women could not win. If women did not develop feminine qualities as girls (assuming that such qualities do not spring automatically from female biology) then they would be forced to deal with the world in the aggressive terms of men. They would lose every source of power their feminine abilities now give them and they would gain nothing. . . .

The most crucial of the feminist fallacies involves the confusion of cause and function. We need not involve ourselves in a detailed discussion of causation here; a simple example should suffice. A jockey is small because biology made him that way. There may be an element of feedback here in that the jockey might well weigh more if society did not reward his weighing as little as possible, but the causation involved in the determination of his physical characteristics is certainly primarily biological. The function that his size plays in society, its manifestation in his role of jockey, is not biological, but society's putting his size to use. Likewise, the economic functions that sexual differentiation requires do not cause the differentiation. The biological element of male aggression will manifest itself in any economic system. . . . Because the social and economic must conform to the biological, we can change any variable and patriarchy will not be diminished. Political rule is male whether the institutions relevant to private property, control of the means of production, and class stratification are as minimally present as is possible or as advanced as is found in any society. It is male whether a society is patrilineal, matrilineal, or bilateral; patrilocal, matrilocal, or neolocal; white, black, or heterogeneous; racist, separatist, or equalitarian; primitive, preindustrial, or technological; Shintoist, Catholic, or Zoroastrian; monarchical, totalitarian, or democratic; Spartan, Quaker, or Bourbon; ascetic, hedonist, or libertine. It makes no difference whether a society has a value system that specifically forbids women from entering areas of authority or, like Communist China, an ideological and political commitment to equal distribution of authority positions. One cannot "disprove" the inevitability of biological factors manifesting themselves by demonstrating the function that they serve in a political or economic system. No system could operate that did not conform to, and utilize, the reality that constitutes it. In short, . . . reasoning that concludes that men rule because of the nature of the political-economic system . . . ignores the reality that the possible varieties of political-economic systems are limited by, and must conform to, the nature of man.

QUESTIONS

1. Construct a debate between Mill and Goldberg on the following issue: Social practices which accord unequal treatment to the sexes are morally justified.

2. Millett and Goldberg give different analyses of the roots of male political dominance. Argue in support of either Millett or Goldberg.

Joyce Trebilcot

SEX ROLES: THE ARGUMENT FROM NATURE

Biographical Information. Joyce Trebilcot teaches in the Philosophy Department at Washington University. She has also taught at Bryn Mawr College. Trebilcot has published articles on various philosophical topics in publications such as the Monist *and the* Philosophical Quarterly.

Argument in the Selection. Trebilcot examines and evaluates the following three arguments frequently given in support of the claim that natural psychological differences between the sexes are relevant to the issue of whether some roles in society should be assigned on the basis of sex. (1) The argument from inevitability. Since the alleged psychological differences between the sexes and the concomitant differences in behavior are inevitable, society will inevitably be structured to enforce sex roles. Therefore, sex roles are inevitable. (2) The argument from well-being. Because there are natural psychological differences between the sexes, members of each sex will be happier in certain roles than in others; the roles tending to promote happiness will differ according to sex. Thus, society should encourage individuals to make the right role choices so that happiness will be maximized. (3) The argument from efficiency. If there are natural differences in the capacities of the sexes to perform specified tasks, then, for the sake of efficiency, these tasks should be assigned to the sex with the greatest innate ability to perform them.

I am concerned here with the normative question of whether, in an ideal society, certain roles should be assigned to females and others to males. In discussions of this issue, a great deal of attention is given to the claim that there are natural psychological differences between the sexes. Those who hold that at least some roles should be sex roles generally base their view primarily on an appeal to such natural differences, while many of those advocating a society without sex roles argue either that the sexes do not differ in innate psychological traits or that there is no evidence that they do.[1] In this paper I argue that whether there are natural psychological differences between females and males has little bearing on the issue of whether society should reserve certain roles for females and others for males.

Let me begin by saying something about the claim that there are natural psychological differences between the sexes. The issue we are dealing with arises, of course, because there are biological differences among human beings which are bases for designating some as females and others as males. Now it is held by some that, in addition to biological differences between the sexes, there are also natural differences in temperament, interests, abilities, and the like. In this paper I am concerned only with arguments which appeal to these psychological differences as bases of sex roles. Thus I exclude, for example, arguments that the role of jockey should be female because women are smaller than men or that boxers should be male because men are more muscular than women. Nor do I discuss arguments which appeal directly to the reproductive functions peculiar to each sex. If the physiological processes of gestation or of depositing sperm in a vaginia are, apart from any psychological correlates they may have, bases for sex roles, these roles are outside the scope of the present discussion.

It should be noted, however, that virtually all those who hold that there are natural psychological differences between the sexes assume that these differences are determined primarily by differences in biology. According to one hypothesis, natural psychological differences between the sexes are due at least in part to differences between female and male nervous systems. As the male fetus develops in the womb, the testes secrete a hormone which is held to influence the growth of the central nervous system. The female fetus does not produce this hormone, nor is there an analogous female hormone which is significant at this stage. Hence it is suggested that female and male brains differ in structure, that this difference is due to the prenatal influence of testicular hormone, and that the difference in brains is the basis of some later differences in behavior.[2]

A second view about the origin of allegedly natural psychological differences between the sexes, a view not incompatible with the first, is psychoanalytical. It conceives of feminine or masculine behavior as, in part the individual's response to bodily structure. On this view, one's more or less unconscious experience of one's own body (and in some versions, of the bodies of others) is a major factor in producing sex-specific personality traits. The classic theories of this kind are, of course, Freud's; penis envy and the castration complex are supposed to arise largely from perceptions of differences between female and male bodies. Other

---

[1] For support of sex roles, see, for example, Aristotle, *Politics*, book 1; and Erik Erikson, "Womanhood and the Inner Space," *Identity: Youth and Crisis* (New York: W.W. Norton & Co., 1968). Arguments against sex roles may be found, for example, in J. S. Mill, "The Subjection of Women," in *Essays on Sex Equality: John Stuart Mill and Harriet Taylor Mill*, ed. Alice S. Rossi (Chicago: University of Chicago Press, 1970); and Naomi Weisstein, "Psychology Constructs the Female," in *Women in Sexist Society*, ed. Vivian Gornick and Barbara K. Moran (New York: Basic Books, 1971).

[2] See John Money and Anke A. Ehrhardt, *Man and Woman, Boy and Girl* (Baltimore: Johns Hopkins Press, 1972).

writers make much of the analogies between genitals and genders: the uterus is passive and receptive, and so are females; penises are active and penetrating, and so are males.[3] But here we are concerned not with the etiology of allegedly natural differences between the sexes but rather with the question of whether such differences, if they exist, are grounds for holding that there should be sex roles.

That a certain psychological disposition is natural only to one sex is generally taken to mean in part that members of that sex are more likely to have the disposition, or to have it to a greater degree, than persons of the other sex. The situation is thought to be similar to that of height. In a given population, females are on the average shorter than males, but some females are taller than some males, as suggested by figure 1. The shortest members of the population are all

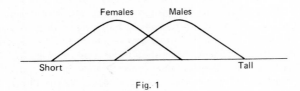

Fig. 1

females, and the tallest are all males, but there is an area of overlap. For psychological traits, it is usually assumed that there is some degree of overlap and that the degree of overlap is different for different characteristics. Because of the difficulty of identifying natural psychological characteristics, we have of course little or no data as to the actual distribution of such traits.

I shall not undertake here to define the concept of role, but examples include voter, librarian, wife, president. A broad concept of role might also comprise, for example, being a joker, a person who walks gracefully, a compassionate person. The genders, femininity and masculinity, may also be conceived as roles. On this view, each of the gender roles includes a number of more specific sex roles, some of which may be essential to it. For example, the concept of femininity may be construed in such a way that it is necessary to raise a child in order to be fully feminine, while other feminine roles—teacher, nurse, charity worker—are not essential to gender. In the arguments discussed below, the focus is on sex roles rather than genders, but, on the assumption that the genders are roles, much of what is said applies, *mutatis mutandis*, to them.

A sex role is a role performed only or primarily by persons of a particular sex. Now if this is all we mean by "sex role," the problem of whether there should be sex roles must be dealt with as two separate issues: "Are sex roles a good thing?" and "Should society enforce sex roles?" One might argue, for example, that sex roles have value but that, even so, the demands of individual autonomy and freedom are such that societal institutions and practices should not enforce

[3] For Freud, see, for example, "Some Psychological Consequences of the Anatomical Distinctions between the Sexes," in *Sigmund Freud: Collected Papers*, ed. James Strachey (New York: Basic Books, 1959), 5:186–97. See also Karl Stern, *The Flight from Woman* (New York: Farrar, Straus & Giroux, 1965), chap. 2; and Erikson.

correlations between roles and sex. But the debate over sex roles is of course mainly a discussion about the second question, whether society should enforce these correlations. The judgment that there should be sex roles is generally taken to mean not just that sex-exclusive roles are a good thing, but that society should promote such exclusivity.

In view of this, I use the term "sex role" in such a way that to ask whether there should be sex roles is to ask whether society should direct women into certain roles and away from others, and similarly for men. A role is a sex role then (or perhaps an "institutionalized sex role") only if it is performed exclusively or primarily by persons of a particular sex *and* societal factors tend to encourage this correlation. These factors may be of various kinds. Parents guide children into what are taken to be sex-appropriate roles. Schools direct students into occupations according to sex. Marriage customs prescribe different roles for females and males. Employers and unions may refuse to consider applications from persons of the "wrong" sex. The media carry tales of the happiness of those who conform and the suffering of the others. The law sometimes penalizes deviators. Individuals may ridicule and condemn role crossing and smile on conformity. Societal sanctions such as these are essential to the notion of sex role employed here.

I turn now to a discussion of the three major ways the claim that there are natural psychological differences between the sexes is held to be relevant to the issue of whether there should be sex roles.

1. *Inevitability.* It is sometimes held that if there are innate psychological differences between females and males, sex roles are inevitable. The point of this argument is not, of course, to urge that there should be sex roles, but rather to show that the normative question is out of place, that there will be sex roles, whatever we decide. The argument assumes first that the alleged natural differences between the sexes are inevitable; but if such differences are inevitable, differences in behavior are inevitable; and if differences in behavior are inevitable, society will inevitably be structured so as to enforce role differences according to sex. Thus, sex roles are inevitable.

For the purpose of this discussion, let us accept the claim that natural psychological differences are inevitable. We assume that there are such differences and ignore the possiblity of their being altered, for example, by evolutionary change or direct biological intervention. Let us also accept the second claim, that behavioral differences are inevitable. Behavioral differences could perhaps be eliminated even given the assumption of natural differences in disposition (for example, those with no natural inclination to a certain kind of behavior might nevertheless learn it), but let us waive this point. We assume then that behavioral differences, and hence also role differences, between the sexes are inevitable. Does it follow that there must be sex roles, that is, that the institutions and practices of society must enforce correlations between roles and sex?

Surely not. Indeed, such sanctions would be pointless. Why bother to direct women into some roles and men into others if the pattern occurs regardless of the nature of society? Mill makes the point elegantly in *The Subjection of Women*: "The anxiety of mankind to interfere in behalf of nature, for fear lest nature should not succeed in effecting its purpose, is an altogether unnecessary solicitude."[4]

---

[4] Mill, p. 154.

It may be objected that if correlations between sex and roles are inevitable, societal sanctions enforcing these correlations will develop because people will expect the sexes to perform different roles and these expectations will lead to behavior which encourages their fulfillment. This can happen, of course, but it is surely not inevitable. One need not act so as to bring about what one expects.

Indeed, there could be a society in which it is held that there are inevitable correlations between roles and sex but institutionalization of these correlations is deliberately avoided. What is inevitable is presumably not, for example, that every woman will perform a certain role and no man will perform it, but rather that most women will perform the role and most men will not. For any individual, then, a particular role may not be inevitable. Now suppose it is a value in the society in question that people should be free to choose roles according to their individual needs and interests. But then there should not be sanctions enforcing correlations between roles and sex, for such sanctions tend to force some individuals into roles for which they have no natural inclination and which they might otherwise choose against.

I conclude then that, even granting the assumptions that natural psychological differences, and therefore role differences, between the sexes are inevitable, it does not follow that there must be sanctions enforcing correlations between roles and sex. Indeed, if individual freedom is valued, those who vary from the statistical norm should not be required to conform to it.

2. Well-being. The argument from well-being begins with the claim that, because of natural psychological differences between the sexes, members of each sex are happier in certain roles than in others, and the roles which tend to promote happiness are different for each sex. It is also held that if all roles are equally available to everyone regardless of sex, some individuals will choose against their own well-being. Hence, the argument concludes, for the sake of maximizing well-being there should be sex roles: society should encourage individuals to make "correct" role choices.

Suppose that women, on the average, are more compassionate than men. Suppose also that there are two sets of roles, "female" and "male", and that because of the natural compassion of women, women are happier in female than in male roles. Now if females and males overlap with respect to compassion, some men have as much natural compassion as some women, so they too will be happier in female than in male roles. Thus, the first premise of the argument from well-being should read: Suppose that, because of natural psychological differences between the sexes, *most* women are happier in female roles and *most* men in male roles. The argument continues: If all roles are equally available to everyone, some of the women who would be happier in female roles will choose against their own well-being, and similarly for men.

Now if the conclusion that there should be sex roles is to be based on these premises, another assumption must be added—that the loss of potential well-being resulting from societally produced adoption of unsuitable roles by individuals in the overlapping areas of the distribution is *less* than the loss that would result from "mistaken" free choices if there were no sex roles. With sex roles, some individuals who would be happier in roles assigned to the other sex perform roles assigned to their own sex, and so there is a loss of potential happiness. Without sex roles, some individuals, we assume, choose against their own well-being. But surely we are not now in a position to compare the two systems with

146

respect to the number of mismatches produced. Hence, the additional premise required for the argument, that overall well-being is greater with sex roles than without them, is entirely unsupported.

Even if we grant, then, that because of innate psychological differences between the sexes members of each sex achieve greater well-being in some roles than in others, the argument from well-being does not support the conclusion that there should be sex roles. In our present state of knowledge, there is no reason to suppose that a sex role system which makes no discriminations within a sex would produce fewer mismatches between individuals and roles than a system in which all roles are open equally to both sexes.

3. *Efficiency.* If there are natural differences between the sexes in the capacity to perform socially valuable tasks, then, it is sometimes argued, efficiency is served if these tasks are assigned to the sex with the greatest innate ability for them. Suppose, for example, that females are naturally better than males at learning foreign languages. This means that, if everything else is equal and females and males are given the same training in a foreign language, females, on the average, will achieve a higher level of skill than males. Now suppose that society needs interpreters and translators and that in order to have such a job one must complete a special training program whose only purpose is to provide persons for these roles. Clearly, efficiency is served if only individuals with a good deal of natural ability are selected for training, for the time and effort required to bring them to a given level of proficiency is less than that required for the less talented. But suppose that the innate ability in question is normally distributed within each sex and that the sexes overlap (see fig. 2). If we assume that a

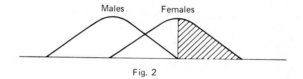

Fig. 2

sufficient number of candidates can be recruited by considering only persons in the shaded area, they are the only ones who should be eligible. There are no men in this group. Hence, although screening is necessary in order to exclude nontalented women, it would be inefficient even to consider men, for it is known that no man is as talented as the talented women. In the interest of efficiency, then, the occupational roles of interpreter and translator should be sex roles; men should be denied access to these roles but women who are interested in them, especially talented women, should be encouraged to pursue them.

This argument is sound. That is, if we grant the factual assumptions and suppose also that efficiency for the society we are concerned with has some value, the argument from efficiency provides one reason for holding that some roles should be sex roles. This conclusion of course is only prima facie. In order to determine whether there should be sex roles, one would have to weigh efficiency, together with other reasons for such roles, against reasons for holding that there should not be sex roles. The reasons against sex roles are very strong. They are couched in terms of individual rights—in terms of liberty, justice, equality of

147

opportunity. Efficiency by itself does not outweigh these moral values. Neverthe-less, the appeal to nature, if true, combined with an appeal to the value of efficiency, does provide one reason for the view that there should be sex roles.

The arguments I have discussed here are not the only ones which appeal to natural psychological differences between the sexes in defense of sex roles, but these three arguments—from inevitability, well-being, and efficiency—are, I believe, the most common and the most plausible ones. The argument from efficiency alone, among them, provides a reason—albeit a rather weak reason—for thinking that there should be sex roles. I suggest, therefore, that the issue of natural psychological differences between women and men does not deserve the central place it is given, both traditionally and currently, in the literature on this topic.

It is frequently pointed out that the argument from nature functions as a cover, as a myth to make patriarchy palatable to both women and men. Insofar as this is so, it is surely worthwhile exploring and exposing the myth. But of course most of those who use the argument from nature take it seriously and literally, and this is the spirit in which I have dealt with it. Considering the argument in this way, I conclude that whether there should be sex roles does not depend primarily on whether there are innate psychological differences between the sexes. The question is, after all, not what women and men naturally are, but what kind of society is morally justifiable. In order to answer this question, we must appeal to the notions of justice, equality, and liberty. It is these moral concepts, not the empirical issue of sex differences, which should have pride of place in the philosophical discussion of sex roles.

QUESTIONS

1. Summarize Trebilcot's criticisms of the arguments based on appeals to well-being and inevitability. Are her criticisms well-taken?

2. If there are innate psychological differences between the sexes, should society enforce differentiated sexual roles?

3. If there are innate psychological sexual differences, should society attempt to minimize such differences?

J. R. Lucas

'BECAUSE YOU ARE A WOMAN'

Biographical Information. J. R. Lucas is a fellow and tutor in philosophy at Merton College, Oxford. He is the author of The Principles of Politics, The Concept of Probability, *and* The Freedom of the Will. *Among his published articles is "Justice,"* Philosophy *(1972).*

148

Argument in the Selection. *Lucas asks what differences between men and women would justify treating them differently. He answers that sex may sometimes be relevant, especially when general rules are being framed or social institutions are being established by appeal either to the principle of utility or to tradition. Social utility may require that rules be framed to fit the general or average case rather than the exceptional one. Tradition may require that where there is a strong reluctance to accept women in certain institutionalized roles, those roles should be denied to women. If this is counter to the Humanitarian Principle, Lucas argues, special institutions should be formed in which women can fulfill their vocations.*

If it could be established that there were no innate intellectual or emotional differences between men and women, the feminists' case would be pretty well made; but it does not follow that to admit that there are differences carries with it an adequate justification for every sort of discrimination, and it is useful to consider what sort of bearing various types of difference might have. Suppose, for example, that mathematical ability were distributed unevenly and according to the same pattern as haemophilia, so that only one in n males have it and only one in n^2 females. This would be a highly relevant factor in framing our educational policy. It would justify the provision of far more opportunities for boys to study higher mathematics than for girls. But it would not justify the total exclusion of girls. Most girls prefer nursing to numeracy, but those few who would rather solve differential equations ought not to be prevented from doing so on the grounds that they are female. Two principles underlie this judgment. First that the connexion between sex and mathematical ability is purely contingent; and secondly that we are in a position in which considerations of the individual's interests and deserts are paramount. Even if there are very few female mathematicians, there is no reason why any particular woman should not be a mathematician. And if any particular woman is, then her being a woman is irrelevant to her actual performance in mathematics. Her being a woman created a presumption, a purely contingent although usually reliable presumption, that she was no good at mathematics. It is like presumptive evidence in a court of law, which could be rebutted, and in this case was, and having been rebutted is of no more relevance in this individual situation, which is all we are concerned with.

Female mathematicians are rare. Few disciplines are so pure as mathematics. In most human activities—even in most academic pursuits—the whole personality is much more involved, and the irrelevance of a person's sex far more dubious. Differences between the sexes are likely to come into play most in ordinary human relations where one person tells another what to do, or persuades, or cajoles or encourages or warns or threatens or acquiesces. In so far as most positions in society are concerned with social relations, it cannot be argued that the differences between the sexes are, of necessity, irrelevant. Although it might be the case that working men would as readily take orders from a fore-woman as a foreman, or that customers would be as pleased to find a handsome boy receptionist as a pretty girl, there is no reason to suppose that it must be so. Moreover, life is not normally either an examination or a trial. It is one of the disadvantages of our meritocratic age that we too readily assume that all social transactions are exclusively concerned with the individual, who needs to be given every opportunity and whose rights must be zealously safeguarded. But examinations and trials are artificial and cumbersome exceptions to the general rule, in which no one individual is the centre of concern. To deny people the fruits of their examination success or to deprive them of their liberty on any grounds irrelevant to their own desert is wrong: but it is not so evidently wrong to frustrate Miss Amazon's hopes of a military career in the Grenadier Guards on the grounds not that she would make a bad soldier but that she would be a disturbing influence in the mess room. Laws and institutions are characteristically two-faced. They set norms for the behaviour of different parties, and need to take into consideration the interests and claims of more than one person. They also need to apply generally, and cannot be tailor-made to each particular situation: they define rôles rather than fit actual personalities, and rôles need to fit the typical rather than the special case. Even if Miss Amazon is sure not to attract sidelong glances from the licentious soldiery, her sisters may not be; and it may be easier to operate an absolute bar than leave it to the recruiting officer to decide whether a particular woman is sufficiently unattractive to be safe. This type of case turns up in many other laws and public regulations. We lay down rigid speed limits because they are easier to apply. There are many towns in which to drive at 30 mph would be dangerous, and many suburbs in which to drive at 45 mph would sometimes be safe. Some boys of ten are better informed about public affairs than other voters of thirty. But the advantage of having a fixed speed limit or a fixed voting age outweighs its admitted unfairness.

We can now see what sort of facts would bring what sort of principles to bear upon our individual decisions and the general structure of our laws and institutions. We need to know not only whether there are differences, but whether these differences are integrally or only contingently connected with a person's sex, and whether they apply in all cases or only as a rule. The more integrally and the more invariably a difference is connected with a person's sex, the more we are entitled to insist that the mere fact of being male or female can constitute a conclusive reason against being allowed to do something. The less integral a difference is, the more the arguments from Formal Equality (or Universalizability) and from Justice will come into play, requiring us to base our decisions only on the features relevant to the case in hand. The less invariable a difference is, the more the arguments from Humanity and again from Justice will come into play, requiring us to pay respect to the interests and inclinations of each individual person, and to weigh her actual interests, as against those of the community at large, on the basis of her actual situation and actual and reasonable desires.

However much I, a male, want to be a mother, a wife or a girlfriend, I am disqualified from those rôles on account of my sex, and I cannot reasonably complain. Not only can I not complain if individuals refuse to regard me as suitable in those rôles, but I have to acknowledge that it is reasonable for society generally to do so, and for the state to legislate accordingly. The state is justified in not countenancing homosexual 'marriages', because of our general understanding of what marriage really is, and the importance we attach to family life. For exactly the same reasons, women are debarred from being regarded in a fatherly or husbandly light; and hence also in those parts of the Christian Church that regard

150

priests as being essentially fathers in God from being clergymen or bishops. How far rôles should be regarded as being integrally dependent on sex is a matter of dispute. In very intimate and personal relationships it is evident that the whole personality is involved, and that since a man—or at least many, non-Platonic men—responds to a woman in a different way from that in which he responds to a man or a woman to a woman, it is natural that these rôles should be essentially dependent on sex. But as the rôles become more limited, so the dependence becomes less. I could hardly complain if I was not given the part of Desdemona or a job as an *au pair* boy on account of my sex: but if I had very feminine features and had grown my hair long and golden, or if I were particularly deft at changing nappies, I might feel a little aggrieved, and certainly I could call in question any law that forbade a man to play the part of a woman or be a nursemaid. Some substantial public good would need to be shown to justify a legal decision enforceable by penal sanctions being uniformly based not on my actual inability to fill the rôle required but only my supposed unsuitability on account of my sex. We demand a higher standard of cogency in arguments justifying what laws there should be than in those concerned only with individual decisions; and although this standard can be satisfied, often by admitting considerations of the public good, yet the arguments need to be adduced, because, in framing laws, we need to be sensitive to individual rights and careful about our criteria of relevance. Although it may be the case that a nurse is a better nurse for having the feminine touch, we hesitate to deem it absolutely essential; and although many more women than men have been good nurses, we do not believe that it must invariably be so. There are male nurses. We reckon it reasonable to prefer a woman in individual cases, but do not insist upon it in all cases by law. We are reluctant to impose severe legal disqualifications, but equally would hesitate to impose upon employers an obligation not to prefer women to play female parts or to be nurses or to join a family in an *au pair* capacity. For we recognize that a person's sex can reasonably be regarded as relevant to his or her suitability for particular posts, and that many institutions will operate on this basis, and are entitled to. I am justified in refusing to employ a male *au pair* girl or a female foreman, although if there are many males anxious to be looking after young children or many women anxious to supervise the work of others, it may be desirable on grounds of Humanity to establish special institutions in which they can fulfil their vocations. If we will not let Miss Amazon join the Grenadier Guards, let there be an ATS or WRAC for her to join instead.

Athough we are rightly reluctant to impose legal disqualifications on individuals on grounds extraneous to their individual circumstances, it is inherent in all political thinking that we may find considerations of the general case over-riding those of the individual one; and often we frame our laws with an eye to what men and women are generally like rather than what they invariably are. A man may not adopt an infant girl unless she is more than twenty-five years younger than he; for some men might otherwise use adoption to acquire not so much a daughter as a wife. In many societies women have less freedom in disposing of their property than men; for else, things being as they are, some women would be prevailed upon to divest themselves of it to their long-term disadvantage. Ardent feminists have chafed at the shackles of marriage, and demand freedom from this degrading institution for their sisters as well as themselves. But if this freedom were established it would be the libertine males who would enjoy the benefits of

151

liberation, being then free to leave the women to bear the burdens of parenthood all on their own. If most mothers care more for their children and their homes than most fathers do, then in the absence of institutions that recognize the fact they will in fact be disadvantaged. Some discrimination is needed to redress the balance. But discrimination, even positive discrimination, can work to the disadvantage of individuals, however much it may benefit most people on the whole.

The would-be female Stakhanovite is penalized by the law forbidding firms to employ female labour for sixty hours a week, just as the youthful entrepreneur is handicapped by his legal incapacity, as a minor, to pledge his credit except for the necessities of life, and the skilled racing motorist by the law forbidding him to drive, however safely, at more than 70 miles per hour. In each case the justification is the same: the restriction imposed on the individual, although real and burdensome, is not so severe as to outweigh the benefits that are likely to accrue in the long run to women in general, or to minors, or to motorists. It is in the nature of political society that we forgo some freedoms in order that either we ourselves or other people can secure some good. All we can in general demand is that our sacrifices should not be fruitless, and that if we give up some liberty or immunity it is at least arguable that it will be on balance for the best.

Arguments in politics are nearly always mixed, and involve appeals to different principles, according to how the question is construed. We can elucidate some canons of relevance for some of the principles which may be invoked. Where the principle is that of Universal Humanity, the reason 'Because you are a woman' is always irrelevant to its general applicability, though it may affect the way it is specified: perhaps women feel more strongly about their homes than men do, so that although we ought not, on grounds of humanity, to hurt either men or women, deprivation of her home would constitute a greater hurt to a woman than to a man. The principle of Universal Humanity is pervasive in its applications, but is conclusive only over a much more limited range. It is always wrong to torture; but often we cannot help hurting people's feelings or harming their interests if other values—justice, liberty, the public good—are to be preserved. And therefore arguments based on the principle of universal humanity may be over-ridden by ones based on other principles, also valuable. When the principle invoked is that of Formal Equality (or Universalizability) the reason 'Because you are a woman' cannot be dismissed out of hand as necessarily irrelevant. A person's sex is not a 'mere fact', evidently and necessarily separate from all other facts, and such that it is immediately obvious that no serious argument can be founded upon it. Particularly with those rôles that involve relationships with other people, and especially where those relationships are fairly personal ones, it is likely to matter whether it is a man or a woman that is chosen. When some principle of Justice is at stake, the criteria of relevance become fairly stringent. We are concerned only with the individual's actions, attitudes and abilities, and the reason 'Because you are a woman' must either be integrally connected with matter in issue (as in 'Why cannot I marry the girl I love?') or be reliably, although only contingently, connected with it (as in 'Why cannot I get myself employed for 60 hours a week?'); and in the latter case we feel that Justice has been compromised, although perhaps acceptably so, if there is no way whereby an individual can prove she is an exception to the rule and be treated as such. As the interests of the individual become more peripheral, or can be satisfied in alternative ways that are available, the principle of justice recedes, and we are more ready to accept rules and institutions based on general principles of social utility or tradition, and designed only to fit the general case. It is legitimate to base public feeling on such differences as seem to be relevant, but the more a law or an institution is based on merely a contingent, and not an integral, concomitance, the more ready we should be to cater for exceptions.

With sufficient care we may be able to disentangle what is true in the feminists' contention from what is false. At least we should be able to avoid the dilemma, which seems to be taken for granted by most participants in the debate, that we must say that women either are in all respects exactly the same as men or else are in all respects different from, and inferior to, them, and not members of the same universe of discourse at all. I do not share Plato's feelings about sex. I think the sexes are different, and incomparable. No doubt, women are not quite as good as men, *in some respects:* but since men are not nearly as good as women in others, this carries with it no derogatory implication of uniform inferiority. Exactly what these differences are, and, indeed, what sort of differences they are, is a matter for further research; and exactly what bearing they should have in the application of the various principles we value in making up our mind about social matters is a matter for further philosophical thought. But without any further thought we can align our emotions with the proponents of Women's Lib on the most important issue of all. What angers them most is the depersonalization of women in the Admass society: and one cannot but sympathize with their protest against women being treated as mere objects of sexual gratification by men; but cannot avoid the conclusion that their arguments and activities in fact lead towards just that result which they deplore. If we are insensitive to the essential femininity of the female sex, we shall adopt an easy egalitarianism which, while denying that there are any genetic differences, allows us to conclude in most individual cases that women, judged by male standards of excellence, are less good than their male rivals. Egalitarianism ends by depersonalizing women and men alike.

QUESTIONS

1. If the majority of Americans object to women plumbers, would the plumbers' union be justified in refusing to admit women?

2. Try to state Lucas's principle of Universal Humanity as precisely as possible. Then, using the principle, try to make Lucas's argument if you can do so.

Susan Haack

A REJOINDER TO LUCAS

Biographical Information. *Susan Haack is a lecturer in philosophy at the University of Warwick. She was formerly fellow of New Hall, Cambridge.*

Haack has published articles in Analysis, Philosophy, Mind, *and the* Philosophical Quarterly.

Argument in the Selection. Haack attacks Lucas's arguments by focusing on the ambiguity of his language. She examines the possible senses of expressions such as "involvement of the whole personality" and criticizes Lucas for appealing to principles such as the principle of Formal Equality and the principle of Universal Humanity without specifying just what he means by these expressions.

Mr. Lucas remarks several times that it is possible that women are less mathematically talented than men. Now he observes that female mathematicians are, in fact, rare. He leaves it conveniently vague whether by 'mathematician' he means 'professional mathematician' or 'person with mathematical ability'. He goes on to comment that few disciplines are so 'pure' as mathematics. The impression is thus most economically conveyed that women are so woolly-minded and emotional that they are unable to cope with so abstract a subject. However, Lucas next contrasts the purity of mathematics with the 'involvement of the whole personality' in other disciplines and pursuits, and concludes that in these other disciplines and pursuits, therefore, sex is not wholly irrelevant. At this point he seems to have fallen victim to his own rhetoric; previously mathematical ability had been his most highly stressed example of a possibly sex-linked characteristic, whereas now he is committed to the thesis that the 'purer' a pursuit is, the less relevant to it a person's sex is likely to be. This confusion is, however, essential to the next step of the argument. Lucas has previously envisaged the exclusion of women from various pursuits, but only on the basis of their incapacity: although innumerate females were to be excluded, the 'exceptional' female mathematician (the phrase has, incidentally, a splendid ambiguity) was to be permitted to pursue her profession. But now Lucas allows other, far more questionable, grounds of discrimination, viz. the adverse reactions of other people. This argument applies to those pursuits where 'the whole personality is involved'. It rests, however, on a rather serious equivocation. There are importantly different ways in which the whole personality may be involved in a discipline or a job: it might be argued, for instance, that the study of literature requires *personal involvement* in a way the study of mathematics does not; quite differently, it might be argued that the job of foreman or public relations officer requires *involvement with other people* in a way production line jobs do not. It is the first kind of 'personal involvement' which is suggested by the contrast with the 'purity' of mathematics and might, *if* personality were shown to be sex-dependent, be relevant to a person's ability in, say, literature. It is the second kind of 'personal involvement' which is relevant to Lucas's claim that the adverse reactions of other people would justify discrimination. Lucas's examples include (1) that it might be proper to refuse to employ a woman as foreman, because other (i.e. male) employees would be unwilling to take orders from her, and (2) that it might not be improper 'to frustrate Miss Amazon's hopes of a military career in the Grenadier Guards on the grounds not

154

that she would make a bad soldier but that she would be a disturbing influence in the mess room' [p. 150]. The first of these examples allows discrimination on grounds, not of the incompetence of an applicant for a job, but purely of the prejudice of other employees. This is certainly unacceptable in the case of racial discrimination; employers refusing to employ black workers on the ground that white employees would object are, quite rightly, liable to the attentions of the Race Relations Board. It is no less unacceptable where discrimination is on the basis of sex rather than race. The second example is, if possible, more alarming. For one thing, the assumption that men are so licentious that women cannot be allowed to work with them for fear of the resulting havoc clearly betrays that view of women as sexual objects which Lucas subsequently [p. 153] claims, less than convincingly, to deplore. For another, the principles employed in this case rapidly lead, if taken seriously, to absurdity—for presumably they would equally well justify the exclusion of men from the Grenadier Guards for fear that male recruits might provoke licentious behaviour on the part of their homosexual colleagues.

It is bad enough that Lucas is prepared to support discrimination on the strength of other people's reactions even when those reactions are the result of sheer prejudice; worse, that his argument entails that this kind can be more pervasive than discrimination on grounds of incapacity. But this turns out to be the case, since to the objection that a particular woman may be so unattractive as to pose no threat to the Guards' peace of mind, Lucas replies that all women ought, nevertheless, to be excluded, apparently because of the simplicity of such an inclusive rule. He supports this claim by an analogy with other cases where, he claims, considerations of generality outweigh considerations of fairness, e.g. the imposition of a uniform speed limit or voting age. The analogy is used in a misleading way. In the first place, it is not made as clear as it should be that the analogy is not relevant to the claim that women sufficiently attractive to disturb the Guards should be excluded, but only to the claim that even women not sufficiently attractive to be disturbing should also be excluded. One suspects, however, one is intended to suppose that Lucas has shown that considerations of the public good support the exclusion of attractive women. The analogy used is in any case dubious, since the prohibitions on driving over a certain speed, or on voting under a certain age, are based on the presumed *incapacity* of motorists to drive safely above a certain speed, or of minors to vote sensibly, whereas the case with which these are compared is of a prohibition based on something other than incapacity.

It is important to notice how Lucas's apparent moderation, in allowing competent women to pursue careers for which they are suited, is now entirely nullified. For Lucas must allow that a competent woman may properly be excluded from any profession on the grounds of the prejudice or boorishness of her (male?) colleagues. . . .

[Lucas's paper] addresses itself to the question: what differences between men and women would warrant treating them differently, but contributes little by way of an answer except (1) that it is *possible* that sex is sometimes relevant, and (2) that unfairness to individuals may sometimes be outweighed by public good. . . . And he suggests that sex is relevant to 'Formal Equality' rather than 'Universal Humanity', but the usefulness of this cannot be assessed while the content of these principles remains unspecified.

QUESTIONS

1. Summarize Haack's criticisms of Lucas; then defend Lucas against Haack's criticisms.
2. What differences between the sexes would warrant treating them differently?

SUGGESTED ADDITIONAL READINGS

Davidson, Kenneth M., Ruth B. Ginsburg, and Herma H. Kay, eds. *Sex-Based Discrimination: Text, Cases, and Materials.* Minneapolis: West Publishing Company, 1974. This is a record and discussion of court cases centering on issues such as the inequality of the legal rights of men and women and the unequal treatment of the sexes in education.

Jaggar, Alison. "On Sexual Equality." *Ethics,* vol. 84, 1974. This is one of the more difficult articles on the subject. At issue is whether sexual social equality requires integration or complete separation. By "sexual equality" Jaggar means that a situation of equality exists between the sexes in society, so that one group is not in a socially advantageous position in relation to the other.

The Philosophical Forum, vol. V, Nos. 1 and 2, Fall–Winter 1973-1974. This edition of *The Philosophical Forum* is directed to the theme: "Women and Philosophy." It presents a number of philosophical approaches to the social problem discussed in this chapter, the oppression and liberation of women. The articles are divided into three sections preceded by a discussion of the methodological issues involved. The three sections are (1) Historical Critique; (2) Analysis: Critique of the Present; (3) What is to Be Done? Contemporary Social, Ethical and Political Issues.

Rossi, Alice S., ed. *The Feminist Papers.* New York: Bantam Books, 1974. This is a collection of feminist writings, most of them written in the eighteenth and nineteenth centuries. It is interesting as a history of feminist thought and feminist movements.

FIVE

Discrimination and Reverse Discrimination

What does society owe to groups whose treatment in the past has not been consistent with the principle of equality?[1] What does it owe to a minority group whose members have been systematically discriminated against in the past, to groups whose members have not had the same opportunities as white males to enter the most desirable professions and graduate schools because of discriminatory quotas, or to Indians who have lost land and water rights because of government exploitation? If we agree that these groups have been unjustly accorded unequal treatment in the past and that we ought to compensate them in some way for these past injustices, then we are appealing to the *principle of compensatory justice.* The principle of compensatory justice says that whenever an injustice has been committed, just compensation or reparation must be made to the injured parties.

Such compensatory measures can take various forms. In the case of American Indians, for example, financial reparation has sometimes been given as compensation for past injustice. In the case of blacks and other minority groups special educational programs have been established. One example of such a program is the SEEK program in New York State. Applicants who would not ordinarily gain admittance to colleges in the state simply on the basis of their precollege grades and test scores, but who are judged capable of doing college-level work on the basis of other criteria, are enrolled in special preparatory courses. Their college expenses are paid and they are given an allowance as well. The SEEK preparatory courses are designed to make up for past economic and educational disadvantages by training the students with

[1] The principle of equality is discussed in the introduction to Chapter 4.

157

disadvantaged backgrounds to compete eventually in the regular college curriculum.

Compensatory measures have taken other forms as well. Governmental *affirmative action* and *equal opportunity* programs have been designed to eliminate the effects of past discrimination and to prevent further discrimination. Some of these compensatory programs have involved the *preferential treatment* of minority group members. That is, members of minority groups have been hired or admitted into educational institutions on the basis of criteria other than those used to evaluate the members of nonminority groups. One such case of preferential treatment resulted in the lawsuit by Marco DeFunis against the University of Washington Law School, which is included in the readings in this chapter.

DeFunis, a nonminority applicant, was denied admission to the University of Washington Law School's first-year law class in 1971. He filed a suit claiming that he had been unfairly discriminated against on the basis of race by the Admissions Committee of the Law School. Preferential treatment that year was accorded to blacks, American Indians, Chicanos, and Filipinos. The Law School had 150 available spaces in its first-year law class. There were 1,601 applicants. In order to enroll 150 students, 275 applicants were offered acceptances. Among the 275 who were accepted there were 37 minority applicants. Of these 37, 18 actually enrolled. The Law School Admission Test (LSAT) scores and Projected Grade Point Averages (PGAs) of almost all these minority applicants were lower than those of some of the rejected nonminority applicants. These nonminority applicants were denied admission simply because their PGAs and LSAT scores fell below a certain level. Minority applicants, however, whose scores fell even below the level of some rejected nonminority applicants were evaluated on the basis of other criteria and then admitted to the school.

The legal aspects of the case do not concern us here. They are presented in this chapter in Justice Neill's opinion and in Carl Cohen's discussion of the constitutionality of any preferential treatment programs based on racial or ethnic classifications. What primarily concerns us here is the ethical dilemma arising out of such preferential treatment programs. Consider our earlier discussion of the principle of equality. We said that when two or more individuals compete for the same position, some of the characteristics of these individuals are relevant to the position in question; other characteristics are not relevant. The principle of equality is violated whenever individuals are denied equal treatment simply on the basis of generally irrelevant characteristics such as sex or race. This is precisely what happened to Marco DeFunis. He was not accorded the same treatment as the members of the favored minority groups. If test scores (and not race or ethnic background) are the relevant characteristics when admission to law school is in question, the treatment of DeFunis was morally incorrect according to the principle of equality. The inequality of treatment accorded to individuals such as DeFunis is sometimes cited as an example of *reverse discrimination.* There is reverse discrimination whenever an action or a practice discriminates against an individual or a group on the basis of some normally irrelevant criterion (such as race, sex, or ethnic origin) because preference is being given to members of previously discriminated-against groups.

Compensatory programs which produce reverse discrimination may involve blanket preferential treatment or treatment that is more selective. Blanket preferential treatment is that extended to individuals simply because they are women or members of specified minority groups. Under such treatment no weight is given to the fact that a favored black or Chicano applicant may belong to a family with an income of $50,000 a year. But compensatory programs productive of reverse discrimination also may be more selective: preferential treatment may be extended to individuals only if two conditions are met. First, these individuals must be members of previously discriminated-against groups. Second, they must themselves have been individually disadvantaged educationally and economically. For example, a hiring or admission program could be set up in which preferential treatment would be extended only to those blacks whose family income fell below $5,000. But whether the preferential treatment is blanket or selective, compensatory measures involving such treatment may and often do result in reverse discrimination, and reverse discrimination violates the principle of equality. Thus, according to the principle of equality practices productive of reverse discrimination are not morally acceptable. But compensatory programs, as we noted above, are morally correct according to the principle of compensatory justice, and programs involving preferential treatment are one kind of compensatory program. So, the preferential treatment accorded to minority applicants by the University of Washington Law School may be viewed as morally correct according to the principle of compensatory justice, even though the treatment of nonminority applicants in these cases may be viewed as morally incorrect according to the principle of equality.

Ought we, then, as a matter of public policy, to institute compensatory programs which may produce reverse discrimination? That is, what is the morally correct course to adopt in a case such as this when the moral decision reached by an appeal to the principle of equality is at odds with the one reached by an appeal to the principle of compensatory justice? Some argue that the principle of equality always takes precedence. This is the position taken by Lisa Newton in this chapter. Reverse discrimination can never be justified, she claims, because such discrimination is not permitted by the principle of equality. Others maintain that under specified circumstances, the principle of compensatory justice takes precedence. The moral obligation to compensate for injustice justifies compensatory programs even when such programs result in reverse discrimination. In attempting to mediate these opposing claims, ethicists such as Tom L. Beauchamp in this chapter sometimes take a third approach. This approach involves the use of a third moral principle, the *principle of utility*.

According to the principle of utility, that action or practice is morally correct which in the circumstances produces the greatest possible balance of good over evil for the members of the group affected.

Suppose we need to decide whether or not there should be gun-control laws. We consider the consequences which might follow from such laws. Fewer accidental shootings and fewer homicides committed impulsively during family arguments are potential good consequences. Potential bad consequences of gun-control laws are also considered. For example, criminals will find some way to acquire guns, but law-abiding citizens will not possess such weapons. This will make storeowners and homeowners even more vulnerable to criminal attacks than they presently are. Suppose that after weighing all the possible consequences, we decide that the potential good consequences of gun-control laws outweigh the potential bad ones. Such laws will then be judged morally correct according to the principle of utility.

This kind of reasoning can be applied to the issues raised by compensatory programs productive of reverse discrimination. If the potential good consequences of such programs outweigh their potential bad consequences, then according to the principle of utility these programs are morally acceptable, and perhaps even morally required; but if the potential bad consequences outweigh the potential good ones, then such programs are morally unacceptable. The compensatory programs in question will produce good consequences, of course, insofar as they rectify past injustices and help to eliminate present and future discriminatory practices against blacks, women, Chicanos, and other favored minority groups. But they will also produce undesirable consequences, such as the denial of equal treatment to male applicants who do not belong to the favored minority groups. Among these applicants will be members of other minority groups which were also discriminated against in the past (eg., Poles, Italians, Irish, and Jews). The individuals in these latter groups will bear a large part of the burden of the cost of compensating the favored groups.

Another alleged undesirable consequence is the deterioration of economic, educational, and government institutions. Such deterioration will supposedly result if individuals are hired on the basis of race, sex, or ethnic origin rather than on the basis of individual merit. Sidney Hook in this chapter, for example, argues that the use of affirmative action programs to end sexual, racial, and ethnic discrimination will result in the hiring of the unqualified and the rejection of the qualified. Others deny that such consequences will follow from preferential treatment programs. They argue that, in fact, individual merit is not the decisive criterion in our present social situation when the qualifications of competing applicants are being weighed.

Those who like Beauchamp use the principle of utility to determine the moral correctness of preferential treatment programs must pay special attention to the factual questions raised by discussions of the potential consequences of such programs. They must attempt to answer questions such as the following. Is racial, sexual, and ethnic discrimination still prevalent in our society? If it is, can present discriminatory practices against women and minority applicants be eliminated without quota systems or other measures requiring preferential treatment? Are racist and sexist attitudes so pervasive in our society that mandatory quota systems are required to eliminate continued discrimination?

Answers to such factual questions are important in evaluating the potential consequences of either adopting or not adopting preferential treatment programs. The answers given help to determine the answer to the moral question: Can compensatory programs productive of reverse discrimination be justified by the principle of utility? If this question can be answered affirmatively, then we will have given one possible answer to the more general question: Can compensatory measures productive of reverse discrimination ever be morally justified?

J. S. Z.

Justice Marshall A. Neill

MAJORITY OPINION IN *DeFUNIS v. ODEGAARD*

Biographical Information. *Marshall A. Neill (b. 1914) was admitted to the Washington bar in 1938. He was a judge on the Washington Supreme Court from 1967 to 1972. Since then, he has served as a district judge in Spokane, Washington.*

Argument in the Selection. *The Marco Defunis v. Odegaard case is the first case involving "reverse discrimination" to come before the Supreme Court of the United States. After DeFunis was denied admission to the first-year law class of the University of Washington Law School in 1971, he filed suit against the university. DeFunis charged that he had been discriminated against simply on the basis of race. He had been denied admission to the law school while minority applicants with lower test scores were admitted. Because DeFunis was granted an injunction by a lower court enabling him to be enrolled by the University of Washington*

Law School, he was in his last semester of law school by the time the case reached the Supreme Court of the United States. Therefore, the case was declared moot by the Court since DeFunis would gain nothing even from a favorable verdict.

The opinion reprinted here is excerpted from the majority opinion of the Supreme Court of the State of Washington issued when that court ruled in favor of the University of Washington. In this opinion, Justice Neill expresses the following view: (1) Racial classifications are not unconstitutional in themselves. A state university can take race and ethnic background into account when considering applicants. (2) If there is a compelling state interest which can be served only through the use of racial classifications, such use is acceptable. (3) The shortage of minority attorneys and, therefore, also minority prosecutors, judges, and public officials constitutes an undeniably compelling state interest.

Broadly phrased, the major question presented herein is whether the law school may, in consonance with the equal protection provisions of the state and federal constitutions, consider the racial or ethnic background of applicants as one factor in the selection of students. . . .

In considering minority applicants, the committee was guided by a University-wide policy which sought to eliminate the continued effects of past segregation and discrimination against Blacks, Chicanos, American Indians and other disadvantaged racial and ethnic minority groups. At trial, the President of the University of Washington testified as to the origin of this policy:

> More and more it became evident to us that just an open door, as it were, at the point of entry to the University, somehow or other seemed insufficient to deal with what was emerging as the greatest internal problem of the United States of America, a problem which obviously could not be resolved without some kind of contribution being made not only by the schools, but obviously, also, by the colleges in the University and the University of Washington, in particular, given the racial distribution of this state. . . .
>
> So that was the beginning of a growing awareness that just an open-door sheer equality in view of the cultural circumstances that produced something other than equality, was not enough; that some more positive contribution had to be made to the resolution of this problem in American life, and something had to be done by the University of Washington.

Thus, the University sought to achieve a reasonable representation within the student body of persons from these groups which have been historically suppressed by encouraging their enrollment within the various programs offered at the University. Policies for admission of minorities throughout the University recognized that the conventional "mechanical" credentializing system does not always produce good indicators of the full potential of such culturally separated or deprived individuals, and that to rely solely on such formal credentials could well result in unfairly denying to qualified minority persons the chance to pursue the educational opportunities available at the University.

The law school sought to carry forward this University policy in its admission program, not only to obtain a reasonable representation from minorities within its classes, but to increase participation within the legal profession by persons from racial and ethnic groups which have been historically denied access to the profession and which, consequently, are grossly underrepresented within the legal system. In doing so, the Admissions Committee followed certain procedures which are the crux of plantiff's claimed denial of equal protection of the laws.

First, in reviewing the files of minority applicants, the committee attached less weight to the PFYA in making a total judgmental evaluation as to the relative ability of the particular applicant to succeed in law school. Also, the chairman testified that although the same standard was applied to all applicants (*i.e.*, the relative probability of the individual succeeding in law school), minority applicants were directly compared to one another, but were not compared to applicants outside of the minority group. The committee sought to identify, within the minority category, those persons who had the highest probability of succeeding in law school. Thus, the law school included within its admitted group minority applicants whose PFYAs were lower than those of some other applicants, but whose entire record showed the committee that they were capable of successfully completing the law school program.[1]

As a result of this process, the committee admitted a group of minority applicants, placed a group of such applicants on a waiting list, and rejected other minority applications. The dean of the law school testified that the law school has no fixed admissions quota for minority students, but that the committee sought a reasonable representation of such groups in the law school. He added that the law school has accepted no unqualified minority applicants, but only those whose records indicated that they were capable of successfully completing the law school program. . . .

The trial court found that some minority applicants with college grades and LSAT scores so low that had they been of the white race their applications would have been summarily denied, were given invitations for admission; that some such students were admitted instead of plaintiff; that since no more than 150 applicants were to be admitted to the law school, the admission of less qualified students resulted in a denial of places to those better qualified; and that plaintiff had better "qualifications" than many of the students admitted by the committee. The trial court also found that plaintiff was and is fully qualified and capable of satisfactorily attending the law school.

The trial court concluded . . . that, in denying plaintiff admission to the law school, the University of Washington discriminated against him and did not accord to him equal protection of the laws as guaranteed by the Fourteenth Amendment to the United States Constitution; and therefore, that plaintiff should be admitted to the law school for the class of 1974, beginning September 22, 1971. . . .

The essence of plaintiff's Fourteenth Amendment argument is that the law school violated his right to equal protection of the laws by denying him admission, yet accepting certain minority applicants with lower PFYAs than plaintiff who, but for their minority status, would not have been admitted.

---

[1] For example, many of the minority group applicants were first screened through special compensatory summer programs, operated primarily by CLEO.

To answer this contention we consider three implicit, subordinate questions: (A) whether race can ever be considered as one factor in the admissions policy of a state law school or whether racial classifications are *per se* unconstitutional because the equal protection of the laws requires that law school admissions be "colorblind"; (B) if consideration of race is not *per se* unconstitutional, what is the appropriate standard of review to be applied in determining the constitutionality of such a classification; and (C) when the appropriate standard is applied does the specific minority admissions policy employed by the law school pass constitutional muster? . . .

A

In Brown v. Board of Education (1954), the Supreme Court addressed a question of primary importance:

> Does segregation of children in public schools solely on the basis of race, even though the physical facilities and other "tangible" factors may be equal, deprive the children of the minority group of equal educational opportunities? We believe that it does.

The Court in *Brown* held the equal protection clause of the Fourteenth Amendment prohibits state law from requiring the operation of racially segregated, dual school systems of public education and requires that the system be converted into a unitary, nonracially segregated system. In so holding, the Court noted that segregation inevitably stigmatizes Black children:

> To separate them from others of similar age and qualifications solely because of their race generates a feeling of inferiority as to their status in the community that may affect their hearts and minds in a way unlikely ever to be undone.

Moreover, "The impact is greater when it has the sanction of the law; for the policy of separating the races is usually interpreted as denoting the inferiority of the negro group."

Brown did not hold that all racial classifications are *per se* unconstitutional; rather, it held that invidious racial classifications—i.e., those that stigmatize a racial group with the stamp of inferiority—are unconstitutional. Even viewed in a light most favorable to plaintiff, the "preferential" minority admissions policy administered by the law school is clearly not a form of invidious discrimination. The goal of this policy is not to separate the races, but to bring them together. And, as has been observed,

> Preferential admissions do not represent a covert attempt to stigmatize the majority race as inferior; nor is it reasonable to expect that a possible effect of the extension of educational preferences to certain disadvantaged racial minorities will be to stigmatize whites. . . .

While Brown v. Board of Education, *supra*, certainly provides a starting point for our analysis of the instant case, we do not agree with the trial court that *Brown* is dispositive here. Subsequent decisions of the United States Supreme Court have made it clear that in some circumstances a racial criterion *may* be used—and indeed in some circumstances *must* be used—by public educational institutions in bringing about racial balance. School systems which were formerly segregated de jure now have an affirmative duty to remedy racial imbalance. . . .

Thus, the Constitution is color conscious to prevent the perpetuation of discrimination and to undo the effects of past segregation. In holding invalid North Carolina's anti-bussing law, which flatly forbade assignment of any student on account of race or for the purpose of creating a racial balance or ratio in the schools and which prohibited bussing for such purposes, the Court stated:

> [T]he statute exploits an apparently neutral form to control school assignment plans by directing that they be "color blind"; that requirement, against the background of segregation, would render illusory the promise of Brown v. Board of Education. Just as the race of students must be considered in determining whether a constitutional violation has occurred, so also must race be considered in formulating a remedy. . . .

Clearly, consideration of race by school authorities does not violate the Fourteenth Amendment where the purpose is to bring together, rather than separate, the races. The "minority" admissions policy of the law school, aimed at insuring a reasonable representation of minority persons in the student body, is not invidious. Consideration of race is permissible to carry out the mandate of *Brown,* and, as noted, has been required in some circumstances. . . .

We conclude that the consideration of race as a factor in the admissions policy of a state law school is not a *per se* violation of the equal protection clause of the Fourteenth Amendment. We proceed, therefore, to the question of what standard of review is appropriate to determine the constitutionality of such a classification.

B

Generally, when reviewing a state-created classification alleged to be in violation of the equal protection clause of the Fourteenth Amendment, the question is whether the classification is reasonably related to a legitimate public purpose. And, in applying this "rational basis" test "[A] discrimination will not be set aside if any state of facts reasonably may be conceived to justify it."

However, where the classification is based upon race, a heavier burden of justification is imposed upon the state. In overturning Virginia's antimiscegenation law, the Supreme Court explained this stricter standard of review:

> The clear and central purpose of the Fourteenth Amendment was to eliminate all official state sources of invidious racial discrimination in the States.
> . . . At the very least, the Equal Protection Clause demands that racial classifications, especially suspect in criminal statutes, be subjected to the "most rigid scrutiny," [citation omitted] and, if they are ever to be upheld, they must be shown to be necessary to the accomplishment of some permissible state objective, independent of the racial discrimination which it was the object of the Fourteenth Amendment to eliminate . . .
> There is patently no legitimate overriding purpose independent of invidious racial discrimination which justifies this classification. . . .

165

It has been suggested that the less strict "rational basis" test should be applied to the consideration of race here, since the racial distinction is being used to redress the effects of past discrimination; thus, because the persons normally stigmatized by racial classifications are being benefited, the action complained of should be considered "benign" and reviewed under the more permissive standard. However, the minority admissions policy is certainly not benign with respect to nonminority students who are displaced by it. The burden is upon the law school to show that its consideration of race in admitting students is necessary to the accomplishment of a compelling state interest.

C

It can hardly be gainsaid that the minorities have been, and are, grossly underrepresented in the law schools—and consequently in the legal profession—of this state and this nation. We believe the state has an overriding interest in promoting integration in public education. In light of the serious underrepresentation of minority groups in the law schools, and considering that minority groups participate on an equal basis in the tax support of the law school, we find the state interest in eliminating racial imbalance within public legal education to be compelling. . . .

The legal profession plays a critical role in the policy making sector of our society, whether decisions be public or private, state or local. That lawyers, in making and influencing these decisions, should be cognizant of the views, needs and demands of all segments of society is a principle beyond dispute. The educational interest of the state in producing a racially balanced student body at the law school is compelling.

Finally, the shortage of minority attorneys—and, consequently, minority prosecutors, judges and public officials—constitutes an undeniably compelling state interest. If minorities are to live within the rule of law, they must enjoy equal representation within our legal system.

Once a constitutionally valid state interest has been established, it remains for the state to show the requisite connection between the racial classification employed and that interest. The consideration of race in the law school admissions policy meets the test of necessity here because racial imbalance in the law school and the legal profession is the evil to be corrected, and it can only be corrected by providing legal education to those minority groups which have been previously deprived.

It has been suggested that the minority admissions policy is not necessary, since the same objective could be accomplished by improving the elementary and secondary education of minority students to a point where they could secure equal representation in law schools through direct competition with nonminority applicants on the basis of the same academic criteria. This would be highly desirable, but 18 years have passed since the decision in Brown v. Board of Education, *supra*, and minority groups are still grossly underrepresented in law schools. If the law school is forbidden from taking affirmative action, this underrepresentation may be perpetuated indefinitely. No less restrictive means would serve the governmental interest here; we believe the minority admissions policy of the law school to be the only feasible "plan that promises realistically to work, and promises realistically to work *now.*"

We conclude that defendants have shown the necessity of the racial classification herein to the accomplishment of an overriding state interest, and have thus sustained the heavy burden imposed upon them under the equal protection provision of the Fourteenth Amendment.

There remains a further question as to the scope of the classification. A validly drawn classification is one "which includes all [and only those] persons who are similarly situated with respect to the purpose of the law." The classification used by defendants does not include all racial minorities, but only four (Blacks, Chicanos, Indians and Philippine Americans). However, the purpose of the racial classification here is to give special consideration to those racial minority groups which are underrepresented in the law schools and legal profession, and which cannot secure proportionate representation if strictly subjected to the standardized mathematical criteria for admission to the law school.

In selecting minority groups for special consideration, the law school sought to identify those groups most in need of help. The chairman of the admissions committee testified that Asian-Americans, e. g., were not treated as minority applicants for admissions purposes since a significant number could be admitted on the same basis as general applicants. In light of the purpose of the minority admissions policy, the racial classification need not include all racial minority groups. The state may identify and correct the most serious examples of racial imbalance, even though in so doing it does not provide an immediate solution to the entire problem of equal representation within the legal system.

We hold that the minority admissions policy of the law school, and the denial by the law school of admission to plaintiff, violate neither the equal protection clause of the Fourteenth Amendment to the United States Constitution nor Article 1, § 12 of the Washington State Constitution.

QUESTIONS

1. Should the goods of society (such as job and educational opportunities) be dispensed simply on the basis of individual talent and merit?
2. Give reasons to justify having two sets of criteria for judging applicants to institutions of higher learning.

Carl Cohen

RACE AND THE CONSTITUTION

Biographical Information. *Carl Cohen is an associate professor of philosophy at the University of Michigan. He is the author of* Democracy *and*

Civil Disobedience: Conscience, Tactics and the Law *as well as editor of* Communism, Fascism, and Democracy: The Theoretical Foundations.

Argument in the Selection. Cohen criticizes the decision in the DeFunis case and argues that classification on the basis of race for purposes of law school admissions or the distribution of other benefits under the laws is per se unconstitutional. Preferential admission systems, although intended to achieve important ends, are unconstitutional since they result in the discriminatory distribution of benefits on the basis of race or ethnicity. Cohen notes that at different times some particular objective — such as national security or racial justice—will seem to provide a compelling reason to justify a practice violating constitutional rights. He cautions that sacrificing a constitutional principle in order to achieve some honorable end will weaken the force of the principle and the fragile network of principles that is constitutional government.

Much controversy in the *DeFunis* case arose over the operating procedures of this particular Law School, the qualifications of the student members of its Admissions Committee, and so on. DeFunis claimed (and some justices strongly agreed) that the entire process in the Law School, apart from the matter of racial classification, was arbitrary and capricious. He was not sustained in this. The issue, although a fascinating sidelight on university practice, was not central to the main thrust of the decision.

That decision could have gone the other way. A minority of the Washington Supreme Court, led by its Chief Justice, expressed dissenting judgment firmly. Justice William Douglas of the U.S. Supreme Court (concurring with Justices Brennan, Marshall and White that the case was not moot), separately attacked the Law School's efforts to effect proportional representation based on race or ethnicity. But a full response to the Washington Court, developed with careful attention to the logic of its argument, has been missing. I try now to supply that want.

Each of the three steps of that argument must be questioned. Preferential treatment for some racial or ethnic groups is what the words of the U.S. Constitution, given their plainest meaning, seem to prohibit. A great burden clearly falls upon those who defend such preference. If the chain constructed by the Court to carry that burden breaks at any link, the case falls. In fact, upon careful scrutiny— and in spite of the most laudable aims of the Law School and the Court—not one, but all three of the links in their argument crumble.

... Are classifications on the basis of race, for purposes of law school admission and the like, *per se* unconstitutional? The correct answer is yes. Indeed, the Fourteenth Amendment was deliberately formulated to prohibit precisely such classifications. The Constitution is and always must be, in that sense, color blind. It cannot be, from time to time and at the discretion of certain agencies or administrators, color conscious in order to become color blind at some future date. The principle that a person's race is simply not relevant in the application of the laws is a treasured one. If we are prepared to sacrifice that principle now and then, in an attempt to achieve some very pressing and very honorable objective, we will have given up its force as constitutional principle. No doubt intentions here are of the best, but so, often, are the intentions of those who would from time to time sacrifice other constitutional principles for the attainment of other very worthy ends. The enforcement of justice, the redistribution of wealth, the very protection of the nation, might all be more conveniently, more efficiently, even more effectively accomplished if, from time to time, we winked at the Constitution and did what, as we will be told with honest fervor, is of absolutely overriding importance. In this way is the Congressional authority to declare war conveniently ignored; in this way is the constitutional protection of our persons, houses, papers and effects from unreasonable search and seizure effectively (of course only temporarily) by-passed. In this way, in sum, constitutional government, fragile network of principles that it is, comes apart.

But, some will reply, those other objectives—national security, protection against crime, etc.—are only claimed to be compelling; racial justice, so long deliberately denied, really is so. Of course. And every person and every group has, at some time, objectives that are, to its complete and profound conviction, so utterly compelling that nothing must be allowed to stand in the way of their accomplishment.[1] But every such party must yield in turn to the restrictions of constitutional government; if those in authority do not enforce these restrictions, the Constitution is but paper. A constitution, ideally, is not an expression of particular social ends; rather, it identifies very general common purposes and lays down principles according to which the many specific ends of the body politic may be decided upon and pursued. Its most critical provisions will be those which absolutely preclude certain means. Thus to say that a protection afforded citizens is "constitutional" is at least to affirm that it will be respected, come what may. The specific constitutional provision that each citizen is entitled to equal protection of the laws is assurance that, no matter how vital the government alleges its interest to be, or how laudable the objective of those who would temporarily suspend that principle, it will stand. The highest obligation to respect it is owed by public institutions and government agencies.[2]

Preferential admission systems present instances of this sometimes agonizing tension between important ends and impermissible means. Hence the persuasiveness of the argument on both sides. In facing dilemmas of this kind long experience has taught the supremacy of the procedural principle. With societies, as with individuals, the use of means in themselves corrupt tends to corrupt the user, and

---

[1] Justice Douglas, in his dissenting opinion in *DeFunis* writes: "The argument is that a 'compelling' state interest can justify the racial discrimination that is practiced here. . . . If discrimination based on race is constitutionally permissible when those who hold the reins can come up with 'compelling' reasons to justify it, then constitutional guarantees acquire an accordionlike quality." [40 L. Ed 2d 184.]

[2] The only previous suspension of this constitutional protection was a national moral disaster. To meet the alleged danger of sabotage and espionage during the Second World War, American citizens of Japanese descent were peremptorily rounded up, moved, and excluded from large sections of our West Coast. The Supreme Court was pained, but found this roundup and detention justified by "pressing public necessity." (*Korematsu v. United States,* 323 U.S. 216, 1944.) Never before or since has the use of race in applying constitutional protection been expressly approved by our highest Court.

to infect the result. So it is with wiretapping, with censorship, with torture. So it is with discriminatory preference by racial grouping for racial balance.

But this is racial classification, the Court insisted, not racial discrimination. The latter is indeed ruled out, said they, but the former is not; *Brown* and other powerful precedents forbid invidious racial classification, not all racial classification. This argument misses the central point—the sharpest bite of *Brown* and like cases—that in the distribution of benefits under the laws *all* racial classifications are necessarily invidious. Invidious distinctions are those tending to excite ill will, or envy, those likely to be viewed as unfair—and that is what racial classifications are likely to do and be when used as instrument for the apportionment of goods or opportunities.

Perhaps the Court would respond: Some such invidiousness is difficult to deny, but our main point is that the racial classifications condemned by *Brown* and succeeding cases are those that stigmatize one of the groups distinguished, stamping it with inferiority. But the change of phrase provides no rescue. To stigmatize is to brand, or label, generally with disgrace—and that is exactly what is done by racial classification in this context. Indeed, put to the service of preferential admissions such classification is doubly stigmatizing. It marks one racial group as formally to be handicapped, its members burdened specifically by virtue of race; for the majority applicant (as formerly for the minority) earned personal qualifications will not be enough. Persons in the other racial category are to be officially treated as though unable to compete for the good in question on an equal basis; by physical characteristic the minority applicant is marked as in need of special help. On both sides morale is subverted, accomplishments clouded. On the one side all carry the handicap, regardless of their past deeds or capacity to bear it; on the other, all are received with the supposition of inferiority, regardless of their personal attainments or hatred of condescension. For all, the stigmata are visually prominent and permanent.[3]

I conclude that the first and fundamental step of the Court's argument in defense of preferential admissions cannot be justly taken. Racial classifications, in the application of the laws, or in the distribution of benefits under the laws, are always invidious, always stigmatizing. That is why they are, *per se*, unconstitutional. . . .

Preferential admission procedures certainly do result in the discriminatory apportionment of benefits on the basis of race or ethnicity. When any resource is in short supply, and some by virtue of their race are given more of it, others by virtue of their race get less. If that resource be seats in a law school, procedures that assure preference to certain racial groups in allotting those seats necessarily produce a correlative denial of access to those not in the preferred categories. This plain consequence should not be overlooked. Whether the numbers be fixed or flexible; whether "quotas" be established and called "benign"; whether they be measured by percentages or absolute quantities; whether the objective be "reasonable proportionality" or "appropriate representation"—the setting of benefit

[3] Justice Douglas writes in his dissenting opinion: "A segregated admission process creates suggestions of stigma and caste no less than a segregated classroom, and in the end it may produce that result despite its contrary intentions. . . . [T]hat Blacks or Browns cannot make it on their individual merit . . . is a stamp of inferiority that a state is not permitted to place on any lawyer." [40 L Ed 2d 184.]

floors for some groups in this context inescapably entails benefit ceilings for other groups.

By fuzzing the numbers and softening the names some manage to hide this conclusion from themselves. The majority of the Washington Court, to their credit, did not do that. Although eager to minimize the discriminatory character of the instrument, they recognized candidly its inevitable result. They wrote: "The minority admissions policy is certainly not benign with respect to non-minority students who are displaced by it." Preference by race is malign; its malignity has no clearer or more fitting name than racism. Widespread in American universities, this well-meant racism will indeed be found, upon reflection, to deny the equal protection of the laws. . . .

QUESTIONS

1. Cohen claims that worthwhile ends do not justify social policies which violate constitutional principles. Is he correct?
2. Is all racial classification invidious as Cohen maintains?

Sidney Hook

DISCRIMINATION AGAINST THE QUALIFIED?

A biographical sketch of Sidney Hook is found on page 95.

Argument in the Selection. Sidney Hook argues against reverse discrimination. He criticizes some government attempts to end sexual, racial, ethnic, and religious discrimination by institutions of higher learning. (1) Hook questions the validity of inferring the existence of discriminatory practices from statistical evidence about the number of women and minority group members employed on university teaching and research staffs. (2) He criticizes what he takes to be one of the consequences of preferential treatment programs—the hiring of the less qualified rather than the more qualified. Merit is the only criterion, Hook claims, which should be used in judging applicants.

Every humane and fair-minded person must approve of the Presidential Executive Order of 1965 which forbade discrimination with respect to race, religion, national origin or sex by any organization or group that receives financial support from the Government in the course of fulfilling its contractual obligations with it.

171

The difficulties in enforcing this order flow not from its ethical motivation and intent, but in establishing the criteria of evidence that discrimination has been practiced. Very rarely are the inequities explicitly expressed in the provisions guiding or regulating employment. They must be inferred.

There is, unfortunately, evidence that some foolish and unperceptive persons in the office of civil rights of the Department of Health, Education and Welfare are mechanically inferring from actual figures of academic employment in institutions of higher learning the existence of discriminatory practices. What is worse, they are threatening to cancel Federal financial support, without which many universities cannot survive, unless, within a certain period of time, the proportion of members of minorities on the teaching and research staffs of universities approximate their proportion in the general population.

In the light of this evidence, a persuasive case can be made that those who have issued these guidelines and ultimata to universities, whether they are male or female, black or white, Catholic, Jewish or Protestant are unqualified for the offices they hold and therefore unable properly to enforce the Presidential Executive Order. For they are guilty of fostering the very racialism and discrimination the Executive Order was issued to correct and forestall. The faculties of many Negro colleges are overwhelmingly black out of all proportion to their numbers in the country, state, or even local community. It would be a grim jest therefore to tax them with discriminatory practices. Until recently, they have been pathetically eager to employ qualified white teachers, but they have been unable to attract them.

The fact that H.E.W. makes a distinction between women and minorities, judging sexual discrimination not by simple proportion of women teachers and researchers in universities to their proportion in the general population, but only to their proportion among applicants, shows that it has a dim understanding of the relevant issue. There are obviously various occupational fields—military, mining, aeronautical—for which women have, until now, shown little inclination. Neither the schools nor the department can be faulted for the scarcity of female applications. But the main point is this: no matter how many applicants there are for a post, whether they are male or female, the only relevant criterion is whether or not they are qualified.

The effect of the ultimata to universities to hire blacks and women under threat of losing crucial financial support is to compel them to hire unqualified Negroes and women and to discriminate against qualified nonblacks and men. This is just as much a manifestation of racism, even if originally unintended, as the racism the original Presidential directive was designed to correct. Intelligent, self-respecting Negroes and women would scorn such preferential treatment.

The universities should not yield to the illiberal ultimata of the office of civil rights of H.E.W. There is sufficient work for it to do in enforcing the Presidential directive in areas where minorities are obviously qualified and are obviously suffering from unfair discrimination. It undoubtedly is true that some educational institutions or their departments have been guilty of obvious religious and racial discrimination. The evidence of this was flagrant and open and required no elaborate questionnaires to establish.

The office of civil rights could cooperate with the Department of Justice here. Currently, its activities in the field of higher education are not only wasting time, effort, and the taxpayer's money but debasing educational standards as well.

QUESTIONS

1. Two candidates are applying for a position in a law office. Both of them meet the appropriate criteria, but one of them is an Anglo-Saxon male and the other is a black woman. Which one ought to get the position? Justify your answer by using some or all of the following three ethical principles: (a) the principle of equality, (b) the principle of compensatory justice, (c) the principle of utility.

2. Argue for or against the following set of claims: (a) The use of quotas will result in the hiring of the "unqualified" and the rejection of the "qualified." (b) This will lead to the deterioration of the educational, political, and economic institutions in our society. (c) Therefore, we should not use quota systems.

Lisa H. Newton

REVERSE DISCRIMINATION AS UNJUSTIFIED

Biographical Information. Lisa H. Newton teaches at Fairfield University, where she is an associate professor of philosophy. Among her publications is "Dimensions of a Right of Revolution," published in the Journal of Value Inquiry, vol. 7, Spring 1973.

Argument in the Selection. Newton makes the following claims in arguing against programs productive of reverse discrimination: (1) All discrimination, including reverse discrimination, is wrong because it violates the principle of equality. (2) The practice of reverse discrimination raises insoluble problems. Among these problems are the difficulties in determining both (a) which groups have been sufficiently discriminated against in the past to warrant preferential treatment in the present and (b) the amount of reverse discrimination which will compensate the favored groups for the initial discrimination.

I have heard it argued that "simple justice" requires that we favor women and blacks in employment and educational opportunities, since women and blacks were "unjustly" excluded from such opportunities for so many years in the not so distant past. It is a strange argument, an example of a possible implication of a true proposition advanced to dispute the proposition itself, like an octopus absent-mindedly slicing off his head with a stray tentacle. A fatal confusion underlies this argument, a confusion fundamentally relevant to our understanding of the notion of the rule of law.

Two senses of justice and equality are involved in this confusion. The root notion of justice, progenitor of the other, is the one that Aristotle (*Nichomachean*

Ethics 5.6; *Politics* 1.2; 3.1) assumes to be the foundation and proper virtue of the political association. It is the condition which free men establish among themselves when they "share a common life in order that their association bring them self-sufficiency"—the regulation of their relationship by law, and the establishment, by law, of equality before the law. Rule of law is the name and pattern of this justice; its equality stands against the inequalities—of wealth, talent, etc.—otherwise obtaining among its participants, who by virtue of that equality are called "citizens." It is an achievement—complete, or, more frequently, partial—of certain people in certain concrete situations. It is fragile and easily disrupted by powerful individuals who discover that the blind equality of rule of law is inconvenient for their interests. Despite its obvious instability, Aristotle assumed that the establishment of justice in this sense, the creation of citizenship, was a permanent possibility for men and that the resultant association of citizens was the natural home of the species. At levels below the political association, this rule-governed equality is easily found; it is exemplified by any group of children agreeing together to play a game. At the level of the political association, the attainment of this justice is more difficult, simply because the stakes are so much higher for each participant. The equality of citizenship is not something that happens of its own accord, and without the expenditure of a fair amount of effort it will collapse into the rule of a powerful few over an apathetic many. But at least it has been achieved, at some times in some places; it is always worth trying to achieve, and eminently worth trying to maintain, wherever and to whatever degree it has been brought into being.

Aristotle's parochialism is notorious; he really did not imagine that persons other than Greeks could associate freely in justice, and the only form of association he had in mind was the Greek *polis*. With the decline of the *polis* and the shift in the center of political thought, his notion of justice underwent a sea change. To be exact, it ceased to represent a political type and became a moral ideal: the ideal of equality as we know it. This ideal demands that all men be included in citizenship—that one Law govern all equally, that all men regard all other men as fellow citizens, with the same guarantees, rights, and protections. Briefly, it demands that the circle of citizenship achieved by any group be extended to include the entire human race. Properly understood, its effect on our associations can be excellent: it congratulates us on our achievement of rule of law as a process of government but refuses to let us remain complacent until we have expanded the associations to include others within the ambit of the rules, as often and as far as possible. While one man is a slave, none of us may feel truly free. We are constantly prodded by this ideal to look for possible unjustifiable discrimination, for inequalities not absolutely required for the functioning of the society and advantageous to all. And after twenty centuries of pressure, not at all constant, from this ideal, it might be said that some progress has been made. To take the cases in point for this problem, we are now prepared to assert, as Aristotle would never have been, the equality of sexes and of persons of different colors. The ambit of American citizenship, once restricted to white males of property, has been extended to include all adult free men, then all adult males including ex-slaves, then all women. The process of acquisition of full citizenship was for these groups a sporadic trail of half-measures, even now not complete; the steps on the road to full equality are marked by legislation and judicial decisions which are only recently concluded and still often not enforced. But the fact that we can now discuss the possibility of favoring such groups in hiring shows that over the area that concerns us, at least, full equality is presupposed as a basis for discussion. To that extent, they are full citizens, fully protected by the law of the land.

It is important for my argument that the moral ideal of equality be recognized as logically distinct from the condition (or virtue) of justice in the political sense. Justice in this sense exists *among* a citizenry, irrespective of the number of the populace included in that citizenry. Further, the moral ideal is parasitic upon the political virtue, for "equality" is unspecified—it means nothing until we are told in what respect that equality is to be realized. In a political context, "equality" is specified as "equal rights"—equal access to the public realm, public goods and offices, equal treatment under the law—in brief, the equality of citizenship. If citizenship is not a possibility, political equality is unintelligible. The ideal emerges as a generalization of the real condition and refers back to that condition for its content.

Now, if justice (Aristotle's justice in the political sense) is equal treatment under law for all citizens, what is injustice? Clearly, injustice is the violation of that equality, discriminating for or against a group of citizens, favoring them with special immunities and privileges or depriving them of those guaranteed to the others. When the southern employer refuses to hire blacks in white-collar jobs, when Wall Street will only hire women as secretaries with new titles, when Mississippi high schools routinely flunk all black boys above ninth grade, we have examples of injustice, and we work to restore the equality of the public realm by ensuring that equal opportunity will be provided in such cases in the future. But of course, when the employers and the schools *favor* women and blacks, the same injustice is done. Just as the previous discrimination did, this reverse discrimination violates the public equality which defines citizenship and destroys the rule of law for the areas in which these favors are granted. To the extent that we adopt a program of discrimination, reverse or otherwise, justice in the political sense is destroyed, and none of us, specifically affected or not, is a citizen, a bearer of rights—we are all petitioners for favors. And to the same extent, the ideal of equality is undermined, for it has content only where justice obtains, and by destroying justice we render the ideal meaningless. It is, then, an ironic paradox, if not a contradiction in terms, to assert that the ideal of equality justifies the violation of justice; it is as if one should argue, with William Buckley, that an ideal of humanity can justify the destruction of the human race.

Logically, the conclusion is simple enough: all discrimination is wrong prima facie because it violates justice, and that goes for reverse discrimination too. No violation of justice among the citizens may be justified (may overcome the prima facie objection) by appeal to the ideal of equality, for that ideal is logically dependent upon the notion of justice. Reverse discrimination, then, which attempts no other justification than an appeal to equality, is wrong. But let us try to make the conclusion more plausible by suggesting some of the implications of the suggested practice of reverse discrimination in employment and education. My argument will be that the problems raised there are insoluble, not only in practice but in principle.

We may argue, if we like, about what "discrimination" consists of. Do I discriminate against blacks if I admit none to my school when none of the black applicants are qualified by the tests I always give? How far must I go to root out cultural bias from my application forms and tests before I can say that I have not discriminated against those of different cultures? Can I assume that women are not strong enough to be roughnecks on my oil rigs, or must I test them individually? But this controversy, the most popular and well-argued aspect of the issue, is not as fatal as two others which cannot be avoided: if we are regarding the blacks as a "minority" victimized by discrimination, what is a "minority"? And for any group—blacks, women, whatever—that has been discriminated against, what amount of reverse discrimination wipes out the initial discrimination? Let us grant as true that women and blacks were discriminated against, even where laws forbade such discrimination, and grant for the sake of argument that a history of discrimination must be wiped out by reverse discrimination. What follows?

First, are there other groups which have been discriminated against? For they should have the same right of restitution. What about American Indians, Chicanos, Appalachian Mountain whites, Puerto Ricans, Jews, Cajuns, and Orientals? And if these are to be included, the principle according to which we specify a "minority" is simply the criterion of "ethnic (sub) group," and we're stuck with every hyphenated American in the lower-middle class clamoring for special privileges for *his* group—and with equal justification. For be it noted, when we run down the Harvard roster, we find not only a scarcity of blacks (in comparison with the proportion in the population) but an even more striking scarcity of those second-, third-, and fourth-generation ethnics who make up the loudest voice of Middle America. Shouldn't they demand *their* share? And eventually, the WASPs will have to form their own lobby, for they too are a minority. The point is simply this: there is no "majority" in America who will not mind giving up just a bit of their rights to make room for a favored minority. There are only other minorities, each of which is discriminated against by the favoring. The initial injustice is then repeated dozens of times, and if each minority is granted the same right of restitution as the others, an entire area of rule governance is dissolved into a pushing and shoving match between self-interested groups. Each works to catch the public eye and political popularity by whatever means of advertising and power politics lend themselves to the effort, to capitalize as much as possible on temporary popularity until the restless mob picks another group to feel sorry for. Hardly an edifying spectacle, and in the long run no one can benefit: the pie is no larger—it's just that instead of setting up and enforcing rules for getting a piece, we've turned the contest into a free-for-all, requiring much more effort for no larger a reward. It would be in the interests of all the participants to reestablish an objective rule to govern the process, carefully enforced and the same for all.

Second, supposing that we do manage to agree in general that women and blacks (and all the others) have some right of restitution, some right to a privileged place in the structure of opportunities for a while, how will we know when that while is up? How much privilege is enough? When will the guilt be gone, the price paid, the balance restored? What recompense is right for centuries of exclusion? What criterion tells us when we are done? Our experience with the Civil Rights movement shows us that agreement on these terms cannot be presupposed: a process that appears to some to be going at a mad gallop into a black takeover appears to the rest of us to be at a standstill. Should a practice of reverse discrimination be adopted, we may safely predict that just as some of us begin to see "a satisfactory start toward righting the balance," others of us will see that we "have already gone too far in the other direction" and will suggest that the discrimination ought to be reversed again. And such disagreement is inevitable, for the point is that we could not *possibly* have any criteria for evaluating the kind of recompense we have in mind. The context presumed by any discussion of restitution is the context of rule of law: law sets the rights of men and simultaneously sets the method for remedying the violation of those rights. You may exact suffering from others and/or damage payments for yourself if and only if the others have violated your rights; the suffering you have endured is not sufficient reason for them to suffer. And remedial rights exist only where there is law: primary human rights are useful guides to legislation but cannot stand as reasons for awarding remedies for injuries sustained. But then, the context presupposed by any discussion of restitution is the context of preexistent full citizenship. No remedial rights could exist for the excluded; neither in law nor in logic does there exist a right to *sue* for a standing to sue.

From these two considerations, then, the difficulties with reverse discrimination become evident. Restitution for a disadvantaged group whose rights under the law have been violated is possible by legal means, but restitution for a disadvantaged group whose grievance is that there was no law to protect them simply is not. First, outside of the area of justice defined by the law, no sense can be made of "the group's rights," for no law recognizes that group or the individuals in it, qua members, as bearers of rights (hence *any* group can constitute itself as a disadvantaged minority in some sense and demand similar restitution). Second, outside of the area of protection of law, no sense can be made of the violation of rights (hence the amount of the recompense cannot be decided by any objective criterion). For both reasons, the practice of reverse discrimination undermines the foundation of the very ideal in whose name it is advocated; it destroys justice, law, equality, and citizenship itself, and replaces them with power struggles and popularity contests.

QUESTIONS

1. Specify criteria for determining that a group had been sufficiently discriminated against in the past to warrant preferential treatment in the present.

2. Argue for or against the following set of claims: (a) The present economic and social status of blacks is a disadvantaged one. (b) This present unfavorable status is the result of past discriminatory treatment. (c) Therefore, we ought to institute programs which will improve the social and economic status of blacks even if such programs produce reverse discrimination.

Irving Thalberg

VISCERAL RACISM

Biographical Information. *Irving Thalberg is a professor of philosophy at the University of Illinois, Chicago Circle. He was educated at Stanford*

177

University and has taught at Oberlin College and the University of Washington. Thalberg is a member of the American Civil Liberties Union and NAACP. He is the author of Enigmas of Agency *and numerous articles. His interest in social issues is reflected not only in the article from which this selection is excerpted but also in "Justifications of Institutional Racism"* (Philosophical Forum, *1971–1972).*

Argument in the Selection. Thalberg is concerned with the lack of progress made by blacks. He ascribes this lack of progress to "visceral racism"—a set of unacknowledged attitudes held by "unprejudiced" whites. These attitudes, he maintains, blind visceral racists to social inequalities which are obvious to blacks. Whites simply do not perceive themselves as privileged in comparison to blacks. Therefore, they do not see that measures need to be taken to eliminate inequalities. Thalberg distinguishes between white supremacists and visceral racists. The former group recognizes inequalities and wants to preserve them. The latter simply fail to perceive them.

At a meeting shortly before his death, Malcolm X was asked by a young white listener: "What contribution can youth, especially students who are disgusted with racism, make to the black struggle for freedom?" Malcolm X's reply has become a familiar one: "Whites who are sincere should organize among themselves and figure out some strategy to break down prejudice that exists in white communities. . . . This has never been done."[1]

I will not offer strategies, but I will do what I can with fairly standard philosophical techniques to delineate one target for action. I hope that the social phenomenon I analyze is what polemical writers had in view when they coined the term 'visceral racism.' At any rate the phenomenon is worth bringing into sharper focus; and therefore I will keep the emotively charged term 'racism' out of my discussion as much as possible. Nevertheless when I do for convenience use the expression 'visceral racism', I want it to be clear that I am not belaboring old-fashioned white supremacy doctrines and practices. Adherents of white supremacy are still both numerous and influential; but I doubt that further analysis is needed to understand or to attack their position. What I examine here is more protectively camouflaged and philosophically challenging. . . .

By visceral racism I will mean a set of unacknowledged attitudes that afflict me and most other 'unprejudiced' whites, especially middle-class liberals. These attitudes are mainly dispositions to perceive and to describe social events in which black people figure. Our most noticeable proclivities are, first, to structure and report such events in a manner that 'screens out' social inequalities which are glaringly evident to black observers; and secondly to represent black people as helplessly dependent upon the white majority. The overall tendency is for 'visceral' whites to regard themselves as doing just about as well as can be expected

[1] In G. Breitman, ed., *Malcolm X Speaks* (New York: Grove Press, 1966), p. 221.

with 'the race problem'. Of course they never regard themselves as the problem! Examples will emphasize how the visceral racist does not want to think of himself as hostile toward blacks or indifferent to their individual and collective aspirations.

This sketch explains why the visceral inclinations that I shall analyze here are not dissimulated white supremacy attitudes. To recognize your viscerally racist dispositions is *not* to avow that deep down you think black people are all over-sexed savages, or that you really like the caste system we have. It is to notice the protective cocoon of ignorance and distortion that we have spun about ourselves. . . .

I want to answer a natural objection from liberal white readers. Many will indignantly complain, "I've never had any hostile feelings toward black people, so how can you call me a visceral or any other kind of racist?" . . .

The visceral racist will not throw a brick through the window of a new black neighbor. He won't assault black children who are bussed to the neighborhood school. But what does he do to protect them? Doesn't he let the redneck do his dirty-work for him? In general, doesn't he support institutions that oppress black people in nearly every area of social life? Right; and that is why I want to diagnose his visceral inclinations to misperceive our society as progressing with all deliberate speed toward equality.

For the benefit of nonmilitants, I will explain briefly the claim that there is almost no practical difference for the majority of blacks under liberals and their 'reformed' institutions, in comparison with the old days. No doubt there are more lucky blacks who 'make it' nowadays. Certainly more vote. Fewer lynchings occur. Blacks are no longer obliged to display humility and gratitude. Otherwise the statistics on the vast *majority* of black people in America show little alteration. Except for temporary economic gains during World War II and the Korean War, most blacks have continued to enjoy a very small share of the nation's fabled prosperity. Typically, the 500 largest industrial corporations earn around 40% of the gross national product. About 7,000 companies with 100 or more employees do 90% of manufacturing and 80% of the sales. About 1.6% of the population owns more than 80% of the stock of these top corporations and others. As you would expect, members of this group control corporate and government policy. Blacks have not gotten into this 1.6% group that owns and runs the country. The few whites who belong to it are usually inheritors of wealth. Most stock ends up in the hands of white women, because of their longevity.[2]

Turning to black wage-earners, experts attribute to them between 55% and 70% of the salary that whites receive for equivalent work.[3] Incidentally, the

---

[2] For convenient and abundant documentation, largely based on government statistics and other 'respectable' sources, consult Ferdinand Lundberg, *The Rich and the Super Rich* (New York: Bantam Books, 1969), esp. pp. 12–20, 295–298, 354–355, 927–946.

[3] The lower figure is given by Thomas F. Mayer, on the basis of U.S. Bureau of Census figures for 1939 and 1947–62, in his useful résumé, "The Position and Progress of Black America," reprinted by Radical Education Project (Ann Arbor, 1967). *The Report of the National Advisory Commission on Civil Disorders* (Washington, D.C.: Government Printing Office, 1968) gives the higher figure for 23 cities it surveyed. Since Mayer draws upon a wide variety of official and scholarly sources, I generally paraphrase his summary of the situation in jobs, housing, and education.

percentage *declines* when we consider blacks with 'higher' positions and more formal education, thus refuting the myth that serious study and 'drive' will be differentially rewarded. Working-class blacks are twice as likely to be unemployed or laid off. In nearly every profession—including our own, academic philosophy—blacks are grossly under-represented. The same is true with skilled trades. Labor unions have driven blacks out of some fields. This happened with locomotive engineers and firemen in the South. Construction workers' unions have kept blacks out. And in automotive industry, unions have confined blacks to low-paying no-seniority positions.[4]

Black consumers face similar hindrances. They pay more to buy or rent deteriorated housing. Mortgages are nearly unavailable to a black homebuyer. If he obtains one, he will pay higher interest than whites do. Neighborhood segregation is rising, and black children attend increasingly segregated schools, where considerably less is spent per pupil than in white areas. Barely 2% of elective offices at all levels of government are held by blacks—and this marks a relatively big step forward during the last few years. In their relations with government, notably police, most blacks have made no progress at all. Black citizens and property-owners are virtually without police protection, while harrassment from police has grown. Ten to seventeen times as many black people are arrested for major violent crimes.[5] Large numbers, including 'bystanders', fall victims of unprovoked attacks by police. Their property rights, and Fourth Amendment immunity to arbitrary search and seizure, are violated constantly by police. Blacks still constitute the majority of the more than 200,000 inmates of federal and state prisons and reformatories, and are the least likely to have received an impartial trial.

All in all, this lack of progress since the passing of white supremacy appears to confirm Dr. King's foreboding. He wrote in 1963:

> I have almost reached the regrettable conclusion that the Negro's great stumbling block in the stride toward freedom is not the White Citizen's Counciler or the Ku Klux Klanner, but the white moderate who is more devoted to "order" than to justice. . . . Shallow understanding from people of goodwill is more frustrating than absolute misunderstanding from people of ill will.[6]

It's hard to believe that the visceral racist manages to ignore all this. But as I shall illustrate, he sometimes even turns the situation upside down, and imagines

---

[4] For typical railroad cases, see *Steele v. L. and N. R. Co.*, 323 U.S. 192 (1944), and *Railroad Trainmen v. Howard*, 343 U.S. 768 (1951). In Chicago during the summer of 1969, the Coalition for United Community Action established that of 87,783 union workers in 19 building trades, only 2,251 were black, Latin, or from a similar minority. On the automotive industry, my source is Robert Dudnick, *Black Workers in Revolt* (New York: Guardian Pamphlets, 1969). For broader background, see Ray Marshall, *The Negro and Organized Labor* (New York: John Wiley & Sons, Inc., 1965), and (with V. M. Briggs, Jr.) *The Negro and Apprenticeship* (Baltimore: Johns Hopkins, 1967).

[5] This last figure comes from a report by the National Commission on the Causes and Prevention of Violence, summarized in the *Chicago Sun-Times*, November 24, 1969, pp. 5, 18.

[6] "Letter from a Birmingham City Jail," reprinted in *Civil Disobedience*, ed. by H. A. Bedau (New York: Pegasus, 1969), p. 81.

that with all the current 'favoritism' toward blacks, there is discrimination against whites! In any case, my method is straightforward. Rather than suspect most 'well-meaning' whites of hypocrisy, I will look for patterns of selective and distorted perception of this background when they describe social occurrences involving black people. . . .

The test for my analysis is therefore simple. I will ask, of readily available though relatively crude data, whether or not they qualify as evidence for a viscerally racist outlook. Take this pungent interview:

Ray Walczak, 44, works as a gig grinder . . . in Milwaukee. As he walked off his shift not long ago, he saw across the street the Rev. James Groppi and a group of black militants picketing for more jobs.

"Look at that," Ray Walczak said. "Bastards don't want jobs. If you offered them jobs now, 90 per cent of them would run like hell. I tell you, people on relief get better jobs, got better homes, than I've got. You're better off now not working. The colored people are eating steak, and this Polack bastard is eating chicken."

"Damn right I'm bitter. The Polish race years ago didn't go out and riot and ruin people's property. I've been in the shops since I was 16 . . . if I live to be a hundred I'll probably be doing the same job.

"The only raise I ever got was a union raise . . . never a merit raise . . . We're peons, just numbers."[7]

That particular worker does not think himself privileged: but if you compare his situation with that of his potential black competitors, he is. There is an interesting distortion in his claim that blacks do not really want the meagre opportunities he has. There is even a slight contradiction between his statement that they "don't want jobs" and his complaint that "people on relief get better jobs"; but perhaps this indicates that he is candidly expressing attitudes that conflict. Naturally he assumes that black protesters are on relief!

More explicit animosity toward blacks appears in another interview:

Ernest (Pee Wee) Hayes is 58, and for 37 years he has worked at the Armco steel plant in Middletown, Ohio. . . .

"We do all the work and the niggers have got it made. They keep closing and closing in, working their way into everything. Last 3 or 4 months you can't even turn on that damn TV without seeing a nigger. They're even playing cowboys. We briarhoppers ain't gonna stand for it. And 90% of Middletown is briarhoppers.

"My man got beat, Wallace. We need someone to wake 'em up. Shake 'em up. Kill 'em."[8]

This second worker is clearly a white supremacist, because in addition to being hostile toward blacks, he recognizes that they do not presently have the same opportunities he has, and he intends to keep things that way.

How about the first worker? I think that my analysis helps us notice distortions as well as white supremacist elements in his diatribe. One particular theme

---

[7] From Lemon, *The Troubled American*, as serialized in the Chicago *Daily News*, October 29, 1970, p. 6.

[8] Lemon, *The Troubled American*, as serialized in the Chicago *Daily News*, October 30, 1970, p. 6.

in that interview is worth examining further, because it is so common in discussions I've heard. The theme is that workers like this man have suffered to win the few advantages they have. They started working before they could complete high school, and they accepted miserable wages for long hours, under hazardous conditions. They joined the union movement, got fired and took beatings. How can you expect them to give up the few advantages they won, and step aside to benefit blacks? On this view, schemes for preferential recruitment of blacks, admission to apprenticeship programs, and promotion, all seem like 'favoritism' and 'discrimination in reverse'.

Why are these misdescriptions of economic reality? First, while it is true that white workers suffered, fought and took their knocks, it is a distortion to forget that black workers did also. Moreover, as we noticed [earlier], labor unions regularly betrayed black workers, forcing companies to put them out of jobs they already had, and refusing to admit and represent them. Thus fatal ambiguities begin to appear in the claim that white workers gained the advantages they have by struggling. If you ask, "Struggling against whom, and advantages over whom?", the answer in each case is: "Employers and black workers." Now the struggle does not sound so much like 'the good fight' any more. And the privileges no longer appear to be *privileges for laborers in general*. We notice that they are to a considerable extent 'white-skin privileges', unfair advantages over potential black competitors. The case for white workers looks very twisted.

How about the 'sacrifice' and 'favoritism' themes? These are again gross distortions. In the first place, there is a confusion between actuality and possibility. So far, very few blacks have gotten into industrial and craft unions, apprenticeship programs and supervisory positions. Thus in actual fact, whites have made no sacrifices, and no favoritism has been shown to black workers. At most the complaint might be that *if* blacks eventually get what they demand, this *would be* the result. But the second point to raise here is: 'Would it be favoritism, and would there be sacrifices?' If you agree that white workers' advantages are unfair advantages, then how can you describe it as a 'sacrifice' when they must renounce them? Black workers have not called for the firing of whites. No renunciation of their legitimate privileges *as workers* is at issue: only their undeserved privileges as *white* workers. To end these privileges is no more a sacrifice than it is a sacrifice when you must return someone's property, whether you took it deliberately or by mistake, or whether you got it from your parents.

In connection with the 'favoritism' theme, what distorts things is the omission of all-important historical background. Consider preferential hiring programs in the setting of 350 years of gross favoritism toward white laborers and craftsmen. Then it hardly sounds unfair when blacks announce: "Until we get our share, you will have to *wait longer* than usual for the new jobs, for promotions and for admission to apprenticeship programs." It is not favoritism toward blacks when whites lose their illegal monopoly.

White workers and their union representatives who describe economic circumstances in the manner I've been analyzing certainly display visceral racism. But the hitch is that when you expose these and similar distortions, many workers will become explicitly antagonistic towards blacks. How many? That is for trained interviewers to find out. At this stage of exploring a person's attitudes, does it make any difference whether you have a visceral racist or a white supremacist on your hands? Besides the ideological and theoretical differences I've noted, there

182

might be a practical difference when someone is intellectually 'up against the wall'. The acknowledged white supremacist will want to preserve current inequalities. Visceral racists like ourselves, once we have stopped misperceiving things, have strong professed reasons to work for immediate and drastic change.[9]

QUESTIONS

1. Would any evidence conclusively prove or disprove the claim that visceral racism is a widespread phenomenon?

2. Using Thalberg's discussion of visceral racism as a model, make a case for the claim: Because of visceral sexism, males fail to perceive the discriminatory inequality of treatment accorded women by the institutions in our society.

3. Has Thalberg succeeded in drawing a clear distinction between white supremacists and visceral racists?

Tom L. Beauchamp

THE JUSTIFICATION OF REVERSE DISCRIMINATION

A biographical sketch of Tom L. Beauchamp is found on page 67.

Argument in the Selection. Beauchamp argues that reverse discrimination can be morally justified. He concedes that reverse discrimination does violate the principle of equality and so appears to be immoral. But the need to compensate for past discrimination creates a strong obligation to ensure that such discrimination does not continue. Beauchamp maintains that in our present situation reverse discrimination is necessary as a means to an undeniably justified end. Measures productive of reverse discrimination are necessary to eliminate present and future discriminatory practices and not simply to compensate for past injustices. Beauchamp's argument is in large measure based on the following set of factual claims: (1) Sexual and racial discrimination still exists in our society. (2) The judgments of those who evaluate competing applicants are often affected by subtle sexist and racist attitudes. (3) It is in part because of such attitudes that judgments supposedly based on objective criteria of merit are frequently subjective and discriminatory. (4) In this kind of situation present and future discrimination will not be

[9] For comments on an earlier draft of this paper, I am grateful to Kathryn Pyne Parsons, Ruth Barcan Marcus, George Favors and Robert Coburn and Peter Stone. I thank Richard Lemon, Simon & Schuster and the Chicago *Daily News* for permission to quote from Lemon's book (see n. 7 and n. 8). I first noticed the term 'visceral racism' in Kenneth Clark, *Dark Ghetto* (Boston: Beacon Press, 1964), p. 20.

eliminated unless social measures productive of reverse discrimination are employed.

In recent years government policies intended to ensure fairer employment and educational opportunities for women and minority groups have engendered alarm. Target goals, timetables, and quotas seem to many citizens to discriminate against more talented applicants who are excluded yet would be accepted on their merits were it not for the preferential advancement of others. Such government policies are said to create a situation of "reverse discrimination." By balancing or compensating for past discrimination against persons on the basis of morally irrelevant characteristics (race, sex, nationality, and religion), these policies now require discrimination in favor of such persons and therefore against the members of other previously favored classes. These policies seem unfairly discriminatory to some because they violate basic principles of justice and equal protection. I believe this conclusion to be reasonable but incorrect, and in this paper I argue that some government policies which would result in reverse discrimination are appropriate and justifiable.

Most all published discussions on this subject known to me are opposed to public policies which would permit reverse discrimination. Among those writers who would permit policies of reverse discrimination, a fairly standard approach is taken: They attempt to justify reverse discrimination by showing that under certain conditions compensation owed for *past* wrongs justifies (for varying reasons) *present* policies productive of reverse discrimination. *This is not my argument;* and it is important to see that it is not. I draw only weak obligations from the claims of compensatory justice; I contend only that because of past wrongs to classes of persons we have *special and strong* obligations to see that these wrongs do not continue. My argument differs from more usual ones since I hold that reverse discrimination is permitted and even required in order that we might eliminate *present* discriminatory practices against classes of persons. I adduce factual evidence for this claim of present, continuing discrimination.

As will become apparent, I construe the issue of reverse discrimination as *primarily* a factual one, and as only secondarily an ethical one. My factual argument is based on factual evidence which establishes the following: there exist discriminatory social attitudes and selection procedures so deeply entrenched in contemporary society that they are almost certainly ineradicable by good faith measures in an acceptable period of time. My ethical contention is that because these crippling conditions exist, policies producing reverse discrimination are justified. These policies are morally *permitted* because they are social measures necessary for the protection of those harmed by invidious social attitudes and selection procedures.[1] A stronger thesis is that such policies are morally *required*

---

[1] I do not claim that policies productive of reverse discrimination are necessary for the elimination of every particular case of invidious discriminatory treatment. Obviously some non-reverse discriminatory measures will on some occasions suffice. My claim is that without such policies the problems of intractable discriminatory treatment in society at large cannot be resolved.

184

and not merely morally permitted. I also support this stronger contention on grounds that past discriminatory practices have created a special and strong obligation to erase invidious discrimination and ensure equal protection of the law. Hence these policies are morally required (by compensatory justice) under the kind of incorrigible social conditions I discuss in my factual arguments.

I proceed by first establishing a principled framework for resolving moral issues about the justifiability of reverse discrimination (I). I then discuss the factual evidence of present discriminatory practices and the difficulties which attend weak attempts to offset or overcome such bias (II).

(I) ETHICAL PRINCIPLES AND REVERSE DISCRIMINATION

My moral argument is intended to show that policies productive of reverse discrimination are compatible with basic principles of justice and utility. This is not to say that no injustices result from the occurrence of reverse discrimination, but it is to say that these injustices can be justified.

For moral philosophy the main issues of reverse discrimination may be formulated as follows: Under what conditions, if any, are policies resulting in reverse discrimination justified? Can basic ethical principles of justice and utility be successfully employed for the justification of reverse discrimination? Conceivably other ethical principles, such as beneficence, might be invoked. But since justice and utility are universally recognized as the most directly relevant principles, I shall confine my discussion to them, beginning with justice.

An initial difficulty must be faced in any appeal to principles of justice. Since there are different theories of justice, and different kinds of justice recognized within the different theories, it might be thought that a comprehensive theory of justice must be defended before problems of reverse discrimination can be intelligently discussed. Fortunately, for our purposes, this difficulty may be largely ignored, for two reasons. First, we can without prejudicing the arguments successfully operate with two rather minimal principles of justice, both of which derive from Aristotle and both of which receive wide acceptance as at least necessary, even if not sufficient, conditions of justice. The first is the principle of *formal equality*. It says that equals must be treated equally and unequals unequally; or, more fully stated, it says that "No person should be treated unequally, despite all differences with other persons, until such time as it has been shown that there is a difference between them relevant to the treatment at stake." One demand of the principle is the egalitarian ideal of equal consideration of persons: every person is to be evaluated on his or her merit when there is equal opportunity to compete. The problem with the principle is notoriously more in its abstractness than in any deficiency of content. That equals ought to be treated equally, by law and elsewhere, is not likely to stir disagreement. But who is equal and who unequal? Presumably all citizens should have equal political rights, equal access to public services, and should receive equal treatment under the law. But almost all would allow that distinctions based on experience, merit, and position do sometimes introduce criteria justifying differential treatment. Whether race, sex, and religion similarly justify differential treatment under some conditions is more controversial. This issue of the appropriate *application* of the principle of formal equality is one that we shall be considering.

The second principle of justice deserving explicit statement is the principle of *compensatory justice*. It says that whenever an injustice has been committed, just compensation or reparation is owed the injured parties. The idea is to restore, so far as possible, the state of affairs prior to the injury or injustice which created the need for compensation, and also to benefit the injured parties in a manner proportional to the injury or loss suffered. The compensation might be to groups or to individuals, but in either case the same justifying principle is used. It is now a widespread view that groups invidiously discriminated against in the proximate and remote past, including women, blacks, North American Indians, and French Canadians, should be recompensed for these injustices by compensatory policies, at least in those cases where injury is traceable to particular persons. I shall be discussing not merely whether some form of compensation is deserved, but the more controversial question whether such compensation might justifiably result in reverse discrimination. I shall not, however, argue that compensatory claims by themselves justify direct monetary reparations or quota allotments to classes of persons. My account is weaker: compensatory justice both (1) demands that we make an especially vigorous attempt to discover *present* discrimination against classes of persons discriminated against in the past and (2) creates a *special* obligation to eliminate such present discriminatory treatment wherever it is found. I will take for granted that this weakened claim about obligations generated by compensatory justice is reasonable, and that any society which fails to act on this obligation is an unjust society, whether or not this failure is intentional.

Recently a rather large literature has emerged in which the attempt is made to show that policies causing reverse discrimination violate the above (and perhaps other) principles of justice. It is argued in this literature that since reverse discriminatory policies create injustices they cannot be justified. The most widely circulated form of the argument makes a direct appeal to the principle of formal equality. The following is a typical example of this basic argument:

> Now, if justice (Aristotle's justice in the political sense) is equal treatment under the law for all citizens, what is injustice? Clearly, injustice is the violation of that equality, discriminating for or against a group of citizens, favoring them with special immunities and privileges or depriving them of those guaranteed to the others. . . . But, of course, when the employers and the schools *favor* women and blacks, the same injustice is done. Just as the previous discrimination did, this reverse discrimination violates the public equality which defines citizenship and destroys the rule of law for the areas in which these favors are granted. To the extent that we adopt a program of discrimination, reverse or otherwise, justice in the political sense is destroyed, . . . [and] the ideal of equality is undermined, for it has content only where justice obtains. . . . [Reverse discrimination] destroys justice, law, equality, and citizenship itself, and replaces them with power struggles and popularity contests.[2]

---

[2] Lisa H. Newton, "Reverse Discrimination as Unjustified," *Ethics*, Vol. 83 (1973), pp. 310, 312. Also reprinted in *Today's Moral Problems*, ed. Richard Wasserstrom (New York: MacMillan, 1975).

I want to concede from the outset that policies of reverse discrimination can create serious and perhaps even tragic injustices. One must be careful, however, not to draw an overzealous conclusion from this admission. Those who argue that reverse discrimination creates injustices often say that because of the injustice such policies are *unjust*. I think by this use of "unjust" they generally mean "not justified" (rather than "not sanctioned by justice"). But this conclusion does not follow merely from the arguments thus far mentioned. A policy can create and even perpetuate injustices, as violations of the principle of formal equality, and yet be justified by other reasons. It would be an injustice in this sense to fire either one of two assistant professors with exactly similar professional credentials, while retaining the other of the two; yet the financial condition of the university or compensation owed the person retained might provide compelling reasons which justify the action. The first reason supporting the dismissal is utilitarian in character, and the other derives from the principle of compensatory justice. This shows both that there can be conflicts between different justice-regarding reasons and also that violations of the principle of formal equality are not in themselves sufficient to render an action unjustifiable.

A proper conclusion, then—and one which I accept—is that all discrimination, including reverse discrimination, is prima facie immoral, because a basic principle of justice creates a prima facie duty to abstain from such treatment of persons. But no absolute duty is created come what may, for we might have conflicting duties of sufficient weight to justify such injustices. The latter is the larger thesis I wish to defend: considerations of compensatory justice and utility are conjointly of sufficient weight in contemporary society to neutralize and overcome the quite proper presumption of immorality in the case of some policies productive of reverse discrimination.

(II) FACTUAL EVIDENCE OF INCORRIGIBLE DISCRIMINATORY PRACTICES

I now turn away from moral considerations to factual ones. It is difficult to avoid accepting two important claims: (a) that the law ought never to sanction any discriminatory practices (whether plain old unadorned discrimination or reverse discrimination), and (b) that such practices can be eradicated by bringing the full weight of the law down on those who engage in discriminatory practices. The first claim is a moral one, the second a factual one. I contend in this section that it is unrealistic to believe, as *b* suggests, that in contemporary society discriminatory practices *can* be eradicated by legal measures which do not permit reverse discrimination. And because they cannot be eradicated, I think we ought to relax our otherwise unimpeachably sound reservations (as recorded in *a* and discussed in the first section) against allowing any discriminatory practices whatever.

My argument is motivated by the belief that racial, sexual, and no doubt other forms of discrimination are not antique relics but are living patterns which continue to warp selection and ranking procedures. In my view the difference between the present and the past is that discriminatory treatment is today less widespread and considerably less blatant. But its reduction has produced apathy; its subtleness has made it less visible and considerably more difficult to detect.

187

SOCIAL ETHICS

Largely because of the reduced visibility of racism and sexism, I suggest, reverse discrimination now strikes us as all too harsh and unfair. After all, quotas and preferential treatment have no appeal if one assumes a just, primarily non-discriminatory society. Since the presence or absence of seriously discriminatory conditions in our society is a factual matter, empirical evidence must be adduced to show that the set of discriminatory attitudes and selection procedures I have alleged to exist do in fact exist. The data I shall mention derive primarily from historical, linguistic, sociological, and legal sources.

Statistical Evidence. Statistical imbalances in employment and admission are often discounted, because so many variables can be hypothesized to explain why, for non-discriminatory reasons, an imbalance exists. We can all think of plausible non-discriminatory reasons why 22% of Harvard's graduate students in 1969 were women but its tenured Arts and Sciences Faculty in the Graduate School consisted of 411 males and 0 females.[3] But sometimes we are able to discover evidence which supports the claim that skewed statistics are the result of discrimination. Quantities of such discriminatory findings, in turn, raise serious questions about the real reasons for suspicious statistics in those cases where we have not been able to determine these reasons—perhaps because they are so subtle and unnoticed. I shall discuss each factor in turn: (a) statistics which constitute prima facie but indecisive evidence of discrimination; (b) findings concerning discriminatory reasons for some of these statistics; and (c) cases where the discrimination is probably undetectable because of its subtleness, and yet the statistical evidence is overwhelming.

(a) A massive body of statistics constituting prima facie evidence of discrimination has been assembled in recent years. Here is a tiny but diverse fragment of some of these statistical findings.[4] (1) Women college teachers with identical credentials in terms of publications and experience are promoted at almost exactly one-half the rate of their male counterparts. (2) In the United States women graduates of medical schools in 1965 stood at 7%, as compared with 36% in Germany. The gap in the number of women physicians was similar. (3) Of 3,000 leading law firms surveyed in 1957 only 32 reported a woman partner, and even these women were paid much less (increasingly so for every year of employment) than their male counterparts. (4) 40% of the white collar positions in the United States are presently held by women, but only 10% of the management positions

[3] From "Statement of Dr. Bernice Sandler," *Discrimination Against Women: Congressional Hearings on Equal Rights in Education and Employment* (New York: R. R. Bowker Company, 1973), ed. Catharine R. Stimpson, pp. 61, 415. Hereafter *Discrimination Against Women.*

[4] All of the statistics and quotations cited are taken from the compilations of data in the following sources: (1) Kenneth M. Davidson, Ruth B. Ginsburg, and Herma H. Kay, eds., *Sex-Based Discrimination: Text, Cases, and Materials* (Minneapolis: West Publishing Company, 1974), esp. Ch. III. Hereafter *Sex-Based Discrimination.* (2) *Discrimination Against Women,* esp. pp. 397-441 and 449-502. (3) Alfred W. Blumrosen, *Black Employment and the Law* (New Brunswick, New Jersey: Rutgers University Press, 1971), esp. pp. 107, 122f. (4) *The Federal Civil Rights Enforcement Effort—1971,* A Report of the United States Commission on Civil Rights.

are held by women, and their pay again is significantly less (70% of clerical workers are women). (5) 8,000 workers were employed in May 1967 in the construction of BART (Bay Area Rapid Transit), but not a single electrician, ironworker, or plumber was black. (6) In the population as a whole in the United States, 3 out of 7 employees hold white collar positions, but only 1 of 7 blacks holds such a position, and these latter jobs are clustered in professions which have the fewest jobs to offer in top-paying positions.

(b) I concede that such statistics are far from decisive indicators of discrimination. But when further evidence concerning the reasons for the statistics is uncovered, they are put in a perspective affording them greater power—clinching power in my view. Consider (3)—the statistics on the lack of women lawyers. A survey of Harvard Law School alumnae in 1970 provided evidence about male lawyers' attitudes.[5] It showed that business and legal firms do not generally expect the women they hire to become lawyers, that they believe women cannot become good litigators, and that they believe only limited numbers of women should be hired since clients generally prefer male lawyers. Surveys of women applicants for legal positions indicate they are frequently either told that women will not be hired, or are warned that "senior partners" will likely object, or are told that women will be hired to do only probate, trusts, and estate work. (Other statistics confirm that these are the sorts of tasks dominantly given to women.) Consider also (5)—a particular but typical case of hiring in non-white-collar positions. Innumerable studies have shown that most of these positions are filled by word-of-mouth recruitment policies conducted by all-white interviewers (usually all-male as well). In a number of decisions of the Equal Employment Opportunity Commission, it has been shown that the interviewers have racially biased attitudes and that the applications of blacks and women are systematically handled in unusual ways, such as never even being filed. So serious and consistent have such violations been that the EEOC has publicly stated its belief that word-of-mouth recruitment policies without demonstrable supplementary and simultaneous recruitment in minority group communities is in itself a "prima facie violation of Title VII."[6] Gertrude Ezorsky has argued, convincingly I believe, that this pattern of "special ties" is no less present in professional white collar hiring, which is neither less discriminatory nor more sensitive to hiring strictly on the basis of merit.[7]

(c) Consider, finally, (1)—statistics pertaining to the treatment of women college teachers. The Carnegie Commission and others have assembled statistical evidence to show that in even the most favorable construal of relevant variables, women teachers have been discriminated against in hiring, tenuring, and ranking. But instead of summarizing this mountain of material, I wish here to take a particular case in order to illustrate the difficulty in determining, on the basis of statistics and similar empirical data, whether discrimination is occurring; and yet where even courts have been forced to find satisfactory evidence of discrimina-

[5] *Discrimination Against Women*, pp. 505f.
[6] *Sex-Based Discrimination*, p. 516.
[7] "The Fight Over University Women," *The New York Review of Books*, Vol. XXI (May 16, 1974), pp. 32-39.

tion. In December 1974 a decision was reached by the Commission Against Discrimination of the Executive Department of the State of Massachusetts regarding a case at Smith College where the two Complainants were women who were denied tenure and dismissed by the English Department.[8] The women claimed sex discrimination and based their case on the following: (1) Women at the full professor level in the university declined from 54% in 1958 to 21% in 1972, and in the English department from 57% in 1960 to 11% in 1972. These statistics compare unfavorably at all levels with Mt. Holyoke's, a comparable institution (since both have an all female student body and are located in Western Massachusetts). (2) Thirteen of the department's fifteen associate and full professorships belonged to men. (3) The two tenured women had obtained tenure under "distinctly peculiar experiences" including a stipulation that one be only part-time and that the other not be promoted when given tenure. (4) The department's faculty members conceded that tenure standards were applied subjectively, were vague, and lacked the kind of precision which would avoid discriminatory application. (5) The women denied tenure were at no time given advance warning that their work was deficient. Rather, they were given favorable evaluations of their teaching and were encouraged to believe they would receive tenure. (6) Some stated reasons for the dismissals were later demonstrated to be rationalizations, and one letter from a senior member to the tenure and promotion committee contradicted his own appraisal of teaching ability filed with the department. (7) The court accepted expert testimony that any deficiencies in the women candidates were also found in male candidates promoted and given tenure during this same period, and that the women's positive credentials were at least as good as the men's.

The Commissioner's opinion found that "the Complainants properly used statistics to demonstrate that the Respondents' practices operate with a discriminatory effect." Citing *Parham v. Southwestern Bell Telephone Co.,*[9] the Commissioner argued that "in such cases extreme statistics may establish discrimination as a matter of law, without additional supportive evidence." But in this case the Commissioner found abundant additional evidence in the form of "the historical absence of women," "word-of-mouth recruitment policies" which operate discriminatorily, and a number of "subtle and not so subtle, societal patterns" existent at Smith.[10] On December 30, 1974 the Commissioner ordered the two women reinstated with tenure and ordered the department to submit an affirmative action program within 60 days.

This Case is interesting because there is little in the way of clinching proof that the members of the English department actually held discriminatory attitudes. Yet so consistent a pattern of *apparently* discriminatory treatment must be regarded, according to this decision, as *de facto* discriminatory. The Commissioner's ruling and other laws are quite explicit that "intent or lack thereof is of no consequence." If a procedure constitutes discriminatory treatment, then the parties discriminated against must be recompensed. Here we have a case where

---

[8] *Maurianne Adams and Mary Schroeder v. Smith College,* Massachusetts Commission Against Discrimination, Nos. 72-S-53, 72-S-54 (December 30, 1974). Hereafter *The Smith College Case.*

[9] 433 F.2d 421, 426 (8 Cir. 1970).

[10] *The Smith College Case,* pp. 23, 26.

irresistible statistics and other sociological evidence of "social exclusion" and "subtle societal patterns" provide convincing evidence that strong, court backed measures must be taken because nothing short of such measures is sufficiently strong to overcome the discriminatory pattern, as the Respondent's testimony in the case verifies.[11]

Some understanding of the attitudes underlying the statistical evidence thus far surveyed can be gained by consideration of some linguistic evidence now to be mentioned. It further supports the charge of widespread discrimination in the case of women and of the difficulty in changing discriminatory attitudes.

Linguistic Evidence. Robert Baker has assembled some impressive linguistic evidence which indicates that our language is male-slanted, perhaps male chauvinistic, and that language about women relates something of fundamental importance concerning the males' most fundamental conceptions of women.[12] Baker argues that as the term "boy" once expressed a paternalistic and dominating attitude toward blacks (and was replaced in our conceptual structure because of this denigrating association), so there are other English terms which serve similar functions in regard to women (but are not replaced because not considered by men as in need of replacement). Baker assembles evidence both from the language itself and from surveys of users of the language to show the following.

(a) Substitutions for "woman". The term "woman" is broadly substitutable for and frequently interchanged in English sentences such as "Who is that_____ over there?" by terms such as those in the following divisions:

A. Neutral Categories	B. Animal Categories	C. Plaything Categories	D. Gender Categories	E. Sexual Categories
lady	chick	babe	skirt	snatch
gal	bird	doll	hem	cunt
girl	fox	cuddly thing		ass
broad	vixen			twat
(sister)	filly			piece
	bitch			lay
				pussy

Baker notes that (1) while there are differences in the frequency of usage, all of these terms are standard enough to be recognizable at least by most male users of the language; (2) women do not typically identify themselves in sexual categories; and (3) typically only males use the non-neutral categories (B–E). He takes this to be evidence—and I agree—that the male conception of women differs significantly from the female conception and that the categories used by the male in

---

[11] *Ibid.,* pp. 26f.

[12] Robert Baker, "'Pricks' and 'Chicks': A Plea for Persons," in Richard Wasserstrom, ed., *Today's Moral Problems* (New York: Macmillan Publishing Company, 1975), pp. 152-70.

classifying women are "prima facie denigrating." He then argues that it is clearly and not merely prima facie denigrating when categories such as C and E are used, as they are either derived from playboy male images or are outright vulgarities. Baker argues that it is most likely that B and D are similarly used in denigrating ways. His arguments center on the metaphorical associations of these terms, but the evidence cannot be further pursued here.

Although Baker does not remark that women do not have a similar language for men, it seems to me important to notice this fact. Generally, any negative categories used by women to refer to men are as frequently or more frequently used by men to apply to women. This asymmetrical relation does not hold, of course, for the language used by whites and blacks for denigrating reference. This fact perhaps says something about how blacks have caught onto the impact of the language as a tool of denigrating identification in a way women have yet to do, at least in equal numbers. It may also say something about the image of submissiveness which many women still bear about themselves—an image blacks are no longer willing to accept.

(b) The language of sexual intercourse. Baker argues that the conception of sexual intercourse in our culture depicts women more as objects of sexual exploitation than as persons with the same entitlements as males. He analyzes the many terms that are synonymously used with "had sexual intercourse with" ("screwed," "layed," "fucked," "balled," "humped," "diddled with," etc.). He shows—again quite convincingly in my view—that: (1) Male names are the subjects of sentences with active constructions, while names for females require passive constructions. That is, we conceive of the male as doing the action and the female as the recipient, and therefore conceive of the two as having different sexual roles. (2) This linguistic difference cannot be explained merely in terms of the sexual differences in physiology (as "screw," e.g. suggests), since many other words could be chosen ("engulfing," e.g.) but never are. (3) Most of the terms used to portray the male's action are also terms used to indicate that a person is harming another person ("screwed," "had," and "fucked," e.g.) and that the language itself would indicate that we see the woman as "being taken advantage of." (4) Similarly terms such as "prick" used expressly to refer to the male are words in our language for one who hurts or is abusive or brutalizing.

Baker concludes from his linguistic studies that "sexual discrimination permeates our conceptual structure. Such discrimination is clearly inimical to any movement toward sexual egalitarianism and virtually defeats its purpose at the outset."[13] His conclusion may somewhat overreach his premises, but when combined with the corroborating statistical evidence previously adduced, it seems apt. Linguistic dispositions lead us to categorize persons and events in discriminatory ways which are sometimes glaringly obvious to the categorized, but accepted as "objective" by the categorizer. My contention, derived from Baker's, is that cautious, good faith movements toward egalitarianism such as affirmative action guidelines *cannot* succeed short of fundamental conceptual and ethical revisions. And since the probability of such revisions approximates zero (because discriminatory attitudes are covertly embedded in language and cultural habit), radical expedients are required to bring about the desired egalitarian results, expedients which may result in reverse discrimination.

[13] *Ibid.*, p. 170.

Conclusions. Irving Thalberg has argued, correctly I believe, that the gravest contemporary problems with racism stem from its "protectively camouflaged" status, which he calls "visceral." Thalberg skillfully points to a number of attitudes held by those whites normally classified as unprejudiced which indicate that racism still colors their conception of social facts.[14] John Stuart Mill argued a similar thesis in the Nineteenth Century about sexism.[15] Virginia Held has recently argued the additional thesis that under present, legally acceptable policies and programs of "gradual improvement" in the hiring of women and non-whites, it will take decades to achieve equality of occupational opportunity.[16] My alliance with such positions ought by now to be obvious. But my overall intentions and conclusions are somewhat different. I hold that because of the peculiarly concealed nature of the protective camouflage under which sexism and racism have so long thrived, it is not a reasonable expectation that the lightweight programs now administered under the heading of affirmative action will succeed in overcoming discriminatory treatment. . . .

[14]"Visceral Racism," *The Monist,* Vol. 56 (October 1972), pp. 43-63, and reprinted in Wasserstrom, *op. cit.*

[15] *On the Subjection of Women* (London: Longmans, Green, Reades, and Dyer, 1869), and especially as partially reprinted in Tom L. Beauchamp, ed., *Ethics and Public Policy* (Englewood Cliffs, New Jersey: Prentice-Hall, Inc., 1975), pp. 11-19.

[16]"Reasonable Progress and Self-Respect," *The Monist,* Vol. 57 (1973), pp. 12-27, and reprinted in Beauchamp, *op. cit.*

QUESTIONS

1. What other types of evidence can you suggest which will either support or refute Beauchamp's factual claim that discrimination against women and blacks will not be eliminated without measures productive of reverse discrimination?

2. The principle of utility states that one should always perform that action, or adopt that practice, which in the circumstances produces the greatest balance of good over evil. Using the principle of utility, argue that when the claims of compensatory justice conflict with the claims based on the principle of equality (as in the DeFunis case), it is the principle of equality which should not be violated.

SUGGESTED ADDITIONAL READINGS

Blackstone, William T., and Robert Heslep, eds. *Social Justice and Preferential Treatment.* Athens: University of Georgia Press, 1976. This is a collection of diverse essays, on the topic indicated, written by philosophers, lawyers, businessmen, and government officials.

Ezorsky, Gertrude. "The Fight over University Women." *New York Review of Books*, XXI, 8, 1974. Ezorsky's article is a critique of the kind of position represented by Sidney Hook in this chapter (page 171).

Held, Virginia. "Reasonable Progress and Self-Respect." *The Monist*, vol. 57, no. 1, 1973. Reprinted in *Ethics and Public Policy*, ed. by Tom L. Beauchamp. Englewood Cliffs, N.J.: Prentice-Hall, Inc., 1975. Held focuses on two questions: How long is it reasonable to expect the victims of past discrimination to wait for a redress of their wrongs? What reasonable rate of progress would not involve a loss of self-respect?

Katzner, Louis. "Is the Favoring of Women and Blacks in Employment and Educational Opportunities Justified?" In *Philosophy of Law*, ed. by Joel Feinberg and Hyman Gross. Encino, Calif.: Dickenson Publishing Company, 1975. Katzner's argument *for* the justification of reverse discrimination is based on the claim that the obligation to compensate for past wrongs justifies present policies productive of reverse discrimination.

Nagel, Thomas. "Equal Treatment and Compensatory Discrimination." *Philosophy and Public Affairs*, vol. 2, no. 4, 1973. Also reprinted in Beauchamp, cited above, under Held. This is one of the most difficult, yet one of the most interesting articles on the subject of preferential policies. Nagel questions the whole system of social rewards which bases such awards on superior merit. The most serious injustice, he claims, is a subtle economic injustice grounded in the attitude that talent and effort ought first and foremost to be rewarded.

Thalberg, Irving. "Justifications of Institutional Racism." *Philosophical Forum*, vol. III, 1971–1972. Thalberg critiques the recent arguments against the kinds of changes which he believes are needed to equalize the economic and political status of blacks.

194

SIX
Sexual Integrity

Someone who is said to have "loose morals" is thought to have taken more liberty in sexual matters than is appropriate. But assessments of what is appropriate in the area of sexual expression vary enormously. Many traditionalists consider sex appropriate only within the bounds of marriage. Some even consider morally objectionable any sexual expression between husband and wife that is not a standard act of intercourse. More liberal thinkers espouse various degrees of permissiveness. Some would allow a full and open promiscuity; some would not. Some would allow homosexual behavior; some would not. Let us investigate the grounds of these several positions.

SOME INITIAL MORAL CONSIDERATIONS

It is initially clear that those cases of sexual activity in which one person manifestly harms another person are morally objectionable. There is no doubt, for example, that rape is a moral outrage, involving as it does the forcible violation of one person by another. Likewise, the seduction of a minor who does not even know "what it's all about" is morally objectionable on the grounds that the minor will almost inevitably be psychologically harmed. But it is also often asserted that *all* sex outside of marriage is morally objectionable. (The category of *sex outside of marriage* is taken here to include any sexual relation other than that between marriage partners. Thus it includes sexual relations between unmarried people as well as adulterous sexual relations.) What grounds can be advanced in support of such a claim? It can be argued, of course, that *many* cases of sex outside of marriage are morally objectionable on the grounds that they involve one person in taking advantage of, or "using," another person. Both deception—"I told her that I loved her and would like to marry her"—and the application of psychological force—"I told him that he would not really be a man until he tried it"—can be freely recruited to bend another person to one's own sexual will. But even if the presence of such factors render *some* cases of sex outside of marriage morally objectionable, there yet remains the (presumably) typical case in which two unmarried, freely consenting adults engage in sexual intercourse. There may be present some degree of mutual affection or love, or there may be present merely the common desire to attain sexual satisfaction. Is such sexual expression still to be judged morally objectionable? If so, on what grounds?

The general category of sex outside of marriage includes as a special case *adultery,* which is understood as a married person having sexual relations with someone other than his or her marriage partner. It is commonly asserted that *all* adultery is wrong, and as the marriage bond is usually understood, it seems clear that there is present in cases of adultery a distinctive ground of moral condemnation. If marriage involves a pledge of sexual exclusivity, and this is surely the normal understanding, then it is hard to see that adulterous behavior does not involve a serious breaking of trust. Of course, if marriage partners have entered upon a so-called "open marriage," where there has been no pledge of sexual exclusivity, then this special ground of moral condemnation seems to evaporate. Is the "adulterous" behavior of the partners in an open marriage still to be judged morally objectionable? If so, on what grounds?

THE TRADITIONAL REJECTION OF SEX OUTSIDE OF MARRIAGE

Perhaps the most common defense of the traditional convention that sex is permissible only within the bounds of marriage is one that is based on considerations of *social utility.* It takes the following form: A stable family life is absolutely essential for the proper raising of children and the consequent welfare of society as a whole. But the limitation of sex to marriage is a necessary condition of forming and maintaining stable family units. The availability of sex within marriage will reinforce the loving relationship between husband and wife, the *exclusive* availability of sex within marriage will lead most people to get married and to stay married, and the unavailability of sex outside of marriage will keep the marriage strong. Therefore, the convention that sex is permissible only within the bounds of marriage is solidly based on considerations of social utility.

This argument is attacked in many ways. Sometimes it is argued that stable family units are not really so essential. More commonly, it is argued that the availability of sex outside of marriage does not really undercut family life. Whereas adultery might very well undermine a marital relationship, it is argued, premarital sex often prepares one for marriage. At any rate, it is pointed out, people continue to marry even after they have had somewhat free access to sexual relations.

SEX WITH LOVE AND SEX WITHOUT LOVE

One may find the absolute prohibition of sex outside of marriage unwarranted and yet stop short of supporting an unbridled promiscuity. Many thinkers who reject the traditional view are reluctant to endorse promiscuity, on the grounds that such a way of life will lead to the dehumanization of the person. On this view, promiscuity is thought to reduce a humanly significant activity to a merely mechanical performance, which in turn leads to the disintegration of the human personality. In an effort to avoid such alleged consequences, many have adopted the view that sexual expression ought to be limited only by the condition that sexual partners have some measure of love and affection for one another. Defenders of this *sex with love* attitude differ themselves as to whether the love necessary to warrant a sexual relationship must be an *exclusive* love or whether it may be a *nonexclusive* love. Those who argue that it must be exclusive nevertheless grant that *successive* sexual liaisons are not objectionable. Those who argue that the love may be nonexclusive necessarily presume that a person is capable of simultaneously loving several persons. On their view, even *simultaneous* love affairs are not objectionable. Whether exclusive or nonexclusive love is taken to be the relevant standard, proponents of the sex with love attitude usually argue that their view allows for sexual freedom in a way that avoids the alleged dehumanizing effects of mere promiscuity. Where sex and love remain united, it is argued, there is no danger of dehumanization and psychological disintegration.

Others wish to take the case for sexual freedom even further, defending *sex without love*. Some defenders of sex without love go so far as to argue against the desirability of sex with love. Such an attitude is often based on the view that sex is a source of pleasure that can best be cultivated by removing it altogether from the sphere of human involvement. Inasmuch as this kind of glorification of sex without love is especially open to objections of dehumanization, many defenders of sex without love do not wish to argue against the desirability of sex with love. They simply argue that there is good reason to leave open the possibility of sex without love. Some people, it is said, derive great pleasure from sex without love and/or have no access to sex with love.

Unless it can be shown that some definitive harm results from such sexual expression, they maintain, it should nowise be considered objectionable. On the other hand, those who argue against sex without love usually contend that such sexual expression has a dehumanizing impact on human existence and moreover, in various ways, tends to undermine the more desirable expression of sex with love.

HOMOSEXUALITY

A homosexual, in the most generic sense, is a person (male or female) whose dominant sexual preference is for a person of the same sex. In common parlance, however, the term "homosexual" usually designates a male, whereas the term "lesbian" is used to designate a female. It is an interesting fact that the male variety of homosexuality seems to occasion a higher degree of societal indignation than the female variety does. Though there is presently a strong movement toward the decriminalization of homosexual behavior between consenting adults, homosexual behavior remains a criminal offense in the vast majority of states; but whereas there is often strong pressure on law enforcement agencies to prosecute male homosexual "criminals," there is virtually no pressure to prosecute lesbian "criminals." At any rate, whatever reasons of our collective depth psychology may be adduced to explain the apparently greater societal aversion to the male variety of homosexuality, it is difficult to see any morally relevant distinction between the two varieties.

There is no lack of invective against the homosexual and against homosexual behavior. For example, the following things are often said: "Homosexual behavior is repulsive and highly offensive." "Homosexuality as a way of life is totally given over to promiscuity and is little susceptible of enduring human relationships." "Homosexuality is a perversion, a sin against nature." "Homosexuals make the streets unsafe for our children." It is difficult to assess whether or not such claims can be justifiably recruited in support of the claim that homosexual behavior is morally objectionable. It may in fact be true that many people find homosexual behavior repulsive and offensive, but it is also true that many people find eating liver repulsive and offensive, and we could hardly think that this fact alone could render the eating of liver morally objectionable. (The fact that many people find homosexual behavior repulsive and offensive, however, may be a reason to prohibit public displays of homosexuality.) Again, it may be true that homosexuality is typically a promiscuous way of life, but it can be argued that society's attitude toward homosexuality is responsible for making stable homosexual relationships impossible. Again, it may be true that *some* homosexuals prey upon children, and surely this is morally reprehensible, but still we find ourselves left with the more typical case in which homosexual relations take place between consenting adults.

One argument, mentioned above, has a long philosophical history. It directly asserts that homosexual behavior is unnatural and therefore immoral. This argument, which might be called the "unnaturalness argument," has typically been applied not only against homosexuality but also against other "perversions," such as masturbation, oral-genital sex practices, etc. The argument is based on the contention that there is one primary function of the sex organs—procreation. Thus, any sex practice that bypasses this essential function is judged unnatural and therefore immoral. The "unnaturalness argument" as applied against homosexuality is thoroughly discussed in the selection by Burton M. Leiser.

T. A. M.

Justice Byron R. White

CONCURRING OPINION IN *GRISWOLD v. STATE OF CONNECTICUT*

A biographical sketch of Justice Byron R. White is found on page 10.

Argument in the Selection. *This case centers around the constitutionality of two closely related Connecticut statutes. An "anticontraceptive" statute prohibited any person from using "any drug, medicinal article or instrument for the purpose of preventing conception." An "aiding and abetting" statute prohibited any person from assisting or counseling another with regard to the use of contraceptives. The executive director of the Planned Parenthood League of Connecticut (Griswold) and a medical doctor associated with the League were both convicted under the "aiding and abetting" statute. The Supreme Court ultimately reversed these convictions.*

Justice White, in his concurring opinion, contends that these Connecticut statutes violate the Fourteenth Amendment because they deprive married persons of liberty without due process of law. He considers the state's claim that these statutes are justified by serving the state's policy against "promiscuous or illicit sexual relationships." Justice White affirms the legitimacy of this particular legislative goal, but he argues that prohibiting married persons from using contraceptives is at best of marginal utility to the declared objective.

In my view this Connecticut law as applied to married couples deprives them of "liberty" without due process of law, as that concept is used in the Fourteenth Amendment. I therefore concur in the judgment of the Court reversing these convictions under Connecticut's aiding and abetting statute.

It would be unduly repetitious, and belaboring the obvious, to expound on the impact of this statute on the liberty guaranteed by the Fourteenth Amendment against arbitrary or capricious denials or on the nature of this liberty. . . . [Previous] decisions affirm that there is a "realm of family life which the state cannot enter" without substantial justification. Surely the right invoked in this case, to be free of regulation of the intimacies of the marriage relationship, "come[s] to this Court with a momentum for respect lacking when appeal is made to liberties which derive merely from shifting economic arrangements."

The Connecticut anti-contraceptive statute deals rather substantially with this relationship. For it forbids all married persons the right to use birth-control devices, regardless of whether their use is dictated by considerations of family planning, health, or indeed even of life itself. The anti-use statute, together with the general aiding and abetting statute, prohibits doctors from affording advice to married persons on proper and effective methods of birth control. And the clear effect of these statutes, as enforced, is to deny disadvantaged citizens of Connecticut, those without either adequate knowledge or resources to obtain private counseling, access to medical assistance and up-to-date information in respect to proper methods of birth control. In my view, a statute with these effects bears a substantial burden of justification when attacked under the Fourteenth Amendment.

An examination of the justification offered, however, cannot be avoided by saying that the Connecticut anti-use statute invades a protected area of privacy and association or that it demeans the marriage relationship. The nature of the right invaded is pertinent, to be sure, for statutes regulating sensitive areas of liberty do, under the cases of this Court, require "strict scrutiny," and "must be viewed in the light of less drastic means for achieving the same basic purpose." "Where there is a significant encroachment upon personal liberty, the State may prevail only upon showing a subordinating interest which is compelling." But such statutes, if reasonably necessary for the effectuation of a legitimate and substantial state interest, and not arbitrary or capricious in application, are not invalid under the Due Process Clause.

As I read the opinions of the Connecticut courts and the argument of Connecticut in this Court, the State claims but one justification for its anti-use statute. There is no serious contention that Connecticut thinks the use of artificial or external methods of contraception immoral or unwise in itself, or that the anti-use statute is founded upon any policy of promoting population expansion. Rather, the statute is said to serve the State's policy against all forms of promiscuous or illicit sexual relationships, be they premarital or extramarital, concededly a permissible and legitimate legislative goal.

200

Without taking issue with the premise that the fear of conception operates as a deterrent to such relationships in addition to the criminal proscriptions Connecticut has against such conduct, I wholly fail to see how the ban on the use of contraceptives by married couples in any way reinforces the State's ban on illicit sexual relationships. Connecticut does not bar the importation or possession of contraceptive devices; they are not considered contraband material under state law, and their availability in that State is not seriously disputed. The only way Connecticut seeks to limit or control the availability of such devices is through its general aiding and abetting statute whose operation in this context has been quite obviously ineffective and whose most serious use has been against birth-control clinics rendering advice to married, rather than unmarried, persons. Indeed, after over 80 years of the State's proscription of use, the legality of the sale of such devices to prevent disease has never been expressly passed upon, although it appears that sales have long occurred and have only infrequently been challenged. This "undeviating policy . . . throughout all the long years . . . bespeaks more than prosecutorial paralysis." Moreover, it would appear that the sale of contraceptives to prevent disease is plainly legal under Connecticut law.

In these circumstances one is rather hard pressed to explain how the ban on use by married persons in any way prevents use of such devices by persons engaging in illicit sexual relations and thereby contributes to the State's policy against such relationships. Neither the state courts nor the State before the bar of this Court has tendered such an explanation. It is purely fanciful to believe that the broad proscription on use facilitates discovery of use by persons engaging in a prohibited relationship or for some other reason makes such use more unlikely and thus can be supported by any sort of administrative consideration. Perhaps the theory is that the flat ban on use prevents married people from possessing contraceptives and without the ready availability of such devices for use in the marital relationship, there will be no or less temptation to use them in extramarital ones. This reasoning rests on the premise that married people will comply with the ban in regard to their marital relationship, notwithstanding total nonenforcement in this context and apparent nonenforcibility, but will not comply with criminal statutes prohibiting extramarital affairs and the anti-use statute in respect to illicit sexual relationships, a premise whose validity has not been demonstrated and whose intrinsic validity is not very evident. At most the broad ban is of marginal utility to the declared objective. A statute limiting its prohibition on use to persons engaging in the prohibited relationship would serve the end posited by Connecticut in the same way, and with the same effectiveness, or ineffectiveness, as the broad anti-use statute under attack in this case. I find nothing in this record justifying the sweeping scope of this statute, with its telling effect on the freedoms of married persons, and therefore conclude that it deprives such persons of liberty without due process of law.

QUESTIONS

1. Apparently Justice White would find constitutionally acceptable a law prohibiting the use of contraceptives by unmarried persons. Would such a law effectively serve the common good?

2. Advance arguments for or against the following claim: Private sexual activities between consenting adults should in no way be legally restricted.

Richard Taylor

EROS, OR THE LOVE OF THE SEXES

Biographical Information. Richard Taylor (b. 1919) is professor of philosophy at the University of Rochester (N.Y.). Several of his works are in the field of ethics, including Good and Evil *(1970), from which this selection is excerpted. But perhaps best known of his published works is* Metaphysics *(1963; rev. ed., 1974).*

Argument in the Selection. Taylor takes up the question of the relationship of eros (sexual passion) and love. He maintains that human sexual passion differs in no significant way from the sexual passion of brute animals. He argues that sexual passion, in the human person as well as in the brute animal, is simply a blind and immensely powerful force. Taylor's primary thesis is that sexual passion and love are totally distinct sentiments. He does not wish to deny that sexual passion and love can coexist; he only denies that they are one and the same. On his view, the acting out of sexual passion is not in itself an expression of love. He even goes so far as to object to using the common expression "making love" as a designation for human copulation.

In [considering the sexual passion as having no essential connection with love and friendship] I think the ancients were basically right, and to see this we need to examine the sexual passion, as objectively as possible, to see what is its explanation and what connection it has, if any, with love and friendship and with good and evil.

The general conception most persons seem quite unthinkingly to have formed is something like this: Sexual union is a great good, an allurement that presents itself to the mind and the imagination; and, because it is thus viewed, one who is thus seized with this vision directs his will to the attainment of it. But this is to put the whole thing backward. The sexual embrace is not first seen as a great good and delight, and for that reason pursued; it is the reverse of this. That is, it is because it is keenly, and blindly, desired, that it is deemed a great good. The impulse and passion are what first make themselves felt and, in the younger portion of mankind, sometimes quite irresistably felt. Then, in response to this impulse, which lacks any intellectual direction whatever, that which is imagined as fulfilling it is deemed a great good. Men want to think otherwise because they like to

202

think they have reasons and even conscious reasons for pursuing the things they pursue. And what could the reason be, in the present case, other than the great goodness and delight of the thing sought? But this is to overlook what is in general true of all willing: the things men deem good are so considered because they are sought. They are not sought because they are first deemed good. Indeed, the good and evil of things generally is simply a consequence, and not a cause, of their promising fulfillment or threatening frustration of one's aims and purposes.

This becomes obvious, I think, if we consider the urge to sexual union as it finds expression in other creatures, and then note how unessential are the differences between these and ourselves. Certain fishes, such as the salmon and herring, for example, leave the salty oceans in vast numbers at a certain time of the year, seeking out the fresh waters where they spawn. This is nothing they would do ordinarily, for the environmental change, to which their bodily functions are so delicately attuned, is very great and abrupt. Evidently they are driven by a powerful force. This becomes more evident when we observe how they persevere against every obstacle, constantly exposing themselves to every danger, to sudden destruction among the rocks and in shallow waters, leaping against the powerful currents and high waterfalls, often persisting in this time after time, until one would suppose their energy and even their lives would long since have been spent in the effort. Finally, some of them do make it. Now then, after all this struggle, struggle against which no obstacle or danger can ever avail, and from which no force or danger can divert them, with what great good are they then rewarded? What allurement awaited them in the spawning beds, solicited from them such feats and exertions, and made it all so worthwhile? What actually happens is nothing more than this: the female fishes go about laying eggs, and the males follow behind to fertilize them, the two having no more concern for or contact with each other than is described here.

This is, of course, pretty much how the sexual urge expresses itself throughout nature, as anyone having any acquaintance with animals knows. It would be strange indeed if, coming to man, we were to find this picture suddenly reversed. What we do find is an impulse that is absolutely blind, at least from the point of view of that creature in whom it arises. From another point of view, it is of course not blind, for the function it actually serves is the perpetuation of the species. That this is no conscious or deliberate aim of other animals is perfectly obvious, for it would be laughable to suppose that one of these—one of the fishes just described, for example—framed in his mind the objective of producing others like himself and then embarked on the means he thought might lead to the goal. Nor is it just that such creatures lack the necessary wit to have purposes and plan the means to their attainment. It is more absurd than that. For if we could somehow imagine them endowed with the necessary intelligence, then we could not imagine them applying it in that fashion. What their intelligence or reason would tell them, if they had any, is that it is not worth it. Few animals show any interest in or concern for their young, once they have produced them, and in those that do, it persists only until the young are able to shift for themselves. Clearly, it was no hope of begetting these that lured them on. It was, instead, a blind urge that goaded them on, then produced this result. One might say that nature's great plan is thereby fulfilled, which would be rather poetic; but beneath the poetry there is, of course, a truth that could be expressed scientifically.

If one looks at eros in this way and considers that its human expression is not

203

Not fundamentally different from its expression throughout nature, then many apparent mysteries begin to dissolve. They dissolve when one considers the blindness
of eros, its incredible power, and its unfailing result, this latter being the perpetuation of the race—which is not, however, the end that is consciously sought
even in the case of men, who can foresee it. We get inklings of its great power
when we see what must give way before it. Prudence and good sense collapse
almost at once, the moment an outlet for this demonic urge presents itself, even if
but for a moment; it is no wonder, then, that heroic efforts are made, continuously
and on every side, to cage and confine it. These take the form of conventions and
attitudes of shame and modesty that are instilled in one from the tenderest age,
and are woven so tightly that they often enable men and women to dwell in close
proximity, day after day, without breaking them. All such efforts notwithstanding,
however, we continuously see great careers brought to ruin, even thrones abandoned, and sometimes the interests of nations endangered by the insufficiency of
such efforts, in the face of what they seek to restrain. This urge usurps a large part
of the thinking of youth and infects all its emotions, day and night. No allusion
to it fails to quicken immediate interest and, more often than not, to shove from
the stage for the time being whatever other interests one has. No crime is so
heinous that it has not been committed in response to this impulse, and no deed
seems too heroic to attempt in response to the same. Thus does it become the
central ingredient of most song, poetry, and story—and, oddly enough, of much
humor. For most humor appears to result simply from this: someone, seemingly
aware and knowing what he is up to, is nevertheless guided in his actions by
things over which he has no control, and in such a way that he is carried to some
absurd end that he could not really ever have intended. It is the surprise of this
outcome, a surprise produced by the tension between planning and fate, that so
often produces the inner tension that is expressed in laughter. Thus, the clown,
apparently knowing what he is about, suddenly has something blow up in his
face, precisely as a result of what he was so deliberately doing—and onlookers are
bent over in laughter. The inebriate, similarly, plans his own motions, but is
constantly foiled by a force he cannot control, presenting a ridiculous spectacle of
thought versus force that culminates in a victory of force at the actor's expense.
This is at the heart of much that presents itself to the mind as ridiculous, and it
finds its purest and clearest expression in the sexual passion. For here we have,
par excellence, the spectacle of an agent apparently planning and executing his
own actions—deliberately, and often at great pains and expense of time, fortune,
and effort—seemingly knowing what he is doing and why, yet all the time being
entirely goaded from behind by a force that he never created and can now in no
way abate or ignore. Like the clown, his labor carries him to a result that his mind
or reason could never have chosen, and he is landed precisely in what all can at
least dimly see as absurd. If one tries to divest the thing of its passional associations—so as to be blinded as little as possible—and brings clearly before his mind
an actual image of the culmination and goal of the erotic drive, he can see that
nothing could possibly be more totally absurd, nothing less likely as a candidate
for a sane being's aspiration. It is without doubt our perception of this, of the
unsurpassable ridiculousness in the image of sexual union, that prompts men
everywhere to conceal it as nothing else on earth is concealed, and almost to
pretend that it does not exist. It is not mere shame begotten by custom, for no mere
custom could be so universally and tenaciously held—and in any case it is

204

everywhere declared not to be shameful when certain conditions are met. It is, therefore, its inherent absurdity to the mind, together with its ineluctable appeal to the will, that has invested it with this feeling of embarrassment and shame that without fail leads lovers to places of darkness and concealment. What they do must never be seen, for it is so immensely absurd.

This is of course a large subject, and an intriguing one, about which much more could be said; but perhaps the brief and general description before us will suffice to answer the questions that now arise. Namely, is eros, or the sexual passion, an expression of love? What has it to do with love? And what is its moral significance?

Clearly, it is no form of love at all, beyond the fact that it happens to be called by that name, and it has almost nothing to do with love, in any sense in which this is of special moral significance. Eros, or the attraction of the sexes, is found in virtually everything that lives and appears to differ in men only in certain accidental details. Men, for example, are aware of this drive, can formulate and act on deliberate plans with respect to it, can to some degree at least understand it, and can foresee its consequences; but none of these things changes its essential nature. It is in us as irrational, blind, and unchosen as in any insect; it is something that is simply thrust on us by nature, we then to act out our response to it. The fact that we know what we are doing and are aware of what is going on does not change this in the least, for no more did any man ever choose *not* to be impelled by its urging, than did any ever choose to be so impelled. One could not aptly describe a pair of copulating grasshoppers, or mice, or dogs, as making *love*; they are simply copulating. The expression is no less inept when applied to people—except that here we feel some euphemism is needed, and this one serves.

Love, as a sentiment, expresses itself naturally in sympathetic kindness, even sometimes in a kind of identification of oneself with the thought, feelings, and aspirations of another. It is compatible with sexual passion, but it by no means rests on it nor, contrary to what so many would like to believe, does it find its highest expression there. This is made obvious by a number of things; for example, by the natural love of parents for their children, and by the fact that sentiments of genuine love and friendship can exist and sometimes persist through a lifetime among persons of either sex, wherein the erotic element is entirely absent. And on the other side, it is notorious that the sexual passion can be kindled by one for whom one cares nothing at all, and equally, that one may have a friend who is truly beloved who nevertheless stirs this passion not in the least. Looking at it from still another point of view, it is obvious to anyone having a knowledge of human affairs that genuine love, as St. Paul put it, "never fails"; that is to say, it is inseparable from loving kindness in action, and absolutely ennobles everything that it touches. The erotic passion, on the other hand, left to itself seldom succeeds, for it is a notoriously fertile source of folly, of madness, sometimes of human degradation, and very often of cruelty and unspeakable crime.

None of this is of course intended to deny that the two can dwell together; it is only meant to deny that they are one and the same, and even spring from a common source—all of which would probably be obvious if men did not insist on adorning in their own case whatever behavior they share with other animals. Certainly the adoration of lovers is increased by erotic fulfillment, and the latter is itself ennobled by loving sympathy, but an excursus on that theme belongs in manuals for lovers rather than in a philosophical treatise.

QUESTIONS

1. Specify the arguments adduced by Taylor in defense of his claim that sexual passion and love are totally distinct sentiments.
2. On Taylor's view, it is a gross abuse of language to describe the act of human copulation as "making love." Do you agree with his explanation of why people are inclined to describe the act in this way?
3. Do you think that at least some instances of human copulation can justifiably be described as "making love"? If so, specify what conditions must be met and explain why such conditions are relevant.

Peter A. Bertocci

THE HUMAN VENTURE IN SEX, LOVE AND MARRIAGE

Biographical Information. Peter A. Bertocci (b. 1910 in Italy) is professor of philosophy at Boston University. He has written many books, most of which are in the area of philosophy of religion, such as Religion as Creative Insecurity *(1958) and* Is God for Real? *(1971). Two of his books, however, are explicitly concerned with matters of sexual ethics:* The Human Venture in Sex, Love and Marriage *(1949), from which this selection is excerpted, and* Sex, Love and the Person *(1967).*

Argument in the Selection. Bertocci's primary contention is that sex can provide its most enduring and enriching satisfactions only when it is entered into as a "symbolic expression of other human values." He attacks the tendency of some authors, such as Taylor in the previous selection, to portray human sexuality as akin to animal sexuality. Bertocci thinks that such a portrayal neglects the special human significance of sex. On Bertocci's account, the human significance of sex is essentially bound up with love. He develops the notion of a "love progression," whereby love naturally leads to marriage and marriage naturally leads to procreation. Thus, love, marriage, and the family are seen as human values that sex must "symbolically express" in order to provide its most profound satisfactions.

THE HUMAN EXPERIENCE OF SEX

When a person decides that he is going to get all he can out of sex *as* sex, he is driven into an almost endless progression: he must find a new fancy, a new variety of sexual experience, real or imaginary, for he soon tires of the last mode of sexual exploration. Having made sex an end in itself, as a miser makes money an end in itself, or as a glutton makes food an end in itself, there is nothing more to do but seek some more thrilling or novel sexual experience. Many sexual perverts are products of this chase for new forms of pleasure. They teach us that sexual expression for its own sake brings diminishing returns. I am not, of course, trying to say that every incontinent person becomes a sex pervert, but he invites trouble for himself and others when he tries to find in sex what sex as such cannot give him. Sex experience for its own sake, and certainly when the other person is simply "used," hardens the arteries of tender feeling. Though sexual perversion is by no means a necessary result, the loss of tenderness and sympathy, let alone self-confidence, is a tremendous price to pay for sex pleasure.

On the other hand, sex is an increasing source of personal enrichment when dedicated to objectives other than mere self-satisfaction. The fact of human experience seems to be that persons enjoy deeper, more lasting, and more profound satisfaction when the normal experience of sex lust is not primarily an end in itself but a symbolic expression of other values. This, after all, is true not only about sex but about other desires also. We enjoy eating at a banquet in honor of a friend more than eating in solitude. Before elaborating this theme, several remarks must be made about a counter-theme that has pervaded, sometimes quite subtly, much thinking about the functioning of sex in human life.

There is a tendency to think of sex in human experience as a continuation of the sex function in animals. Man's life, including sex, is more complicated but not essentially different from that of the higher animals. The prevalence of this view has sometimes led us to suppose that sex education is hardly necessary since at the right time the biological organism will react effectively and appropriately as it does among animals. Thinking of man as a complicated animal, we falsely reasoned that his sex behavior is as mechanical and automatic with him as it is with animals. Indeed some of us added, to expect him to control himself sexually is like expecting an animal in heat to reject sexual advances. The best we can do, according to this view, is to realize that man is a higher animal and teach him enough of the physiology of sex to avoid disease.

This line of reasoning neglects the *human* significance of sex. Sex in the human is so interwoven with his total psychological being that, once allowance is made for some physiological similarities, the contrasts are more illuminating than the likenesses. To compare the sounds an animal makes with the poetry of word symbols gives some notion of the range of differences possible. The biological transaction of sexual intercourse in animals has at its best nowhere near the possible meaning that a similar biological transaction can have in human experience. Sex education has failed to make enough of the function of sex as human experience. In consequence we have talked as if the biology of sex measures its importance as a human function.

Consequently the argument against intercourse has emphasized the physical effects of sexual promiscuity, the danger of sexual diseases and of pregnancy. These must not be minimized, but they have played such a large part in the so-called "case for chastity" that both young and old have wondered, with justification, what possible case can be made against promiscuity once knowledge of the methods of disease prevention and contraceptives has been increased and disseminated. The concern of the military during World War II did not go beyond educating young men and women for physical efficiency. The general impression was left that sin is not in sexual intercourse but in the infection that may result from carelessness. We seemed to be bankrupt of really adequate reasons why human beings should abstain from promiscuity when they are confident that impregnation or venereal diseases can be prevented.

The situation will not be greatly changed until we become more fully aware of the conditions in human experience under which sexual intercourse makes its deepest contributions. Here we are clearly in the area of the interpretation of the value of sex as part of the meaning of life. If we cannot interpret the higher values of sex as clearly as we have explained physiological, and even psychological, details, we shall go on "expressing" sex and "avoiding frustration" when we might be finding, through sex experience, a creative human joy.

THE HUMAN CHALLENGE IN LOVE

The assumption at this stage of the argument is that love, marriage, and the home are among the supreme values of human existence; that the human beings who cannot enjoy the blessings that love, marriage, and the home bestow are relatively poverty-stricken. We shall try to show that the experience of sex may bless or endanger love, that it may bless or be a constant source of friction in marriage, that it may be a solid foundation for co-operative family life or a source of frustrating disharmony.

As already suggested, there is a "love progression" in human life. This progression is affected by the sexual progression, but it has its own laws. The love progression protects the satisfactions of sex, but sex, unless mastered, will endanger the progression of love and enslave the person. The individual in love invests his energies and abilities in joyous concern for the security and growth of another. He finds fulfillment of his own life in consecration to the needs and development of his beloved. As his love grows, his self-discipline increases with a view to insuring the happiness of his sweetheart. He rethinks and replans the goals of his life so that she may find opportunity and realization within them. "To love a person productively implies to care, to feel responsible for his life, not only for his physical existence, but for the growth and development of all his human powers."[1]

Loving, therefore, is a kind of growing. Love inspires one to live with at least one other person in mind. The circle of self-enjoyment grows into an ellipse in which the two poles are included. But, as Plato long ago reminded us, love is a suffering yearning for what one does not possess completely. The individual must refocus his mind and body, re-form his ideas and dreams, so that the good he wants for himself and for his sweetheart may be realized. Love means growth; it means work; it means moral progress. Thus *love, inclusive of sex, needs marriage to protect and nourish its values. And marriage, to be a most fruitful and inclusive experience which protects and nourishes the values of both love and sex, must be put to work in building a family and a society.* This is the inner progression of love.

[1] Fromm, Eric. *Man for Himself.* (New York: Farrar & Rinehart)

It is evident that there will be many obstacles on the way to realizing personality and character built around love. The deception in the progression of love is just the opposite of that in the sexual progression. For now the individual will be tempted to stop short of more complete fulfillment. It will be easy to think that a sexual experience enjoyed by two persons will remain an adequate source of joy, that the pleasure of sex and love without marriage will endure, that marriage without commitment to objectives greater than the union of two married lovers will maintain a challenging equilibrium. For there is no doubt that sex lust usually brings pleasure sufficiently gratifying to seem entirely satisfactory, especially to those who do not know the quality of sex love. So also with this next step in the progression of love: sex love without marriage can bring so much satisfaction, at least for a time, that two persons may be tempted to forego the more complete satisfaction of married love. Then there are some who, having reached a high level of married love, may be tempted to forfeit the more creative experience that children and a home can bring.

Let the sexual act be the expression of the conscious desire and decision to become parents, and that act reaches its zenith in human feeling, inspiration, and fulfillment. It is almost foolish to try to make this experience clear to those who have not known it. Words that receive their content from other levels of sex experience are quite inadequate for this. Let two persons extend their love for each other into the tender and responsible decision to have and care for children, and they will find the meaning of the sexual experience immeasurably enriched.

Sex, love, marriage, family, and social responsibility are human ventures all along the line. The question is: Which venture brings completeness, invites to growth in character and personality, enables the individual to feel that he has accepted the role that his abilities allow in the achievement of a dependable social order? It is our thesis that love, including sex love, is the more radiant and satisfying when it becomes a means of communicating one's concern for the wider range of values that purposeful living together makes possible. Sex without love, love without marriage, and marriage without creative commitments to children (or the equivalent) are in constant danger of vanishing away. Persons disregard the laws of growth and development in human nature only to find that they have forfeited their heritage.

Love, at its best, is the supreme victory over parasitism and egoism. It is a unique fruition of human experience, so unique and so different from anything in the physical and biological world, that it stands as the richest product of human effort. It is not, however, a fruit which just comes with maturation. It will be no greater than the person in love; it will reflect and challenge the intelligence, emotion, and discipline dedicated to its development.

QUESTIONS

1. To what extent, if at all, does Bertocci successfully defend traditional sexual morality?
2. If you disagree with Bertocci's analysis of the "human significance" of sex, draw out your own analysis of its human significance.
3. Does Bertocci think that the sex life of a childless married couple will be less satisfying than the sex life of a married couple with children? Explain and evaluate his view.

Albert Ellis

THE JUSTIFICATION OF SEX WITHOUT LOVE

Biographical Information. *Albert Ellis (b. 1913) is a clinical psychologist whose private practice for many years centered on psychotherapy and marriage counseling. Among his many publications on the multiple facets of human sexuality are* The Art and Science of Love *(1960),* Creative Marriage *(1961),* The Case for Sexual Liberty *(1964), and* Homosexuality: Its Causes and Cure *(1965).*

Argument in the Selection. *Ellis contends that we ought to accept a very liberal attitude toward sex without love. He acknowledges that sex with love (affectional sex) is usually more desirable than sex without love (nonaffectional sex). Nevertheless, he argues that we ought not to condemn sex without love; a repressive attitude would needlessly deprive many people of an effective channel of satisfaction, or at least cause them to feel needless guilt. Ellis concludes by considering and attempting to provide answers to the following arguments that might be raised against his position. (1) Sex without love is self-defeating because it allows immediate gratification to triumph over greater long-term enjoyments. (2) The toleration of sex without love will lead to the demise of sex with love.*

A scientific colleague of mine, who holds a professorial post in the department of sociology and anthropology at one of our leading universities, recently asked me about my stand on the question of human beings having sex relations without love. Although I have taken something of a position on this issue in my book, *The American Sexual Tragedy*, I have never quite considered the problem in sufficient detail. So here goes.

In general, I feel that affectional, as against non-affectional, sex relations are *desirable* but not *necessary*. It is usually desirable that an association between coitus and affection exist—particularly in marriage, because it is often difficult for two individuals to keep finely tuned to each other over a period of years, and if there is not a good deal of love between them, one may tend to feel sexually imposed upon by the other.

The fact, however, that the co-existence of sex and love may be desirable does not, to my mind, make it necessary. My reasons for this view are several:

1. Many individuals—including, even, many married couples—do find great satisfaction in having sex relations without love. I do not consider it fair to label these individuals as criminal just because they may be in the minority.

Moreover, even if they are in the minority (as may well *not* be the case), I am sure that they number literally millions of men and women. If so, they constitute a sizeable subgroup of humans whose rights to sex satisfaction should be fully acknowledged and protected.

(2.) Even if we consider the supposed majority of individuals who find greater satisfaction in sex-love than in sex-sans-love relations, it is doubtful if all or most of them do so for *all* their lives. During much of their existence, especially their younger years, these people tend to find sex-without-love quite satisfying, and even to prefer it to affectional sex.

When they become older, and their sex drives tend to wane, they may well emphasize coitus with rather than without affection. But why should we condemn them *while* they still prefer sex to sex-love affairs?

(3) Many individuals, especially females in our culture, who say that they only enjoy sex when it is accompanied by affection are actually being unthinkingly conformist and unconsciously hypocritical. If they were able to contemplate themselves objectively, and had the courage of their inner convictions, they would find sex without love eminently gratifying.

This is not to say that they would *only* enjoy non-affectional coitus, nor that they would always find it *more* satisfying than affectional sex. But, in the depths of their psyche and soma, they would deem sex without love pleasurable *too.*

And why should they not? And why should we, by our puritanical know-nothingness, force these individuals to drive a considerable portion of their sex feelings and potential satisfactions underground?

If, in other words, we view sexuo-amative relations as desirable rather than necessary, we sanction the innermost thoughts and drives of many of our fellow-men and fellowwomen to have sex *and* sex-love relations. If we take the opposing view, we hardly destroy these innermost thoughts and drives, but frequently tend to intensify them while denying them open and honest outlet. This, as Freud pointed out, is one of the main (though by no means the only) source of rampant neurosis.

(4) I firmly believe that sex is a biological, as well as a social, drive, and that in its biological phases it is essentially non-affectional. If this is so, then we can expect that, however we try to civilize the sex drives—and civilize them to *some* degree we certainly must—there will always be an underlying tendency for them to escape from our society-inculcated shackles and to be still partly felt in the raw.

When so felt, when our biosocial sex urges lead us to desire and enjoy sex without (as well as with), love, I do not see why we should make their experiences feel needlessly guilty.

(5) Many individuals—many millions in our society, I am afraid—have little or no capacity for affection or love. The majority of these individuals, perhaps, are emotionally disturbed, and should preferably be helped to increase their affectional propensities. But a large number are not particularly disturbed, and instead are neurologically or cerebrally deficient.

Mentally deficient persons, for example, as well as many dull normals (who, together, include several million citizens of our nation) are notoriously shallow in their feelings, and probably intrinsically so. Since these kinds of individuals—like the neurotic and the organically deficient—are for the most part, in our day and age, *not* going to be properly treated and *not* going to overcome their deficiencies, and since most of them definitely *do* have sex desires, I again see no point in making them guilty when they have non-loving sex relations.

Surely these unfortunate individuals are sufficiently handicapped by their *really?* disturbances or impairments without our adding to their woes by anathematizing them when they manage to achieve some non-amative sexual release.

211

6 Under some circumstances—though these, I admit, may be rare—some people find more satisfaction in non-loving coitus even though, under other circumstances, these *same* people may find more satisfaction in sex-love affairs. Thus, the man who *normally* enjoys being with his girlfriend because he loves as well as is sexually attracted to her, may occasionally find immense satisfaction in being with another girl with whom he has distinctly non-loving relations. Granting that this may be (or is it?) unusual, I do not see why it should be condemnable.

7 If many people get along excellently and most cooperatively with business partners, employees, professors, laboratory associates, acquaintances, and even spouses for whom they have little or no love or affection, but with whom they have certain specific things in common, I do not see why there cannot be individuals who get along excellently and most cooperatively with sex mates with whom they may have little else in common.

I personally can easily see the tragic plight of a man who spends much time with a girl with whom he has nothing in common but sex: since I believe that life is too short to be well consumed in relatively one-track or intellectually low-level pursuits. I would also think it rather unrewarding for a girl to spend much time with a male with whom she had mutually satisfying sex, friendship, and cultural interests but no love involvement. This is because I would like to see people, in their 70-odd years of life, have maximum rather than minimum satisfactions with individuals of the other sex with whom they spend considerable time.

I can easily see, however, even the most intelligent and highly cultured individuals spending a *little* time with members of the other sex with whom they have common sex and cultural but no real love interests. And I feel that, for the time expended in this manner, their lives may be immeasurably enriched.

Moreover, when I encounter friends or psychotherapy clients who become enamored and spend considerable time and effort thinking about and being with a member of the other sex with whom they are largely sexually obsessed, and for whom they have little or no love, I mainly view these sexual infatuations as one of the penalties of their being human. For humans are the kind of animals who are easily disposed to this type of behavior.

I believe that one of the distinct inconveniences or tragedies of human sexuality is that it endows us, and perhaps particularly the males among us, with a propensity to become exceptionally involved and infatuated with members of the other sex whom, had we no sex urges, we would hardly notice. That is too bad; and it might well be a better world if it were otherwise. But it is *not* otherwise, and I think it is silly and pernicious for us to condemn ourselves because we are the way that we are in this respect.

We had better *accept* our biosocial tendencies, or our fallible humanity—instead of constantly blaming ourselves and futilely trying to change certain of its relatively harmless, though still somewhat tragic, aspects.

For reasons such as these, I feel that although it is usually—if not always—*desirable* for human beings to have sex relations with those they love rather than with those they do not love, it is by no means *necessary* that they do so. When we teach that it *is* necessary, we only needlessly condemn millions of our citizens to self-blame and atonement.

The position which I take—that there are several good reasons why affectional, as against non-affectional, sex relations are desirable but not necessary—can be assailed on several counts. I shall now consider some of the objections to this position to see if they cannot be effectively answered.

It may be said that an individual who has non-loving instead of loving sex relations is not necessarily wicked but that he is self-defeating because, while going for immediate gratification, he will miss out on even greater enjoyments. But this would only be true if such an individual (whom we shall assume, for the sake of discussion, *would* get greater enjoyment from affectional sex relations than from non-affectional ones) were *usually* or *always* having non-affectionate coitus. If he were *occasionally* or *sometimes* having love with sex, and the rest of the time having sex without love, he would be missing out on very little, if any, enjoyment.

Under these circumstances, in fact, he would normally get *more* pleasure from *sometimes* having sex without love. For the fact remains, and must not be unrealistically ignored, that in our present-day society sex without love is *much more frequently* available than sex with love.

Consequently, to ignore non-affectional coitus when affectional coitus is not available would, from the standpoint of enlightened self-interest, be sheer folly. In relation both to immediate *and* greater enjoyment, the individual would thereby be losing out.

The claim can be made of course that if an individual sacrifices sex without love *now* he will experience more pleasure by having sex with love in the future. This is an interesting claim; but I find no empirical evidence to sustain it. In fact, on theoretical grounds it seems most unlikely that it will be sustained. It is akin to the claim that if an individual starves himself for several days in a row he will greatly enjoy eating a meal at the end of a week or a month. I am sure he will—provided that he is then not too sick or debilitated to enjoy anything! But, even assuming that such an individual derives enormous satisfaction from his one meal a week or a month, is his *total* satisfaction greater than it would have been had he enjoyed three good meals a day for that same period of time? I doubt it.

So with sex. Anyone who starves himself sexually for a long period of time—as virtually everyone who rigidly sticks to the sex with love doctrine must—will (perhaps) *ultimately* achieve greater satisfaction when he does find sex with love than he would have had, had he been sexually freer. But, even assuming that this is so, will his *total* satisfaction be greater?

It may be held that if both sex with and without love are permitted in any society, the non-affectional sex will drive out affectional sex, somewhat in accordance with Gresham's laws of currency. On the contrary, however, there is much reason to believe that just because an individual has sex relations, for quite a period, on a non-affectional basis, he will be more than eager to replace it, eventually, with sex with love.

From my clinical experience, I have often found that males who most want to settle down to having a single mistress or wife are those who have tried numerous lighter affairs and found them wanting. The view that sex without love eradicates the need for affectional sex relationships is somewhat akin to the ignorance is bliss theory. For it virtually says that if people never experienced sex with love they would never realize how good it was and therefore would never strive for it. Or else the proponents of this theory seem to be saying that sex without love is so greatly satisfying, and sex with love so intrinsically difficult and disadvanta-geous to attain, that given the choice between the two, most people would pick the former. If this is so, then by all means let them pick the former: with which, in terms of their greater and total happiness, they would presumably be better off.

I doubt however, that this hypothesis is factually sustainable. From clinical experience, again, I can say that individuals who are capable of sex with love usually seek and find it; while those who remain non-affectional in their sex affairs generally are not particularly capable of sex with love and need psycho-therapeutic help before they can become thus capable.

QUESTIONS

1. If society as a whole openly adopted the attitude promulgated by Ellis, would the overall result in terms of human happiness be positive or negative? Explain and defend your view.

2. Do you think that Ellis's overall argument is insightful and telling, or do you think it is shortsighted and simplistic? Explain and defend your view.

3. Argue for or against the following claim: Prostitution is an ethically acceptable practice.

Burton M. Leiser

HOMOSEXUALITY AND THE "UNNATURALNESS ARGUMENT"

Biographical Information. *Burton M. Leiser, professor and chairperson of the department of philosophy at Drake University, has also taught at the State University College at Buffalo and at Sir George Williams University. His publications include* Custom, Law, and Morality *(1969) and* Liberty, Justice and Morals *(1973), as well as articles in philosophy and other fields—biblical criticism, religion, and archaeology.*

Argument in the Selection. *Leiser critiques an argument which is often advanced to show the immorality of homosexual behavior: Homosexual behavior is unnatural and therefore immoral. On Leiser's analysis, an adequate "unnaturalness argument" would have to provide the follow-ing: (1) a clearly specified sense of "unnatural" according to which homosexual behavior is rightly identified as unnatural; (2) substantia-tion for thinking that the unnaturalness of homosexual behavior is linked with the production of harm and is thus a ground of moral condemnation. Leiser analyzes four possible senses that proponents of the argument might attribute to "unnatural." Finding that each sugges-*

tion fails to satisfy one or both of the conditions necessary to sustain the argument, he concludes that the argument must be rejected. ✗

[The alleged "unnaturalness" of homosexuality] raises the question of the meaning of *nature, natural,* and similar terms. Theologians and other moralists have said that [homosexual acts] violate the "natural law," and that they are therefore immoral and ought to be prohibited by the state.

The word *nature* has a built-in ambiguity that can lead to serious misunderstandings. When something is said to be "natural" or in conformity with "natural law" or the "law of nature," this may mean either (1) that it is in conformity with the descriptive laws of nature, or (2) that it is not artificial, that man has not imposed his will or his devices upon events or conditions as they exist or would have existed without such interference.

1. *The Descriptive Laws of Nature.* The laws of nature, as these are understood by the scientist, differ from the laws of man. The former are purely descriptive, whereas the latter are prescriptive. When a scientist says that water boils at 212° Fahrenheit or that the volume of a gas varies directly with the heat that is applied to it and inversely with the pressure, he means merely that as a matter of recorded and observable fact, pure water under standard conditions always boils at precisely 212° Fahrenheit and that as a matter of observed fact, the volume of a gas rises as it is heated and falls as pressure is applied to it. These "laws" merely describe the manner in which physical substances *actually behave.* They differ from municipal and federal laws in that they *do not prescribe behavior.* Unlike manmade laws, natural laws are not passed by any legislator or group of legislators; they are not proclaimed or announced; they impose no obligation upon anyone or anything; their "violation" entails no penalty, and there is no reward for "following" them or "abiding by" them. When a scientist says that the air in a tire "obeys" the laws of nature that "govern" gases, he does *not* mean that the air, having been informed that it *ought* to behave in a certain way, behaves appropriately under the right conditions. He means, rather, that as a matter of fact, the air in a tire *will* behave like all other gases. In saying that Boyle's law "governs" the behavior of gases, he means merely that gases do, as a matter of fact, behave in accordance with Boyle's law, and that Boyle's law enables one to predict accurately what will happen to a given quantity of a gas as its pressure is raised; he does *not* mean to suggest that some heavenly voice has proclaimed that all gases should henceforth behave in accordance with the terms of Boyle's law and that a ghostly policeman patrols the world, ready to mete out punishments to any gases that "violate" the heavenly decree. In fact, according to the scientist, it does not make sense to speak of a natural law being violated. For if there were a true exception to a so-called law of nature, the exception would require a change in the description of those phenomena, and the "law" would have been shown to be no law at all. The laws of nature are revised as scientists discover new phenomena that require new refinements in their descriptions of the way things actually happen. In this respect they differ fundamentally from human laws, which are

215

revised periodically by legislators who are not so interested in *describing* human behavior as they are in *prescribing what human behavior should* be.

2. *The Artificial as a Form of the Unnatural.* On occasion when we say that something is not natural, we mean that it is a product of human artifice. My typewriter is not a natural object, in this sense, for the substances of which it is composed have been removed from their natural state—the state in which they existed before men came along—and have been transformed by a series of chemical and physical and mechanical processes into other substances. They have been rearranged into a whole that is quite different from anything found in nature. In short, my typewriter is an artificial object. In this sense, the clothing that I wear as I lecture before my students is not natural, for it has been transformed considerably from the state in which it was found in nature; and my wearing of clothing as I lecture before my students is also not natural, in this sense, for in my natural state, before the application of anything artificial, before any human interference with things as they are, I am quite naked. Human laws, being artificial conventions designed to exercise a degree of control over the natural inclinations and propensities of men, may in this sense be considered to be unnatural.

Now when theologians and moralists speak of homosexuality, contraception, abortion, and other forms of human behavior as being unnatural, and say that for that reason such behavior must be considered to be wrong, in what sense are they using the word *unnatural*? Are they saying that homosexual behavior and the use of contraceptives are contrary to the scientific laws of nature, are they saying that they are artificial forms of behavior, or are they using the terms *natural* and *unnatural* in some third sense?

They cannot mean that homosexual behavior (to stick to the subject presently under discussion) violates the laws of nature in the first sense, for, as we have pointed out, in *that* sense it is impossible to violate the laws of nature. Those laws, being merely descriptive of what actually does happen, would have to *include* homosexual behavior if such behavior does actually take place. Even if the defenders of the theological view that homosexuality is unnatural were to appeal to a statistical analysis by pointing out that such behavior is not normal from a statistical point of view, and therefore not what the laws of nature require, it would be open to their critics to reply that any descriptive law of nature must account for and incorporate all statistical deviations, and that the laws of nature, in this sense, do not require anything. These critics might also note that the best statistics available reveal that about half of all American males engage in homosexual activity at some time in their lives, and that a very large percentage of American males have exclusively homosexual relations for a fairly extensive period of time; from which it would follow that such behavior is natural, for them, at any rate, in this sense of the word *natural*.

If those who say that homosexual behavior is unnatural are using the term *unnatural* in the second sense, it is difficult to see why they should be fussing over it. Certainly nothing is intrinsically wrong with going against nature (if that is how it should be put) in this sense. That which is artificial is often far better than what is natural. Artificial homes seem, at any rate, to be more suited to human habitation and more conducive to longer life and better health than caves and other natural shelters. There are distinct advantages to the use of such unnatural (i.e. artificial) amenities as clothes, furniture, and books. Although we may dream of an idyllic return to nature in our more wistful moments, we would soon

216

discover, as Thoreau did in his attempt to escape from the artificiality of civilization, that needles and thread, knives and matches, ploughs and nails, and countless other products of human artifice are essential to human life. We would discover, as Plato pointed out in the *Republic*, that no man can be truly self-sufficient. Some of the by-products of industry are less than desirable; but neither industry itself, nor the products of industry, are intrinsically evil, even though both are unnatural in this sense of the word.

Interference with nature is not evil in itself. Nature, as some writers have put it, must be tamed. In some respects man must look upon it as an enemy to be conquered. If nature were left to its own devices, without the intervention of human artifice, men would be consumed with disease, they would be plagued by insects, they would be chained to the places where they were born with no means of swift communication or transport, and they would suffer the discomforts and the torments of wind and weather and flood and fire with no practical means of combating any of them. Interfering with nature, doing battle with nature, using human will and reason and skill to thwart what might otherwise follow from the conditions that prevail in the world, is a peculiarly human enterprise, one that can hardly be condemned merely because it does what is not natural.

Homosexual behavior can hardly be considered to be unnatural in this sense. There is nothing "artificial" about such behavior. On the contrary, it is quite natural, in this sense, to those who engage in it. And even if it were not, even if it were quite artificial, this is not in itself a ground for condemning it.

It would seem, then, that those who condemn homosexuality as an unnatural form of behavior must mean something else by the word *unnatural*, something not covered by either of the preceding definitions. A third possibility is this:

3. *Anything Uncommon or Abnormal is Unnatural*. If this is what is meant by those who condemn homosexuality on the ground that it is unnatural, it is quite obvious that their condemnation cannot be accepted without further argument. For the fact that a given form of behavior is uncommon provides no justification for condemning it. Playing viola in a string quartet is no doubt an uncommon form of human behavior. I do not know what percentage of the human race engages in such behavior, or what percentage of his life any given violist devotes to such behavior, but I suspect that the number of such people must be very small indeed, and that the total number of manhours spent in such activity would justify our calling that form of activity uncommon, abnormal (in the sense that it is statistically not the kind of thing that people are ordinarily inclined to do), and therefore unnatural, in this sense of the word. Yet there is no reason to suppose that such uncommon, abnormal behavior is, by virtue of its uncommonness, deserving of condemnation or ethically or morally wrong. On the contrary, many forms of behavior are praised precisely because they are so uncommon. Great artists, poets, musicians, and scientists are "abnormal" in this sense; but clearly the world is better off for having them, and it would be absurd to condemn them or their activities for their failure to be common and normal. If homosexual behavior is wrong, then, it must be for some reason other than its "unnaturalness" in this sense of the word.

4. *Any Use of an Organ or an Instrument That Is Contrary to Its Principal Purpose or Function Is Unnatural*. Every organ and every instrument—perhaps even every creature—has a function to perform, one for which it is particularly designed. Any use of those instruments and organs that is consonant with their

217

purposes is natural and proper, but any use that is inconsistent with their principal functions is unnatural and improper, and to that extent, evil or harmful. Human teeth, for example, are admirably designed for their principal functions— biting and chewing the kinds of food suitable for human consumption. But they are not particularly well suited for prying the caps from beer bottles. If they are used for the latter purpose, which is not natural to them, they are liable to crack or break under the strain. The abuse of one's teeth leads to their destruction and to a consequent deterioration in one's overall health. If they are used only for their proper function, however, they may continue to serve well for many years. Similarly, a given drug may have a proper function. If used in the furtherance of that end, it can preserve life and restore health. But if it is abused, and employed for purposes for which it was never intended, it may cause serious harm and even death. The natural uses of things are good and proper, but their unnatural uses are bad and harmful.

What we must do, then, is to find the proper use, or the true purpose, of each organ in our bodies. Once we have discovered that, we will know what constitutes the natural use of each organ, and what constitutes an unnatural, abusive, and potentially harmful employment of the various parts of our bodies. If we are rational, we will be careful to confine our behavior to our proper functions and to refrain from unnatural behavior. According to those philosophers who follow this line of reasoning, the way to discover the "proper" use of any organ is to determine what it is peculiarly suited to do. The eye is suited for seeing, the ear for hearing, the nerves for transmitting impulses from one part of the body to another, and so on.

What are the sex organs peculiarly suited to do? Obviously, they are peculiarly suited to enable men and women to reproduce their own kind. No other organ in the body is capable of fulfilling that function. It follows, according to those who follow the natural-law line, that the "proper" or "natural" function of the sex organs is reproduction, and that strictly speaking, any use of those organs for other purposes is unnatural, abusive, potentially harmful, and therefore wrong. The sex organs have been given to us in order to enable us to maintain the continued existence of mankind on this earth. All perversions—including masturbation, homosexual behavior, and heterosexual intercourse that deliberately frustrates the design of the sexual organs—are unnatural and bad. As Pope Pius XI once said, "Private individuals have no other power over the members of their bodies than that which pertains to their natural ends."

But the problem is not so easily resolved. Is it true that every organ has one and only one proper function? A hammer may have been designed to pound nails, and it may perform that particular job best. But it is not sinful to employ a hammer to crack nuts if I have no other more suitable tool immediately available. The hammer, being a relatively versatile tool, may be employed in a number of ways. It has no one "proper" or "natural" function. A woman's eyes are well adapted to seeing, it is true. But they seem also to be well adapted to flirting. Is a woman's use of her eyes for the latter purpose sinful merely because she is not using them, at that moment, for their "primary" purpose of seeing? Our sexual organs are uniquely adapted for procreation, but that is obviously not the only function for which they are adapted. Human beings may—and do—use those organs for a great many other purposes, and it is difficult to see why any *one* use should be considered to be the only proper one. The sex organs, for one thing, seem to be particularly well adapted to give their owners and others intense sensations of pleasure. Unless one believes that pleasure itself is bad, there seems to be little reason to believe that the use of the sex organs for the production of pleasure in oneself or in others is evil. In view of the peculiar design of these organs, with their great concentration of nerve endings, it would seem that they were designed (if they *were* designed) with that very goal in mind, and that their use for such purposes would be no more unnatural than their use for the purpose of procreation.

Nor should we overlook the fact that human sex organs may be and are used to express, in the deepest and most intimate way open to man, the love of one person for another. Even the most ardent opponents of "unfruitful" intercourse admit that sex does serve this function. They have accordingly conceded that a man and his wife may have intercourse even though she is pregnant, or past the age of child bearing, or in the infertile period of her menstrual cycle.

Human beings are remarkably complex and adaptable creatures. Neither they nor their organs can properly be compared to hammers or to other tools. The analogy quickly breaks down. The generalization that a given organ or instrument has one and only one proper function does not hold up, even with regard to the simplest manufactured tools, for, as we have seen, a tool may be used for more than one purpose—less effectively than one especially designed for a given task, perhaps, but "properly" and certainly not *sinfully*. A woman may use her eyes not only to see and to flirt, but also to earn money—if she is, for example, an actress or a model. Though neither of the latter functions seems to have been a part of the original "design," if one may speak sensibly of *design* in this context, of the eye, it is difficult to see why such a use of the eyes of a woman should be considered sinful, perverse, or unnatural. Her sex organs have the unique capacity of producing ova and nurturing human embryos, under the right conditions; but why should any other use of those organs, including their use to bring pleasure to their owner or to someone else, or to manifest love to another person, or even, perhaps, to earn money, be regarded as perverse, sinful, or unnatural? Similarly, a man's sexual organs possess the unique capacity of causing the generation of another human being, but if a man chooses to use them for pleasure, or for the expression of love, or for some other purpose—so long as he does not interfere with the rights of some other person—the fact that his sex organs do have their unique capabilities does not constitute a convincing justification for condemning their other uses as being perverse, sinful, unnatural, or criminal. If a man "perverts" himself by wiggling his ears for the entertainment of his neighbors instead of using them exclusively for their "natural" function of hearing, no one thinks of consigning him to prison. If he abuses his teeth by using them to pull staples from memos—a function for which teeth were clearly not designed—he is not accused of being immoral, degraded, and degenerate. The fact that people *are* condemned for using their sex organs for their own pleasure or profit, or for that of others, may be more revealing about the prejudices and taboos of our society than it is about our perception of the true nature or purpose or "end" (whatever that might be) of our bodies.

To sum up, then, the proposition that any use of an organ that is contrary to its principal purpose or function is unnatural assumes that organs have a principal purpose or function, but this may be denied on the ground that the purpose or function of a given organ may vary according to the needs or desires of its owner.

It may be denied on the ground that a given organ may have more than one principal purpose or function, and any attempt to call one use or another the only natural one seems to be arbitrary, if not questionbegging. Also, the proposition suggests that what is unnatural is evil or depraved. This goes beyond the pure description of things, and enters into the problem of the evaluation of human behavior, which leads us to the fifth meaning of "natural."

5.) *That Which Is Natural Is Good, and Whatever Is Unnatural Is Bad.* When one condemns homosexuality or masturbation or the use of contraceptives on the ground that it is unnatural, one implies that whatever is unnatural is bad, wrongful, or perverse. But as we have seen, in some senses of the word, the unnatural (i.e., the artificial) is often very good, whereas that which is natural (i.e., that which has not been subjected to human artifice or improvement) may be very bad indeed. Of course, interference with nature may be bad. Ecologists have made us more aware than we have ever been of the dangers of unplanned and uninformed interference with nature. But this is not to say that *all* interference with nature is bad. Every time a man cuts down a tree to make room for a home for himself, or catches a fish to feed himself or his family, he is interfering with nature. If men did not interfere with nature, they would have no homes, they could eat no fish, and, in fact, they could not survive. What, then, can be meant by those who say that whatever is natural is good and whatever is unnatural is bad? Clearly, they cannot have intended merely to reduce the word *natural* to a synonym of *good, right,* and *proper,* and *unnatural* to a synonym of *evil, wrong, improper, corrupt,* and *depraved.* If that were all they had intended to do, there would be very little to discuss as to whether a given form of behavior might be proper even though it is not in strict conformity with someone's views of what is natural; for good and natural being synonyms, it would follow inevitably that whatever is good must be natural, and vice versa, by definition. This is certainly not what the opponents of homosexuality have been saying when they claim that homosexuality, being unnatural, is evil. For if it were, their claim would be quite empty. They would be saying merely that homosexuality, being evil, is evil—a redundancy that could as easily be reduced to the simpler assertion that homosexuality is evil. This assertion, however, is not an argument. Those who oppose homosexuality and other sexual "perversions" on the ground that they are "unnatural" are saying that there is some objectively identifiable quality in such behavior that is unnatural; and that that quality, once it has been identified by some kind of scientific observation, can be seen to be detrimental to those who engage in such behavior, or to those around them; and that *because* of the harm (physical, mental, moral, or spiritual) that results from engaging in any behavior possessing the attribute of unnaturalness, such behavior must be considered to be wrongful, and should be discouraged by society. "Unnaturalness" and "wrongfulness" are not synonyms, then, but different concepts. The problem with which we are wrestling is that we are unable to find a meaning for *unnatural* that enables us to arrive at the conclusion that homosexuality is unnatural or that if homosexuality is unnatural, it is therefore wrongful behavior. We have examined four common meanings of *natural* and *unnatural,* and have seen that none of them performs the task that it must perform if the advocates of this argument are to prevail. Without some more satisfactory explanation of the connection between the wrongfulness of homosexuality and its alleged unnaturalness, the argument must be rejected.

QUESTIONS

1. Do you think that the "unnaturalness argument" can be developed in a way that avoids the criticisms leveled by Leiser? If so, draw out such an argument.

2. Advance arguments for or against the following claim: Homosexual behavior is immoral.

3. Critically assess the following argument: It is necessary that homosexual behavior, even between consenting adults, be considered a criminal offense; toleration of homosexual behavior will have long-term consequences disastrous for society.

John Wilson

LOGIC, SEXUAL MORALITY, AND HOMOSEXUALITY

Biographical Information. *John Wilson (b. 1928), an Englishman, is a philosopher who has taught at the University of Toronto and at the University of Sussex. He has maintained a long-standing interest in matters of applied ethics and moral education. His several books include* Reason and Morals, Introduction to Moral Education, *and* Logic and Sexual Morality, *from which this selection is excerpted.*

Argument in the Selection. *Wilson argues that society, given the emerging powers of behavioral engineering, may eventually be confronted with basic choices concerning the direction(s) in which human sexuality is to be channeled. Should we raise a child to be exclusively heterosexual, exclusively homosexual, or perhaps bisexual? On Wilson's view, such questions can be adequately answered only by appeal to two permanent features of human welfare: (1) the stability and integration of the human person and (2) the development and expansion of the human personality. Holding that all matters of sexual morality ought to be decided in the light of these two criteria, Wilson proceeds to use them in an evaluation of homosexuality. He concludes, at least in a tentative and provisional way, that homosexuality is not as acceptable as heterosexuality.*

To ask what our sexual lives ideally ought to be is to ask what sort of creatures human beings ought to be; and, given wide powers of changing human nature, we plainly cannot give a permanent answer to such a question. We might conceive of an 'ideal' human being, with an 'ideal' sex life; but even if we cannot detect any faults in our picture, it would always be open for someone far in the future, armed with more knowledge of the possibilities of changing human nature, to make a more exciting and fuller picture, to which we would have given our assent if we had only been imaginative enough to form it for ourselves. To ask this question

221

would be like asking what the 'ideal' symphony is. We might answer that (say) Beethoven's Ninth was as near the ideal as anyone had yet got, but of course there might be a super-Beethoven in the future, someone who had learned to do more things with music than Beethoven could. He too could not claim to have 'achieved the ideal', since a super-super-Beethoven might in due course make *him* look small.

Even the depth psychologists can give us little help, if we insist on looking as far ahead as we are looking now. Our conception of 'human nature' is more superficial than theirs, in that we take more for granted and regard more features as immutable—features which they might claim to be alterable by undergoing a deep psychoanalysis. But their conception of 'human nature' is based on what are, for the present, immutable facts also. No psychoanalyst has yet suggested, to my knowledge, the possibility of (say) abolishing human aggression altogether, or making human beings asexual, or in any other way making a complete alteration of the human life-story: nor would any such suggestion have much practical point, since we are very far from being able to do such things. Yet such things are *logically* possible and it may be that some day we shall do them.

There are some choices, however, which may not lie far in the future, and to which we shall have to accustom ourselves. For instance, we may have to choose between bringing up human beings to be heterosexual, bringing them up to be homosexual, and bringing them up to be ambisexual. We may have the power to add to 'normal' sexual pleasures the pleasures of those we now characterize as 'masochist' and 'sadist'. We may be able to make societies that are monogamous, polygamous, or promiscuous, just as we choose. Moreover, certain facts that may now deter us from one or the other choice—which, as it were, take care of the problem for us—may soon be alterable. Thus the argument that we cannot have homosexuality if the race is to survive falls down as soon as we can produce children artificially; the argument that sadism is bad, because the poor sadist cannot enjoy normal sexual expression, will not do if we can produce people who enjoy normal expression *and* sadism; and the argument that monogamy is desirable, because children need two (and only two) permanent parental figures, falls down if it turns out that children are actually much happier with a larger number of 'parents'.

In making such choices we shall have to look for features, or principles, of a more permanent kind. Two of these [are]: the importance of stability and integration on the one hand, and of the development and expansion of the personality on the other. It would, indeed, be difficult to conceive of a human being, who, whatever he might think or feel, and whatever powers he had, did not wish (a) to remain a whole person, consciously in control of his personality and not subject to disruptive and unstabilizing influences, and (b) to increase his satisfaction, enlarging and developing his personality along new lines. Not to desire these things is, almost by definition, not to accept life and consciousness as good. Of course this is a logically possible position, and I do not know of any argument which could force anyone to accept life rather than reject it, for all arguments would have to point to some desirable feature within life, and if the whole of life is rejected no such pointing is going to be effective. It is quite possible for people to abdicate altogether, to refuse to play the game of life; and then it is no good showing them how they might improve their position in the game, if they are really serious in thinking that the game as a whole is not worth playing under any conditions. I do not think one can, in a strict sense, *argue* somebody out of suicide, though this is not to say that suicide is, in a wider sense, always a rational action.

However that may be, those of us who wish to stay in the game are bound to use these two criteria, the criteria of integration and development, in some form or other. Our judgements on sexual morality will be—or ought to be—based on them, and we shall always have to consider what effect our sexual behaviour has on the rest of our personality, in relation to the criteria. Thus, if it is true now (of course it may not always be true in the future) that early sexual experience for girls is disruptive, and puts them into a state of instability, this would be an adequate argument against it. The argument would not be overwhelming, since it might be true that such experience satisfies the second criterion, and makes them develop in new and exciting ways. We should then have to balance the two factors, and no doubt arrive at some kind of compromise. Again, if we found that promiscuity was addictive and compulsive, i.e. it restricted our general development and the acquisition of new and important experiences, that would count fairly against it; but if we regarded it as a useful means of learning and communicating, that would count for it.

It is evident that these are not moral arguments, in the sense of 'moral' to which we are accustomed. What we normally describe as 'moral' matters fall in quite different spheres: the sphere of law-making, bringing up young children, responding to our social and individual consciences, keeping the conventions, and so on. We have already seen that these contexts have their own importance. But in the present context, where our concern is with long-range choices and decisions, what we normally call 'morality' itself becomes part of our subject-matter, and has to be inspected as such. The arguments which we now have to use are moral in a deeper sense: that is, they are concerned with the characters of human beings and with what is best for those characters. But since we have the power to change both the individual character and the social framework we have to use arguments which do not depend on specific characteristics of individuals and society.

An example will help to make this clear. There are two current attitudes to homosexuality in our society. Some think it a vice, a crime, a piece of wickedness; others think it a disease, a neurosis, an unfortunate maladjustment of the personality. It is fairly plain, without the need for lengthy argument, that these are, as it were, short-range attitudes and not long-term ones. They derive from the kind of consciences and upbringing we have, and the kind of social morality we are accustomed to. If we took the standard libertarian line we could argue, first, that adult homosexuality cannot reasonably be said to interfere with other people, so that there is no case for making laws against it or applying social sanctions to it. Secondly, we say that there is no *obvious* way in which homosexuality damages the human personality, as drug addiction damages it. To produce children, enjoy sleeping with women, and have a happy marriage are objectives which may not commend themselves to all people, and it is not easy to prove that they ought to commend themselves to all people. Certainly we cannot prove this on any meta-physical theory. And thirdly, when we view the lives of homosexuals (in so far as these are not deranged or made unhappy by social pressures or feelings of guilt induced by society), we do not observe that they are in any obvious way less productive, happy, or well-balanced than the lives of heterosexuals.

But we do not thereby commit ourselves to saying that it is a matter of taste whether we should be homosexual or not. For of any two lives, it is possible to say that one satisfies our two criteria better than the other, and though there is no question of *proving* this in any strict sense of 'prove', there are ways of showing it. Our objection to the homosexual life is that it is too restrictive and, in a sense, too easy. A male homosexual does not become involved, at least as deeply, with one half of the world, the half consisting of women. His experience, understanding, and capacity for feeling and demonstrating love are thereby grossly curtailed. This is not to say that other curtailments, perhaps just as severe or more so, may not vitiate the lives of some heterosexuals: but at least, so to speak, they enter the arena. If our sexual preferences have to be focused on one sex or the other (an important condition which is by no means proven), then there is a lot to be said for focusing on people who are different from ourselves, and who hence have more to teach us. Although we require much more knowledge to make a proper choice— for instance, if the homosexual life compensates for this deficiency by greater cultural creativity we might have to think again—in principle we can say that we would more reasonably choose the heterosexual life.

Of course all this is not only tentative, but in a sense academic, since at present we do not know enough about the psychology of homosexuals or hetero-sexuals to know how far their sexual behaviour affects the rest of their personali-ties. But it may help to give some idea of how the criteria of choice, in this kind of long-range context, should operate. Both criteria have to be firmly kept in the forefront of our vision, since there is always a temptation to forget one or the other. Thus, it is possible to be the sort of person who wants to try out all the heights and depths of new experience, without regard for the loss of control and integration that may ensue; or the sort of person who keeps his whole life calm and balanced, on an even keel, and thereby misses all sorts of chances of learning and develop-ing his personality. These two mistakes, two forms of extremism, are open to us today; and they will always be open—more open, indeed, as we acquire fuller and fuller powers over our own natures. We shall always be able to be either cowardly or foolhardy.

QUESTIONS

1. Critically assess Wilson's evaluation of homosexuality.
2. Utilizing the criteria suggested by Wilson, assess the acceptability of a life-style predicated upon sex without love.

SUGGESTED ADDITIONAL READINGS

Atkinson, Ronald. *Sexual Morality.* New York: Harcourt, Brace & World, 1965. In this book, Atkinson treats many aspects of sexual morality. He concentrates on analyzing the arguments that can be offered in support of various views.

Baker, Robert, and Frederick Elliston. *Philosophy and Sex.* Buffalo, N.Y.: Prometheus

Books, 1975. This anthology provides several relevant articles, representing diverse viewpoints on various problems of sexual morality.

Leiser, Burton M. *Liberty, Justice and Morals.* New York: Macmillan, 1973. Chapter 2 of this book is concerned with homosexuality. In the course of constructing a case against criminal sanctions, Leiser analyzes the arguments commonly made in support of the condemnation of homosexual behavior.

Nagel, Thomas. "Sexual Perversion." *Journal of Philosophy,* 66 (1969). Also reprinted in *Moral Problems,* ed. by James Rachels. New York: Harper & Row, 1971, 2d ed. 1975. In this difficult article, Nagel attempts to clarify the somewhat unwieldy concept of sexual perversion.

Russell, Bertrand. *Marriage and Morals.* New York: Liveright, 1929. This highly readable statement against conventional sexual morality, by one of the most famous philosophers of our time, is now slightly dated but still worthy of attention.

Wasserstrom, Richard. "Is Adultery Immoral?" In Richard Wasserstrom, ed., *Today's Moral Problems.* New York: Macmillan, 1975. Wasserstrom, in this very helpful article, investigates the various arguments that can plausibly be made in support of the claim that adultery is immoral. His analysis is especially valuable in focusing attention on the presuppositions of such arguments.

Wellman, Carl. *Morals and Ethics.* Glenview, Ill.: Scott, Foresman and Company, 1975. Chapter 5 of this book provides a highly readable analysis of the arguments that may be given for and against the moral acceptability of premarital sex.

Whiteley, C. H., and W. M. Whiteley. *Sex and Morals.* New York: Basic Books, 1967. This book as a whole is useful, but chap. 5 on "Unfruitful Sex" is especially germane. In this chapter, the Whiteleys examine the morality of masturbation, homosexual behavior, and other types of sexual activity that exclude the possibility of procreation.

SEVEN

Pornography
and Censorship

In 1967, the Congress of the United States, labeling the traffic in obscene and pornographic materials "a matter of national concern," established the Commission on Obscenity and Pornography. This advisory commission, whose members were appointed by the President in January of 1968, was charged with initiating a thorough study of obscenity and pornography and, on the basis of such a study, submitting recommendations for the regulation of obscene and pornographic materials. In September of 1970 the Commission transmitted its final report to the President and to the Congress. Its fundamental recommendation was that all legislation prohibiting the sale, exhibition, or distribution of sexual materials to *consenting adults* be repealed. However, the Commission recommended the continuance of legislation intended to protect nonconsenting adults from being confronted with sexually explicit material through public displays and unsolicited mailings. The Commission based its fundamental recommendation largely, though not exclusively, on its central factual finding⟨There is no evidence to support the contention that exposure to explicit sexual materials is a significant causal factor in antisocial behavior.⟩

The report of the Commission on Obscenity and Pornography was unwelcome in many quarters. To begin with, only twelve of the Commission's eighteen members voted in support of its fundamental recommendation. In fact, the report itself features a substantial minority report that questions the factual findings as well as the recommendations of the Commission. President Richard Nixon contended that the report was completely unsatisfactory. Many members of Congress were also displeased, and there was a substantial public outcry that the conclusions of the Commission were "morally bankrupt." As a result, there has been little movement to implement its fundamental recommendation.

The developments just described encourage us to pose, as the cen-

226

tral issue of this chapter, the following ethical question: Is a government justified in limiting the access of consenting adults to pornographic materials?

LIBERTY-LIMITING PRINCIPLES

Laws limiting the access of consenting adults to pornographic materials, like all laws, inevitably involve limitation of individual liberty. Accordingly, one way of approaching our central question is to take notice of the kinds of grounds that may be advanced to justify the limitation of individual liberty. Four suggested liberty-limiting principles are especially noteworthy:[1]

1. The Harm Principle—Individual liberty is justifiably limited to prevent *harm to others*.
2. The Principle of Legal Paternalism—Individual liberty is justifiably limited to prevent *harm to self*.
3. The Principle of Legal Moralism—Individual liberty is justifiably limited to prevent *immoral behavior*.
4. The Offense Principle—Individual liberty is justifiably limited to prevent *offense to others*.

The Harm Principle is the most widely accepted liberty-limiting principle. Few will dispute that the law is within its proper bounds when it restricts actions whereby one person causes harm to others. (The category of *harm to others* is understood as encompassing not only personal injury but also damage to the general welfare of society.) What remains a lively source of debate is whether any, or all, of the other suggested principles are legitimate liberty-limiting principles.

According to the Principle of Legal Paternalism, the law may justifiably be invoked to prevent self-harm, and thus "to protect individuals against themselves." Supporters of this principle think that the law rightfully serves much as a benevolent father who limits his child's liberty in order to save the child from harm. Some hotly contest the legitimacy of the Principle of Legal Paternalism. It is said, for example, that government does not have the right to meddle in the private life of its citizens. There is little doubt, however, that there are presently numerous paternalistic features in our legal system. One apparent example is the widespread law that requires motorcyclists to wear protective headgear.

[1]Joel Feinberg's discussion of such principles served as a guide for the formulations adopted here. *Social Philosophy* (Englewood Cliffs, N.J.: Prentice-Hall, 1973), chap. 2.

According to the Principle of Legal Moralism, the law may justifiably be invoked to prevent immoral behavior or, as it is often expressed, to "enforce morals." Such things as kidnapping, murder, and fraud are undoubtedly immoral, but there would seem to be no need to appeal to the Principle of Legal Moralism to justify laws against them. An appeal to the Harm Principle already provides a widely accepted independent justification. As a result, the Principle of Legal Moralism usually comes to the fore only when so-called "victimless" crimes are under discussion. Is it justifiable to legislate against homosexual relations, gambling, and smoking marijuana simply on the ground that such activities are thought to be morally unacceptable? There are many such laws, and presumably they are intended to enforce conventional morality, but some people continue to call for their repeal on the grounds that the Principle of Legal Moralism is an unacceptable liberty-limiting principle. To accept the Principle of Legal Moralism, it is said, is tantamount to permitting a "tyranny of the majority."

According to the Offense Principle, the law may justifiably be invoked to prevent "offensive" behavior in public. "Offensive" behavior is understood as behavior that causes shame, embarrassment, discomfort, etc., to be experienced by onlookers. In this chapter's final reading, Joel Feinberg argues that a suitably formulated Offense Principle ought to be accepted as a legitimate liberty-limiting principle.

THE CASE FOR CENSORSHIP

Arguments in support of laws that would limit the access of consenting adults to pornographic materials can conveniently be organized in terms of the liberty-limiting principles upon which they are based.

1. *Arguments Based on the Harm Principle.* It is often alleged, against pornography, that exposure to it is a direct cause of crime. It is thought, on this view, that exposure to pornography is a significant causal factor in sex-related crimes such as rape. Defenders of this thesis often argue for their claim by citing examples where a person is exposed to pornographic material and subsequently commits a sex-related crime. Such examples, however, fail to establish that the crime, which follows exposure to pornography, is a causal result of exposure to pornography. Indeed, the Commission on Obscenity and Pornography reported that there is no evidence to support such a causal connection. Since the Harm Principle is a widely accepted liberty-limiting principle, if a causal connection between the use of pornography and antisocial behavior were ever to be demonstrated, a formidable argument for censorship would emerge.

A second line of argument based on the Harm Principle emphasizes alleged disastrous effects of the widespread exposure to pornography on the overall welfare of society. It is said, for example, that society will become obsessed with impersonal expressions of sexuality, that love will disappear, and that children entering such a society will be psychologically deprived. Such an argument is developed by Edward J. Mishan in one of the readings of this chapter. Two related responses are possible: (1) It is argued that the anticipated effects will not follow. (2) It is argued that the anticipated effects are so speculative as not to constitute a "clear and present danger."

   2. *Arguments Based on the Principle of Legal Paternalism.* It is often said, against pornography, that those exposed to it will themselves be harmed by such exposure. It is said, for example, that those exposed to pornography will develop or reinforce emotional problems, that they will render themselves incapable of love and other human relationships necessary for a happy and satisfying life. In a more abstract and possibly rhetorical version of this argument, it is alleged that frequent exposure to pornography "depersonalizes" or "dehumanizes," and presumably such effects are at least in a broad sense harmful to the individual. Arguments based on the Principle of Legal Paternalism are answered in two ways: (1) It is argued that the alleged self-harm does not occur. (2) Regardless of the truth or falsity of the claim of self-harm, it is argued, the Principle of Legal Paternalism is not an acceptable liberty-limiting principle.

   3. *Arguments Based on the Principle of Legal Moralism.* It is frequently claimed that there is a widespread consensus to the effect that pornography is morally repugnant. Inasmuch as one construal of the Principle of Legal Moralism allows a community to enforce its moral convictions, it follows that the access of consenting adults to pornographic materials may rightfully be restricted. Arguments thus based on the Principle of Legal Moralism are answered in two ways: (1) It is argued that the alleged consensus of moral opinion is nonexistent. (2) Regardless of the truth or falsity of the claim of an existing moral consensus, it is argued, the Principle of Legal Moralism is not an acceptable liberty-limiting principle.

   The Offense Principle, unlike the other principles discussed above, is not ordinarily advanced to justify laws that would limit access of *consenting* adults to pornographic materials. The Offense Principle, however, is sometimes advanced to justify laws that protect *nonconsenting* adults from "offensive" displays of pornography.

THE CASE AGAINST CENSORSHIP

The overall case against laws limiting the access of consenting adults to pornographic materials usually takes the following direction: The Principle of Legal Paternalism is an unacceptable liberty-limiting principle;

the government has no business meddling in the private affairs of its citizens since such meddling is likely to produce more harm than it prevents. The Principle of Legal Moralism is an unacceptable liberty-limiting principle; to enforce the moral views of the majority is in effect to allow a "tyranny of the majority." A government can rightfully legislate against the private activity of consenting adults only on the grounds that such activity is *harmful to others*. At the present time, however, there is no evidence that the access of consenting adults to pornographic materials presents a "clear and present danger." Thus, censorship is unwarranted.

It is sometimes further argued by opponents of censorship, in conjunction with the claim that pornography has no socially damaging consequences, that it is positively beneficial to those exposed to it and to society as a whole. Here it is said, for example, that exposure to pornography can aid normal sexual development, that it can invigorate sexual relationships, and that it can provide a socially harmless release from sexual tension. Such considerations are developed by G. L. Simons in one of the readings in this chapter.

T. A. M.

Chief Justice Warren Burger

MAJORITY OPINION IN *PARIS ADULT THEATRE I v. SLATON*

A biographical sketch of Chief Justice Warren Burger is found on page 87.

Argument in the Selection. *The state of Georgia sought an injunction against the showing of two films—It All Comes Out in the End and Magic Mirror—by the Paris Adult Theatres I and II (Atlanta). The state claimed that the films were obscene under the relevant Georgia standards. The trial court refused to grant the injunction, holding that the showing of the films could be prohibited only if it were proved that they were shown to minors or nonconsenting adults. The Supreme Court of Georgia reversed the decision of the trial court, and the Supreme Court of the United States upheld the reversal.*

In Chief Justice Burger's majority opinion, he argues that there are legitimate state interests at stake in the state regulation of consenting adults' access to obscene material. According to Chief Justice Burger,

230

such interests include the maintenance of a decent society, the tone of commerce in large cities, and "possibly" the public safety. Chief Justice Burger acknowledges that there is no conclusive proof of a connection between obscene material and antisocial behavior, but he nevertheless considers the belief in such a connection to be a reasonable one. In arguing that state regulation of obscene material is constitutionally acceptable, he emphasizes two points: (1) State regulation of obscene material in no way violates the constitutionally protected right to privacy. (2) State regulation of obscene material is not tantamount to restricting the communication of ideas and thus does not violate the First Amendment.

We categorically disapprove the theory, apparently adopted by the trial judge, that obscene, pornographic films acquire constitutional immunity from state regulation simply because they are exhibited for consenting adults only. This holding was properly rejected by the Georgia Supreme Court. Although we have often pointedly recognized the high importance of the state interest in regulating the exposure of obscene materials to juveniles and unconsenting adults, this Court has never declared these to be the only legitimate state interests permitting regulation of obscene material. The States have a long-recognized legitimate interest in regulating the use of obscene material in local commerce and in all places of public accommodation, as long as these regulations do not run afoul of specific constitutional prohibitions. "In an unbroken series of cases extending over a long stretch of this Court's history, it has been accepted as a postulate that 'the primary requirements of decency may be enforced against obscene publications.'"

In particular, we hold that there are legitimate state interests at stake in stemming the tide of commercialized obscenity, even assuming it is feasible to enforce effective safeguards against exposure to juveniles and to the passerby. Rights and interests "other than those of the advocates are involved." These include the interest of the public in the quality of life and the total community environment, the tone of commerce in the great city centers, and, possibly, the public safety itself. The Hill-Link Minority Report of the Commission on Obscenity and Pornography indicates that there is at least an arguable correlation between obscene material and crime. Quite apart from sex crimes, however, there remains one problem of large proportions aptly described by Professor Bickel:

> It concerns the tone of the society, the mode, or to use terms that have perhaps greater currency, the style and quality of life, now and in the future. A man may be entitled to read an obscene book in his room, or expose himself indecently there. . . . We should protect his privacy. But if he demands a right to obtain the books and pictures he wants in the market and to foregather in public places—discreet, if you will, but accessible to all—with others who share his tastes, then to grant him his right is to affect the world about the rest of us, and to impinge on other privacies. Even supposing that each of us can, if he wishes, effectively avert the eye and stop the ear (which, in truth, we

cannot), what is commonly read and seen and heard and done intrudes upon us all, want it or not.
22 The Public Interest 25, 25–26 (Winter, 1971). (Emphasis supplied.)

As Chief Justice Warren stated there is a "right of the Nation and of the States to maintain a decent society. . . ." But, it is argued, there is no scientific data which conclusively demonstrates that exposure to obscene materials adversely affects men and women or their society. It is urged on behalf of the petitioner that, absent such a demonstration, any kind of state regulation is "impermissible." We reject this argument. It is not for us to resolve empirical uncertainties underlying state legislation, save in the exceptional case where that legislation plainly impinges upon rights protected by the Constitution itself. Mr. Justice Brennan, speaking for the Court in Ginsberg v. New York (1968), said "We do not demand of legislatures 'scientifically certain criteria of legislation.'" Although there is no conclusive proof of a connection between antisocial behavior and obscene material, the legislature of Georgia could quite reasonably determine that such a connection does or might exist. . . .

If we accept the unprovable assumption that a complete education requires certain books, and the well nigh universal belief that good books, plays, and art lift the spirit, improve the mind, enrich the human personality and develop character, can we then say that a state legislature may not act on the corollary assumption that commerce in obscene books, or public exhibitions focused on obscene conduct, have a tendency to exert a corrupting and debasing impact leading to antisocial behavior? "Many of these effects may be intangible and indistinct, but they are nonetheless real." Mr. Justice Cardozo said that all laws in Western civilization are "guided by a robust common sense. . . ." The sum of experience, including that of the past two decades, affords an ample basis for legislatures to conclude that a sensitive, key relationship of human existence, central to family life, community welfare, and the development of human personality, can be debased and distorted by crass commercial exploitation of sex. Nothing in the Constitution prohibits a State from reaching such a conclusion and acting on it legislatively simply because there is no conclusive evidence or empirical data.

It is argued that individual "free will" must govern, even in activities beyond the protection of the First Amendment and other constitutional guarantees of privacy, and that Government cannot legitimately impede an individual's desire to see or acquire obscene plays, movies, and books. We do indeed base our society on certain assumptions that people have the capacity for free choice. Most exercises of individual free choice—those in politics, religion, and expression of ideas—are explicitly protected by the Constitution. Totally unlimited play for free will, however, is not allowed in ours or any other society. We have just noted, for example, that neither the First Amendment nor "free will" precludes States from having "blue sky" laws to regulate what sellers of securities may write or publish about their wares. Such laws are to protect the weak, the uninformed, the unsuspecting, and the gullible from the exercise of their own volition. Nor do modern societies leave disposal of garbage and sewage up to the individual "free will," but impose regulation to protect both public health and the appearance of public places. States are told by some that they must await a "laissez faire" market solution to the obscenity-pornography problem, paradoxically "by people who have never otherwise had a kind word to say for laissez-faire," particularly in solving urban, commercial, and environmental pollution problems.

The States, of course, may follow such a "laissez faire" policy and drop all controls on commercialized obscenity, if that is what they prefer, just as they can ignore consumer protection in the market place, but nothing in the Constitution *compels* the States to do so with regard to matters falling within state jurisdiction. . . .

It is asserted, however, that standards for evaluating state commercial regulations are inapposite in the present context, as state regulation of access by consenting adults to obscene material violates the constitutionally protected right to privacy enjoyed by petitioners' customers. Even assuming that petitioners have vicarious standing to assert potential customers' rights, it is unavailing to compare a theatre, open to the public for a fee, with the private home of Stanley v. Georgia (1969), and the marital bedroom of Griswold v. Connecticut (1965). This Court, has, on numerous occasions, refused to hold that commercial ventures such as a motion-picture house are "private" for the purpose of civil rights litigation and civil rights statutes. The Civil Rights Act of 1964 specifically defines motion-picture houses and theatres as places of "public accommodation" covered by the Act as operations affecting commerce.

Our prior decisions recognizing a right to privacy guaranteed by the Fourteenth Amendment included "only those personal rights that can be deemed 'fundamental' or 'implicit in the concept of ordered liberty.' This privacy right encompasses and protects the personal intimacies of the home, the family, marriage, motherhood, procreation, and child rearing. Nothing, however, in this Court's decisions intimates that there is any "fundamental" privacy right "implicit in the concept of ordered liberty" to watch obscene movies in places of public accommodation.

If obscene material unprotected by the First Amendment in itself carried with it a "penumbra" of constitutionally protected privacy, this Court would not have found it necessary to decide *Stanley* on the narrow basis of the "privacy of the home," which was hardly more than a reaffirmation that "a man's home is his castle." Moreover, we have declined to equate the privacy of the home relied on in *Stanley* with a "zone" of "privacy" that follows a distributor or a consumer of obscene materials wherever he goes. The idea of a "privacy" right and a place of public accommodation are, in this context, mutually exclusive. Conduct or depictions of conduct that the state police power can prohibit on a public street does not become automatically protected by the Constitution merely because the conduct is moved to a bar or a "live" theatre stage, any more than a "live" performance of a man and woman locked in a sexual embrace at high noon in Times Square is protected by the Constitution because they simultaneously engage in a valid political dialogue.

It is also argued that the State has no legitimate interest in "control [of] the moral content of a person's thoughts," and we need not quarrel with this. But we reject the claim that the State of Georgia is here attempting to control the minds or thoughts of those who patronize theatres. Preventing unlimited display or distribution of obscene material, which by definition lacks any serious literary, artistic, political, or scientific value as communication, is distinct from a control of reason and the intellect. Where communication of ideas, protected by the First Amend-

233

ment, is not involved, nor the particular privacy of the home protected by *Stanley*, nor any of the other "areas or zones" of constitutionally protected privacy, the mere fact that, as a consequence, some human "utterances" or "thoughts" may be incidentally affected does not bar the State from acting to protect legitimate state interests. The fantasies of a drug addict are his own and beyond the reach of government, but government regulation of drug sales is not prohibited by the Constitution.

Finally, petitioners argue that conduct which directly involves "consenting adults" only has, for that sole reason, a special claim to constitutional protection. Our Constitution establishes a broad range of conditions on the exercise of power by the States, but for us to say that our Constitution incorporates the proposition that conduct involving consenting adults only is always beyond state regulation, that is a step we are unable to take. Commercial exploitation of depictions, descriptions, or exhibitions of obscene conduct on commercial premises open to the adult public falls within a State's broad power to regulate commerce and protect the public environment. The issue in this context goes beyond whether someone, or even the majority, considers the conduct depicted as "wrong" or "sinful." The States have the power to make a morally neutral judgment that public exhibition of obscene material, or commerce in such material, has a tendency to injure the community as a whole, to endanger the public safety, or to jeopardize in Chief Justice Warren's words, the States' "right . . . to maintain a decent society."

To summarize, we have today reaffirmed the basic holding of Roth v. United States (1957) that obscene material has no protection under the First Amendment. We have directed our holdings, not at thoughts or speech, but at depiction and description of specifically defined sexual conduct that States may regulate within limits designed to prevent infringement of First Amendment rights. We have also reaffirmed the holdings of United States v. Reidel (1971) and United States v. Thirty-Seven Photographs (1971) that commerce in obscene material is unprotected by any constitutional doctrine of privacy. In this case we hold that the States have a legitimate interest in regulating commerce in obscene material and in regulating exhibition of obscene material in places of public accommodation, including so-called "adult" theatres from which minors are excluded. In light of these holdings, nothing precludes the State of Georgia from the regulation of the allegedly obscene materials exhibited in Paris Adult Theatre I or II, provided that the applicable Georgia law, as written or authoritatively interpreted by the Georgia courts, meets the First Amendment standards set forth in Miller v. California (1973). . . .

QUESTIONS

1. To what extent, if at all, does the opinion of Chief Justice Burger reveal a commitment to the Principle of Legal Moralism and/or the Principle of Legal Paternalism?

2. Critically analyze the argument advanced by Chief Justice Burger in support of his claim that the state regulation of obscene material is not tantamount to restricting the communication of ideas and thus does not violate the First Amendment.

Justice William Brennan

DISSENTING OPINION IN *PARIS ADULT THEATRE I v. SLATON*

Biographical Information. *William Brennan (b. 1906), associate justice of the United States Supreme Court, is a graduate of Harvard Law School. He maintained a private law practice in Newark, New Jersey, until 1949. He then served as superior court judge (1949–1959), appellate division judge (1950–1952) and justice of the Supreme Court of New Jersey (1952– 1956). In 1956 Justice Brennan received his appointment to the United States Supreme Court.*

Argument in the Selection. *Justice Brennan acknowledges that there may be a class of material—obscene material—that in itself is not protected by the First Amendment guarantee of free speech. He argues, however, that it is impossible to specifically define "obscenity," and, as a result, that state efforts to totally suppress obscene material inevitably lead to the erosion of protected speech, thus infringing on the First Amendment. Likewise, he contends, such state efforts inevitably infringe on the Fourteenth Amendment and generate "costly institutional harms." He analyzes the interests of the state in suppressing obscene material and concludes that such interests are not sufficient to "justify the substantial damage to constitutional rights and to this nation's judicial machinery."*

Our experience since Roth v. United States (1957) requires us not only to abandon the effort to pick out obscene materials on a case-by-case basis, but also to reconsider a fundamental postulate of *Roth*: that there exists a definable class of sexually oriented expression that may be totally suppressed by the Federal and State Governments. Assuming that such a class of expression does in fact exist, I am forced to conclude that the concept of "obscenity" cannot be defined with sufficient specificity and clarity to provide fair notice to persons who create and distribute sexually oriented materials, to prevent substantial erosion of protected speech as a by-product of the attempt to suppress unprotected speech, and to avoid very costly institutional harms. Given these inevitable side-effects of state efforts to suppress what is assumed to be *unprotected* speech, we must scrutinize with care the state interest that is asserted to justify the suppression. For in the absence of some very substantial interest in suppressing such speech, we can hardly condone the ill-effects that seem to flow inevitably from the effort. . . .

Because we assumed—incorrectly, as experience has proven—that obscenity could be separated from other sexually oriented expression without significant costs either to the First Amendment or to the judicial machinery charged with the task of safeguarding First Amendment freedoms, we had no occasion in *Roth* to probe the asserted state interest in curtailing unprotected, sexually oriented

235

speech. Yet as we have increasingly come to appreciate the vagueness of the concept of obscenity, we have begun to recognize and articulate the state interests at stake. Significantly, in *Redrup v. New York* (1967), where we set aside findings of obscenity with regard to three sets of material, we pointed out that

> [i]n none of the cases was there a claim that the statute in question reflected a specific and limited state concern for juveniles. In none was there any suggestion of an assault upon individual privacy by publication in a manner so obtrusive as to make it impossible for an unwilling individual to avoid exposure to it. And in none was there evidence of the sort of 'pandering' which the Court found significant in Ginzburg v. United States (1966).

The opinions in *Redrup* and Stanley v. Georgia (1969) reflected our emerging view that the state interests in protecting children and in protecting unconsenting adults may stand on a different footing from the other asserted state interests. . . .

But whatever the strength of the state interests in protecting juveniles and unconsenting adults from exposure to sexually oriented materials, those interests cannot be asserted in defense of the holding of the Georgia Supreme Court in this case. That court assumed for the purposes of its decision that the films in issue were exhibited only to persons over the age of 21 who viewed them willingly and with prior knowledge of the nature of their contents. And on that assumption the state court held that the films could still be suppressed. The justification for the suppression must be found, therefore, in some independent interest in regulating the reading and viewing habits of consenting adults.

At the outset it should be noted that virtually all of the interests that might be asserted in defense of suppression, laying aside the special interests associated with distribution to juveniles and unconsenting adults, were also posited in Stanley v. Georgia where we held that the State could not make the "mere private possession of obscene material a crime." That decision presages the conclusions I reach here today.

In *Stanley* we pointed out that "[t]here appears to be little empirical basis for" the assertion that "exposure to obscene materials may lead to deviant sexual behavior or crimes of sexual violence." In any event, we added that "if the State is only concerned about printed or filmed materials inducing antisocial conduct, we believe that in the context of private consumption of ideas and information we should adhere to the view that '[a]mong free men, the deterrents ordinarily to be applied to prevent crime are education and punishment for violations of the law. . . .'"

Moreover, in *Stanley* we rejected as "wholly inconsistent with the philosophy of the First Amendment," the notion that there is a legitimate state concern in the "control [of] the moral content of a person's thoughts," and we held that a State "cannot constitutionally premise legislation on the desirability of controlling a person's private thoughts." That is not to say, of course, that a State must remain utterly indifferent to—and take no action bearing on—the morality of the community. The traditional description of state police power does embrace the regulation of morals as well as the health, safety, and general welfare of the citizenry. And much legislation—compulsory public education laws, civil rights laws, even the abolition of capital punishment—are grounded at least in part on a concern with the morality of the community. But the State's interest in regulating morality by suppressing obscenity, while often asserted, remains essentially unfocused and ill-defined. And, since the attempt to curtail unprotected speech necessarily spills over into the area of protected speech, the effort to serve this speculative interest through the suppression of obscene material must tread heavily on rights protected by the First Amendment.

In Roe v. Wade (1973), we held constitutionally invalid a state abortion law, even though we were aware of

> the sensitive and emotional nature of the abortion controversy, of the vigorous opposing views, even among physicians, and of the deep and seemingly absolute convictions that the subject inspires. One's philosophy, one's experiences, one's exposure to the raw edges of human existence, one's religious training, one's attitudes toward life and family and their values, and the moral standards one establishes and seeks to observe, are all likely to influence and to color one's thinking and conclusions about abortion.

Like the proscription of abortions, the effort to suppress obscenity is predicated on unprovable, although strongly held, assumptions about human behavior, morality, sex, and religion. The existence of these assumptions cannot validate a statute that substantially undermines the guarantees of the First Amendment, any more than the existence of similar assumptions on the issue of abortion can validate a statute that infringes the constitutionally protected privacy interests of a pregnant woman.

If, as the Court today assumes, "a state legislature may . . . act on the . . . assumption that . . . commerce in obscene books, or public exhibitions focused on obscene conduct, have a tendency to exert a corrupting and debasing impact leading to antisocial behavior," then it is hard to see how state-ordered regimentation of our minds can ever be forestalled. For if a State may, in an effort to maintain or create a particular moral tone, prescribe what its citizens cannot read or cannot see, then it would seem to follow that in pursuit of that same objective a State could decree that its citizens must read certain books or must view certain films. However laudable its goal—and that is obviously a question on which reasonable minds may differ—the State cannot proceed by means that violate the Constitution. . . .

Recognizing these principles, we have held that so-called thematic obscenity—obscenity which might persuade the viewer or reader to engage in "obscene" conduct—is not outside the protection of the First Amendment:

> It is contended that the State's action was justified because the motion picture attractively portrays a relationship which is contrary to the moral standards, the religious precepts, and the legal code of its citizenry. This argument misconceives what it is that the Constitution protects. Its guarantee is not confined to the expression of ideas that are conventional or shared by a majority. It protects advocacy of the opinion that adultery may sometimes be proper, no less than advocacy of socialism or the single tax. And in the realm of ideas it protects expression which is eloquent no less than that which is unconvincing. Kingsley Int'l Pictures Corp. v. Regents (1959).

Even a legitimate, sharply focused state concern for the morality of the community cannot, in other words, justify an assault on the protections of the First Amendment. Where the state interest in regulation of morality is vague and ill-defined, interference with the guarantees of the First Amendment is even more difficult to justify.

237

In short, while I cannot say that the interests of the State—apart from the question of juveniles and unconsenting adults—are trivial or nonexistent, I am compelled to conclude that these interests cannot justify the substantial damage to constitutional rights and to this Nation's judicial machinery that inevitably results from state efforts to bar the distribution even of unprotected material to consenting adults. I would hold, therefore, that at least in the absence of distribution to juveniles or obtrusive exposure to unconsenting adults, the First and Fourteenth Amendments prohibit the state and federal governments from attempting wholly to suppress sexually oriented materials on the basis of their allegedly "obscene" contents. Nothing in this approach precludes those governments from taking action to serve what may be strong and legitimate interests through regulation of the manner of distribution of sexually oriented material.

QUESTIONS

1. If you disagree with Justice Brennan's claim that it is impossible to specifically define "obscenity," advance and defend a workable definition.
2. Critically analyze Justice Brennan's assessment of the constitutional difficulties occasioned by censoring obscene materials when there is no specific definition of "obscenity."
3. To what extent, if at all, does the opinion of Justice Brennan reveal a commitment to the Principle of Legal Moralism?

John Stuart Mill

THE HARM PRINCIPLE

A biographical sketch of John Stuart Mill is found on page 122.

Argument in the Selection. In this excerpt from his classic work On Liberty *(1859), Mill contends that society is warranted in restricting individual liberty only if an action is harmful to others, never because an action in one way or another is harmful to the person who performs the action. Mill argues on utilitarian grounds for an exclusive adherence to the Harm Principle, holding that society will be better off by tolerating all expressions of individual liberty that involve no harm to others, rather than by "compelling each to live as seems good to the rest." While alluding to offenses against decency, he makes it clear that certain actions may be exclusively "self-harming" when done in private and yet, when done in public, may constitute an offense against others.*

The object of this Essay is to assert one very simple principle, as entitled to govern absolutely the dealings of society with the individual in the way of compulsion and control, whether the means used be physical force in the form of legal penalties, or the moral coercion of public opinion. That principle is, that the sole end for which mankind are warranted, individually or collectively, in interfering with the liberty of action of any of their number, is self-protection. That the only purpose for which power can be rightfully exercised over any member of a civilized community, against his will, is to prevent harm to others. His own good, either physical or moral, is not a sufficient warrant. He cannot rightfully be compelled to do or forbear because it will be better for him to do so, because it will make him happier, because, in the opinions of others, to do so would be wise, or even right. These are good reasons for remonstrating with him, or reasoning with him, or persuading him, or entreating him, but not for compelling him, or visiting him with any evil in case he do otherwise. To justify that, the conduct from which it is desired to deter him, must be calculated to produce evil to some one else. The only part of the conduct of any one, for which he is amenable to society, is that which concerns others. In the part which merely concerns himself, his independence is, of right, absolute. Over himself, over his own body and mind, the individual is sovereign.

It is, perhaps, hardly necessary to say that this doctrine is meant to apply only to human beings in the maturity of their faculties. We are not speaking of children, or of young persons below the age which the law may fix as that of manhood and womanhood. Those who are still in a state to require being taken care of by others, must be protected against their own actions as well as against external injury. . . .

There is a sphere of action in which society, as distinguished from the individual, has, if any, only an indirect interest; comprehending all that portion of a person's life and conduct which affects only himself, or if it also affects others, only with their free, voluntary, and undeceived consent and participation. When I say only himself, I mean directly, and in the first instance: for whatever affects himself, may affect others *through* himself; and the objection which may be grounded on this contingency, will receive consideration in the sequel. This, then, is the appropriate region of human liberty. It comprises, first, the inward domain of consciousness; demanding liberty of conscience, in the most comprehensive sense; liberty of thought and feeling; absolute freedom of opinion and sentiment on all subjects, practical or speculative, scientific, moral, or theological. The liberty of expressing and publishing opinions may seem to fall under a different principle, since it belongs to that part of the conduct of an individual which concerns other people; but, being almost of as much importance as the liberty of thought itself, and resting in great part on the same reasons, is practically inseparable from it. Secondly, the principle requires liberty of tastes and pursuits; of framing the plan of our life to suit our own character; of doing as we like, subject to such consequences as may follow; without impediment from our fellow-creatures, so long as what we do does not harm them, even though they should think our conduct foolish, perverse, or wrong. Thirdly, from this liberty of each individual, follows the liberty, within the same limits, of combination among individuals; freedom to unite, for any purpose not involving harm to others: the persons combining being supposed to be of full age, and not forced or deceived.

No society in which these liberties are not, on the whole, respected, is free, whatever may be its form of government; and none is completely free in which

239

they do not exist absolute and unqualified. The only freedom which deserves the name, is that of pursuing our own good in our own way, so long as we do not attempt to deprive others of theirs, or impede their efforts to obtain it. Each is the proper guardian of his own health, whether bodily, or mental and spiritual. Mankind are greater gainers by suffering each other to live as seems good to themselves, than by compelling each to live as seems good to the rest. . . .

Again, there are many acts which, being directly injurious only to the agents themselves, ought not to be legally interdicted, but which, if done publicly, are a violation of good manners, and coming thus within the category of offences against others, may rightfully be prohibited. Of this kind are offences against decency; on which it is unnecessary to dwell, the rather as they are only connected indirectly with our subject, the objection to publicity being equally strong in the case of many actions not in themselves condemnable, nor supposed to be so. . . .

QUESTIONS

1. Would Mill find permissible laws restricting the access of consenting adults to pornography? Would Mill find permissible laws restricting the access of minors to pornography? Would Mill find permissible laws prohibiting pornographic billboards? Explain.
2. Argue for or against Mill's claim: "Mankind are greater gainers by suffering each other to live as seems good to themselves, than by compelling each to live as seems good to the rest."

Burton M. Leiser

THE EFFECTS OF OBSCENITY

A biographical sketch of Burton M. Leiser is found on page 214.

Argument in the Selection. *Leiser reviews the findings of the Commission on Obscenity and Pornography in regard to the effects of "erotic materials." He suggests that the minority report of the Commission may embody several fallacies of causal reasoning. Cautiously assessing the available evidence, Leiser concludes that we simply do not know, at this date, whether or not erotic materials have socially undesirable effects.*

If no satisfactory definition of *obscenity* has thus far been developed, it cannot be for lack of effort. When the nine justices on a single court cannot arrive at a single definition that they can work with, but consistently come up with as many as seven or eight separate views on the meaning of the term in a given case, it is obvious that the problem is not only a difficult one, but that it has serious practical consequences. For the student who is interested in studying the effects of obscene materials, such a state of affairs must be most disconcerting; for if no definition of the key term can be found, then it is impossible to inquire meaningfully into the effects of obscene materials, because there is no way to distinguish such materials from those that are not obscene.

Until quite recently no sustained scientific research had been done in this area. But the Commission on Obscenity and Pornography, armed with a $2 million appropriation from Congress, was able to initiate a number of studies that have started to provide some answers to some of the most troublesome questions.

Instead of attempting to define *obscenity*, the commission chose to discuss "erotic materials," without passing moral or legal judgment on them. The problem, then, was to determine what effects erotic materials of various sorts have upon people in a variety of contexts.

Some of the research findings can be dismissed as trivial. Surveys, for example, revealed that at least half the population believes that explicit sexual materials provide information about sex, and that more than half of all police chiefs believe that obscene materials contribute to juvenile delinquency. They have also found that erotic materials cause sexual arousal in many males and females and that females are not as aroused by material designed to arouse male homosexuals as they are by material depicting heterosexual conduct.

Other findings, however, are more important for our purposes. The commission's studies concluded that a significant number of persons increased their masturbatory activity after exposure to erotic materials. Persons who reported increased rates of intercourse were generally those who were already experienced and had established sexual partners. In general, the commission concluded, any such increase in sexual activity tended to be temporary and was not significantly different from the kind of sexual behavior in which the individual had engaged prior to his or her exposure to the erotic materials. Erotic dreams, sexual fantasies, and conversation about sexual matters all tended to increase after exposure to such materials. Some married couples reported more agreeable relations and greater willingness to discuss sexual matters after such exposure than before.

One might have expected delinquent youth to have more and earlier exposure to erotic materials than nondelinquent youth. Both of these expectations turn out to be ill founded, according to the commission. Both delinquent and nondelinquent youth have wide exposure to such materials.

According to the commission's report, there is no statistical correlation between sex crimes and exposure to erotic materials. Although the United States has experienced a significant increase in arrests for rape during the past decade of relaxed restrictions on erotic material, arrests for juvenile sex crimes decreased during the same period. In Denmark there was a notable decrease in sex crimes after Danish law was changed to permit virtually unrestricted access to erotic materials.

The commission's overall conclusion was that "empirical research designed to clarify the question has found no evidence to date that exposure to explicit sexual materials plays a significant role in the causation of delinquent or criminal behavior among youth or adults. The commission cannot conclude that exposure to erotic materials is a factor in the causation of sex crime or sex delinquency."[1]

Other authorities had earlier come to much the same conclusion, but without the benefit of the extensive studies sponsored by the commission.

This is not the place for a detailed summary or evaluation of the commission's report or the data on which it based its findings. It is appropriate to note, however, that several members of the commission protested its findings, and wrote a minority report that contained the following major disagreements with it: A number of studies available to the commission were ignored or underrated by it in its final report. Thus, one research team found that there was a definite correlation between juvenile exposure to pornography and precocious heterosexual and deviant sexual behavior. Another study found that there was a direct relation between the frequency with which adolescents saw movies depicting sexual intercourse and the extent to which the adolescents themselves engaged in premarital sexual intercourse. In a third study it was found that "the rapists were the group reporting the highest 'excitation to masturbation' rates by pornography both in the adult (80%) as well as teen (90%) years." The dissenters add, "Considering the crime they were imprisoned for, this suggests that pornography (with accompanying masturbation) did not serve adequately as a catharsis [as some researchers have suggested it might], prevent a sex crime, or 'keep them off the streets.'" The same study reported that 80 per cent of prisoners who had had experience with erotica reported that they "wished to try the act" they had witnessed in the erotic films they had seen, and when asked whether they *had* followed through, between 30 and 38 per cent replied that they had. In still another study, 39 per cent of sex offenders reported that "pornography had something to do with their committing the offense" of which they were convicted.[2]

In addition, the minority accused the majority of being biased, of suppressing evidence, of misinterpreting statistics and conclusions of researchers, and of misrepresentation.

No attempt will be made here to analyze these findings. However, a number of venerable fallacies may have been perpetrated in them. One, known by its Latin description, *post hoc ergo propter hoc*, consists of supposing that because one phenomenon follows another, the later phenomenon must be caused by the earlier one. But this is not necessarily the case. I know a man who begins to eat his lunch every day promptly after the whistle at the steel mill blows; but the blowing of the whistle is not the cause of his eating, or even of his eating at that particular time. He eats at that time because that happens to be the beginning of his lunch hour. Nor, contrary to David Hume's opinion, is the fact that one phenomenon regularly accompanies another evidence that the one is necessarily the cause of, or caused by, the other. They may both be caused by some unknown third factor. Thus, in the cases before us, both the delinquent behavior and the reading of erotica may have been caused by some other factors in the lives of the adolescents who were surveyed; there is no way, with the information presently available, to show that

[1] *The Report of the Commission on Obscenity and Pornography* (New York: Bantam Books, 1970), p. 32.
[2] *Ibid.*, Part IV, pp. 443 ff.

the erotic material caused the delinquent behavior. Nor is the fact that some sex criminals report that they read pornographic books or saw pornographic films prior to the commission of their crimes an unequivocal indication that the pornography contributed to their criminal behavior. For one thing, they may have been seeking some excuse for their behavior or a scapegoat on whom to fasten the guilt. It would be useful if a rapist could claim that he is really not to blame for his crime. The man who should be in jail, he might claim, is the one who published the obscene book he read just before he raped his victim, or the governor who signed the liberalized censorship law, or the Supreme Court Justice who removed the ban on it. But this will not do at all, because so many persons read the same pornographic works and do not commit sex crimes.

This is not to say that there is no causal connection between erotic literature and sexual behavior. It is to suggest merely that the answers are not in yet, and that even such research as is presently available must be approached with considerable caution.

Thus far, one must conclude that available evidence does not support the thesis that erotic materials have socially undesirable effects upon the people who are exposed to them, but it does not support the thesis that such materials do *not* have such effects either.

QUESTIONS

1. Suppose someone says that he is certain that pornography is a cause of crime because he saw a man leave a pornographic film theater and later that night the man sexually assaulted a small girl. How would Leiser respond to this claim of certainty?

2. Argue for or against the following claim: Even though there is presently no proof that pornography is causally linked with socially undesirable behavior, we had better take the path of caution and limit the access of consenting adults to pornography.

G. L. Simons

IS PORNOGRAPHY BENEFICIAL?

Biographical Information. G. L. Simons, an Englishman, is an author whose principal works center on various aspects of human sexuality. His books include A History of Sex *(1970),* A Place for Pleasure, The History of the Brothel *(1975), and* Pornography without Prejudice *(1972), from which this selection is excerpted.*

Argument in the Selection. Simons argues in favor of easy access to pornography on the grounds that it provides pleasure without producing any significant harms. Moreover, Simons argues, pornography is socially _beneficial_. He cites evidence in support of the view that pornography can aid normal sexual development. He also contends that pornography can provide "sex by proxy" for those who otherwise would be sexually frustrated. Finally, he contends, it is at least plausible to think that the availability of pornography provides release for sexual desires that might otherwise be released through socially harmful behavior.

It is not sufficient, for the objectors' case, that they demonstrate that some harm has flowed from pornography. It would be extremely difficult to show that pornography had *never* had unfortunate consequences, but we should not make too much of this. Harm has flowed from religion, patriotism, alcohol and cigarettes without this fact impelling people to demand abolition. The harm, if established, has to be weighed against a variety of considerations before a decision can be reached as to the propriety of certain laws. Of the British Obscenity Laws the Arts Council Report comments[1] that 'the harm would need to be both indisputable and very dire indeed before it could be judged to outweigh the evils and anomalies inherent in the Acts we have been asked to examine'.

The onus therefore is upon the anti-pornographers to demonstrate not only that harm is caused by certain types of sexual material but that the harm is considerable; if the first is difficult the second is necessarily more so, and the attempts to date have not been impressive. It is even possible to argue that easily available pornography has a number of benefits. Many people will be familiar with the *catharsis* argument whereby pornography is said to cut down on delinquency by providing would-be criminals with substitute satisfactions. This is considered later but we mention it here to indicate that access to pornography may be socially beneficial in certain instances, and that where this is possible the requirement for anti-pornographers to *justify* their objections must be stressed.

The general conclusion[2] of the U.S. Commission was that no adequate proof had been provided that pornography was harmful to individual or society—'if a case is to be made out against "pornography" [in 1970] it will have to be made on grounds other than demonstrated effects of a damaging personal or social nature.'
. . .

The heresy (to some ears) that pornography is harmless is compounded by the even greater impiety that it may be beneficial. Some of us are managing to adjust to the notion that pornography is unlikely to bring down the world in moral ruin, but the idea that it may actually do good is altogether another thing. When we read of Professor Emeritus E. T. Rasmussen, a pioneer of psychological studies in Denmark, and a government adviser, saying that there is a possibility 'that pornography can be beneficial', many of us are likely to have *mixed* reactions, to say the least. In fact this thesis can be argued in a number of ways.

[1] _The Obscenity Laws_, André Deutsch, 1969, p. 33.
[2] _The Report of the Commission on Obscenity and Pornography_, Part Three, II, Bantam Books, 1970, p. 169.

The simplest approach is to remark that people enjoy it. This can be seen to be true whether we rely on personal testimony or the most respectable index of all in capitalist society—'preparedness to pay'. The appeal that pornography has for many people is hardly in dispute, and in a more sober social climate that would be justification enough. Today we are not quite puritan enough to deny that *pleasure* has a worthwhile place in human life: not many of us object to our food being tasty or our clothes being attractive. It was not always like this. In sterner times it was *de rigueur* to prepare food without spices and to wear the plainest clothes. The cult of puritanism reached its apotheosis in the most fanatical asceticism, where it was fashionable for holy men to wander off into a convenient desert and neglect the body to the point of cultivating its lice as 'pearls of God'. In such a bizarre philosophy pleasure was not only condemned in its sexual manifestations but in all areas where the body could conceivably take satisfaction. These days we are able to countenance pleasure in most fields but in many instances still the case for *sexual* pleasure has to be argued.

Pleasure is not of course its own justification. If it clearly leads to serious malaise, early death, or the displeasure of others, then there is something to be said against it. But the serious consequences have to be demonstrated: it is not enough to condemn certain forms of pleasurable experience on the grounds of *possible* ill effect. With such an approach *any* human activity could be censured and freedom would have no place. In short, if something is pleasurable and its bad effects are small or nonexistent then it is to be encouraged: opposition to such a creed should be recognized as an unwholesome antipathy to human potential. Pleasure is a good except where it is harmful (and where the harmfulness is *significant*). . . .

That pornography is enjoyable to many people is the first of the arguments in its favour. In any other field this would be argument enough. It is certainly sufficient to justify many activities that have—unlike a taste for pornography—demonstrably harmful consequences. Only in a sexually neurotic society could a tool for heightening sexual enjoyment be regarded as reprehensible and such as to warrant suppression by law. The position is well summarized[3] in the *first* of the Arts Council's twelve reasons for advocating the repeal of the Obscenity Publications Acts:

> 'It is not for the State to prohibit private citizens from choosing what they may or may not enjoy in literature or art unless there were incontrovertible evidence that the result would be injurious to society. There is no such evidence.'

A further point is that availability of pornography may *aid*, rather than frustrate normal sexual development. Thus in 1966, for example, the New Jersey Committee for the Right to Read presented the findings of a survey conducted among nearly a thousand psychiatrists and psychologists of that state. Amongst the various personal statements included was the view that 'sexually stimulating materials' might help particular people develop a normal sex-drive.[4] In similar

---

[3] *The Obscenity Laws*, André Deutsch, 1969, p. 35.
[4] Quoted by Isadore Rubin, 'What Should Parents Do About Pornography?' *Sex in the Adolescent Years*, Fontana, 1969, p. 202.

spirit, Dr. John Money writes[5] that pornography 'may encourage normal sexual development and broadmindedness', a view that may not sound well to the anti-pornographers. And even in circumstances where possible dangers of pornography are pointed out conceivable good effects are sometimes acknowledged. In a paper issued[6] by The Danish Forensic Medicine Council it is pointed out that neurotic and sexually shy people may, by reading pornographic descriptions of normal sexual activity, be freed from some of their apprehension regarding sex and may thereby attain a freer and less frustrated attitude to the sexual side of life. . . .

One argument in favour of pornography is that it can serve as a substitute for actual sexual activity involving another person or other people. This argument has two parts, relating as it does to (1) people who fantasize over *socially acceptable* modes of sexual involvement, and (2) people who fantasize over types of sexual activity that would be regarded as illegal or at least immoral. The first type relates to lonely and deprived people who for one reason or another have been unable to form 'normal' sexual contacts with other people; the second type are instances of the much quoted *catharsis* argument.

One writer notes[7] that pornography can serve as a substitute for both the knowledge of which some people have been deprived and the pleasure in sexual experience which they have not enjoyed. One can well imagine men or women too inhibited to secure sexual satisfaction with other adults and where explicit sexual material can alleviate some of their misery. It is facile to remark that such people should seek psychiatric assistance or even 'make an effort': the factors that prevent the forming of effective sexual liaisons are just as likely to inhibit any efforts to seek medical or other assistance. Pornography provides sex *by proxy*, and in such usage it can have a clear justification.

It is also possible to imagine circumstances in which men or women—for reasons of illness, travel or bereavement—are unable to seek sexual satisfaction with spouse or other loved one. Pornography can help here too. Again it is easy to suggest that a person abstain from sexual experience, or, if having *permanently* lost a spouse, seek out another partner. Needless to say such advice is often quite impractical—and the alternative to pornography may be prostitution or adultery. Montagu notes that pornography can serve the same purpose as 'dirty jokes', allowing a person to discharge harmlessly repressed and unsatisfied sexual desires.

In this spirit, Mercier (1970) is quoted by the U.S. Commission:

' . . . it is in periods of sexual deprivation—to which the young and the old are far more subject than those in their prime—that males, at any rate, are likely to reap psychological benefit from pornography.'

And also Kenneth Tynan (1970):

[5] John Money, contribution to 'Is Pornography Harmful to Young Children?' *Sex in the Childhood Years*, Fontana, 1971, p. 181–5.

[6] Paper from The Danish Forensic Medicine Council to The Danish Penal Code Council, published in The Penal Code Council Report on Penalty for Pornography, Report No. 435, Copenhagen, 1966, pp. 78–80, and as appendix to *The Obscenity Laws*, pp. 120–4.

[7] Ashley Montagu, 'Is Pornography Harmful to Young Children?' *Sex in the Childhood Years*, Fontana, 1971, p. 182.

'For men on long journeys, geographically cut off from wives and mistresses, pornography can act as a portable memory, a welcome shortcut to remembered bliss, relieving tension without involving disloyalty.'

It is difficult to see how anyone could object to the use of pornography in such circumstances, other than on the grounds of a morbid anti-sexuality. The *catharsis argument* has long been put forward to suggest that availability of pornography will neutralize 'aberrant' sexual tendencies and so reduce the incidence of sex crime or clearly immoral behaviour in related fields. (Before evidence is put forward for this thesis it is worth remarking that it should not be necessary to demonstrate a *reduction* in sex crime to justify repeal of the Obscenity Laws. It should be quite sufficient to show that an *increase* in crime will not ensue following repeal. We may even argue that a small increase may be tolerable if other benefits from easy access to pornography could be shown: but it is no part of the present argument to put this latter contention.)

Many psychiatrists and psychologists have favoured the catharsis argument. Chesser, for instance, sees[8] pornography as a form of voyeurism in which—as with sado-masochistic material—the desire to hurt is satisfied passively. If this is so and the analogy can be extended we have only to look at the character of the voyeur—generally furtive and clandestine—to realize that we have little to fear from the pornography addict. Where consumers are preoccupied with fantasy there is little danger to the rest of us. Karpman (1959), quoted by the U.S. Commission, notes that people reading 'salacious literature' are less likely to become sexual offenders than those who do not since the reading often neutralizes 'aberrant sexual interests'. Similarly the Kronhausens have argued that 'these "unholy" instruments' may be a safety-valve for the sexual deviate and potential sex offender. And Cairns, Paul and Wishner (1962) have remarked that *obscene materials* provide a way of releasing strong sexual urges without doing harm to others.

It is easy to see the plausibility of this argument. The popularity of all forms of sexual literature—from the superficial, *sexless*, sentimentality of the popular women's magazine to the clearest 'hard-core' porn—has demonstrated over the ages the perennial appetite that people have for fantasy. To an extent, a great extent with many single people and frustrated married ones, the fantasy constitutes an important part of the sex-life. The experience may be vicarious and sterile but it self-evidently fills a need for many individuals. If literature, as a *symbol* of reality, can so involve human sensitivities it is highly likely that when the sensitivities are *distorted* for one reason or another the same sublimatory function can occur: the 'perverted' or potentially criminal mentality can gain satisfaction, as does the lonely unfortunate, in sex *by proxy*. If we wanted to force the potential sex criminal on to the streets in search of a human victim perhaps we would do well to deny him his sublimatory substitutes: deny him fantasy and he will be forced to go after the real thing. . . .

The importance of this possibility should be fully faced. If a causal connection *does* exist between availability of pornographic material and a *reduction* in the amount of sex crime—and the evidence is wholly consistent with this possibility rather than its converse—then people who deliberately restrict pornography

---

[8] Eustace Chesser, *The Human Aspects of Sexual Deviation*, Arrow Books, 1971, p. 39.

by supporting repressive legislation are prime architects of sexual offences against the individual. The anti-pornographers would do well to note that their anxieties may be driving them into a position the exact opposite of the one they explicitly maintain—their commitment to reduce the amount of sexual delinquency in society.

The most that the anti-pornographers can argue is that at present the evidence is inconclusive—a point that would be taken by Kutschinsky *et al*. But if the inconclusive character of the data is once admitted then the case for repressive legislation falls at once. For in a *free* society, or one supposedly aiming after freedom, social phenomena are, like individuals, innocent until proven guilty—and an activity will be permitted unless there is clear evidence of its harmful consequences. This point was well put—in the specific connection with pornography—by Bertrand Russell, talking[9] when he was well over 90 to Rupert Crawshay-Williams.

After noting how people beg the question of causation in instances such as the Moors murders (where the murders and the reading of de Sade *may* have a common cause), Russell ('Bertie') said that on the whole he disapproved of sadistic pornography being available. But when Crawshay-Williams put the catharsis view, that such material might provide a harmless release for individuals who otherwise may be dangerous, Russell said at once—'Oh, well, if that's true, then I don't see that there is anything against sadistic pornography. In fact it should be encouraged. . . .' When it was stressed that there was no preponderating evidence either way Russell argued that we should fall back on an overriding principle—'in this case the principle of free speech'.

Thus in the absence of evidence of harm we should be permissive. Any other view is totalitarian. . . .

If human enjoyment *per se* is not to be condemned then it is not too rash to say that we *know* pornography does good. We can easily produce our witnesses to testify to experiencing pleasure. If in the face of this—and no other favourable argument—we are unable to demonstrate a countervailing harm, then the case for easy availability of pornography is unassailable. If, in such circumstances, we find some people unconvinced it is futile to seek out further empirical data. Once we commit ourselves to the notion that the evil nature of something is axiomatic we tacitly concede that evidence is largely irrelevant to our position. If pornography never fails to fill us with predictable loathing then statistics on crime, or measured statements by careful specialists, will not be useful: our reactions will stay the same. But in this event we would do well to reflect on what our emotions tell us of our own mentality. . . .

QUESTIONS

1. Critically evaluate the extent to which Simons offers support for his contention that pornography is beneficial.

[9] Rupert Crawshay-Williams, *Russell Remembered*, Oxford University Press, 1970, p. 144.

2. Assess the soundness of the "catharsis argument."

3. Argue for or against the following claim: The immediate pleasure that people derive from pornography is not in their long-term self-interest because it is outweighed by the long-term effect of dehumanization.

Edward J. Mishan

THE PORNOGRAPHIC SOCIETY

Biographical Information. *Edward J. Mishan is reader in economics at the London School of Economics. Among his books are* The Costs of Economic Growth *(1967) and* Twenty-one Economic Fallacies *(1969). He also writes on more general social issues and has been a frequent contributor to the magazine* Encounter.

Argument in the Selection. *Mishan maintains that failure to restrict access to pornography will have harmful long-term consequences. He imagines a "pornographic society" and suggests the following very grave consequences as possible in such a society: (1) The emotional health of children will be adversely affected by the "apprehension of a society obsessed with carnal indulgence." (2) The quality of love will be thoroughly undermined. (3) The very existence of an orderly and civilized society will be threatened. Mishan contends that such possibilities are "clear and present dangers" that warrant various restraints on sexual permissiveness.*

Familiar arguments, used to persuade us that the growth of sexual permissiveness has wholesome effects on the personality, and increases the capacity for enjoyment, are, to say the least, inconclusive, while those attempting to persuade us that, no matter what the degree of depravity in a work, it cannot really harm anyone, are wholly unconvincing. It is time, therefore, to bring some thought to bear on the harmful consequences society may suffer if current trends toward increasing pornography continue.

I begin by acknowledging the fact that not all those favouring the abolition of censorship are equally comfortable at the turn of events. Some are prepared to admit that things have gone "too far," or far enough. Yet, as indicated, they continue for the most part to rest their hopes for containment, or improvement, on some eventual recoil from current excesses, or on some re-assertion of an imagined natural law that is latent in liberal democracies, or, in the last resort, on the gradual onset of ennui. However, since there is no evidence at present of any slackening in the growth of the market in pornography, hard or soft, it is just possible that—unless the state takes action—our innocent Sex Lobbyists will be proved wrong by events. If so, the question of the consequences for Western societies of an unarrested trend toward increased public pornography becomes very pertinent. In addressing myself to so large a question, I admittedly enter the realm of speculation though without, I hope, forsaking the conventions of reasoned discourse.

In order to avoid tedious qualifications at every turn in the argument, let us project existing trends and think in terms of an emergent "Pornographic Society," one in which all existing restraints have vanished. There are no legal checks on any form of erotic experience, "natural" or "unnatural," and no limit with respect to place, time, scale, or medium, in the depiction of what today would be called the carnal and lascivious. Neither are there any limits placed on the facilities for auto-eroticism, or for participating in any activity, heterosexual, homosexual, bestial, or incestuous, sado-masochistic, fetishistic, or just plain cruel. Provided actors, audience, and participants are willing, provided there is a market for the "product," no objection is entertained.

Any who would accuse me of being an alarmist merely for proposing the concept as an aid to enquiry would surely be revealing also that, were such a society to come into being, there would indeed be grounds for alarm. Since, however, they would reject this possible outcome (in the absence of state action) it would be of some interest if they could be more articulate on the nature and strength of the forces they believe can be depended upon to stem the tide. It would be of further interest to know just how far they expect society to travel along the primrose path to all-out pornography. How far would they themselves wish to travel along this road or, to be more fastidious, what existing or possible features would they wish to admit or prohibit, extend or contract? In short, where would they wish to "draw the line," and, having drawn it, on what principles would they defend it, and by what sanctions? Finally, if they could be persuaded that the forces they once relied upon to restore some sort of equilibrium are too weak to operate, what measures would they favour now in order to stay the pace of movement toward the pornographic society? . . .

It is time to turn about in our minds some of the facets of the problem posed by the concept of the Pornographic Society; namely, whether such a society is compatible with the Good Life, any good life.

First, allowing that family life will continue in such a society, what are we to make of the effect on the child's psychology of his apprehension of a society obsessed with carnal indulgence? It has been alleged, occasionally, that children are immune to pornography; that, up to a certain age, it does not signify. Though this allegation cannot draw on any evidence since they are not in fact exposed, when young, to sexual circuses, we need not pursue this controversial question here because, presumably, there does come an age when they begin to understand the significance of what is happening about them. It is appropriate, then, to question the effect on the child's emotional life, in particular his regard and feelings for his parents.

Is it not just possible that the child needs not only to love his parents but to esteem them? In his first gropings for order and security in a world of threatening impulse, does he not need to look up to beings who provide assurance, who appear to him as "good" and wise and just? Will such emotional needs not be thwarted in a society of uninhibited sexual device? I do not pretend to know the answers to these questions, but no one will gainsay their importance. In view of the possibly very grave consequences on our children's children, would it not be an act of culpable negligence to allow current trends toward an increasingly promiscuous society to continue without being in sight of the answers?

Consider next the quality of love in such a society. Three closely related questions arise.

Treated simply as a physical exploit with another body, and divorced from the intrusion of sentiment, is sexual fulfilment possible?[1] David Holbrook, for one, has doubts whether this is possible. Indeed, he concludes that the so-called sexual revolution is "placing limits on people's capacities to develop a rich enjoyment of sexual love by reducing it to sexuality."[2] Nor has Irving Kristol any brief for the more visible manifestations of the sexual revolution:

> There are human sentiments . . . involved in this animal activity. But when sex is public the viewer does not—cannot—see the sentiments. . . . He can only see the animal coupling. And that is why, when men and women make love, as we say, they prefer to be alone—because it is only when you are alone that you can make love, as distinct from merely copulating in an animal and casual way.

The second question that comes to mind in this connection is whether romantic love will become obsolete in a society of unfettered sexual recourse.

The "savage" in Aldous Huxley's brilliant satire, *Brave New World,* who commits suicide in despair, tried for romantic love but could obtain only instant sex. There might well continue to be sexual friendships, sexual rivalries, sexual jealousies. But the sublimation of sex, thought to be the well-spring of creative imagination and of romantic love, would be no more. One of the great sources of inspiration of poetry and song, of chivalry and dedication, throughout the ages would have dried up. To the denizens of the pornographic society the story of Abelard and Heloise or even the theories of Stendhal *On Love* would be implausible, if not incomprehensible.

The third related question is about the quality of love in general that can be expected to emerge along the road to such a society. One wonders if it would really be possible to love other people very much, or to care for them as persons very much in a world without opportunity for sublimation. Can such virtues as loyalty, honour, compassion, sacrifice, charity, or tenderness, flourish in an environment of uninhibited public exhibitionism and pornography?

Taking a wider perspective of the scene, one wonders whether it is possible to unite unchecked public sexual indulgence with the continued progress of any civilisation—thinking of civilisation in terms not merely of increasing scientific advance and technological innovation but in those, also, of a refinement of taste and sensibility. Let the reader ponder on the question at his leisure, bearing in mind the reflection that whereas the emergence in the past of a new civilisation, or of a new age within the matrix of an existing civilisation, has indeed always been

---

[1] In order to avoid turning the question into a semantic issue, it could be rephrased more precisely as follows: Does suspension of sentiment *vis-à-vis* the sexual partner strengthen the physical sensations of pleasure or does it weaken them?

[2] See his review of the books written by Dr. Viktor Frankl, *The Doctor and the Soul* and *Psychotherapy and Existentialism,* and that written by Dr. Rollo May, *Love and the Will,* in *The Times,* 20 March 1971.

associated with a rapid displacement of old conceptions, values, and purposes by new ones, it has never been associated with a mass movement toward unbridled sexual licentiousness. For, aside from the sexually neurotic elements at large in Western societies, there are in each of us—among "normal" people, that is— infantile and regressive elements that are for the most part dormant though deeply imbedded. "Emotional maturity" is a frail plant that can sustain itself only by clinging to an appropriate social structure. Familiar tabus that place a variety of constraints on freedom of sexual practices reflect a society's desire to guard against the activation of such elements. Until recently the laws of all Western societies sanctioned and reinforced tabus against an unlimited sexual freedom that, if actively sought, could be destructive of organised society.

Thus, a first experiment of this kind just might be the last experiment ever. Goaded on by the predatory forces of commercial opportunism, expectations of carnal gratification—aroused by increasingly salacious spectacles, and increasing facilities for new sexual perversions—would soar beyond the physical limits of attainments. In the unrelenting search for the uttermost in orgiastic experience, cruel passions might be unleashed, impelling humanity into regions beyond barbarism. One has only to recall the fantastic sadistic barbarities of the Nazi era— and to recall also that in 1941 the Nazis were within an ace of winning the War— to accept this conjecture as neither far-fetched nor fanciful, and to recognise that civilisation is indeed but skin-deep. . . .

Such questions need not be regarded as merely rhetorical. They may be thought of as genuine questions. But unless the answers to them are quite other than what I suspect they are, there are clear and present dangers in the current drift toward increased sexual permissiveness.

QUESTIONS

1. Mishan argues that the long-term consequences he discusses pose "clear and present dangers." Assess this claim.
2. Suppose that the access of consenting adults to pornography was left totally unregulated by the government. What would be the long-term impact on the general welfare? Would the results be desirable or undesirable?

Joel Feinberg

THE OFFENSE PRINCIPLE

Biographical Information. *Joel Feinberg (b. 1926) is professor of philosophy at the Rockefeller University. He has taught also at Princeton University and UCLA. Among his books are* Doing and Deserving *(1970) and* Social Philosophy *(1973). Feinberg is also the editor of* Reason and

Responsibility (1965), Moral Concepts (1969), and Philosophy of Law (1975). In addition, he has published many articles in the fields of social, legal, and ethical philosophy.

Argument in the Selection. Feinberg is primarily concerned to argue for the acceptance of a carefully formulated offense principle as a supplement to the Harm Principle. (He speaks of "harm principles" because he formally distinguishes between private and public harm.) He confronts us with certain cases—e.g., obscene billboards, public nudity—where it is widely believed that free expression ought to be legally restricted. Since it is not plausible to think that any significant harm could arise from such displays, Feinberg argues, we are driven to accept the offense principle if we are to have grounds for the legal restriction that seems appropriate. He then explicates the application of the offense principle by appealing to two mediating principles: (1) the standard of universality and (2) the standard of reasonable avoidability. On this construal Feinberg argues that the offense principle cannot be invoked to warrant the suppression of obscene literature.

The American Civil Liberties Union, adopting an approach characteristic of both the friends and the foes of censorship in an earlier period, insists that the offensiveness of obscenity is much too trivial a ground to warrant prior restraint or censorship.[1] The A.C.L.U. argument for this position treats literature, drama, and painting as forms of expression subject to the same rules as expressions of opinion. The power to censor and punish, it maintains, involves risks of great magnitude that socially valuable material will be repressed along with the "filth"; and the overall effect of suppression, it insists, can only be to discourage nonconformist and eccentric expression generally. In order to override these serious risks, the A.C.L.U. concludes, there must be in a given case an even more clear and present danger that the obscene material, if not squelched, will cause even greater harm; and evidence of this countervailing kind is never forthcoming (especially when "mere offense" is not counted as a kind of harm).

The A.C.L.U. stand on obscenity seems clearly to be the position dictated by the unsupplemented harm principles and their corollary, the clear and present danger test. Is there any reason at this point to introduce the offense principle into the discussion? Unhappily, we may be forced to do just that if we are to do justice

---

[1] "Obscenity and Censorship" (New York: American Civil Liberties Union, March, 1963.) The approach that was characteristic of the late fifties and early sixties was to assimilate the obscenity question to developed free speech doctrine requiring a showing of a "clear and present danger" of substantive harm to justify government suppression. Obscene materials pertaining to sex (but not excretion!) were taken to be dangerous, if at all, because they are *alluring* and thus capable of tempting persons into anti-social (harmful) conduct. As Herbert Packer points out (*Limits of Criminal Sanction*, p. 319) the clear and present danger test is virtually certain to be passed by even the most offensive materials.

253

to all of our particular intuitions in the most harmonious way. Consider an example suggested by Louis B. Schwartz. By the provisions of the new Model Penal Code, he writes, "a rich homosexual may not use a billboard on Times Square to promulgate to the general populace the techniques and pleasures of sodomy."[2] If the notion of "harm" is restricted to its narrow sense that is contrasted with "offense," it will be hard to reconstruct a rationale for this prohibition that is based on a harm principle. It is unlikely that there would be evidence that a lurid and obscene public poster in Times Square would create a clear and present danger of injury to those unfortunate persons who fail to avert their eyes in time as they come blinking out of the subway stations. And yet it will be surpassingly difficult even for the most dedicated liberal to advocate freedom of expression in a case of this kind. Hence, if we are to justify coercion in this case, we will likely be driven, however reluctantly, to the offense principle.

There is good reason to be "reluctant" to embrace the offense principle until driven to it by an example of the above kind. People take offense—perfectly genuine offense—at many socially useful or harmless activities, from commercial advertisements to inane chatter. Moreover, as we have seen, irrational prejudices of a very widespread kind can lead people to be disgusted, shocked, even morally repelled by perfectly innocent activities, and we should be loath to permit their groundless repugnance to override the innocence. The offense principle, therefore, must be formulated in a very precise way so as not to open the door to wholesale and intuitively unwarranted repression.

It is instructive to note that a strictly drawn offense principle would not only justify prohibition of public conduct and publicly pictured conduct that is in its inherent character repellent (e.g., buggery, bestiality, sexual sado-masochism), but also conduct and pictured conduct that is inoffensive in itself but offensive only when it occurs in inappropriate circumstances. I have in mind so-called indecencies such as public nudity. One can imagine an advocate of the harm principle more extreme (and perhaps more consistent) even than J. S. Mill who argues against the public nudity prohibition on the grounds that the sight of a naked body does no one any harm and that the state has no right to impose any given standards of dress or undress on private citizens. How one chooses to dress, after all, is a form of self-expression. If we do not permit the state to bar clashing colors, or bizarre hair styles, by what right does it prohibit total undress? Perhaps the sight of naked people could lead to riots or other forms of anti-social behavior, but that is precisely the sort of contingency for which we have police. If we don't take away a man's right of free speech for the reason that its exercise may lead others to misbehave, we cannot in consistency deny his right to dress or undress as he chooses for the same reason.

There may be no answering this challenge on its own ground; but the offense principle provides a special rationale of its own for the nudity prohibition. There is no doubt that the sight of nude bodies in public places is for almost everyone acutely *embarrassing*. Part of the explanation, no doubt, rests on the fact that nudity has an irresistible power to draw the eye and focus the thoughts on matters that are normally repressed. The conflict between these attracting and repressing forces, between allure and disgust, is exciting, upsetting, and anxiety-producing.

---

[2] Schwartz, "Morals Offenses," p. 681.

In most persons it will create a kind of painful turmoil at best and at worst, that experience of exposure to oneself of one's "peculiarly sensitive, intimate, vulnerable aspects"[3] which is called shame. When one has not been able to prepare one's defenses, "one's feeling is involuntarily exposed openly in one's face. . . . We are . . . caught unawares, made a fool of."[4] For many people the result is not mere "offense," but a kind of psychic jolt that can be a painful wound. Those better able to cope with their feelings might well resent the necessity to do so and regard it as an irritating distraction and a bore, much the same as any other nuisance.

If we are to accept the offense principle as a supplement to the harm principles, we must accept two mediating norms of interpretation which stand to it in a way similar to that in which the clear and present danger test stands to the harm principles. The first is the standard of universality which has already been touched upon. The interracial couple strolling hand in hand down the streets of Jackson, Mississippi, without question cause shock and mortification, even shame and disgust, to the overwhelming majority of white pedestrians who happen to observe them; but we surely don't want our offense principle applied to justify preventive coercion on that ground. To avoid that consequence let us stipulate that in order for "offense" (repugnance, embarrassment, shame, etc.) to be sufficient to warrant coercion, it should be the reaction that could reasonably be expected from almost any person chosen at random, taking the nation as a whole, and not because the individual selected belongs to some faction, clique, or party.

That qualification should be more than sufficient to protect the interracial couple, but, alas, it may yield undesirable consequences in another class of cases. I have in mind abusive, mocking, insulting behavior or speech attacking specific subgroups of the population—especially ethnic, racial, or religious groups. Public cross-burnings, displays of swastikas, "jokes" that ridicule Americans of Polish descent told on public media, public displays of banners with large and abusive caricatures of the Pope[5] are extremely offensive to the groups so insulted, and no doubt also offensive to large numbers of sympathetic outsiders. But still, there will be many millions of people who will not respond emotionally at all, and many millions more who may secretly approve. Thus, our amended offense principle will not justify the criminal proscription of such speech or conduct. I am inclined, therefore, simply to patch up that principle in an ad hoc fashion once more. For that special class of offensive behavior that consists in the flaunting of abusive, mocking, insulting behavior of a sort bound to upset, alarm, anger, or irritate those it insults, I would allow the offense principle to apply, even though the behavior would not offend the entire population. Those who are taunted by such conduct will understandably suffer intense and complicated emotions. They might be frightened or wounded; and their blood might boil in wrath. Yet the law cannot permit them to accept the challenge and vent their anger in retaliatory aggression. But again, having to cope with one's rage is as burdensome a bore as having to

[3] Helen Lynd, On Shame and the Search for Identity (New York: Science Editions, 1961), p. 33.
[4] Ibid., p. 32.
[5] For a penetrating discussion of an actual case of this description see Zechariah Chafee, Free Speech in the United States (Cambridge, Mass.: Harvard University Press, 1964), p. 161.

suffer shame, or disgust, or noisome stenches, and the law might well undertake to protect those who are vulnerable, even if they are—indeed, precisely because they are—a minority.

The second mediating principle for the application of the offense principle is the standard of reasonable avoidability. No one has a right to protection from the state against offensive experiences if he can easily and effectively avoid those experiences with no unreasonable effort or inconvenience. If a nude person enters a public bus and takes a seat near the front, there may be no effective way whatever for the other patrons to avoid intensely shameful embarrassment (or other insupportable feelings) short of leaving the bus themselves, which would be an unreasonable inconvenience. Similarly, obscene remarks over a loudspeaker, homosexual billboards in Times Square, pornographic handbills thrust into the hands of passing pedestrians all fail to be reasonably avoidable.

On the other hand, the offense principle, properly qualified, can give no warrant to the suppression of *books* on the grounds of obscenity. When printed words hide decorously behind covers of books sitting passively on the shelves of a bookstore, their offensiveness is easily avoided. The contrary view is no doubt encouraged by the common comparison of obscenity with "smut," "filth," or "dirt." This in turn suggests an analogy to nuisance law, which governs cases where certain activities create loud noises or terrible odors offensive to neighbors, and "the courts must weigh the gravity of the nuisance [substitute "offense"] to the neighbors against the social utility [substitute "redeeming social value"] of the defendant's conduct."[6] There is, however, one vitiating disanalogy in this comparison. In the case of "dirty books," the offense is easily avoidable. There is nothing like the evil smell of rancid garbage oozing right out through the covers of a book whether one looks at it or not. When an "obscene" book sits on a shelf, who is there to be offended? Those who want to read it for the sake of erotic stimulation presumably will not be offended (else they wouldn't read it), and those who choose not to read it will have no experience of it to be offended by. If its covers are too decorous, some innocents may browse through it by mistake and then be offended by what they find, but they need only close the book again to escape the offense. Even this offense, minimal as it is, could be completely avoided by a prior consulting of trusted book reviewers. Moreover, no one forces a customer to browse randomly, and if he is informed in advance of the risk of risqué passages, he should be prepared to shoulder that risk himself without complaint. I conclude that there are no sufficient grounds derived either from the harm or offense principles for suppressing obscene literature, unless that ground be the protection of children; but I see no reason why selective prohibitions for children could not work as well in the case of books as in the cases of cigarettes and whiskey. . . .

I should like to take this opportunity to try one final example and to rest my case on it. It is an example that illustrates not just one but virtually all the categories of offensiveness mentioned in my article; and if the reader fails to concede that it provides a legitimate occasion for legal interference with a citizen's conduct on grounds other than harmfulness, then I must abandon my effort

---

[6] William L. Prosser, *Handbook of the Law of Torts* (St. Paul: West Publishing Co., 1955).

to convince him at all, at least by the use of examples. Consider then the man who walks down the main street of a town at mid-day. In the middle of a block in the central part of town, he stops, opens his briefcase, and pulls out a portable folding camp-toilet. In the prescribed manner, he attaches a plastic bag to its under side, sets it on the sidewalk, and proceeds to defecate in it, to the utter amazement and disgust of the passers-by. While he is thus relieving himself, he unfolds a large banner which reads "This is what I think of the Ruritanians" (substitute "Niggers," "Kikes," "Spics," "Dagos," "Polacks," or "Hunkies"). Another placard placed prominently next to him invites ladies to join him in some of the more bizarre sexual-excretory perversions mentioned in Kraft-Ebbing and includes a large-scale graphic painting of the conduct he solicits. For those who avert their eyes too quickly, he plays an obscene phonograph record on a small portable machine, and accompanies its raunchier parts with grotesquely lewd bodily motions. He concludes his public performance by tasting some of his own excrement, and after savouring it slowly and thoroughly in the manner of a true epicure, he consumes it. He then dresses, ties the plastic bag containing the rest of the excrement, places it carefully in his briefcase, and continues on his way.

Now I would not have the man in the example executed, or severely punished. I'm not sure I would want him punished at all, unless he defied authoritative orders to "move along" or to cease and desist in the future. But I would surely want the coercive arm of the state to protect passers-by (by the most economical and humane means) from being unwilling audiences for such performances. I assume in the example (I hope with some plausibility) that the offensive conduct causes no harm or injury either of a public or a private kind. After all, if the numerous tons of dog dung dropped every day on the streets of New York are no health hazard, then surely the fastidious use of a sanitary plastic bag cannot be seriously unhygienic. . . .

QUESTIONS

1. If you find Feinberg's overall argument unacceptable, develop your criticisms.
2. If you think it might be possible to advance a Feinberglike argument in support of the Principle of Legal Paternalism, advance such an argument.

SUGGESTED ADDITIONAL READINGS

Chandos, John, ed. *"To Deprave and Corrupt . . ."* New York: Association Press, 1962. This anthology contains nine selections, representing a spectrum of views on pornography and censorship.

Clor, Harry M. *Obscenity and Public Morality.* Chicago: The University of Chicago Press, 1969. In this book, Clor develops an overall case for censorship. Chapter 4, concerned with the effects of obscenity, and chap. 5, suggesting a rationale for censorship, are especially relevant to the issues under discussion in our chapter.

Devlin, Patrick. *The Enforcement of Morals.* New York: Oxford University Press, 1965. Lord

Devlin, a prominent English judge, is the foremost contemporary spokesman for the Principle of Legal Moralism. This short book contains seven of his essays.

Feinberg, Joel. *Social Philosophy*. Englewood Cliffs, N.J.: Prentice-Hall, 1973. Chapters 2 and 3 of this book provide a very helpful discussion of liberty-limiting principles.

Holbrook, David, ed. *The Case against Pornography*. New York: The Library Press, 1973. In this anthology, Holbrook has collected nearly thirty selections, all of which develop (from various points of view and to various extents) the case against pornography.

Leiser, Burton M. *Liberty, Justice and Morals*. New York: Macmillan, 1973. Part I of this book features a broad-based discussion of the enforcement of morals. Chapter I critiques the views of Lord Devlin. Successive chapters center on homosexuality, contraception and abortion, divorce, marijuana, and *obscenity and pornography* (chap. VI).

The Report of the Commission on Obscenity and Pornography. Washington, D.C.: U.S. Government Printing Office, 1970. This famous report, whose findings are frequently referred to in contemporary discussions of censorship, contains a wealth of valuable material. Part Three, Section II, of the report centers on the effects of erotic material.

Simons, G. L. *Pornography without Prejudice*. London: Abelard-Schuman, 1972. In this short and highly readable book, Simons provides a vigorous defense of pornography and develops an overall case against censorship. Chapter 2 contains responses to a number of arguments commonly made against pornography.

EIGHT
Violence

Bombings, terrorism, airplane hijackings, increasing crime rates, and riots have all focused public interest on violence. Discussion about the causes, cures, and ethical justification of violence is a commonplace of our time. Many condemn violence, assuming it to be simply equatable with acts involving the illegal use of force. They also assume that violence is always wrong and therefore always to be morally condemned. But philosophers and political theorists who discuss the concept of violence do not always take these two assumptions for granted. Among the questions they ask are: (1) What is violence? (2) Is violence ever morally justified, and if it is, under what conditions is it justified? (3) Is violence in a democracy ever morally justified?

WHAT IS VIOLENCE?

Philosophical analyses of the concept of violence focus on two sets of questions. The first set centers on the scope of the concept of violence. The second set centers on the normative or evaluative content of the term "violence."

THE SCOPE OF THE CONCEPT

Before we can discuss ethical questions concerning the moral justification of violence, we must first determine just what kinds of acts are correctly considered to be violent. For example, must violent acts involve the use of physical force, or can acts involving purely psychological pressure also be categorized as violent ones? Is violence always the illegal use of force, or can legally sanctioned acts of authorities, such as the infliction of capital punishment, also be correctly described as violent? Is violence something which is inflicted only on persons, or can violence be perpetrated on animals, on property, or even on the environment? Is violence always something which is done by persons to other persons, or is there such a thing as institutional violence? Are only intentional acts violent, or can unintentional acts, such as accidental shootings, also be considered violent? There are as many answers as there are questions, and what you choose to include within your definition of violence determines how narrow or how broad you consider the scope of the concept of violence to be.

Philosophers take various positions on the scope of the concept of violence. Some, such as Newton Garver in this chapter, think that the concept of violence is so broad that they would answer all or most of the above questions affirmatively. Robert Audi, one of the writers in this chapter, associates this position on the scope of the concept with liberals and radicals. Others, such as Sidney Hook in our readings, tend to see the concept as a very narrow one, holding that violence is only the illegal and immoral use of physical force. Audi associates such a narrow interpretation of the scope of the concept with conservatives and reactionaries. Whether one agrees with Audi or not, many would claim, against Hook, that the legally sanctioned acts of authorities are often violent acts. Take as an example a situation in which a police officer shoots a gunman, wounding him to keep him from shooting a bystander. Those who hold a very broad view of the concept of violence would call the police officer's act violent even though it is the legally sanctioned act of an authority. Hook and others would claim that this forceful act is not a violent one since the police officer's act is both legal and moral. At issue in the arguments about the scope of the concept is the question of which actions involving the use of force (physical and/or psychological) are to be morally condemned since the word "violence" is often thought to be a condemnatory word. But there is disagreement also about the normative or evaluative content of "violence."

THE NORMATIVE CONTENT OF "VIOLENCE"

Is violence wrong by definition? That is, does the word "violence" function normatively, as, for example, the word "murder" does? If it does, then an act of violence, like an act of murder, is necessarily wrong because it is a part of the very meaning of the word "violence" that violence is wrong. Those who consider violence wrong by definition tend to limit the scope of the concept so that the acts which they consider to be morally correct are not included within those limits. If they consider the police officer's act in our earlier example to be morally correct, they will not call it violent. On the other hand, those who hold that such acts are violent, but not morally wrong, hold that it is not a necessary part of the meaning of "violence" that all violent acts are morally wrong. On this view violence is not wrong simply by definition.

If we reject the claim that violence is wrong by definition, further questions can be considered about the evaluative force of the word "violence." For example, is the term "violence" ethically neutral? If it is, then to call an act violent is to say nothing about its moral rightness or wrongness since the word then does not have any evaluative force. Wrestling, police actions, hitting in self-defense, rape, and murder might all be correctly called violent, even though some of them are considered morally reprehensible and others not.

The claim that "violence" is ethically neutral is as extreme as the claim that all violence is wrong by definition. Some philosophers would reject both extremes and defend a more intermediate position. Perhaps "violence" has some measure of evaluative force, even though it is not a part of its meaning that violent acts are *necessarily* wrong. This would leave open the possibility that violence might be justified under certain conditions even if violent acts are prima facie wrong.[1]

IS VIOLENCE EVER MORALLY JUSTIFIED?

Assuming that violent acts are not morally wrong by definition and that we have at most a prima facie duty to abstain from violent acts, under what conditions is violence morally justified? Writers on this issue usually focus on the use of violence in a political context.

ARGUMENT FOR THE JUSTIFICATION OF VIOLENCE

Arguments for the justification of violence in a political sphere usually center on attempts to specify a set of conditions which should be used to distinguish a violent act that is morally correct from one that is morally incorrect. A typical statement of the conditions under which a violent

---

[1] Because it is difficult to determine both the scope of the concept and the evaluative force of the term "violence," some philosophers, such as Arnold S. Kaufman in this chapter, prefer to sidestep such discussions altogether. At issue for them is not the meaning of a particular term "violence," but the justification of certain kinds of acts such as illegal disorderly acts aimed at harming social institutions. It is always possible to adopt Kaufman's approach, avoid the word "violence," specify the kinds of acts to be morally evaluated (e.g., police killings, ghetto riots, terrorist bombings), and ask which of these kinds of acts are morally justifiable.

act is justified might run as follows. (1) The end that the act is intended to achieve is a morally desirable one such as more freedom for an oppressed group or the establishment of a heretofore denied right. In order to determine whether the end proposed is a morally desirable one, that end is assessed by appeal to ethical principles such as the principle of equality or some principle of distributive justice.[2] For example, we might consider committing a violent act in order to achieve a more equitable distribution of wealth. We would decide that this end is a morally desirable one if we determined that the present distribution of wealth violated our accepted principle of distributive justice. (2) Some violent act is the only effective means which will (within a reasonable length of time) eliminate an existing wrong, such as racial discrimination, or promote the extension of what is taken to be an important human right, such as the right to self-determination. (3) The good consequences of the act will outweigh the bad consequences. Here an appeal is made to the principle of utility since one of the necessary conditions that a morally correct violent act must meet is the condition that on balance it will produce more good consequences than bad ones.

These three major conditions which a violent act must satisfy in order to be morally correct are usually augmented by the following important *qualifications*. (4) In weighing consequences, the injustice and suffering inflicted by the violent act itself must be taken into account. (5) The violence must not intentionally be greater than that which is actually necessary to achieve the morally desirable end. (6) The importance of the end must outweigh the harm perpetrated by the violent act. (7) Wherever possible, violence is to be perpetrated against property rather than against persons.

ARGUMENT AGAINST THE JUSTIFICATION OF VIOLENCE

A typical argument against proposed justifications of violence in political contexts begins with an assumption about the scope of the concept: the acts of authorities in the state are not violent acts; the acts whose moral status is being evaluated are those forceful illegal acts intended to change the status quo. The argument proceeds as follows. A violent act is always morally reprehensible even when the purpose of the act is a morally desirable one, such as the rectification of existing injustices. Such ends are always better achieved by nonviolent means. Violence is always counterproductive. It leads to repression and to a concomitant denial of freedom, whether the violence is "successful" or not. If it is

---

[2]The principle of equality is discussed in the introduction to Chapter 4. Principles of distributive justice are discussed in the introduction to Chapter 9 and in Joel Feinberg's paper in that chapter.

successful, those who achieve victory by the use of violence tend to perpetuate their gains through the continued use of violence. If it is unsuccessful, the use of violence may encourage the use of repressive measures by those holding power. In either case, the result is a loss of freedoms and the denial of just and equal treatment to some members of the society.

IS VIOLENCE IN A DEMOCRACY EVER MORALLY JUSTIFIED?

If we assume that violence can be justified in some political states, the question can still be asked: Is it ever justified in a democracy? Sidney Hook and Justice Vinson in our readings claim that democracy is a special case, that even if violence is justified in a totalitarian state, it is not justified in a democracy. Others, such as Arnold S. Kaufman in this chapter, deny that democracy presents a special case.

DEMOCRACY IS A SPECIAL CASE

The following argument can be given for the claim that violence in a democracy is never justified. Even though violence may be justified in a totalitarian regime, there are at least two sets of reasons why it cannot be justified in a democracy. (1) Democracies, unlike totalitarian states, provide legal means for rectifying existing injustices and alleviating oppressive conditions. In a democracy, the morally desirable end can eventually be achieved by peaceful means. Given the harm which results from violence, peaceful means are always preferable to violent ones. (2) Democracies on the whole are open, free, and just societies. Although they fall short of the social ideal of democracy, they do to some extent already embody the morally desirable ends which violence is supposed to bring about. The use of violence in a democracy can have only undesirable moral consequences, since such an open and free society cannot long exist if violence is tolerated. The result of violence will be either that a minority will rule by force or, at the very least, that the ideal of equal participation in government will be severely jeopardized.

DEMOCRACY IS NOT A SPECIAL CASE

The above reasons are questioned by some philosophers and political scientists. In regard to the first set of reasons, the following argument is sometimes given. Even if existing injustices and oppressive conditions may in time be alleviated in a democracy, the length of time may be very long since those favored by the status quo will tend to retain the status quo. In the meantime, more injustices will occur. The second set of reasons is attacked in two ways. (1) The claims made about the superiority of the democratic form of government are questioned. It is argued, for example, that another type of state might be more conducive to freedom, justice, and equality than a democracy. (2) Questions are raised about the predicted consequences. It is argued, for example, that the threat of violence is necessary to effect desirable social change and that without some cases of actual violence, the threat would lose its effect. The use and threat of violence, instead of jeopardizing democracy, will result in a more just democracy—one in which there is greater freedom, justice, and equality than there would have been without the use of violence.

J. S. Z.

Chief Justice Frederic Moore Vinson

MAJORITY OPINION IN *DENNIS v. UNITED STATES*

Biographical Information. *Frederic Moore Vinson (1880–1953) served as the chief justice of the United States Supreme Court from 1946 until his death. Before he was appointed chief justice by Harry S. Truman, Vinson had a long career both as a lawyer and as a government official. Among the offices held by Vinson were those of director of the Office of Economic Stabilization (1943–1945) and Secretary of the Treasury (1945–1946).*

Argument in the Selection. *Eleven Communist party leaders (including Dennis) were convicted for conspiracy. They appealed to the United States Supreme Court, which upheld the convictions. In the majority opinion, Chief Justice Vinson expresses the view that the actions of the Communist party leaders fall under the Smith act. This act prohibits the organization of any group whose purpose is to "overthrow or encourage the overthrow of any government in the United States by force or violence." Chief Justice Vinson briefly considers the claim that there is such a thing as a "right to rebellion" against dictatorial governments. If there is such a right, he concludes, it does not apply "where the existing structure of the government provides for peaceful and orderly change."*

VIOLENCE

Petitioners were indicted in July, 1948, for violation of the conspiracy provisions of the Smith Act during the period of April, 1945, to July, 1948. . . . A verdict of guilty as to all the petitioners was returned by the jury on October 14, 1949. . . .

Sections 2 and 3 of the Smith Act provide as follows:

Sec. 2
(a) It shall be unlawful for any person—

(1) to knowingly or willfully advocate, abet, advise, or teach the duty, necessity, desirability, or propriety of overthrowing or destroying any government in the United States by force or violence, or by the assassination of any officer of any such government;

(2) with the intent to cause the overthrow or destruction of any government in the United States, to print, publish, edit, issue, circulate, sell, distribute, or publicly display any written or printed matter advocating, advising, or teaching the duty, necessity, desirability, or propriety of overthrowing or destroying any government in the United States by force or violence;

(3) to organize or help to organize any society, group, or assembly of persons who teach, advocate, or encourage the overthrow or destruction of any government in the United States by force or violence; or to be or become a member of, or affiliate with any such society, group, or assembly of persons, knowing the purposes thereof.
(b) For the purposes of this section, the term "government in the United States" means the Government of the United States, the government of any State, Territory, or possession of the United States, the government of the District of Columbia, or the government of any political sub-division of any of them.

Sec. 3. It shall be unlawful for any person to attempt to commit, or to conspire to commit, any of the acts prohibited by the provisions of . . . this title.

The indictment charged the petitioners with wilfully and knowingly conspiring (1) to organize as the Communist Party of the United States of America a society, group and assembly of persons who teach and advocate the overthrow and destruction of the Government of the United States by force and violence, and (2) knowingly and wilfully to advocate and teach the duty and necessity of overthrowing and destroying the Government of the United States by force and violence. The indictment further alleged that § 2 of the Smith Act proscribes these acts and that any conspiracy to take such action is a violation of § 3 of the Act.

The trial of the case extended over nine months, six of which were devoted to the taking of evidence, resulting in a record of 16,000 pages. . . . But the Court of Appeals held that the record supports the following broad conclusions: By virtue of their control over the political apparatus of the Communist Political Association, petitioners were able to transform that organization into the Communist Party; that the policies of the Association were changed from peaceful cooperation with the United States and its economic and political structure to a policy which had existed before the United States and the Soviet Union were fighting a common enemy, namely, a policy which worked for the overthrow of the Government by force and violence; that the Communist Party is a highly disciplined organization, adept at infiltration into strategic positions, use of aliases, and double-meaning language; that the Party is rigidly controlled; that Communists, unlike other political parties, tolerate no dissension from the policy laid down by the guiding

265

forces, but that the approved program is slavishly followed by the members of the Party; that the literature of the Party and the statements and activities of its leaders ... advocate, and the general goal of the Party was, during the period in question, to achieve a successful overthrow of the existing order by force and violence.

   ... The structure and purpose of the statute demand the inclusion of intent as an element of the crime. Congress was concerned with those who advocate and organize for the overthrow of the Government. Certainly those who recruit and combine for the purpose of advocating overthrow intend to bring about that overthrow. We hold that the statute requires as an essential element of the crime proof of the intent of those who are charged with its violation to overthrow the Government by force and violence. ...

   The obvious purpose of the statute is to protect existing Government, not from change by peaceable, lawful and constitutional means, but from change by violence, revolution and terrorism. That it is within the *power* of the Congress to protect the Government of the United States from armed rebellion is a proposition which requires little discussion. Whatever theoretical merit there may be to the argument that there is a "right" to rebellion against dictatorial governments is without force where the existing structure of the government provides for peaceful and orderly change. We reject any principle of governmental helplessness in the face of preparation for revolution, which principle, carried to its logical conclusion, must lead to anarchy. ...

   In this case we are squarely presented with the application of the "clear and present danger" test, and must decide what that phrase imports. We first note that many of the cases in which this Court has reversed convictions by use of this or similar tests have been based on the fact that the interest which the State was attempting to protect was itself too insubstantial to warrant restriction of speech. ... Overthrow of the Government by force and violence is certainly a substantial enough interest for the Government to limit speech. Indeed, this is the ultimate value of any society, for if a society cannot protect its very structure from armed internal attack, it must follow that no subordinate value can be protected. If, then, this interest may be protected, the literal problem which is presented is what has been meant by the use of the phrase "clear and present danger" of the utterances bringing about the evil within the power of Congress to punish.

   ... Obviously, the words cannot mean that before the Government may act, it must wait until the *putsch* is about to be executed, the plans have been laid and the signal is awaited. If Government is aware that a group aiming at its overthrow is attempting to indoctrinate its members and to commit them to a course whereby they will strike when the leaders feel the circumstances permit, action by the Government is required. ...

   The formation by petitioners of such a highly organized conspiracy, with rigidly disciplined members subject to call when the leaders, these petitioners, felt that the time had come for action, coupled with the inflammable nature of world conditions, similar uprisings in other countries, and the touch-and-go nature of our relations with countries with whom petitioners were in the very least ideologically attuned, convince us that their convictions were justified on this score. And this analysis disposes of the contention that a conspiracy to advocate, as distinguished from the advocacy itself, cannot be constitutionally restrained, because it comprises only the preparation. It is the existence of the conspiracy which creates the danger. ...

We hold that § § 2(a) (1), 2(a) (3), and 3 of the Smith Act, do not inherently, or as construed or applied in the instant case, violate the First Amendment and other provisions of the Bill of Rights, or the First and Fifth Amendments because of indefiniteness. Petitioners intended to overthrow the Government of the United States as speedily as the circumstances would permit. Their conspiracy to organize the Communist Party and to teach and advocate the overthrow of the Government of the United States by force and violence created a "clear and present danger" of an attempt to overthrow the Government by force and violence. They were properly and constitutionally convicted for violation of the Smith Act. The Judgments of conviction are affirmed.

QUESTIONS

1. Should the right to free speech include the right to advocate the violent overthrow of the institutions which are established to protect the rights of citizens (including the right to free speech)?

2. Suppose the use of force to overthrow a totalitarian government is morally justified; are there any reasons why such a use of force is not justified in a democracy?

Maurice Cranston

ETHICS AND POLITICS

Biographical Information. *Maurice Cranston (born in London in 1920) was educated at London University. He is presently a professor of political science at the London School of Economics. Cranston has written numerous books and articles. His books include* Freedom—a New Analysis, Human Rights Today, Political Dialogues, *and* The New Left. *Cranston has also written biographies of two philosophers who have made significant contributions to the field of social and political philosophy: John Locke and John Stuart Mill.*

Argument in the Selection. *Cranston examines the changing value connotations associated with the word "violence." In the past, he claims, the word usually had negative connotations. A violent act was wrong by definition. This is no longer true, Cranston maintains, and he speculates about the significance of the change in the evaluative force of the word.*

[C]onsider the word "violence." Until a few years ago, this word was invoked only as a word of condemnation: its use implied the presence of excessive or unjustifed force. Both in moral theory and ordinary conversation, the distinction between force and violence was plainly understood. Force was something always regrettable, but in certain circumstances permissible. The word "force" had no judgment of condemnation built into it as the word "violence" had. We might say: "He used force and was wrong to do so." But we did not need to say, "He used violence and was wrong to do so," because that would be to utter a pleonasm. "Violence" was wrong by definition.

Recently this seems to be changing, and we even find the word "violence" used as a word of praise. And what used to be called force is now called violence. Sometimes this is done deliberately: by Sartre, for example, who argues that violence is what lies behind all civil society, and who would like to see violence used to institute a revolution. Whereas there is permissible force and wrongful force in traditional thinking, for Sartre there is bad violence or good violence. Although I don't think many people subscribe to Sartre's political theory, or even perhaps understand it, many people nowadays have taken to using the word "violence" as he does.

Admittedly, the word "violence" is given a laudatory sense in the writings of several minor political theorists who flourished before the War: but such theorists used to be thought of as fascistic, and indeed it was long regarded as the badge of a fascist to speak in praise of violence. Even as ruthless a tyrant as Stalin never admitted to the use of anything other than force.

Now it is becoming increasingly accepted that the word "violence" may be used either as a neutral or a laudatory word. This may well mean, and I suspect it does, that the fascist *ethos* is coming to life again among us; but it also means that words—and especially the words we use in politics—can gain prestige as well as lose it, and that the normative implications of a word are never fixed and precise.

QUESTIONS

1. Cranston writes as if "violence" had no "fixed" evaluative content because some people use it as if it were normatively neutral. Do concepts change just because the words which refer to them change? (One way of answering this question is to examine whether or not there is a class of acts involving the use of physical force which are held to be morally wrong no matter what term is used to describe those acts.)

2. Today, the word "terrorism" is to many people a condemnatory word. Is every act of terrorism morally unjustified simply by virtue of the meaning of the term?

3. Should an evaluative distinction be made between "force" and "violence," and "violence" used only to refer to those actions involving force which are morally wrong?

Newton Garver

WHAT VIOLENCE IS

Biographical Information. Newton Garver (b. 1928) was educated at Swarthmore College and Cornell University. He has taught philosophy at

Cornell University, the University of Minnesota, and the University of Michigan and is presently teaching at the State University of New York at Buffalo. Among his other publications are "Philosophy and Pacifism" (Philosophy Today, Summer 1967) and "Analyticity and Grammar" (Monist, July 1967).

Argument in the Selection. Garver analyzes the concept of violence. His examination of the etymology of the word leads him to emphasize the relation between the word "violence" and the word "violation." For Garver, violation is a necessary element in violence; force, however, is not a necessary element. Garver identifies four kinds of violence and classifies them on the basis of two sets of criteria: (1) Violence can be personal or institutional. It can be committed by persons or by institutions. (2) Violence can be covert or overt. It is overt when it involves physical force. It is covert when the violence is purely psychological.

I

What I want to do is to present a kind of typology of violence. I want, that is, to try to make clear what some of the different types and kinds and forms of violence are, and thereby to give a perspective of the richness of this topic. Unfortunately, I can't begin saying what the types of violence are without saying first what it is I'm giving you a typology of. So let's begin with a definition of violence.

What is violence? That is a typical philosophical question. The psychiatrists and the sociologists are interested in the questions: why is there violence? what causes violence? That's not my concern—at least not my professional concern nor my concern here. What I'm interested in is the old-fashioned philosophical question: What is the nature or essence of violence? We can make a good start etymologically. The word "violence" comes, of course, from the French, prior to that from the Latin, and you can find Greek roots if you're up to it—which I'm not. The Latin root of the word "violence" is a combination of two Latin words—the word "vis" (force) and the past participle "latus" of the word "fero" (to carry). The Latin word "violare" is itself a combination of these two words, and its present participle "violans" is a plausible source for the word "violence"—so that the word "violence," in its etymological origin, has the sense of to carry force at or toward. An interesting feature of the etymology is that the word "violation" comes from this very same source as the word "violence," which suggests to us the interesting idea that violence is somehow a violation of something: that carrying force against something constitutes in one way or another a violation of it.

The idea of force being connected with violence is a very powerful one. There is no question at all that in many contexts the word "force" is a synonym for the word "violence." This is particularly true if you talk about, for example, a violent blizzard: a violent blizzard is nothing but a blizzard with very great force. The same is true of a violent sea and other bits of violence in nature. It is simply some aspect of nature manifested to us with especially great force. But I don't want to talk about natural phenomena—certainly not meteorological phenomena. I want to talk instead about human phenomena. In human affairs violence cannot be equated with force.

One of the very first things to understand about violence in human affairs is that it is not the same thing as force. It is clear that force is often used on another person's body and there is no violence done. For example, if a man is drowning—thrashing around and apparently unable to save himself—and you use the standard Red Cross life-saving techniques, you will use force against his body although certainly you won't be doing any violence to him. You will, in fact, be saving his life instead. To think so rigidly of force and violence being identical with one another that you call this sort of life-saving an act of violence is to have lost sight entirely of the significance of the concept. Similarly, surgeons and dentists use force on our bodies without doing violence to us.

The idea of violence in human affairs is much more closely connected with the idea of violation than it is with the idea of force. What is fundamental about violence in human affairs is that a person is violated. Now that is a tough notion to explain. It is easy enough to understand how you can violate a moral rule or a parking regulation, but what in the world does it mean to talk about "violating a person"? That, I think, is a very important question, and because it can give a fresh perspective on what it means to be human it deserves fuller consideration than I can give it in this context. If it makes sense to talk about violating a person, that just is because a person has certain rights which are undeniably, indissolubly, connected with his being a person. The very idea of natural rights is controversial since it is redolent of Scholasticism, but I find myself forced to accept natural rights in order to understand the moral dimension of violence. One of the most fundamental rights a person has is a right to his body—to determine what his body does and what is done to his body because without his body he wouldn't be a person anymore. . . .

The right to one's body and the right to autonomy are undoubtedly the most fundamental natural rights of persons. . .

It seems to me that violence in human affairs comes down to violating persons. With that in mind, let me turn now to discussion of the different types and forms of violence. Violence can be usefully classified into four different kinds based on two criteria, whether the violence is personal or institutionalized and whether the violence is overt or a kind of covert or quiet violence.

II

Overt physical assault of one person on the body of another is the most obvious form of violence. Mugging, rape, and murder are the flagrant "crimes of violence," and when people speak of the danger of violence in the streets it is usually visions of these flagrant cases that float before their minds. I share the general concern over the rising rate of these crimes, but at the same time I deplore the tendency to cast our image of violence just in the mold of these flagrant cases. These are cases where an attack on a human body is also clearly an attack on a person and clearly illegal. We must not tie these characteristics in too tight a package, for some acts of

VIOLENCE

violence are intended as a defense of law or a benefit to the person whose body is beaten—e.g. ordinary police activity (not "police brutality")[1] and the corporal punishment of children by parents and teachers. The humbler cases are violence too, although the fact that policemen, teachers, and parents have socially defined roles which they invoke when they resort to violence indicates that these cases have institutional aspects that overshadow the purely personal ones. These institutional overtones make a great deal of difference but they cannot erase that there is violence done. Of course not all cases are so clear: I leave to the reader to ponder whether all sex acts are acts of violence, or just how to distinguish in practical terms those that are from those that are not. Whenever you do something to another person's body without his consent you are attacking not just a physical entity—you are attacking a person. You are doing something by force, so the violence in this case is something that is easily visible, has long been recognized as violence, and is a case of overt, personal violence.

In cases of war, what one group tries to do to another group is what happens to individuals in cases of mugging and murder. The soldiers involved in a war are responsible for acts of violence against "the enemy," at least in the sense that the violence would not have occurred if the soldiers had refused to act. (Of course some other violence might have occurred. But in any case I do not wish to try to assess blame or lesser evils.) The Nuremberg trials after World War II attempted to establish that individual soldiers are responsible morally and legally too, but this attempt overlooked the extent to which the institutionalization of violence changes its moral dimension. On the one hand an individual soldier is not acting on his own initiative and responsibility, and with the enormous difficulty in obtaining reliable information and making a timely confrontation of government claims, not even U.S. Senators, let alone soldiers and private citizens, are in a good position to make the necessary judgments about the justice of a military engagement. On the other hand a group does not have a soul and cannot act except through the agency of individual men. Thus there is a real difficulty in assigning responsibility for such institutional violence. The other side of the violence, its object, is equally ambiguous, for "the enemy" are being attacked as an organized political force rather than as individuals, and yet since a group does not have a body any more than it has a soul "the enemy" is attacked by attacking the bodies of individual men (and women and children). Warfare, therefore, because it is an institutionalized form of violence, differs from murder in certain fundamental respects.

Riots are another form of institutionalized violence, although their warlike character was not widely recognized until the publication of the report of the President's National Advisory Commission on Civil Disorders (the "Riot" Commission). In a riot, as in a war, there are many instances of personal violence, and some persons maintain that the civil disorders are basically massive crime waves. But on the other hand there is also much of a warlike character. One of the characteristics of the Watts riot, as any will know who have read Robert Conot's very interesting book, *The Rivers of Blood, Years of Darkness*, is that in that riot

[1] A persuasive account of the extent to which law itself can be a form of violence, rather than an alternative to it, is to be found in E. Z. Friedenberg's essay "A Violent Country" in the *New York Review*, October 20, 1966.

the people who were supposed to be controlling the situation, the Los Angeles police and their various reinforcements, simply did not know basic facts about the community. In particular they did not know who was the person who could exercise a sort of leadership if the group were left alone and that person's hand was strengthened. One incident illustrates the sort of thing that happened. A Negro policeman was sent in plain clothes into the riot area and told to call back into the precinct whenever there was anything to report. He was told, furthermore, not to identify himself as a policeman under any conditions for fear of jeopardizing himself. At one point, he tried to intervene when some cops were picking on just altogether the wrong person and he ended up getting cursed and having his head bashed in by one of his fellow members of the Los Angeles police force. The police were in such a state that they couldn't even refrain from hitting a Negro policeman who was sent on a plain-clothes assignment into that area. In effect, the Los Angeles police and their various allies conducted what amounted to a kind of a war campaign. . . .

Since these overt forms of violence are, on the whole, fairly easily recognized, let us go on to consider the other forms of violence, the quiet forms which do not necessarily involve any overt physical assault on anybody's person or property. There are both personal and institutional forms of quiet violence, and I would like to begin with a case of what we might call psychological violence, where individuals are involved as individuals and there are not social institutions responsible for the violation of persons that takes place. Consider the following news item:[2]

> PHOENIX, Ariz., Feb. 6 (AP)—Linda Marie Ault killed herself, policemen said today, rather than make her dog Beauty pay for her night with a married man.
> The police quoted her parents, Mr. and Mrs. Joseph Ault, as giving this account:
> Linda failed to return home from a dance in Tempe Friday night. On Saturday she admitted she had spent the night with an Air Force lieutenant.
> The Aults decided on a punishment that would "wake Linda up." They ordered her to shoot the dog she had owned about two years.
> On Sunday, the Aults and Linda took the dog into the desert near their home. They had the girl dig a shallow grave. Then Mrs. Ault grasped the dog between her hands, and Mr. Ault gave his daughter a .22-caliber pistol and told her to shoot the dog.
> Instead, the girl put the pistol to her right temple and shot herself.
> The police said there were no charges that could be filed against the parents except possibly cruelty to animals.

Obviously, the reason there can be no charges is that the parents did no physical damage to Linda. But I think your reaction might be the same as mine—that they really did terrible violence to the girl by the way they behaved in this situation. Of course one must agree that Linda did violence to herself, but that is not the whole account of the violence in this case. The parents did far more violence to the girl than the lieutenant, and the father recognized that when he said to a detective, "I killed her. I killed her. It's just like I killed her myself." If we fail to recognize that there is really a kind of psychological violence that can be perpetrated on people,

---

[2] *New York Times*, February 7, 1968.

a real violation of their autonomy, their dignity, their right to determine things for themselves, their right to be humans rather than dogs, then we fail to realize the full dimension of what it is to do violence to one another. . . .

Psychological violence often involves manipulating people. It often involves degrading people. It often involves a kind of terrorism one way or another. Perhaps these forms that involve manipulation, degradation and terror are best presented in George Orwell's book, *1984*. In that book the hero is deathly afraid of being bitten by a rat. He never is bitten by the rat, but he is threatened with the rat and the threat is such as to break down his character in an extraordinary way. Here what might be called the phenomenology of psychological violence is presented in as convincing a form as I know. . . .

Another form particularly virulent in urban schools—and probably suburban schools too—is the teacher's rebuff. An imaginative child does something out of the ordinary, and the teacher's response is that he is a discipline problem. It now becomes impossible for the child to get out of being a problem. If he tries to do something creative he will be getting out of line and thereby "confirm" that he is a discipline problem. If he stays in line he will be a scholastic problem, thereby "confirming" that he did not have potential for anything but mischief. The result is a kind of stunted person typical of schools in large urban areas, where it is common for a child to enter the public schools half a year behind according to standard tests. Such a child has undoubtedly been a discipline problem during this time and the teacher has spent her effort trying to solve the discipline problem and keep him from getting out of line—that is, from learning anything.[3]

This last variation of the psychological rebuff brings us to the fourth general category of violence, institutionalized quiet violence. The schools are an institution, and teachers are hired not so much to act on their own in the classroom as to fulfill a predetermined role. Violence done by the teacher in the classroom may therefore not be personal but institutional, done while acting as a faithful agent of the educational system. The idea of such institutional violence is a very important one.

A clearer example of quiet institutional violence might be a well established system of slavery or colonial oppression, or the life of contemporary American ghettos. Once established such a system may require relatively little overt violence to maintain it. It is legendary that Southerners used to boast, "We understand our nigras. They are happy here and wouldn't want any other kind of life,"—and there is no reason to doubt that many a Southerner, raised in the system and sheltered from the recurrent lynchings, believed it quite sincerely. In that sort of situation it is possible for an institution to go along placidly, as we might say, with no overt disturbances and yet for that institution to be one that is terribly brutal and that does great harm to its victims and which, incidentally, at the same time brutalizes people who are on top, since they lose a certain measure of their human sensitivity.

[3] Among the many works commenting on this aspect of public education, I have found those of Edgar Friedenberg and Paul Goodman most instructive. See Paul Goodman, *Compulsory Miseducation*, New York, Horizon, 1964; Edgar Z. Friedenberg, *The Vanishing Adolescent*, Boston, Beacon Press, 1959, and *Coming of Age in America*, New York, Knopf, 1963.

There is more violence in the black ghettos than there is anywhere else in America—even when they are quiet. At the time of the Harlem riots in 1964 the Negro psychologist, Kenneth Clark, said that there was more ordinary, day-to-day violence in the life of the ghettos than there was in any day of those disturbances. I'm not sure exactly what he meant. The urban ghettos are places where there is a great deal of overt violence, much of it a kind of reaction to the frustrations of ghetto life. Fanon describes the similar phenomenon of the growth of violence within the oppressed community in the colonial situation in Algeria.[4] When people are suppressed by a colonial regime, when they lack the opportunities which they see other people, white people, around them enjoying, then they become frustrated and have great propensities to violence. The safest target for such angry, frustrated people are their own kind. The Algerians did their first violence to other Algerians, in part because it wasn't safe to do it to a Frenchman. And the same is largely true of the situation that has developed in our urban ghettos. It isn't safe for a person living in the ghettos, if he is feeling frustrated and at the point of explosion, to explode against somebody outside the ghetto; but he can do it to his kids, his wife, his brother and his neighbor, and society will tend to look the other way. So there is a good deal of overt violence in the black ghettos. Perhaps, that is what Clark meant.

But we also have to recognize that there is sometimes a kind of quiet violence in the very operation of the system. Bernard Lafayette, who has worked in urban areas for both the American Friends Service Committee and the Southern Christian Leadership Conference, speaks angrily of the violence of the status quo: "The real issue is that part of the 'good order of society' is the routine oppression and racism committed against millions of Americans every day. That is where the real violence is."[5] The fact [is] that there is a black ghetto in most American cities which operates very like any system of slavery. Relatively little violence is needed to keep the institution going and yet the institution entails a real violation of the human beings involved, because they are systematically denied the options which are obviously open to the vast majority of the members of the society in which they live. A systematic denial of options is one way to deprive men of autonomy. If I systematically deprive a person of the options that are normal in our society, then he is no longer in a position to decide for himself what to do. Any institution which systematically robs certain people of rightful options generally available to others does violence to those people. . . .

These, then, are the main types of violence that I see. By recognizing those types of violence we begin to get the whole question of violence into a much richer perspective than when we hear the Chief of Police deplore violence. Such a richer perspective is vitally necessary, because we cannot do anything about the violence in our society unless we can see it, and most of us do not see it very well. Conceptions and perceptions are closely dependent on one another, and perhaps having a better idea of what violence is will enable us to recognize more readily the many sorts of violence that surround our lives.

[4] Frantz Fanon, *The Wretched of the Earth*, New York, Grove Press, 1966.
[5] In *Soul Force*, February 15, 1968.

III

In concluding I would like to call attention to two aspects of violence. The first is that the concept of violence is a moral concept, but not one of absolute condemnation. Very often psychologists and sociologists and other scientists and students of animal behavior avoid the word "violence" just because it does have a moral connotation. The word "aggression" is sometimes used instead in some of the literature in psychology, and it is prominent in the title of Konrad Lorenz's recent book on animal behavior and aggression.[6] They choose this word "aggression" because it lacks the moral connotations of the term "violence." I think it is important to recognize that the concept of violence is a moral concept, and that the moral elements come in through the fact that an act of violence is a violation of a person. I think that it is also important to recognize that the normal pattern of moral discourse allows for excuses and rationalization. We don't expect people never to do anything which is at all wrong: we allow for excuses.[7] Sartre's very hard line, that excuses undermine the dignity and moral strength of the person being excused, has not really won the day in law courts or in the general moral view; or perhaps what Sartre meant is that we should never allow ourselves excuses rather than that we should never allow them to others. When a person commits an act of violence he is not necessarily to be condemned, though he does have some explaining to do. The fact that we would require an excuse from him, or some justification of his behavior, indicates that a person's doing an act of violence puts the burden of proof on him; but it doesn't suffice to show that the case has gone against him yet.

The second thing I want to say is that it is entirely clear to me that there are degrees of violence. All these various forms of violence are indeed violence, but if I simply say of an act or an institution that it is violent I have not yet said enough to give a clear evaluation of that act. I must also take account of how *much* violence it does to persons affected. Unfortunately this is easier said than done. It might at first be thought that overt violence is always worse than quiet violence, but that rule does not hold generally except in the case of murder; in fact, physical injury often heals more readily than psychological damage. It is more plausible to argue that institutional violence is always of greater harm than personal violence, but that obviously depends on the degree of violence on each side—which means that we must be able to judge the degree of violence in an act or an institution independent of the kind of violence involved. What we need is a scale for measuring degrees of violence, and we don't have one. Still there are degrees of violence, and it is possible to achieve considerable intersubjective agreement about comparisons of pairs of cases.

[6] A classic study in psychology is John Dollard *et al. Frustration and Aggression.* New Haven, Yale, 1939. See also A. Buss, *The Psychology of Aggression,* New York, Wiley, 1961; K. Lorenz, *On Aggression,* New York, Harcourt Brace, 1966.

[7] The late Prof. John L. Austin called the attention of moral philosophers to the importance of excuses in moral discourse. See "A Plea for Excuses," *Philosophical Papers,* London, Oxford University Press, 1961.

QUESTIONS

1. Garver argues that "force" is not equivalent to "violence" since there are acts involving force which are not violent acts. Although the two terms are not synonymous, is force a necessary element in violence?

2. What does it mean to violate somebody? What do the examples of violence which Garver offers have in common that makes them all cases of violation?

3. Is "psychological violence" a good description of the harm done to Linda Marie Ault by her parents, or is the expression "psychological violence" merely a bad metaphor?

Robert Audi

DIMENSIONS OF VIOLENCE

Biographical Information. Robert Audi, who teaches philosophy at the University of Nebraska, Lincoln, has taught also at the University of Texas at Austin. He has written articles on the concepts of intention, wanting, and believing as well as on the concept of violence. In 1970, one of Audi's papers, "On the Meaning and Justification of Violence," was chosen as one of four award-winning essays in a competition sponsored by the Council for Philosophical Studies on the topic of violence. The excerpt below is taken from a more recent paper, "Violence, Legal Sanctions, and Law Enforcement."

Argument in the Selection. Audi examines various philosophical analyses of violence, including Newton Garver's. Audi addresses himself to the following questions: (1) Does violence to persons entail the violation of those persons? (2) Does violence to a person entail the violation of at least one moral right? (3) Is violence unjustified by definition? He answers all the questions in the negative and then offers his own definition of violence.

Except possibly in the waging of war, most violence to persons or property violates someone's moral rights. This, together with the verbal and etymological kinship of 'violence' and 'violation', makes it natural to suppose that the notion of violation of at least one moral right is part of the concept of violence. Thus, one writer has held that

> Violence at its root definition is any violation of the basic human rights of a person. These violations can be social, economic, moral and political.[1]

[1] Peter D. Riga, "Violence: A Christian Perspective," *Philosophy East and West* 19 (1969): 145. Quoted by Ronald B. Miller, "Violence, Force, and Coercion," in Jerome A. Shaffer, ed. *Violence* (New York: David McKay Co., 1971), p. 12.

276

A similar notion is proposed by Newton Garver, who holds that "What is fundamental about violence is that a person is violated," and that "violence in human
affairs amounts to violating persons," where the violation may be "personal or
institutionalized," "overt or covert."[2] F. C. Wade also seems to think that violence
entails some kind of violation. He says that some form of "infringement" is "a
factor" in violence, the other factor being "strong force."[3] Neither Garver nor
Wade does much to clarify the concepts of violation or infringement. It is not clear
whether, for Garver, violation of a person entails the violation of at least one moral
right, nor whether, for Wade, infringement of, say "the holiness of a church, or the
sovereignty of a country" (Wade's examples) entails such violation. But they talk
as though they believe this entailment holds.

Even if it should be true, however, that violence entails the violation of at
least one moral right, it does not clearly follow that it is never justified. For it
would seem that sometimes one moral right conflicts with another and overrides
it, and, if so, the action which is in accord with the overriding right would be
justified though it violates the second right. For instance, perhaps Smith's moral
right to a fair trial could conflict with and override Jones' moral right to mention,
in a conversation with a juror in the case, non-defamatory details of Jones' past
relations with Smith. The former right might override the latter where the details
in question, though non-defamatory, would tend to influence the juror. I state
these points guardedly because one can plausibly argue that Jones' right to
mention such non-defamatory details is only conditional and does not extend to
cases of the sort envisaged, since the right might hold only on the condition that
mentioning the details violates no other moral right. . . .

I want now to assess the above characterizations of violence. I shall argue that
(1) so far as one can gather what is meant by the somewhat metaphorical notion of
violation of a person, even violence to persons does not entail violation of a
person; (2) violence does not entail, though it usually involves, violation of at least
one moral right; and (3) violence is not by definition unjustified, though *most*
forms of it are prima facie unjustified.

In connection with (1), we should first of all bear in mind that violence may be
done to animals and inanimate objects. But presumably Garver was simply ignoring this in saying that violation of persons is fundamental in violence. Yet his
claim seems too strong even as applied to interpersonal violence. Imagine two
friends wrestling vigorously though by the standard collegiate rules. They throw
each other about furiously and sometimes fall to the mat with a loud thud. They
are engaged in violence, yet neither need be injured or even suffer pain. Under
these circumstances, surely, neither need "violate" the other. There is a distinction between merely doing something violently, e.g. shouting with furious but
harmless gestures, and on the other hand *doing violence to* someone or something. One might argue, then, that neither wrestler does violence to the other and
that it is doing violence *to* someone which entails violating him. But imagine that
one of the wrestlers is far superior to the other and throws him around violently,
repeatedly thrusting him hard against the mats, though without injuring him.
Here it becomes plausible to say that the superior wrestler is doing violence to the

[2] Newton Garver, "What Violence Is," *The Nation*, 24 June 1968, reprinted in Thomas
Rose, ed., *Violence in America* (New York: Random House, Vintage Books, 1969), pp. 6, 7.
[3] See Francis C. Wade, "On Violence," *Journal of Philosophy* 68 (1971), esp. p. 370.

other. But it is not plausible to say he violates him. This is partly because the latter has consented to the match and implicitly to its continuation, and partly because none of his rights is being violated.

If I am correct in thinking that violation of at least one of a person's moral rights is a necessary condition for "violating" him, then the many forms of violence that seem justified in self-defense, e.g. punching a would-be mugger, are also cases of doing violence to someone yet not cases of violating that person. It is true that often, and especially in such figurative phrases as 'do violence to the poem' and 'do violence to his good name', the expression 'do violence to' is used with the implication that there is a violation of either a moral right or some other standard of correctness. This makes it initially strange to say that one can do violence to a person without violating him (or his moral rights). But that one can is surely evident when one reflects on the great force and vigor with which, say, a boxer's punch can be delivered. To say that such things are merely acting violently is to ignore the violence that is suffered; and surely if violence is suffered by someone at the hands of another, it is done by the latter to the former. I conclude that violence, even doing violence to someone, does not entail violating him. Nor does the latter entail the former, since one may violate a person by injecting a heavy sedative into him against his will, even if one does so with a tiny and virtually imperceptible needle, and with a gentleness quite untinged by violence.

But let us not dwell on the vague notion of violating a person. I want now to show that violence does not entail the violation of at least one moral right, not even when the violence is done to a person. My examples of vigorous collegiate wrestling and of punching in self-defense seem to me to show this. But there is a different way to make the point. If we leave aside secondary senses of 'violence', such as those illustrated by violence to someone's character or an interpretation's doing violence to a poem, it seems that the notion of violence is an observational notion. That is, roughly speaking, whether violence is being done by a particular agent, at a given time, to a particular person or object, can be ascertained, if at all, by closely observing what the agent is doing at that time with respect to that person or object (there will be borderline cases because the notion of violence is vague, but this applies even to such paradigmatic observation terms as 'red', 'bitter', and 'smooth'). We need not postulate any reason why the agent is doing violence, nor need we interpret his behavior in terms of a rule, such as a moral rule to the effect that one ought not to beat people. But clearly the notion of violating a moral right is not observational in this way: to know whether, in doing A, someone is violating a moral right, we must typically know, or at least have good reason to believe, more than can be grasped simply from closely observing the action. The following contrasts illustrate the distinction between violence as an observational notion and the violation of a moral right as a non-observational notion. If, upon rounding a corner, we see one man sharply club another, we know he is doing the other violence; but since we might have no idea just from closely observing the clubbing by itself whether it is an unavoidable act of self-defense or, say, an act of aggression, we do not know whether it violates the sufferer's moral rights. And if we glimpse a man forcefully slapping a woman's face, we know he is doing violence to her; but since for all we know he may be arresting a fit of hysteria in the only way anyone knows how in her case, we do not know whether he is violating any of her rights, and as in the case of the clubbing we may not (from a very brief look) even have *good reason* to believe the sufferer's moral rights are being violated. Or, consider an example cited in the *Random House Dictionary:* "to take over a government by violence." Surely one could arrive in Saigon just as a contingent of citizens were taking over the government by violence and know by mere observation that they are doing violence; but clearly it is a *further* question whether they are violating anyone's rights in using that violence. But if the writer of the Random House entry were correct and violence (in the sense that occurs in the example) were by definition (morally) unjustified, then it would be contradictory to say they were justified in taking over the government by violence. Thus, if we saw them doing violence it *could* not be a further question whether they were violating anyone's rights. . . .

The main argument is that if violence by definition entailed the violation of at least one moral right, then we could not know just from closely observing an act whether it is an act of violence; for most acts of violence are such that what we can know just from closely observing them leaves open the question whether they violate anyone's moral rights. But what we can know from closely observing them does *not* leave open the question whether they constitute violence. If violence by definition entailed the violation of at least one moral right, then once we observed that an act was one of violence, it could not be an open question whether it violated any moral rights, any more than, once we know that an animal is a vixen, it is an open question whether it is female.

It may be that some violent acts do necessarily violate the victim's rights, e.g. flogging an infant. If so, then merely observing such an act would suffice to tell us that it violates at least one moral right. But few acts are such that merely observing just those acts suffices to establish that they violate a moral right; and most acts of violence, including some that do violate moral rights, are not of this sort. . . .

My distinction between observational and non-observational notions is intended mainly to help *explain* why doing violence does not entail the violation of at least one moral right. *That* the entailment does not hold is shown by the examples I have given and diverse others. Now it seems clear that the same sorts of cases show that neither violence simpliciter, nor even doing violence to someone or something, is by definition unjustified. For just as we can know whether an action we are closely observing is a case of violence while it is an open question whether or not it violates any moral rights, we can know whether an action we are closely observing is a case of violence while it is an open question whether or not the action is justified. If this can be plausibly denied, it is only on the assumption that, *independently* of the claim that violence is by definition unjustified, all acts of violence are unjustified. But this assumption is surely unreasonable. At least in certain kinds of self-defense, such minimal violence as shoving the aggressor away is sometimes justified. Even if one is unqualifiedly dedicated to the idea that we should turn the other cheek, it is not clear that this doctrine rules out all forms of violence in all cases of self-defense. But if it does, then it is simply not plausible for our world, however appropriate it might be on the eve of the Day of Judgment, when all such sacrifices are to be rewarded.

Perhaps there are some people who are careful not to speak of violence being done to someone unless they believe his moral rights are being violated. But not everyone talks this way; and I suspect that even if one resolves to use the term 'violence' this way, it would be difficult to hold to the resolution or to have one's meaning generally understood. For the word 'violence' has many central uses in which violation of moral rights is clearly not entailed, and these uses would constantly tend to exert an influence on one's special use of 'violence'. These central uses would be particularly likely to alter one's special use of the term if the accused perpetrator of violence were oneself.

There is an important reason why I am so concerned to refute the view that violence is by definition unjustifed. This is that the view paves the way for a callous disregard for the enormous amount of violence that most people think is justified. This includes domestic violence done in the name of the law, and violence abroad done in the course of purportedly just wars. I am not saying that most such officially sanctioned violence is unjustified. The point is that it *is* violence, and since so much violence is not justified and causes great suffering, most violence is at least prima facie unjustified and the word itself has connotations that lead people to question the justifiability of the actions to which they apply it. Thus, so far as one thinks violence is by definition unjustified and that what one's government does is by and large justified, one finds it that much easier to give a neutral or even misleading description to what is really extreme violence: violence by police is, say, "rigorous law enforcement"; and napalming may be just "protective reaction." And since the enemy abroad and violators of the law at home are thought of as *not* justified, it tends to be they who are singled out as perpetrators of violence. One can thus easily come to be neither adequately self-critical nor adequately critical of those one tends to approve of.

To be sure, the realization that violence is not necessarily unjustified might lead some people to dismiss as acceptable some violence that ought not to be done. But this is unlikely to be the result of accepting such a weak thesis as that violence is not *necessarily* unjustified, particularly when it is realized that it typically *is* unjustified. By contrast, if we accept the strong thesis that violence is by definition unjustified, then we cannot ask such questions as "Should we be using violence in Southeast Asia?" since what is unjustified should of course not be done. But surely such questions are both intelligible and important.

But if there are dangers in taking the notion of violence too narrowly, there are also dangers in taking it too broadly. For instance, Garver says that

> There is more violence in the black ghettos than anywhere else in America—even when the ghettos are quiet. . . . A black ghetto in American society operates very like any system of slavery. Relatively little overt violence is needed to keep the institution going, and yet the institution violates the human beings involved because they are systematically denied the options given to the vast majority in America.[4]

There are also many who, as Wolff says, "will defend rent strikes, grape boycotts, or lunch counter sit-ins with the argument that unemployment and starvation are a form of violence also."[5] This statement is especially to the point because it indicates both that some people regard even (non-violent) strikes, boycotts, and sit-ins as violence (presumably because they seem to be unjustified uses of force), and that others regard starvation and unemployment as violence when these seem to them to be caused by certain kinds of injustice. Garver, for example, seems to

---

[4] Garver, "What Violence Is," pp. 12-13.
[5] Robert Paul Wolff, "On Violence," *Journal of Philosophy* 66 (1969), p. 614.

VIOLENCE

think that white society is doing violence to blacks insofar as it unjustly maintains conditions under which they cannot achieve equal opportunity with whites.

Now it seems to me that these institutionalized violations of human beings Garver speaks of—meaning such things as widespread inequalities in opportunity—should be called injustices; and the unemployment and starvation Wolff mentions may be forms or results of unjust economic arrangements. These various injustices may be as serious as most forms of violence; but they are different from violence, and it confuses the issue to use the emotively loaded word 'violence' when the grievance can be better described and treated under another name. The term 'injustice' also has much emotive force; but those who want to call (non-violent) injustices violence *also* tend to apply the term 'injustice', so the use of 'violence' here is often not an alternative, but an addition to what is already heated discourse. More important, if such things as (non-violent) social injustice are termed violence by their critics, this opens up the possibility that, at least some of the time, their charges will be dismissed as unfounded by those who point out, rightly, that little or no violence is being done in the disputed cases. Misnaming the disease can lead to the use of the wrong medicine—or none at all.

If discussions of violence are not to ignore much of what governments do in the name of protection of their people, or on the other hand, to spill over into the broad area of social justice, then we need a definition of 'violence' which enables us to avoid both the tendency—especially common among conservatives and reactionaries—to regard as violence only what are believed to be unjustified uses of force, and the tendency—especially common among liberals and radicals—to apply the term 'violence' to a host of non-violent, though, in their view, serious, social injustices. Conservatives, it seems, tend to miss some salient perpetrations of violence in the world; liberals tend to find more violence than there is.

Our definition must also take account of something we have not so far mentioned: psychological violence. Clearly a person can do violence to someone (or even to an animal) by sufficiently vigorous and highly caustic verbal abuse. Psychological violence may also take the form of piercing verbal attacks on someone's sensitive spots. It may take the form of a loud, vehement, nerve-shattering recitation of a person's failures. And there are other forms.[6] The following definition of doing violence is meant to capture both psychological and physical violence:

> Violence is the physical attack upon, or the vigorous physical abuse of, or vigorous physical struggle against, a person or animal; or the highly vigorous psychological abuse of, or the sharp, caustic psychological attack upon, a person or animal; or the highly vigorous, or incendiary, or malicious and vigorous, destruction or damaging of property or potential property.[7]

The "core" notion in this definition is that of vigorous abuse: all the cases that fit the defintion either involve vigorous abuse or at least suggest a fairly clear potential for it. This core notion helps to capture what is valuable in Garver's idea

---

[6] For a discussion of psychological violence, see my "On the Meaning and Justification of Violence," in Jerome A. Shaffer, ed., *Violence* (New York: David McKay Co., 1971), esp. pp. 54-55.

[7] *Ibid.*, pp. 59-60.

that violation of a person is fundamental in violence to persons; for typically—though not always—vigorously abusing a person does in some sense violate him. The definition also helps to explain why we consider violence prima facie unjustified; for clearly, attacking or vigorously abusing persons, and even most violent destructions of property, are prima facie unjustified. Yet the definition does not entail that doing violence is unjustified, or even that doing it entails violations of any moral rights. The definition has several points of serious vagueness, though this seems unavoidable given the vagueness of the notion of violence itself.

QUESTIONS

1. Does Audi distinguish force from violence? Are they distinguishable?
2. Argue for or against the claim: Violence is morally wrong by definition.
3. Philosophers use many examples in their arguments to make their point. One way to criticize a philosopher's argument is to show that the examples used do not prove what they are supposed to prove. Audi, as you have noted, gives examples of what he takes to be violent acts which do not involve the violation of some person's moral right. This use of examples is supposed to support the claim that violence does not entail the violation of someone's moral rights. Argue against Audi that his examples do not support that claim.

Sidney Hook

THE IDEOLOGY OF VIOLENCE

A biographical sketch of Sidney Hook is found on page 95.

Argument in the Selection. *Hook attacks the claim that violence in a democracy can be justified. He examines and criticizes various attempts to support the claim. Hook argues that what is morally permissible under despotism is not morally permissible when peaceful means exist to bring about social change. On his view, the most persuasive argument for the justification of violence in a democracy is the following one: The threat of violence when conjoined with its occasional manifestation is the most effective means to social reform. Hook argues in rebuttal that violence and the threat of violence may be counterproductive, resulting in counterviolence and/or repression.*

[What is] threatening today to world and especially domestic peace is the growth of a family of doctrines that I call the Ideologies of Violence. These ideologies have developed on the peripheries of movements of social protest originally fired by an idealism opposed to war and oppression. Gradually, however, they have acquired a programmatic character of their own. They assert that, to quote one writer,

> The threat of violence, and the occasional outbreak of real violence (which gives the threat credibility) are essential elements in conflict resolution not only in international but also national communities.[1]

Some go further and assert that violence and the threat of violence are necessary and useful in achieving social reforms. The criticism of the use of violence is denounced as hypocritical, as a way of playing the game of the Establishment, as a reaching for a cowardly peace with it. I cannot recall any period in American history in which there has been so much extenuation and glorification of the use of violence not as episodic forays of symbolic character to call attention to shocking evils but as a legitimate strategy in social, political—and even educational reform. (It will be recalled that even John Brown and most of those who rallied to his defence after the raid at Harper's Ferry denied that his original intention was violence against persons or destruction of property, insurrection or murder but only a design to free the slaves and lead them to Canada. Up to the Civil War, the leading abolitionists were pacifists.)

Until recently those who defended the role of violence in social change did so in the main from a revolutionary perspective. . .

What is comparatively novel in our time is the defence of violence by those who are not prepared openly to abandon the standpoint of democracy but who, out of design or confusion, contend that a "healthy" or "just" or "progressive" democratic society will tolerate violence, recognise its productive, even creative role, and eschew any strategy for the control of violence by resort to the force of the civil authorities or to police power. . . .

One of the most frequent confusions in the apologetic literature of violence is the identification of force and violence. Since all government and law rest ultimately—although not exclusively—upon force, the universality of the actual or potential exercise of force prepares the ground for a slide to the view that violence, too, is universal and therefore an inescapable facet of all social life. Those who condemn resort to violence in a democracy are then denounced as themselves confused or hypocritical.

The differing connotations of the words "force" and "violence," the fact that in actual usage there is something strained in substituting one expression for another in all contexts, suggests that they refer to different situations or types of experience. Violence is not physical force *simpliciter* but the "illegal" or "immoral" use of physical force. That is why the term "violence" has a negative and disparaging association except when it anticipates a more acceptable state of affairs, political or moral, in behalf of which physical force is used, *i.e.*, when "revolutionary violence" is approved.

"Force" is normatively neutral in meaning. It cannot be renounced without

[1] H. L. Nieberg, "The Uses of Violence," *Journal of Conflict Resolution* (1963), vol. 7, no. 1, p. 43.

making ideals that encounter resistance ineffectual. Only absolute pacifists can consistently condemn the use of physical force under all circumstances. And their argument can be shown to be self-defeating or irrational, for it is apparent that the very values on behalf of which the use of force is foresworn—the preservation of life, the absence of cruelty, the avoidance of indignity—under some circumstances can be furthered only by the use of force. Force is necessary to sustain or enforce legal rights wherever they are threatened—and human rights, too, which have a moral authority of their own to justify them. Otherwise they are no more than aspirations or pious hopes. When James Meredith was denied the right to study at the University of Mississippi, when Negro women and children were prevented from attending school at Little Rock, after the U.S. Supreme's Court's first school desegregation decision, it was force that protected and redeemed their right against the violence and the threat of violence of the Southern mob.

Whatever rules of the political game are established in order to resolve human conflicts, personal or group, force must ultimately defend or enforce the rules if they are attacked. Where a party resorts to violence in order to breach those rules, to disrupt or destroy the game, it cannot justifiably *equate* its violence with the force used to sustain the rules so long as it professes allegiance to the political system defined by those rules. That is why it makes little sense to discuss the questions of force and violence in the abstract independently of the political context. What holds true for the use and limits of violence in a despotism is not true for the use and limits of violence in a democracy.

One of the most powerful justifications of democracy is that it more readily permits the resolution of human conflicts by argument, persuasion, and debate than is the case under anarchy or despotism. Under anarchy the chaos of recurrent violence defeats the possibility of consensus. Under despotism the appearance of consensus is achieved by terror—the unrestrained and unrestricted use of force. When violence breaks out in a democracy, to that extent it marks the failure or the weakness of the system. Some have therefore concluded that democracy is too noble and rational an ideal to be serviceable to man. Others resign themselves to the suicide of democracy by inactivity in the face of violence. But these do not exhaust the alternatives. A democracy has the moral right to protect itself. Its legitimate use of force to preserve the rules of a democratic society, to enforce the rights without which democracy cannot function, may be wise or unwise, judicious or injudicious. But such use cannot sensibly be classified as violence. The democratic system ideally seeks to make the use of force in human affairs responsible to those who are governed, and to reduce the occasions, frequency and intensity with which physical force is actually employed. In so far as it expresses a moral ideal, independently of the political systems instrumental to its realisation, it is that the reduction of human suffering, the elimination of pain, the avoidance of bloodshed, and the right to collective self-government are desirable. There is much wider agreement among men on the validity of these ideals than on the best way to achieve them. . . .

The importance of considering the question of violence in a *political* context is apparent when we examine some typical syndromes of apologetic justification for violence.

1. The first was exhibited by Mr. Rap Brown, the Black Power militant, in his now classic observation in defending urban riots that "Violence is as American as

cherry-pie." This piece of wisdom actually is the gist of the findings of several task forces of the National Commission on the Causes and Prevention of Violence (the most notable of which has been Skolnick's *Politics of Protest* to which I have already referred). They gravely inform us that violence is customary in American life—as if that were news, as if that made violence more acceptable, as if the prevalence of violence proved anything more than that the democratic process in America had often broken down in the past, as if the relevant question concerned the past rather than the present and future of the democratic political process, as if the fact that something is authentically American necessarily made it as praiseworthy as cherry pie. Certainly, lynching is as American as cherry pie but hardly a cause for boasting!

2. A second popular syndrome of apologetic justification for violence may be called the Boston Tea Party syndrome. Since our patriotic American forbears dumped valuable property into the harbour and engaged in other acts of violence, why is it wrong, we are asked, for present-day rebels to follow suit? Here, too, it is shocking to observe both the source and the frequency of this response to criticism of violence. The SDS invoked the Boston Tea Party in their legal defence of their violence at Columbia University and elsewhere. In their case the exuberance and ignorance of youth may perhaps be pleaded in extenuation. But what shall we say of the adults who in a special foreword to *The Politics of Protest* wrote:

> We take the position that the growth of this country has occurred around a series of violent upheavals and that each one has thrust the nation forward. The Boston Tea Party was an attempt by a few to alter an oppressive system of taxation without representation. The validation of these men rested on their attempts to effect needed social change. If the Boston Tea Party is viewed historically as a legitimate method of producing such change, then present day militancy [i.e., violence] whether by blacks or students, can claim a similar legitimacy. (Greer and Cobb, *The Politics of Protest*, p. xi.)

This total disregard of the fact that the American colonists had no means of remedying their grievances by peaceful constitutional change is symptomatic of the grossly unhistorical approach to problems of social change. It is reinforced by the cool disregard of peaceful changes under our constitutional system of extending representation. Further, what is morally and politically permissible to a democrat struggling for freedom under despotic political conditions is not permissible to him once the mechanisms of democratic consent have been established. Democracy cannot function if political decisions are to be made not through political process but by actions of street mobs, no matter how originally well-intentioned. To be sure, democratic institutions work slowly and, like all institutions, imperfectly. That is the price of democracy which the democrat cheerfully pays because he knows on the basis of history and psychology that the price of any other political alternative is much higher. The democrat who pins his faith on democracy knows that the majority can be wrong but he will not therefore accept the rule of a minority because it occasionally may be right. The integrity of the process by which a minority may peacefully become or win a majority is all-important to him. If the democratic process functions in such a way as to violate the basic moral values of any group of citizens, they have a right to attempt to overthrow it by revolution but they cannot justifiably do so in the name of

285

democracy. And it is open to others to counter these efforts on the basis of their own revolutionary or counter-revolutionary mandate from heaven.[2]

3. The third syndrome challenges the contention that a principled democrat cannot reform an existing democracy by violence without abandoning democratic first principles. This position asserts that existing means of dissent are inadequate, that the wells of public knowledge are poisoned, that the majority has been misled by its education, corrupted by affluence or enslaved by its passions. Allowing for certain changes in time and idiom this indictment against democracy is as old as the Platonic critique. (But Plato did not pretend to be a democrat.) That the institutional life and mechanisms of American democracy are inadequate is undeniable. But just as undeniable is the fact that in many respects they are more adequate today than they have ever been in the past, that dissent has a voice, a platform, a resonance greater than ever before. The issue is, however, this: Does a democrat, dissatisfied with the workings of a democracy, strive to make them more adequate by resorting to violence or by appealing with all the arts of persuasion at his command, from an unenlightened majority to an enlightened one? And what is the test of the inadequacy of existing democratic mechanisms to remedy grievances? That the minority has failed to persuade the majority? This is like saying that a democrat will be convinced that elections are truly democratic only when *he* wins them. Having failed to persuade the majority by democratic and constitutional means, the minority claims the right in the name of a hypothetical, future majority to impose its opinions and rule by violence on the present majority. And by a series of semantic outrages it calls this a democratic method of reforming democracy!

It is easy enough to expose this when it is—as it has often been in the past—a stratagem in the propaganda offensive of totalitarian groups. But the difficulty is greater when these contentions are put forward by individuals who sincerely believe themselves committed to democracy. What they are really saying in their sincere confusion is that in any democratic society that falls short of perfection— that is, in any democratic society in which they fall short of winning a majority— they have a democratic right to resort to violence—which is absurd. Unfortunately, as Cicero once observed, there is no absurdity to which some human beings will not resort to defend another absurdity.

4. The fourth syndrome in the contemporary apologetic literature of violence is the justification of the tactics of violent disruption and confrontation on the ground that the state itself employs force, and sometimes makes an unwise use of it either in war or in preserving domestic peace. Who has not heard militants of the New Left, not only students but their professorial allies, countering rebukes of their irresponsible resort to violence with the cry: "But the Government uses

---

[2] Disregard of these considerations is only one of the failings in the scandalous piece of propaganda for violence which appears under the auspices of the National Commission on the Causes and Prevention of Violence. Of Skolnick's *Politics of Protest*, Professor Milton R. Konvitz of Cornell University, a genuine civil libertarian, outstanding for his compassion and scrupulous sense of fairness, writes: "The main thrust of the book is to validate political violence in America. There is very little in the body of the work that would tend to dispel the myth of violent progress and that would make the value of a constitutional democracy credible—not in some utopian society but in the United States," *Saturday Review*, 15 November 1969.

force! Therefore it cannot be wrong for us to use it. . . ." Only an anarchist who does not recognise any state authority can consistently make this kind of retort— and even anarchists are not likely to be much impressed by it if it were to be mouthed by raiding parties of the Ku Klux Klan and similar groups. In any society, democratic or not, where the state does not have a monopoly of physical force to which all other sanctions are ultimately subordinate, we face incipient civil war.

Nor is the situation any different when the state embarks upon actions that offend the moral sensibilities of some of its citizens. In a debate with Noam Chomsky at Oberlin College last year, I was asked by Professor Chomsky: "How can you reasonably protest against the comparatively limited use of violence by the SDS at Columbia University and elsewhere [of which incidentally he did *not* approve] in view of the massive use of violence by the United States in Viet Nam?" It is a retort frequently heard when student and Black militant violence is condemned. . . .

For one thing these rhetorical questions overlook the obvious fact that one can be opposed *both* to student violence on campus and to the American involvement in Viet Nam just as one could bitterly resist *both* the Stalinist goon squads and Hitler's terrorists who were to clasp arms in fraternal consent a few years later. And even if this were not the case, as we easily can conceive it by changing the illustrations, the comparison is specious and question-begging to boot. Because we disapprove of violence in one context (say, when extremists organise a riot to prevent a dialogue from taking place), we do not have to disapprove of it in another (say, when those who believe in freedom fight to overthrow their oppressors). The assumption that all of these contexts are necessarily involved with each other will not stand examination for a minute. . . .

We must examine what seems to be the most pervasive as well as the most persuasive argument for violence. This maintains that the threat of violence, and its actuality which is necessary to make the threat credible, are the most effective means of achieving reforms, that without the violent extremist the moderate re- former has no chance to implement his programme, that the prospects of reform are always enhanced by the fear generated through the threat of violence and its sporadic outbreaks. *"Kill, burn, ravage!"* exhorts the extremist leader. *"Deal with me, or else face the irresponsibles,"* warns the moderate or reformist leader. His proposed compromises and concessions seem sweetly reasonable against the background mob's shrill cries. On this view it is only because of the multitudinous threats of violence emanating from plural pressure groups that keep each other in check that the democratic system works peacefully *on the whole.* But episodically and fitfully there must be outbreaks of violence to reinforce the readiness to be reasonable, to soften if not to dissolve the stubborn recalcitrance dug in to defend the sacred principles of the Establishment.

Without doubt there is some truth to this view. But it is a half-truth and a dangerous half-truth at that. From the abstract proposition that the threat of exercise of violence *may* facilitate enlightened social change or policy, it is the sheerest dogmatism to assume that in any particular situation violence or its threat will in fact serve a beneficial purpose. It may just as likely set up a cycle of escalating violence and counter-violence that will be more costly and undesirable than the reforms subsequently instituted. It all depends upon the case. . . .

In the democratic community at large the resort to violence, instead of reliance upon the due political process of a self-governing republic, attacks that community at its foundations. And this regardless of the merit of the cause or the sincerity and self-righteousness of the *engagés* and the *enragés*. For every such outbreak of violence makes other outbreaks of violence more likely by serving as a model or precedent to some, or as a provocation to others—in either case escalating the violence.

In this connection Alexander Hamilton was truly prophetic. In the *Federalist Papers* he warned us of this:

> . . .every breach of the fundamental law, though dictated by necessity, impairs that sacred reverence which ought to be maintained in the breast of rulers [who in a self-governing republic are all the people] towards the Constitution of the country, and forms a precedent for other breaches, where the same plea of necessity does not exist at all, or is less urgent and palpable.

Hamilton unerringly cited, on the basis of evidence from the past, the great danger of situations of this kind—the likelihood that citizens "to be more safe . . . at length become more willing to run the risk of becoming less free."

In the end, then, the great paradox and the great truth is that in a democratic society freedom, which is often invoked to justify violence, is itself imperilled by the exercise of violence. The ideologists of violence in a democracy are the sappers and miners of the forces of despotism, the gravediggers, willing or unwilling, of the precious heritage of freedom.

QUESTIONS

1. Hook defines violence as the "illegal or immoral use of physical force." Argue for or against this definition of "violence."

2. Suppose Rap Brown says, "Look, you whites got where you are through the use of violence. You used violence against the red man and against enslaved blacks. Now you try to tell us it's not right for us to use violence to get some of what you've got. How come it was right for you to do it, but it's not right for us to do it?" What answer would you give to Brown?

3. What characteristics of a democratic political system could be used to support the claim that although violence in a political context is sometimes justified it is never justified in a democracy?

Arnold S. Kaufman

DEMOCRACY AND DISORDER

Biographical Information. Arnold S. Kaufman was a promising young political philosopher who died at an early age. During his short career, he taught philosophy at both the University of Michigan and the University of California at Los Angeles. Among his published articles are "A

Sketch of a Liberal Theory of Fundamental Human Rights" (Monist, vol. *52, October 1968) and "The Aims of Scientific Activity"* (Monist, vol. 52, *July 1968). The Spring 1972 volume of* Social Theory and Practice, *which is devoted to a discussion of Kaufman's philosophical work, contains a bibliography of his books, articles, and discussions.*

Argument in the Selection. In this paper, Kaufman does not use the word "violence" but the word "disorder." He defines "acts of disorder" as "violations of law that involve intentionally inflicting harm on persons or property." Kaufman argues that the use of disorder to effect social change is as justified in a democracy as in a nondemocracy. If only peaceful means are used to bring about a social change (such as the end of racial discrimination), Kaufman claims, a great many more injustices will occur while the slow peaceful change is taking place. The harm done by such injustices must be weighed against the harm which results from disorderly acts. Kaufman also maintains that the threat of violence has in the past proved to be an effective instrument of social change; the threat of violence and the occasional use of violence need not be counterproductive.

The tactic of disorder in pursuing political goals is often thought to be morally wrong for members of democracies like Britain and the United States. For those who live in such democracies there are supposed to be reasons against resorting to disorder that do not hold for members of non-democracies. In this view Americans who are plagued by racial discrimination have reasons for rejecting the tactic of disorder as a way of resisting their oppressors that Czechs plagued by tyrannical political masters do not have. I will argue that the presumed distinction between the obligations of citizens in democracies and non-democracies lacks a significant moral basis.

THE ARGUMENT BASED ON PEACEFUL CHANGE

Before developing arguments for my main thesis, certain matters require clarification.

First, for purposes of this discussion, acts of disorder will be understood as violations of law that involve intentionally inflicting physical harm on persons or property. Disorder differs from civil disobedience in that, though both involve illegal action, the former implies an intentional harm which the latter precludes.

Second, democratic political systems are like those that exist in the United States and Great Britain in the following crucial respects. Organized opposition is legally free to form and contest for governmental power through an electoral process. The franchise is widely held, and is, in particular, not limited by political test. There is reasonably little direct governmental interference with speech, press, and inquiry. Finally, the legal system does not normally operate capriciously. That is, given knowledge of statute and precedent, judicial decisions are reasonably easy to predict. . . .

[The] argument turns, not on democracies' overall benefits as compared to non-democracies, but on a specific advantage the former are supposed to have over the latter. It is supposed that in a democracy, peaceful redress of legitimate grievance is always possible, and that a peaceful route is always better than any alternative path that involves disorder. (And here by "peaceful route" all that is meant is "route involving no disorder.") If these claims are true, the argument yields not merely a special reason to reject disorder in a democracy, but a decisive one.

Let us assume at the outset that democracy does guarantee the existence of a peaceful route to any desirable goal. Suppose that one such particular goal, for example racial justice, can be achieved by either a peaceful or a disorderly strategy. In determining which of the two paths is better, all relevant goods and evils should be taken into account—intrinsic and consequential, justice and utility. That is, the moral point of view adopted for purposes of policy judgment is not necessarily utilitarian. Let us suppose also that the relevant goods and evils can be weighed in some balance, a determinate judgment rendered between the alternatives. Is it plausible to suppose that, within democracies, the peaceful path to racial justice is invariably preferable to the disorderly alternative?

One line of reasoning that makes the conclusion seem plausible takes as its point of departure awareness that, in most contexts calling for political judgment, much ignorance of relevant conditions and consequences exists. Hence, it is argued, there are never decisive grounds for excluding the peaceful path. It is always possible that a peaceful path can be found which is less harmful than disorderly alternatives. Peaceful paths to desirable change do, however, tend to produce less harm than disorderly alternatives, for harm is essential to the latter and not to the former. Therefore, within democracies, a peaceful path to racial justice is always better than any disorderly alternative.

But this argument contains two quite common fallacies of political argument.

The first might be called *the fallacy of improbable possibilities*. The general form of the fallacy is to accept judgments based on beliefs about possibilities when only estimates of probabilities will make the argument sound.

In this instance, it is not the *possibility* that a peaceful path will involve less harm than any disorderly alternative that must be established, but the *probability* that this is so. For if, in a particular situation, it is possible that a peaceful strategy is less harmful than a strategy of disorder, but evidence warrants the claim that disorder is *more likely* to involve less harm than a peaceful alternative, then the disorderly route is the one that ought to be traveled. Suppose racial injustice can be eliminated either through electoral effort alone, or through electoral effort in combination with organized violence. Then if the first, entirely peaceful, route *might* involve less harm than the second, disorderly alternative, but the second *probably* involves less harm than the first, from a moral point of view we ought to favor the disorderly alternative. Remember, the harm is judged to be less after *all* relevant values are taken into account, including violations of principles of justice that might be involved in practicing disorder.

The point is that the mere possibility that a peaceful path to desirable change will involve less harm than a partly disorderly alternative is not enough to establish the moral superiority of the former.

The second flaw in the argument might be called the *fallacy of illegitimate tendencies.* One way of giving a bad policy judgment a semblance of validity is by referring to very general *tendencies.* That peaceful tactics generally tend to produce less harm than disorderly ones may be true. That this tendency is greater in democracies than in non-democracies may also be true. But neither admission implies that peaceful paths *are actually* always better than disorderly ones—even within democracies. Not the general tendencies of abstract possibilities, but likely harm or benefit produced by concrete alternatives must be taken into account when specific policy judgments are made. In making political judgments there is no way in which strenuous thought about messy particulars can be safely avoided. To rely on very general tendencies is one way that is least safe.

However, there is one variant of the argument just criticized that is both valid and sound. More than any alternative political system, democracy does increase the likelihood that social advance can be brought about peacefully. Therefore, *in the absence of much knowledge of messy particulars,* within democracies we do have a special reason to suppose that a peaceful route to desirable change that is preferable to any disorderly alternative can always be discovered. However, the special reason that exists is so weak as to be of little practical importance. All it suggests is that, in any particular case, we ought to explore the possibility of finding some peaceful route to change before adopting a path of disorder. It does not guarantee that we will find an alternative that is preferable to a disorderly tactic; nor even that we will discover a possible alternative. Nor does it give us much reason, besides the fact that disorder intrinsically involves harm, to explore peaceful tactics. Thus the argument does nothing but place a slightly heavier burden of proof on those who consider disorderly political tactics when they are members of democratic rather than non-democratic societies. But the extra burden will weigh very lightly on anyone who acknowledges the existence of injustice, and quite properly so. And it will weigh not at all on someone who knows enough about the particulars of the situation in which judgment is required to discount its relevance.

Yet the original argument can be stated in a form which is free of fallacy. Within democracies, it may be assumed, pursuit of desirable change is, in every particular situation, more likely to involve less harm if a peaceful path rather than a disorderly path is taken. But as everyone has an obligation to pursue desirable changes in ways that produce least harm, everyone in any situation has an obligation to act without disorder.

Continuing to assume that a practicable peaceful path always does exist, the assumption that it will invariably, in every concrete situation, involve less harm than some disorderly alternative is, to put it gently, not likely to be true. But, more significantly, there is much reason to doubt what has been granted up till now— that a practicable peaceful path to desirable change always does exist in democracies. Certainly the histories of democracies yield little basis for such optimism. In the United States, for example, it is doubtful that practicable peaceful alternatives to tactics involving much disorder could have ended slavery, widened the effective franchise, organized trade unions. In any society where vast inequalities of power, status, and wealth exist, there is little likelihood that a peaceful path can always be discovered, or that when discovered it will always be preferable to tactics involving disorder.

Indeed, the very persistence of striking inequality indicates that the democratic process has not provided a tolerably efficient means of achieving urgently needed redress of legitimate grievances. In the United States recently, every published report issued by task forces set up under the presidential authorization to study violence carries the same basic message: disorder is a predictable reaction to institutional rigidities of the democratic political system. Even Abraham Lincoln, in his debates with Stephen Douglas, seemed honestly to suppose that slavery would wither away over time, partly through the steady application of democratic remedies. But Douglas had the weight of reason on his side when he insisted that without civil war slavery could not be abolished. On the other hand, Douglas was wrong in assuming that such strife was not a moral price worth paying to end slavery; or so someone can plausibly argue.

While it would not be appropriate here to explore the empirical basis for believing that democracy is a less efficient engine of peaceful social progress than is generally thought, before leaving this topic I do want to explore one reason why so many are inclined to think that peaceful paths to desirable social change always involve less harm than disorderly alternatives. It is an argument that provides insight into the general disposition to accept bad arguments for the claim that all members of democratic societies have a strong obligation to reject disorder.

There is a tendency to ignore the fact that peaceful paths to social progress may be grindingly slow; that disorder will bring the desirable change about much more rapidly. Obviously, if a peaceful strategy takes one hundred years longer than a disorderly alternative, we must question whether the harm done by permitting social evils to fester for a century longer than is necessary outweighs the extra harm involved in the choice of disorder.

And there is good prudential reason why the harm that occurs by permitting chronic social evils to persist for long periods of time is implicitly discounted by many people, especially those who are relatively well off in terms of power, wealth, or status. Those who are relatively advantaged, whose basic position in society is comfortable and secure, are all too often very patient about wrongs that only afflict others. They do not normally suffer the consequences of delaying remedy. They are especially patient about injustice if, as is usual, righting existing wrongs requires that they yield some of their social perquisites. There is good conservative sense in Pareto's idea that social policy is justified only if at least some enjoy gains and no one suffers loss.

Naturally, if those generally elected to powerful offices in democracies are largely drawn from this group of relatively privileged individuals, the problem of resolute indifference to the suffering of underdogs will be intensified. Moreover, even if a leader emerges from among the oppressed, his patience with existing injustice is likely to grow as the perquisites that his office gives are enlarged. That is to say, there is a social dynamic that makes for what many regard as a fundamental tendency of liberal democracies—cooptation.

Finally, in the more affluent democracies, many develop an exaggerated fear of the possibility that steady pressure for desirable radical change will promote right-wing reaction, even fascism. Historically it is true that when societies are forced to choose between order and anarchy, they have tended to choose order however much repressive force has been required to restore stability. In response, those who sought change have been pushed increasingly towards violent revolution as the only effective way to eliminate injustice. However, these historical tendencies have typically occurred, and where they persist still occur, within societies that suffer extreme material scarcity. Resistance to change is quite understandable if one perceives the granting of meaningful reform as certain to result in self-pauperization. That is undoubtedly at least in part why a favorite conservative argument against redistribution of wealth is that it benefits each individual in the mass very little while leveling the aristocratic few. Opposition is then further justified on grounds that this leveling process destroys literature, science, all the cultural amenities of a great civilization.

But as some societies industrialized and became more affluent, an alternative to repression began to emerge. Instead of putting the discontented down with force, buying them off by minimally meeting demands gained favor. Great Britain had a lead time of about fifty years over the other highly industrialized societies. It is not surprising that it was there that the political art of buying discontent off was first brought to a high pitch of development. In particular, one device for facilitating the process of buying off discontent was loosening the reigns of political autocracy; moving in the direction of political democracy. This was especially safe where, as in Britain, the institutions of social despotism remained strong, or where an effective electoral majority of those who were privileged could be constituted. Thus, throughout Britain, scarce access to the best education was a powerful device for maintaining structures of unjust inequality. And in Ulster the democratic hegemony of Protestants has only recently been challenged on the barricades by Catholics. In any event, in a carefully paced, socially controlled way, the franchise within affluent democracies has been gradually extended to underdog minorities. Thus has political democracy been perfected in parallel with the art of buying off discontent.

Marx's prediction that the proletariat in each society would be progressively immiserized has failed principally, I think, because he miscalculated the growing willingness of the advantaged to trade a portion of their advantages for social stability. The democratic process has provided a mechanism for effecting this trade-off with least cost to those who had most. For, generally speaking, political democracy has operated in accordance with the principle of diminishing marginal utility. That is, those most oppressed were generally benefited least by democratically won reforms. This phenomenon is characteristic of almost all advanced industrial democracies, and may be described as *the principle of tokenism*. It must be remembered, however, that by concatenating token gains, significant, even radical changes can, over time, be won.

And this brings us back to the problem of balancing the costs involved in peaceful, but slow, against rapid, but disorderly, redress of legitimate grievance. What tends to happen as democracies become more affluent is that discontent at the moral costs of tokenism grows. That is, the marginal costs of securing social stability rise as expectations thought to be morally legitimate grow. And expectations themselves grow as token gains are more rapidly won. Thus, within political democracies, the very success with which democracy functions tends to inflate the rhetoric of political discontent, tends to enlarge the extent of the criticism of the democratic system itself. A tension develops inside the class of those who are better off. On the one hand they resent what they perceive as unjustifiable escalation of political demands, rising levels of social disorder. This inclines them in the direction of repressive measures. On the other hand, as the increasing level of expectations that produces both demand and disorder is itself a byproduct of the perceived ability of those who are advantaged to yield a portion of what they have without suffering impoverishment, there is also a disposition to trade off more of what one has for social stability. The society is, as it were, seen as balanced on an edge that separates dangerous anarchy and repression from hopeful willingness to pay the price necessary to buy stability.

The point at which this analysis has been driving is that too many emphasize the danger without acknowledging the basis for hope. And many factors—perhaps less dramatically evident than the brutal exercise of police power, or mockery of judicial procedure, or inquisitorial legislative investigation—exist to show why a very affluent democratic society should induce greater payoffs even while the forces of repression grow. Social instability hurts business, jeopardizes personal security, damages the political prospects of office-holders, and so on.[1]

Nothing I am claiming here implies that repression cannot grow, or that democratically won payoffs are bound to grow. But I do think that the overall tendency of the system to respond by facilitating the latter and dampening the former is seriously underestimated by those who think that disorder is invariably counterproductive. Indeed, disorder may often be the catalyst that causes the democratic process to function more efficiently than ever before to eliminate chronic social ills.

Another tendency that develops parallel with the growing, but exaggerated fear of right-wing repression is the effort to dampen the disorderly pressures within society by characterizing them as "immoderate," "irresponsible," "unreasonable," or even "irrational." That is, to a very considerable extent our work-a-day notions of what it is to be reasonable and rational in political affairs are shaped by the implicit tendency of those who are better off to mute the clamor of those who are moved to consider disorder as a political tactic. This subtle and by no means deliberate process by which the very language of rationality is shaped to suit the ideological needs of more conservative social forces is, of course, especially infuriating to those who believe that they have both morality and reason on their side in the struggle to build a good society.

The foregoing analysis of tokenism within democratic societies underlines a claim made previously. The idea that a peaceful route to desirable change can always be charted in democracies may be myth. Under certain conditions, tokenism may be so deeply embedded in institutions that desirable change cannot be won without at least some disorder. It is important to stress, however, that I have not argued that disorder *alone* ever has or can bring about redress of legitimate grievance most efficiently. In fact, disorder may, as I believe, best be viewed as occasionally useful as a means of catalysing electoral effort, or, in other ways, as ancillary to peaceful democratic struggle.

Of course, one can trivialize the claim that peaceful change is always possible by insisting that the possibility of bringing changes about peacefully cannot, in the long run, be discounted. This would be a trivialization first, because the same

---

[1] In research done for the National Advisory Commission on Civil Disorders, a substantial majority of those polled favored providing more money for black Americans if that is what is "necessary to prevent riots." A majority was also willing to absorb tax increases of 10 percent to pay for these programs (cf. Angus Campbell and Howard Schuman, *Racial Attitudes in Fifteen American Cities* [New York, 1968], p. 37). Mounting evidence that this sort of ambivalence is pervasive provides empirical underpinning for my speculations.

is true in any political system; and second, there is no effective way to test an historical prediction that opportunities for peaceful social change are bound to develop after an indefinitely long period of time has elapsed. This is the conservative converse of revolutionary belief that, in the long run, violent revolution must destroy every capitalist society. In any event, that all good things will come about peacefully in the long run if only one is patient does not establish that one should always be patient. And this is the main point at issue.

QUESTIONS

1.   Give a set of criteria for the justification of violence in a political context. Apply it to states with the following political systems: communist, democratic, monarchic. Using your criteria, in which of those states would political violence be justified? In all of them? In some of them? In none of them?

2.   Assume that politically oriented violence in a democracy is morally justified on the basis of some set of criteria such as those given in the introduction to this chapter. Can it also be legally justified? That is, is it possible to enact laws in a democracy which will differentiate between destructive acts which are intended to bring about social reform and those which do not intend some such moral end?

SUGGESTED ADDITIONAL READINGS

Dellinger, Dave. *Revolutionary Nonviolence.* Garden City, N.Y.: Anchor Books, Doubleday & Company, 1971. Dellinger offers a collection of his essays written between 1943 and 1970. These essays center on the use of the tactics of nonviolence to achieve social changes.

Honderich, Ted. "Appraisals of Political Violence." In *Issues in Law and Morality,* ed. by Norman Care and Thomas Trelogan. Cleveland: Case Western Reserve Press, 1973. This is a symposium which includes the Honderich article, a reply to Honderich by Edmund L. Pincoffs and Honderich's reply to Pincoffs. Honderich focuses on the justification of violence in a democracy. A related discussion by Hoenderich is found in "Democratic Violence," *Philosophy and Public Affairs,* vol. 3, 1973.

Marcuse, Herbert. "The Problem of Violence and the Radical Opposition," *Five Lectures.* Boston: Beacon Press, 1970. This is a work on violence by a noted contemporary Marxist philosopher.

Merleau-Ponty, Maurice. *Humanism and Terror.* Boston: Beacon Press, 1969. In this book Merleau-Ponty offers a Marxist perspective on violence.

Murphy, Jeffrie G., ed. *Civil Disobedience and Violence.* Belmont, Calif.: Wadsworth, 1971. This is a brief anthology of classic and contemporary sources with special emphasis on the relation between nonviolence, civil disobedience, and acts of violence.

Shaffer, Jerome A. *Violence.* New York: David McKay Co., Inc., 1971. This book contains four essays dealing with the issues discussed in this chapter—the concept of violence, the justification of violence, and the justification of violence in a society (such as a democracy) governed by the rule of law.

Sibley, Mulford Q., ed. *The Quiet Battle.* Boston: Beacon Press, 1969. Sibley's book is a critique of all strategies of violence by a committed pacifist.

Stanage, Sherman H., ed. *Reason and Violence*. Totowa N.J.: Littlefield, Adams, and Co., 1974. This collection of diverse essays is concerned with the definition, typology, justification, consequences, and history of violence.

Wolff, Robert Paul. "On Violence." *Journal of Philosophy*, vol. 66, 601–616, October 1969. This is an influential article written by an anarchist. Wolff's concept of violence is the broad one discussed in the introduction.

NINE

Economic Injustice

If each individual on earth today were to enjoy an average American standard of living, the world population would probably have to remain under 700 million people; but the world population today is over 4 billion. Among those whose standard of living falls far short of the American one are the 14,000 children in India who go blind each year owing to an insufficiency of protein at the same time that Americans feed their cats and dogs enough protein to meet the daily requirements of 122 million people.[1] Within the United States itself, there are large differences in personal income. Those in the top 5 percent get 20 percent of the income, while those in the bottom 20 percent get about 5 percent.[2] Such unequal distribution of economic goods, both among nations and among individuals within a nation, has been present throughout history. However, the recent famines in sub-Sahara Africa and parts of India and Bangladesh, the economic results of the world energy crisis, and the high unemployment rate among the least-skilled members of American society have heightened public awareness of existing economic inequalities.

That there is an unequal distribution of wealth both among nations and among the members of our society is an unassailable fact. But what, if anything, are we morally obligated to do about such inequalities? Is the United States to be condemned for failing to provide more help to the developing nations of the world while its own citizens live too well, as the critics of the United States at the 1974 World Food Conference in

[1] John Strohm, "Four Billion People," *International Wildlife*, May–June 1975.
[2] "T. R. B. from Washington," *The New Republic*, vol. CLX, no. 12 (March 22, 1969), p. 4.

Rome maintained? Do we as individual members of an affluent society have a moral obligation to deprive ourselves of some comforts in order to prevent starvation in Africa and India? And what about the unequal distribution of wealth within our own society? Are we morally obligated to adopt social practices designed to redistribute that wealth, such as the practice of granting a minimum income to every family within our society? Questions such as these fall in the domain of economic justice. In order to answer them, we need to determine (1) what constitutes an economically just society and (2) whether or not affluent societies have any moral obligation to help meet at least the most basic needs of the members of underdeveloped societies.

AN ECONOMICALLY JUST SOCIETY

In a short story called "The Babylon Lottery," Jorge Luis Borges describes a society in which all societal benefits and obligations are distributed solely on the basis of a periodic lottery. An individual may be a slave at one period, an influential government official the following period, and a person sentenced to jail the third one, simply as the result of chance. No account is taken of the actual contribution the individual has made to society during one of those periods or to the individual's merit, effort, or need, when the temporary economic status of the individual is determined.[3] Such a situation strikes us as capricious. We are accustomed to think that there are some valid principles according to which economic goods are distributed within a society, even though we may disagree about what principles ought to be operative in an economically just society. In the United States, for example, welfare payments and food stamps are said to be distributed on the basis of need, promotions in government offices and business firms are supposedly awarded on the basis of merit and achievement, and the higher incomes of professionals, such as physicians, are assumed to be due them either on the basis of the contribution they make to society or the effort they exert in preparing for their professions.

Whether, and to what extent, merit and achievement, need, effort, or contribution to society ought to be taken into account in the distribution of society's benefits are basic questions of economic justice. Philosophers who attempt to answer such questions usually phrase their question in terms of principles of distributive justice: According to which of the following principles ought the wealth of a society to be distributed?

[3] Jorge Luis Borges, "The Babylon Lottery," in *Ficciones* (New York: Grove Press, Inc., 1956).

1. To each individual an equal share
2. To each individual according to that individual's needs
3. To each individual according to that individual's merit or achievement
4. To each individual according to that individual's contribution to society
5. To each individual according to that individual's effort

We will briefly discuss the first two principles. A thorough discussion of all five principles is found in the Joel Feinberg reading in this chapter.

1. *To Each Individual an Equal Share.* On the strict equalitarian view, each individual in a society is entitled to the same portion of goods as every other individual. All human beings, just because they are human beings, have a right to an equal share in the wealth of their society. This strict equalitarian approach to economic justice leads to the paradoxical view that individual differences are not to be taken into account when the resources of a society are being allocated. When you consider that these resources include food, shelter, and health care, as well as money, it seems absurd to maintain that each individual in society ought to receive a share identical to that of every other individual. Distribution strictly on the basis of the principle of equal sharing would seem to result in an unjust situation in which the 200-pound man would receive the same amount of food as the 140-pound one and the diabetic and paraplegic would receive no more health care than the individual who has no need of either insulin or wheelchairs and physical therapy. Since there are differences between individuals, it would seem more equalitarian to distribute according to the principle of need. Equal distribution would then not involve identical distribution but an equal satisfaction of needs.

2. *To Each Individual according to That Individual's Needs.* If distribution is to be made on the basis of needs, it is necessary to determine just what "needs" are to be considered. Are we to consider only essential or basic needs such as the need for food, clothing, shelter, and health care? Or are we to consider also other human needs such as the need for aesthetic satisfaction and intellectual stimulation? Whether the principle of need is accepted as the sole determinant of a just economic distribution within the society or as only one of those determinants, we need to select some way of ranking needs. If, on the one hand, the principle of need is the sole determinant of economic justice, we must first determine which needs take precedence—which needs must be satisfied before the satisfaction of other, less important needs is even considered. Then, if our society has the means to meet not only these basic needs but other less essential ones, we need to find some way of ranking these less essential ones. For example, does an artist's need for subsidy take precedence over a scientist's need to satisfy his intellectual

curiosity about the existence of life on Mars? If, on the other hand, the principle of need is to be taken as only one of the determinants of economic justice, we need to determine which needs must be satisfied before merit, achievement, contribution, or effort can be used as the basis for distributing the rest of society's wealth.

Note that if either or both of the first two principles are held to be the determinants of distributive justice, the individual's own efforts, achievements, abilities, or contribution to society are not taken into account in determining that individual's benefits. When the claim is made, for example, that each family in a society ought to be guaranteed a minimum yearly income, the moral justification for this claim is usually given either in terms of the principle of need or in terms of the conjunction of that principle and the principle of equal sharing: All human beings, just because they are human beings, are entitled to equal treatment in some important respects; they are entitled, for example, to have at least their most basic needs, such as their need for food and shelter, met by the society of which they are a part.

Suppose we agree that the principle of need ought to be one of the principles of distribution when a society has sufficient means to meet at least the most basic needs of all its citizens.[4] Two questions regarding distributive principles can still arise: (1) Once the minimal needs of all individuals in a society are met, what principles should determine the distribution of the surplus? (2) In a condition of scarcity, when the society cannot meet the minimal needs of all its citizens, whose needs take precedence? In both these cases, appeal can be made to the principles of merit and achievement, effort, or contribution. In this chapter, Feinberg attempts to answer the first question in his paper on economic justice. The second question, however, is not dealt with in any detail.

OUR MORAL OBLIGATIONS TO THE VICTIMS OF FAMINES

Suppose we agree that all human beings, just because they are human beings, are entitled to equal treatment in some respects. Suppose we further agree that they are entitled to at least have their most basic needs satisfied by the society of which they are a part before any members of that society can have a moral right to a more luxurious standard of living. Should we go a step further and say that *all* human beings on

---

[4] Many would not agree that need is an acceptable criterion of distribution in an economically just society. They would argue that all the goods of a society should be distributed on the basis of one or more of the last three criteria: merit and achievement, contribution, or effort.

earth have a right to have one of their most basic needs—the need for food—satisfied, before any individual on earth can have a moral right to the kind of life-style enjoyed by many Americans? If we grant all human beings this right, then we also grant that affluent nations, such as ours, and the members of those nations, have a moral obligation to prevent starvation and malnutrition in the poorer parts of the world.

Some, like Peter Singer in this chapter, contend that we do have such an obligation. Singer bases his contention on the claim that we have an obligation to prevent suffering whenever possible. Singer does not, however, consider the possibility that providing food now to stave off starvation and malnutrition in all the underdeveloped countries might in the long run result in more suffering than it would alleviate. Others, such as Garrett Hardin in this chapter, foresee this very possibility and argue that we are not morally required to aid those nations which are unwilling to adopt the measures necessary to bring their populations into line with their own food resources. The proponents of this view argue that we may have to adopt an ethic of triage toward the poor countries of the world and give help only to those with the best chance of survival. Triage is a method first used by the French during World War I to sort their wounded into three categories. Those with the slightest injuries were given quick first aid. Those who could not be helped were simply allowed to die. The most intensive medical care was given to those in between. The method of triage as applied to the world food problem would also involve a three-way classification: (1) Those nations which will survive even without aid; (2) those with serious food and population problems which will nevertheless survive if given enough aid because they are prepared to take the necessary measures to bring their food resources and populations into line; these nations ought to be given the necessary aid; (3) those whose problems are insoluble in the long run because they are not willing to adopt the necessary measures; according to the ethic of triage, this last group should be given no help.

The argument for the moral acceptability of the proposed treatment of the nations in group 3 is based, at least in part, on the factual claim that economic aid to nations with long-run "insoluble" problems is only a stopgap measure which in the long run will have highly undesirable consequences. Aid to the nations in group 3, it is said, may alleviate current suffering, but it will cause more suffering in the long run for the members of both the needy and affluent nations. Suffering will increase because economic aid will enable more people to survive and reproduce. If no real attempt is made to control the population growth, the ever-increasing population will make ever-increasing demands on the world food supply. Such demands will have a strong adverse effect on the quality of life of the future members of the more affluent societies. In time, it is argued, it will be impossible for the once affluent nations to survive. If help is withheld from the nations in group 3, however, one of two things will follow. Either the needy nations will instigate measures to limit their populations in keeping with their own resources, or else nature itself through famine and disease will decimate the population to the appropriate level. In effect, those who argue in this way maintain that responsibility and rights go hand in hand. Poor nations are entitled to have the most basic needs of their citizens met by the more affluent nations only if they accept the responsibility for limiting their populations so that they will not continue to place an ever-growing burden on the world's food resources.

The adoption of this proposed "survival ethic" by the affluent nations would involve a deliberate decision on their part to let the members of some nations die because those nations are judged to be not worth helping. It is a decision that the United States, which elected recently to give its food aid to the neediest nations, has thus far refused to make. Ethicists argue against the adoption of a survival ethic partly on the ground that the deliberate denial to some human beings of the right to have one of their most basic needs satisfied would weaken our respect for human life and make it easier for us to deny the same right to the needier members within our own society. They agree with Singer that we do have a moral obligation to help the victims of famine and malnutrition. They point out that the United States with less than 6 percent of the world's population consumes between 30 and 40 percent of the world's resources. How can we, they ask, fail to recognize as economically unjust a situation in which we consume such a large share of the world's natural resources while we deny some countries enough food to stave off starvation and malnutrition?

J. S. Z.

Justice William Brennan

MAJORITY OPINION IN *GOLDBERG v. KELLY*

A biographical sketch of Justice William Brennan is found on page 235.

Argument in the Selection. A suit was brought against Jack R. Goldberg, Commissioner of Social Services of the City of New York, by residents of that city who were receiving financial aid under the federally assisted programs of Aid to Families with Dependent Children or under New York State's general Home Relief program. At issue was the right of the officials administering these programs to terminate aid without prior notice and hearing. Such termination, the plaintiffs charged, denied them due process of law. According to the Fourteenth Amendment to the

Constitution, states are prohibited from depriving any person of life, liberty, or property without "due process of law." In using this clause in the amendment to attack the "right" of the officials to deny welfare recipients pretermination hearings, the claim is made that welfare payments are not "gratuities" charitably given, but more like "property" of which an individual cannot be deprived without due process of law. The lower court ruled in favor of the plaintiffs, and the United States Supreme Court upheld that decision. In this majority opinion, Justice Brennan argues that procedural process requires that pretermination evidentiary hearings be held before welfare payments are stopped. He stresses the fact that welfare payments are entitlements and not simply gratuities. For the purposes of this chapter, the case is interesting primarily because it involves a case where need alone, and not effort, contribution, or ability, is held to entitle the members of a society to at least a portion of the goods of that society.

The constitutional issue to be decided . . . is the narrow one whether the Due Process Clause requires that the recipient be afforded an evidentiary hearing before the termination of benefits. The District Court held that only a pre-termination evidentiary hearing would satisfy the constitutional command, and rejected the argument of the state and city officials that the combination of the post-termination "fair hearing" with the informal pre-termination review disposed of all due process claims. The court said: "While post-termination review is relevant, there is one overpowering fact which controls here. By hypothesis, a welfare recipient is destitute, without funds or assets. . . . Suffice it to say that to cut off a welfare recipient in the face of . . . 'brutal need' without a prior hearing of some sort is unconscionable, unless overwhelming considerations justify it." . . . The court rejected the argument that the need to protect the public's tax revenues supplied the requisite "overwhelming consideration." "Against the justified desire to protect public funds must be weighed the individual's overpowering need in this unique situation not to be wrongfully deprived of assistance. . . . While the problem of additional expense must be kept in mind, it does not justify denying a hearing meeting the ordinary standards of due process. Under all the circumstances, we hold that due process requires an adequate hearing before termination of welfare benefits, and the fact that there is a later constitutionally fair proceeding does not alter the result." . . .

Appellant does not contend that procedural due process is not applicable to the termination of welfare benefits. Such benefits are a matter of statutory entitlement for persons qualified to receive them.[1] Their termination involves state

---

[1] It may be realistic today to regard welfare entitlements as more like "property" than a "gratuity." Much of the existing wealth in this country takes the form of rights that do not fall within traditional common-law concepts of property. It has been aptly noted that

"Society today is built around entitlement. The automobile dealer has his franchise, the doctor and lawyer their professional licenses, the worker his union membership,

action that adjudicates important rights. The constitutional challenge cannot be answered by an argument that public assistance benefits are "a 'privilege' and not a 'right'." . . . Relevant constitutional restraints apply as much to the withdrawal of public assistance benefits as to disqualification for unemployment compensation; . . . or to denial of a tax exemption; . . . or to discharge from public employment. The extent to which procedural due process must be afforded the recipient is influenced by the extent to which he may be "condemned to suffer grievous loss," . . . and depends upon whether the recipient's interest in avoiding that loss outweighs the governmental interest in summary adjudication. Accordingly, as we said in Cafeteria & Restaurant Workers Union, etc. v. McElroy, . . . "consideration of what procedures due process may require under any given set of circumstances must begin with a determination of the precise nature of the government function involved as well as of the private interest that has been affected by governmental action." . . .

It is true of course, that some governmental benefits may be administratively terminated without affording the recipient a pre-termination evidentiary hearing.[2] But we agree with the District Court that when welfare is discontinued, only a pre-termination evidentiary hearing provides the recipient with procedural due process. . . . Thus the crucial factor in this context—a factor not present in the case of the blacklisted government contractor, the discharged government employee, the taxpayer denied a tax exemption, or virtually anyone else whose governmental entitlements are ended—is that termination of aid pending resolution of a controversy over eligibility may deprive an eligible recipient of the very means by which to live while he waits. Since he lacks independent resources, his situation becomes immediately desperate. His need to concentrate upon finding the means for daily subsistence, in turn, adversely affects his ability to seek redress from the welfare bureaucracy.

Moreover, important governmental interests are promoted by affording recipients a pre-termination evidentiary hearing. From its founding the Nation's basic commitment has been to foster the dignity and well-being of all persons within its borders. We have come to recognize that forces not within the control of the poor contribute to their poverty. This perception, against the background of our traditions, has significantly influenced the development of the contemporary public

---

contract, and pension rights, the executive his contract and stock options; all are devices to aid security and independence. Many of the most important of these entitlements now flow from government: subsidies to farmers and businessmen, routes for airlines and channels for television stations; long term contracts for defense, space, and education; social security pensions for individuals. Such sources of security, whether private or public, are no longer regarded as luxuries or gratuities; to the recipients they are essentials, fully deserved, and in no sense a form of charity. It is only the poor whose entitlements, although recognized by public policy, have not been effectively enforced."

Reich, Individual Rights and Social Welfare: The Emerging Legal Issues, 74 Yale L. J. 1245, 1255 (1965). See also Reich, The New Property, 73 Yale L. J. 733 (1964).

[2] One Court of Appeals has stated: "In a wide variety of situations, it has long been recognized that where harm to the public is threatened, and the private interest infringed is reasonably deemed to be of less importance, an official body can take summary action pending a later hearing."

assistance system. Welfare, by meeting the basic demands of subsistence, can help bring within the reach of the poor the same opportunities that are available to others to participate meaningfully in the life of the community. At the same time, welfare guards against the societal malaise that may flow from a widespread sense of unjustified frustration and insecurity. Public assistance, then, is not mere charity, but a means to "promote the general Welfare, and secure the Blessings of Liberty to ourselves and our Posterity." The same governmental interests that counsel the provision of welfare, counsel as well its uninterrupted provision to those eligible to receive it; pre-termination evidentiary hearings are indispensable to that end.

Appellant does not challenge the force of these considerations but argues that they are outweighed by countervailing governmental interests in conserving fiscal and administrative resources. These interests, the argument goes, justify the delay of any evidentiary hearing until after discontinuance of the grants. Summary adjudication protects the public fisc by stopping payments promptly upon discovery of reason to believe that a recipient is no longer eligible. Since most terminations are accepted without challenge, summary adjudication also conserves both the fisc and administrative time and energy by reducing the number of evidentiary hearings actually held.

We agree with the District Court, however, that these governmental interests are not overriding in the welfare context. The requirement of a prior hearing doubtless involves some greater expense, and the benefits paid to ineligible recipients pending decision at the hearing probably cannot be recouped, since these recipients are likely to be judgment-proof. But the State is not without weapons to minimize these increased costs. Much of the drain on fiscal and administrative resources can be reduced by developing procedures for prompt pre-termination hearings and by skillful use of personnel and facilities. Indeed, the very provision for a post-termination evidentiary hearing in New York's Home Relief program is itself cogent evidence that the State recognizes the primacy of the public interest in correct eligibility determinations and therefore in the provision of procedural safeguards. Thus, the interest of the eligible recipient in uninterrupted receipt of public assistance, coupled with the State's interest that his payments not be erroneously terminated, clearly outweighs the State's competing concern to prevent any increase in its fiscal and administrative burdens. As the District Court correctly concluded, "the stakes are simply too high for the welfare recipient, and the possibility for honest error or irritable misjudgment too great, to allow termination of aid without giving the recipient a chance, if he so desires, to be fully informed of the case against him so that he may contest its basis and produce evidence in rebuttal."

QUESTIONS

1. Argue for or against the claim: In an affluent society such as ours all individuals who are unable to support themselves should have a *right* to welfare.

2. Suppose that the giving of welfare payments is an act of charity which a society may choose to perform but is not morally obligated to perform. Should a person receiving such aid have the right to a hearing before that aid is withdrawn?

Joel Feinberg

ECONOMIC INCOME AND SOCIAL JUSTICE

A biographical sketch of Joel Feinberg is found on page 252.

Argument in the Selection. *Feinberg discusses five principles of distributive justice: equality, need, merit and achievement, contribution or due return, and effort. His discussion focuses on just distribution within an affluent society which has a surplus to distribute even after it meets the most basic needs of all its citizens. His discussion of the five principles culminates in the tentative conclusion that need, contribution, and effort have the most weight as determinants of economic justice. However, the latter two criteria are applicable only after the basic needs of all the members of society are satisfied.*

The term "distributive justice" traditionally applied to burdens and benefits directly distributed by political authorities, such as appointed offices, welfare doles, taxes, and military conscription, but it has now come to apply also to goods and evils of a nonpolitical kind that can be distributed by private citizens to other private citizens. In fact, in most recent literature, the term is reserved for *economic* distributions, particularly the justice of differences in economic income between classes, and of various schemes of taxation which discriminate in different ways between classes. Further, the phrase can refer not only to acts of distributing but also to de facto states of affairs, such as *the fact that* at present "the five percent at the top get 20 percent [of our national wealth] while the 20 percent at the bottom get about five percent."[1] There is, of course, an ambiguity in the meaning of "distribution." The word may refer to the *process* of distributing, or the *product* of some process of distributing, and either or both of these can be appraised as just or unjust. In addition, a "distribution" can be understood to be a "product" which is *not* the result of any deliberate distributing process, but simply a state of affairs whose production has been too complicated to summarize or to ascribe to any definite group of persons as their deliberate doing. The present "distribution" of American wealth is just such a state of affairs.

Are the 5 percent of Americans "at the top" really different from the 20 percent "at the bottom" in any respect that would justicize the difference between their incomes? It is doubtful that there is any characteristic—relevant or irrelevant—common and peculiar to all members of either group. *Some* injustices, therefore, must surely exist. Perhaps there are some traits, however, that are more or less characteristic of the members of the privileged group, that make the current arrangements at least approximately just. What could (or should) those traits be?

[1] "T. R. B. from Washington" in *The New Republic*, Vol. CLX, No. 12 (March 22, 1969), p. 4.

The answer will state a standard of relevance and a principle of material justice for questions of economic distributions, at least in relatively affluent societies like that of the United States.

At this point there appears to be no appeal possible except to *basic attitudes,* but even at this level we should avoid premature pessimism about the possibility of rational agreement. Some answers to our question have been generally discredited, and if we can see why those answers are inadequate, we might discover some important clues to the properties any adequate answer must possess. Even philosophical adversaries with strongly opposed initial attitudes may hope to come to eventual agreement if they share *some* relevant beliefs and standards and a common commitment to consistency. Let us consider why we all agree (that is the author's assumption) in rejecting the view that differences in race, sex, IQ, or social "rank" are the grounds of just differences in wealth or income. Part of the answer seems obvious. People cannot by their own voluntary choices determine what skin color, sex, or IQ they shall have, or which hereditary caste they shall enter. To make such properties the basis of discrimination between individuals in the distribution of social benefits would be "to treat people differently in ways that profoundly affect their lives because of differences for which they have no responsibility."[2] Differences in a given respect are *relevant* for the aims of distributive justice, then, only if they are differences for which their possessors can be held responsible; properties can be the grounds of just discrimination between persons only if those persons had a *fair opportunity* to acquire or avoid them. Having rejected a number of material principles that clearly fail to satisfy the "fair opportunity" requirement, we are still left with as many as five candidates for our acceptance. (It is in theory open to us to accept two or more of these five as valid principles, there being no a priori necessity that the list be reduced to one.) These are: (1) the principle of perfect equality; (2) the principle[s] of need; (3) the principles of merit and achievement; (4) the principle of contribution (or due return); (5) the principle of effort (or labor). I shall discuss each of these briefly.

(i) EQUALITY

The principle of perfect equality obviously has a place in any adequate social ethic. Every human being is equally a human being, and ... that minimal qualification entitles all human beings equally to certain absolute human rights: positive rights to noneconomic "goods" that by their very natures cannot be in short supply, negative rights not to be treated in cruel or inhuman ways, and negative rights not to be exploited or degraded even in "humane" ways. It is quite another thing, however, to make the minimal qualification of humanity the ground for an absolutely equal distribution of a country's *material wealth* among its citizens. A strict equalitarian could argue that he is merely applying Aristotle's formula of proportionate equality (presumably accepted by all parties to the

---

[2] W. K. Frankena, "Some Beliefs About Justice," *The Lindley Lecture,* Department of Philosophy Pamphlet (Lawrence: University of Kansas, 1966), p. 10.

dispute) with a criterion of relevance borrowed from the human rights theorists. Thus, distributive justice is accomplished between *A* and *B* when the following ratio is satisfied:

$$\frac{A\text{'s share of } P}{B\text{'s share of } P} = \frac{A\text{'s possession of } Q}{B\text{'s possession of } Q}$$

Where *P* stands for economic goods, *Q* must stand simply for "humanity" or "a human nature," and since every human being possesses *that* Q equally, it follows that all should also share a society's economic wealth (the *P* in question) equally.

The trouble with this argument is that its major premise is no less disputable than its conclusion. The standard of relevance it borrows from other contexts where it seems very little short of self-evident, seems controversial, at best, when applied to purely economic contexts. It seems evident to most of us that merely being human entitles *everyone*—bad men as well as good, lazy as well as industrious, inept as well as skilled—to a fair trial if charged with a crime, to equal protection of the law, to equal consideration of his interests by makers of national policy, to be spared torture or other cruel and inhuman treatment, and to be permanently ineligible for the status of chattel slave. Adding a right to an equal share of the economic pie, however, is to add a benefit of a wholly different order, one whose presence on the list of goods for which mere humanity is the sole qualifying condition is not likely to win wide assent without further argument.

It is far more plausible to posit a human right to the satisfaction of (better: to an opportunity to satisfy) one's *basic* economic needs, that is, to enough food and medicine to remain healthy, to minimal clothing, housing, and so on. As Hume pointed out,[3] even these rights cannot exist under conditions of extreme scarcity. Where there is not enough to go around, it cannot be true that everyone has a right to an equal share. But wherever there is moderate abundance or better—wherever a society produces more than enough to satisfy the *basic needs of everyone*—there it seems more plausible to say that mere possession of basic human needs qualifies a person for the opportunity to satisfy them. It would be a rare and calloused sense of justice that would not be offended by an affluent society, with a large annual agricultural surplus and a great abundance of manufactured goods, which permitted some of its citizens to die of starvation, exposure, or easily curable disease. It would certainly be *unfair* for a nation to produce more than it needs and not permit some of its citizens enough to satisfy their basic biological requirements. Strict equalitarianism, then, is a perfectly plausible material principle of distributive justice when confined to affluent societies and basic biological needs, but it loses plausibility when applied to division of the "surplus" left over after basic needs are met. To be sure, the greater the degree of affluence, the higher the level at which we might draw the line between "basic needs" and merely "wanted" benefits, and insofar as social institutions create "artificial needs," it is only fair that society provide all with the opportunity to satisfy them.[4] But once

---

[3] David Hume, *Enquiry Concerning the Principles of Morals* Part III (LaSalle, Ill.: The Open Court Publishing Company, 1947). Originally published in 1777.

[4] This point is well made by Katzner, "An Analysis of the Concept of Justice," pp. 173–203.

the line has been drawn between what is needed to live a minimally decent life by the realistic standards of a given time and place and what is only added "gravy," it is far from evident that justice still insists upon absolutely equal shares of the total. And it is evident that justice does *not* require strict equality wherever there is reason to think that unequal distribution causally determines greater production and is therefore in the interests of everyone, even those who receive the relatively smaller shares.

Still, there is no way to *refute* the strict equalitarian who requires exactly equal shares for everyone whenever that can be arranged without discouraging total productivity to the point where everyone loses. No one would insist upon equal distributions that would diminish the size of the total pie and thus leave smaller slices for *everyone;* that would be opposed to reason. John Rawls makes this condition part of his "rational principle" of justice: "Inequalities are arbitrary unless it is reasonable to expect that they will work out to everyone's advantage. . . ."[5] We are left then with a version of strict equalitarianism that is by no means evidently true and yet is impossible to refute. That is the theory that purports to apply not only to basic needs but to the total wealth of a society, and allows departures from strict equality when, *but only when,* they will work out to everyone's advantage. Although I am not persuaded by this theory, I think that any adequate material principle will have to attach great importance to keeping differences in wealth within reasonable limits, even after all basic needs have been met. One way of doing this would be to raise the standards for a "basic need" as total wealth goes up, so that differences between the richest and poorest citizens (even when there is no real "poverty") are kept within moderate limits.

(ii) NEED

The principle of need is subject to various interpretations, but in most of its forms it is not an independent principle at all, but only a way of mediating the application of the principle of equality. It can, therefore, be grouped with the principle of perfect equality as a member of the equalitarian family and contrasted with the principles of merit, achievement, contribution, and effort, which are all members of the nonequalitarian family. Consider some differences in "needs" as they bear on distributions. Doe is a bachelor with no dependents; Roe has a wife and six children. Roe must satisfy the needs of eight persons out of his paycheck, whereas Doe need satisfy the needs of only one. To give Roe and Doe equal pay would be to treat Doe's interests substantially *more* generously than those of anyone in the Roe family. Similarly, if a small private group is distributing food to its members (say a shipwrecked crew waiting rescue on a desert island), it would not be fair to give precisely the same quantity to a one hundred pounder as to a two hundred pounder, for that might be giving one person all he needs and the other only a fraction of what he needs—a difference in treatment not supported by any relevant difference between them. In short, to distribute goods in proportion to basic needs is not really to depart from a standard of equality, but rather to bring

---

[5] John Rawls, "Justice as Fairness," *The Philosophical Review,* LXVII (1958), 165.

those with some greater initial burden or deficit up to the same level as their fellows.

The concept of a "need" is extremely elastic. In a general sense, to say that S needs X is to say simply that if he doesn't have X he will be harmed. A "basic need" would then be for an X in whose absence a person would be harmed in some crucial and fundamental way, such as suffering injury, malnutrition, illness, madness, or premature death. Thus we all have a basic need for foodstuffs of a certain quantity and variety, fuel to heat our dwellings, a roof over our heads, clothing to keep us warm, and so on. In a different but related sense of need, to say that S needs X is to say that without X he cannot achieve some specific purpose or perform some specific function. If they are to do their work, carpenters need tools, merchants need capital and customers, authors need paper and publishers. Some helpful goods are not strictly needed in this sense: an author with pencil and paper does not really need a typewriter to write a book, but he may need it to write a book speedily, efficiently, and conveniently. We sometimes come to rely upon "merely helpful but unneeded goods" to such a degree that we develop a strong habitual dependence on them, in which case (as it is often said) we have a "psychological" as opposed to a material need for them. If we don't possess that for which we have a strong psychological need, we may be unable to be happy, in which case a merely psychological need for a functional instrument may become a genuine need in the first sense distinguished above, namely, something whose absence is harmful to us. (Cutting across the distinction between material and psychological needs is that between "natural" and "artificial" needs, the former being those that can be expected to develop in any normal person, the latter being those that are manufactured or contrived, and somehow implanted in, or imposed upon, a person.) The more abundant a society's material goods, the higher the level at which we are required (by the force of psychological needs) to fix the distinction between "necessities" and "luxuries"; what *everyone* in a given society regards as "necessary" tends to become an actual, basic need.

(iii) MERIT AND ACHIEVEMENT

The remaining three candidates for material principles of distributive justice belong to the nonequalitarian family. These three principles would each distribute goods in accordance, not with need, but with *desert;* since persons obviously differ in their deserts, economic goods would be distributed unequally. The three principles differ from one another in their conceptions of the relevant *bases of desert* for economic distributions. The first is the principle of *merit.* Unlike the other principles in the nonequalitarian family, this one focuses not on what a person has *done* to deserve his allotment, but rather on what kind of person he is—what characteristics he has.

Two different types of characteristic might be considered meritorious in the appropriate sense: skills and virtues. Native skills and inherited aptitudes will not be appropriate desert bases, since they are forms of merit ruled out by the fair opportunity requirement. No one deserves credit or blame for his genetic inheritance, since no one has the opportunity to select his own genes. Acquired skills may seem more plausible candidates at first, but upon scrutiny they are little better. First, all acquired skills depend to a large degree on native skills. Nobody is born knowing how to read, so reading is an acquired skill, but actual differences in reading skill are to a large degree accounted for by genetic differences that are beyond anyone's control. Some of the differences are no doubt caused by differences in motivation afforded different children, but again the early conditions contributing to a child's motivation are also largely beyond his control. We may still have some differences in acquired skills that are to be accounted for solely or primarily by differences in the degree of practice, drill, and perseverance expended by persons with roughly equal opportunities. In respect to these, we can propitiate the requirement of fair opportunity, but only by nullifying the significance of acquired skill as such, for now skill is a relevant basis of desert only to the extent that it is a product of one's own effort. Hence, *effort* becomes the true basis of desert (as claimed by our fifth principle, discussed below), and not simply skill as such.

Those who would propose rewarding personal *virtues* with a larger than average share of the economic pie, and punishing defects of character with a smaller than average share, advocate assigning to the economic system a task normally done (if it is done at all) by noneconomic institutions. What they propose, in effect, is that we use retributive criteria of distributive justice. Our criminal law, for a variety of good reasons, does not purport to punish people for what they are, but only for what they do. A man can be as arrogant, rude, selfish, cruel, insensitive, irresponsible, cowardly, lazy, or disloyal as he wishes; unless he *does* something prohibited by the criminal law, he will not be made to suffer legal punishment. At least one of the legal system's reasons for refusing to penalize character flaws as such would also explain why such defects should not be listed as relevant differences in a material principle of distributive justice. The apparatus for detecting such flaws (a "moral police"?) would be enormously cumbersome and impractical, and its methods so uncertain and fallible that none of us could feel safe in entrusting the determination of our material allotments to it. We could, of course, give roughly equal shares to all except those few who have *outstanding* virtues—gentleness, kindness, courage, diligence, reliability, warmth, charm, considerateness, generosity. Perhaps these are traits that deserve to be rewarded, but it is doubtful that larger economic allotments are the appropriate vehicles of rewarding. As Benn and Peters remind us, "there are some sorts of 'worth' for which rewards in terms of income seem inappropriate. Great courage in battle is recognized by medals, not by increased pay."[6] Indeed, there is something repugnant, as Socrates and the Stoics insisted, in paying a man to be virtuous. Moreover, the rewards would offer a pecuniary motive for certain forms of excellence that require motives of a different kind, and would thus tend to be self-defeating.

The most plausible nonequalitarian theories are those that locate relevance not in meritorious traits and excellences of any kind, but rather in prior doings: not in what one is, but in what one has done. Actions, too, are sometimes called "meritorious," so there is no impropriety in denominating the remaining families of principles in our survey as "meritarian." One type of action-oriented meritarian might cite *achievement* as a relevant desert basis for pecuniary rewards, so that departures from equality in income are to be justicized only by distinguished

---

[6] Benn and Peters, *Social Principles and the Democratic State*, p. 139.

achievements in science, art, philosophy, music, athletics, and other basic areas of human activity. The attractions and disadvantages of this theory are similar to those of theories which I rejected above that base rewards on skills and virtues. Not all persons have a fair opportunity to achieve great things, and economic rewards seem inappropriate as vehicles for expressing recognition and admiration of noneconomic achievements.

(iv) CONTRIBUTION OR "DUE RETURN"

When the achievements under consideration are themselves contributions to our general economic well-being, the meritarian principle of distributive justice is much more plausible. Often it is conjoined with an economic theory that purports to determine exactly what percentage of our total economic product a given worker or class has produced. Justice, according to this principle, requires that each worker get back exactly that proportion of the national wealth that he has himself created. This sounds very much like a principle of "commutative justice" directing us to *give back* to every worker what is really his own property, that is, the product of his own labor.

The French socialist writer and precursor of Karl Marx, Pierre Joseph Proudhon (1809–1865), is perhaps the classic example of this kind of theorist. In his book *What Is Property?* (1840), Proudhon rejects the standard socialist slogan, "From each according to his ability, to each according to his needs,"[7] in favor of a principle of distributive justice based on contribution, as interpreted by an economic theory that employed a pre-Marxist "theory of surplus value." The famous socialist slogan was not intended, in any case, to express a principle of distributive justice. It was understood to be a rejection of all considerations of "mere" justice for an ethic of human brotherhood. The early socialists thought it unfair, in a way, to give the great contributors to our wealth a disproportionately small share of the product. But in the new socialist society, love of neighbor, community spirit, and absence of avarice would overwhelm such bourgeois notions and put them in their proper (subordinate) place.

Proudhon, on the other hand, based his whole social philosophy not on brotherhood (an ideal he found suitable only for small groups such as families) but on the kind of distributive justice to which even some capitalists gave lip service:

> The key concept was "mutuality" or "reciprocity." "Mutuality, reciprocity exists," he wrote, "when all the workers in an industry, instead of working for an entrepreneur who pays them and keeps their products, work for one another and thus collaborate in the making of a common product whose profits they share among themselves."[8]

---

[7] Traced to Louis Blanc. For a clear brief exposition of Proudhon's view which contrasts it with that of other early socialists and also that of Karl Marx, see Robert Tucker's "Marx and Distributive Justice," in *Nomos VI: Justice,* ed. C. J. Friedrich and J. W. Chapman (New York: Aldine-Atherton Press, 1963), pp. 306–25.

[8] Tucker, "Marx and Distributive Justice," p. 310.

Proudhon's celebrated dictum that "property is theft" did not imply that all *possession* of goods is illicit, but rather that the system of rules that permitted the owner of a factory to hire workers and draw profits ("surplus value") from *their* labor robs the workers of what is rightly theirs. "This profit, consisting of a portion of the proceeds of labor that rightfully belonged to the laborer himself, was 'theft.'"[9] The injustice of capitalism, according to Proudhon, consists in the fact that those who create the wealth (through their labor) get only a small part of what they create, whereas those who "exploit" their labor, like voracious parasites, gather in a greatly disproportionate share. The "return of contribution" principle of distributive justice, then, cannot work in a capitalist system, but requires a *fédération mutualiste* of autonomous producer-cooperatives in which those who create wealth by their work share it in proportion to their real contributions.

Other theorists, employing different notions of what produces or "creates" economic wealth, have used the "return of contribution" principle to support quite opposite conclusions. The contribution principle has even been used to justicize quite unequalitarian capitalistic status quos, for it is said that capital as well as labor creates wealth, as do ingenious ideas, inventions, and adventurous risk-taking. The capitalist who provided the money, the inventor who designed a product to be manufactured, the innovator who thought of a new mode of production and marketing, the advertiser who persuaded millions of customers to buy the finished product, the investor who risked his savings on the success of the enterprise—these are the ones, it is said, who did the most to produce the wealth created by a business, not the workers who contributed only their labor, and of course, these are the ones who tend, on the whole, to receive the largest personal incomes.

Without begging any narrow and technical questions of economics, I should express my general skepticism concerning such facile generalizations about the comparative degrees to which various individuals have contributed to our social wealth. Not only are there impossibly difficult problems of measurement involved, there are also conceptual problems that appear beyond all nonarbitrary solution. I refer to the elements of luck and chance, the social factors not attributable to any assignable individuals, and the contributions of population trends, uncreated natural resources, and the efforts of people now dead, which are often central to the explanation of any given increment of social wealth.

The difficulties of separating out causal factors in the production of social wealth might influence the partisan of the "return of contribution" principle in either or both of two ways. He might become very cautious in his application of the principle, requiring that deviations from average shares be restricted to very clear and demonstrable instances of unusually great or small contributions. But the moral that L. T. Hobhouse[10] drew from these difficulties is that *any* individual contribution will be very small relative to the immeasurably great contribution made by political, social, fortuitous, natural, and "inherited" factors. In particular, strict application of the "return of contribution" principle would tend to support a

[9] Tucker, "Marx and Distributive Justice," p. 311.
[10] L. T. Hobhouse, *The Elements of Social Justice* (London: George Allen and Unwin Ltd., 1922). See especially pp. 161–63.

larger claim for the *community* to its own "due return," through taxation and other devices.

In a way, the principle of contribution is not a principle of mere *desert* at all, no matter how applied. As mentioned above, it resembles a principle of commutative justice requiring repayment of debts, return of borrowed items, or compensation for wrongly inflicted damages. If I lend you my car on the understanding that you will take good care of it and soon return it, or if you steal it, or damage it, it will be too *weak* to say that I "deserve" to have my own car, intact, back from you. After all, the car is *mine* or my due, and questions of ownership are not settled by examination of deserts; neither are considerations of ownership and obligation commonly outbalanced by considerations of desert. It is not merely "unfitting" or "inappropriate" that I should not have my own or my due; it is downright *theft* to withhold it from me. So the return of contribution is not merely a matter of merit deserving reward. It is a matter of a maker demanding that which he has created and is thus properly his. The ratio—*A*'s share of *X* is to *B*'s share of *X* as *A*'s contribution to *X* is to *B*'s contribution to *X*—appears, therefore, to be a very strong and plausible principle of distributive justice, whose main deficiencies, when applied to economic distributions, are of a practical (though severe) kind. If Hobhouse is right in claiming that there are social factors in even the most pronounced individual contributions to social wealth, then the principle of due return serves as a moral basis in support of taxation and other public claims to private goods. In any case, if *A*'s contribution, though apparently much greater than *B*'s, is nevertheless only the tiniest percentage of the total contribution to *X* (whatever that may mean and however it is to be determined), it may seem like the meanest quibbling to distinguish very seriously between *A* and *B* at all.

(v) EFFORT

The principle of due return, as a material principle of distributive justice, does have some vulnerability to the fair opportunity requirement. Given unavoidable variations in genetic endowments and material circumstances, different persons cannot have precisely the same opportunities to make contributions to the public weal. Our final candidate for the status of a material principle of distributive justice, the *principle of effort,* does much better in this respect, for it would distribute economic products not in proportion to successful achievement but according to the degree of effort exerted. According to the principle of effort, justice decrees that hard-working executives and hard-working laborers receive precisely the same remuneration (although there may be reasons having nothing to do with justice for paying more to the executives), and that freeloaders be penalized by allotments of proportionately lesser shares of the joint products of everyone's labor. The most persuasive argument for this principle is that it is the closest approximation to the intuitively valid principle of due return that can pass the fair opportunity requirement. It is doubtful, however, that even the principle of effort fully satisfies the requirements of fair opportunity, since those who inherit or acquire certain kinds of handicap may have little opportunity to *acquire the motivation* even to do their best. In any event, the principle of effort does seem to have intuitive cogency giving it at least some weight as a factor determining the justice of distributions.

In very tentative conclusion, it seems that the principle of equality (in the version that rests on needs rather than that which requires "perfect equality") and the principles of contribution and effort (where nonarbitrarily applicable, and only *after* everyone's basic needs have been satisfied) have the most weight as determinants of economic justice, whereas all forms of the principle of merit are implausible in that role. The reason for the priority of basic needs is that, where there is economic abundance, the claim to life itself and to minimally decent conditions are, like other human rights, claims that all men make with perfect equality. As economic production increases, these claims are given ever greater consideration in the form of rising standards for distinguishing basic needs from other wanted goods. But no matter where that line is drawn, when we go beyond it into the realm of economic surplus or "luxuries," nonequalitarian considerations (especially contribution and effort) come increasingly into play.

QUESTIONS

1. Assume that a society cannot meet even the most basic needs of *all* its citizens, such as the need for food and rudimentary shelter. Should that society adopt a system of distribution which would deny some the necessities of life to ensure the survival of the others?

2. Imagine a society in which all the economic benefits are distributed *solely* on the basis of the contributions made by individuals to the good of that society. Could such a society be an economically just society?

Peter Singer

FAMINE, AFFLUENCE, AND MORALITY

Biographical Information. *Peter Singer has been Radcliffe Lecturer at University College, Oxford, and is now a professor at La Trobe University, Australia. He has published many articles in social and political philosophy. Among these articles are "Animal Liberation," New York Review of Books (Apr. 5, 1973), "The Triviality of the Debate over 'Is-Ought' and the Definition of Moral," American Philosophical Quarterly (January 1973), and "Is Act Utilitarianism Self-Defeating?" Philosophical Review (January 1972).*

Argument in the Selection. *Singer expresses concern over the fact that while members of the more affluent nations spend money on trivia, people in the needier nations are starving. He argues that it is morally wrong not to prevent suffering whenever one can do so without sacrificing anything morally significant. Giving aid to the victims of famine can prevent such suffering. Even if such giving requires a drastic reduction in the standard of living of the members of the more affluent societies, the latter are morally required to meet at least the basic need for food of people who will otherwise starve to death.*

As I write this, in November 1971, people are dying in East Bengal from lack of food, shelter, and medical care. The suffering and death that are occurring there now are not inevitable, not unavoidable in any fatalistic sense of the term. Constant poverty, a cyclone, and a civil war have turned at least nine million people into destitute refugees; nevertheless, it is not beyond the capacity of the richer nations to give enough assistance to reduce any further suffering to very small proportions. The decisions and actions of human beings can prevent this kind of suffering. Unfortunately, human beings have not made the necessary decisions. At the individual level, people have, with very few exceptions, not responded to the situation in any significant way. Generally speaking, people have not given large sums to relief funds; they have not written to their parliamentary representatives demanding increased government assistance; they have not demonstrated in the streets, held symbolic fasts, or done anything else directed toward providing the refugees with the means to satisfy their essential needs. At the government level, no government has given the sort of massive aid that would enable the refugees to survive for more than a few days. Britain, for instance, has given rather more than most countries. It has, to date, given £14,750,000. For comparative purposes, Britain's share of the nonrecoverable development costs of the Anglo-French Concorde project is already in excess of £275,000,000, and on present estimates will reach £440,000,000. The implication is that the British government values a supersonic transport more than thirty times as highly as it values the lives of the nine million refugees. Australia is another country which, on a per capita basis, is well up in the "aid to Bengal" table. Australia's aid, however, amounts to less than one-twelfth of the cost of Sydney's new opera house. The total amount given, from all sources, now stands at about £65,000,-000. The estimated cost of keeping the refugees alive for one year is £464,000,-000. Most of the refugees have now been in the camps for more than six months. The World Bank has said that India needs a minimum of £300,000,000 in assistance from other countries before the end of the year. It seems obvious that assistance on this scale will not be forthcoming. India will be forced to choose between letting the refugees starve or diverting funds from her own development program, which will mean that more of her own people will starve in the future.[1]

These are the essential facts about the present situation in Bengal. So far as it

---

[1] There was also a third possibility: that India would go to war to enable the refugees to return to their lands. Since I wrote this paper, India has taken this way out. The situation is no longer that described above, but this does not affect my argument, as the next paragraph indicates.

concerns us here, there is nothing unique about this situation except its magnitude. The Bengal emergency is just the latest and most acute of a series of major emergencies in various parts of the world, arising both from natural and from man-made causes. There are also many parts of the world in which people die from malnutrition and lack of food independent of any special emergency. I take Bengal as my example only because it is the present concern, and because the size of the problem has ensured that it has been given adequate publicity. Neither individuals nor governments can claim to be unaware of what is happening there.

What are the moral implications of a situation like this? In what follows, I shall argue that the way people in relatively affluent countries react to a situation like that in Bengal cannot be justified; indeed, the whole way we look at moral issues—our moral conceptual scheme—needs to be altered, and with it, the way of life that has come to be taken for granted in our society.

In arguing for this conclusion I will not, of course, claim to be morally neutral. I shall, however, try to argue for the moral position that I take, so that anyone who accepts certain assumptions, to be made explicit, will, I hope, accept my conclusion.

I begin with the assumption that suffering and death from lack of food, shelter, and medical care are bad. I think most people will agree about this, although one may reach the same view by different routes. I shall not argue for this view. People can hold all sorts of eccentric positions, and perhaps from some of them it would not follow that death by starvation is in itself bad. It is difficult, perhaps impossible, to refute such positions, and so for brevity I will henceforth take this assumption as accepted. Those who disagree need read no further.

My next point is this: if it is in our power to prevent something bad from happening, without thereby sacrificing anything of comparable moral importance, we ought, morally, to do it. By "without sacrificing anything of comparable moral importance" I mean without causing anything else comparably bad to happen, or doing something that is wrong in itself, or failing to promote some moral good, comparable in significance to the bad thing that we can prevent. This principle seems almost as uncontroversial as the last one. It requires us only to prevent what is bad, and not to promote what is good, and it requires this of us only when we can do it without sacrificing anything that is, from the moral point of view, comparably important. I could even, as far as the application of my argument to the Bengal emergency is concerned, qualify the point so as to make it: if it is in our power to prevent something very bad from happening, without thereby sacrificing anything morally significant, we ought, morally, to do it. An application of this principle would be as follows: if I am walking past a shallow pond and see a child drowning in it, I ought to wade in and pull the child out. This will mean getting my clothes muddy, but this is insignificant, while the death of the child would presumably be a very bad thing.

The uncontroversial appearance of the principle just stated is deceptive. If it were acted upon, even in its qualified form, our lives, our society, and our world would be fundamentally changed. For the principle takes, firstly, no account of proximity or distance. It makes no moral difference whether the person I can help is a neighbor's child ten yards from me or a Bengali whose name I shall never know, ten thousand miles away. Secondly, the principle makes no distinction between cases in which I am the only person who could possibly do anything and cases in which I am just one among millions in the same position.

I do not think I need to say much in defense of the refusal to take proximity and distance into account. The fact that a person is physically near to us, so that we have personal contact with him, may make it more likely that we *shall* assist him, but this does not show that we *ought* to help him rather than another who happens to be further away. If we accept any principle of impartiality, universalizability, equality, or whatever, we cannot discriminate against someone merely because he is far away from us (or we are far away from him). Admittedly, it is possible that we are in a better position to judge what needs to be done to help a person near to us than one far away, and perhaps also to provide the assistance we judge to be necessary. If this were the case, it would be a reason for helping those near to us first. This may once have been a justification for being more concerned with the poor in one's own town than with famine victims in India. Unfortunately for those who like to keep their moral responsibilities limited, instant communication and swift transportation have changed the situation. From the moral point of view, the development of the world into a "global village" has made an important, though still unrecognized, difference to our moral situation. Expert observers and supervisors, sent out by famine relief organizations or permanently stationed in famine-prone areas, can direct our aid to a refugee in Bengal almost as effectively as we could get it to someone in our own block. There would seem, therefore, to be no possible justification for discriminating on geographical grounds.

There may be a greater need to defend the second implication of my principle—that the fact that there are millions of other people in the same position, in respect to the Bengali refugees, as I am, does not make the situation significantly different from a situation in which I am the only person who can prevent something very bad from occurring. Again, of course, I admit that there is a psychological difference between the cases; one feels less guilty about doing nothing if one can point to others, similarly placed, who have also done nothing. Yet this can make no real difference to our moral obligations. Should I consider that I am less obliged to pull the drowning child out of the pond if on looking around I see other people, no further away than I am, who have also noticed the child but are doing nothing? One has only to ask this question to see the absurdity of the view that numbers lessen obligation. It is a view that is an ideal excuse for inactivity; unfortunately most of the major evils—poverty, overpopulation, pollution—are problems in which everyone is almost equally involved.

The view that numbers do make a difference can be made plausible if stated in this way: if everyone in circumstances like mine gave £5 to the Bengal Relief Fund, there would be enough to provide food, shelter, and medical care for the refugees; there is no reason why I should give more than anyone else in the same circumstances as I am; therefore I have no obligation to give more than £5. Each premise in this argument is true, and the argument looks sound. It may convince us, unless we notice that it is based on a hypothetical premise, although the conclusion is not stated hypothetically. The argument would be sound if the conclusion were: if everyone in circumstances like mine were to give £5, I would have no obligation to give more than £5. If the conclusion were so stated, however, it would be obvious that the argument has no bearing on a situation in which it is not the case that everyone else gives £5. This, of course, is the actual situation. It is more or less certain that not everyone in circumstances like mine will give £5. So there will not be enough to provide the needed food, shelter, and medical care. Therefore by giving more than £5 I will prevent more suffering than I would if I gave just £5.

It might be thought that this argument has an absurd consequence. Since the situation appears to be that very few people are likely to give substantial amounts, it follows that I and everyone else in similar circumstances ought to give as much as possible, that is, at least up to the point at which by giving more one would begin to cause serious suffering for oneself and one's dependents—perhaps even beyond this point to the point of marginal utility, at which by giving more one would cause oneself and one's dependents as much suffering as one would prevent in Bengal. If everyone does this, however, there will be more than can be used for the benefit of the refugees, and some of the sacrifice will have been unnecessary. Thus, if everyone does what he ought to do, the result will not be as good as it would be if everyone did a little less than he ought to do, or if only some do all that they ought to do.

The paradox here arises only if we assume that the actions in question— sending money to the relief funds—are performed more or less simultaneously, and are also unexpected. For if it is to be expected that everyone is going to contribute something, then clearly each is not obliged to give as much as he would have been obliged to had others not been giving too. And if everyone is not acting more or less simultaneously, then those giving later will know how much more is needed, and will have no obligation to give more than is necessary to reach this amount. To say this is not to deny the principle that people in the same circumstances have the same obligations, but to point out that the fact that others have given, or may be expected to give, is a relevant circumstance: those giving after it has become known that many others are giving and those giving before are not in the same circumstances. So the seemingly absurd consequence of the principle I have put forward can occur only if people are in error about the actual circumstances—that is, if they think they are giving when others are not, but in fact they are giving when others are. The result of everyone doing what he really ought to do cannot be worse than the result of everyone doing less than he ought to do, although the result of everyone doing what he reasonably believes he ought to do could be.

If my argument so far has been sound, neither our distance from a preventable evil nor the number of other people who, in respect to that evil, are in the same situation as we are, lessens our obligation to mitigate or prevent that evil. I shall therefore take as established the principle I asserted earlier. As I have already said, I need to assert it only in its qualified form: if it is in our power to prevent something very bad from happening, without thereby sacrificing anything else morally significant, we ought, morally, to do it.

The outcome of this argument is that our traditional moral categories are upset. The traditional distinction between duty and charity cannot be drawn, or at least, not in the place we normally draw it. Giving money to the Bengal Relief Fund is regarded as an act of charity in our society. The bodies which collect money are known as "charities." These organizations see themselves in this way—if you send them a check, you will be thanked for your "generosity." Because giving money is regarded as an act of charity, it is not thought that there is anything wrong with not giving. The charitable man may be praised, but the man who is not charitable is not condemned. People do not feel in any way ashamed or guilty about spending money on new clothes or a new car instead of giving it to famine relief. (Indeed, the alternative does not occur to them.) This way of looking at the matter cannot be justified. When we buy new clothes not to keep ourselves warm but to look "well-dressed" we are not providing for any important need. We would not be sacrificing anything significant if we were to continue to wear our old clothes, and give the money to famine relief. By doing so, we would be preventing another person from starving. It follows from what I have said earlier that we ought to give money away, rather than spend it on clothes which we do not need to keep us warm. To do so is not charitable, or generous. Nor is it the kind of act which philosophers and theologians have called "supererogatory"—an act which it would be good to do, but not wrong not to do. On the contrary, we ought to give the money away, and it is wrong not to do so.

I am not maintaining that there are no acts which are charitable, or that there are no acts which it would be good to do but not wrong not to do. It may be possible to redraw the distinction between duty and charity in some other place. All I am arguing here is that the present way of drawing the distinction, which makes it an act of charity for a man living at the level of affluence which most people in the "developed nations" enjoy to give money to save someone else from starvation, cannot be supported. It is beyond the scope of my argument to consider whether the distinction should be redrawn or abolished altogether. There would be many other possible ways of drawing the distinction—for instance, one might decide that it is good to make other people as happy as possible, but not wrong not to do so.

Despite the limited nature of the revision in our moral conceptual scheme which I am proposing, the revision would, given the extent of both affluence and famine in the world today, have radical implications. These implications may lead to further objections, distinct from those I have already considered. I shall discuss two of these.

One objection to the position I have taken might be simply that it is too drastic a revision of our moral scheme. People do not ordinarily judge in the way I have suggested they should. Most people reserve their moral condemnation for those who violate some moral norm, such as the norm against taking another person's property. They do not condemn those who indulge in luxury instead of giving to famine relief. But given that I did not set out to present a morally neutral description of the way people make moral judgments, the way people do in fact judge has nothing to do with the validity of my conclusion. My conclusion follows from the principle which I advanced earlier, and unless that principle is rejected, or the arguments shown to be unsound, I think the conclusion must stand, however strange it appears. . . .

The second objection to my attack on the present distinction between duty and charity is one which has from time to time been made against utilitarianism. It follows from some forms of utilitarian theory that we all ought, morally, to be working full time to increase the balance of happiness over misery. The position I have taken here would not lead to this conclusion in all circumstances, for if there were no bad occurrences that we could prevent without sacrificing something of comparable moral importance, my argument would have no application. Given the present conditions in many parts of the world, however, it does follow from my argument that we ought, morally, to be working full time to relieve great suffering of the sort that occurs as a result of famine or other disasters. Of course, mitigating circumstances can be adduced—for instance, that if we wear ourselves out through overwork, we shall be less effective than we would otherwise have been. Nevertheless, when all considerations of this sort have been taken into account, the conclusion remains: we ought to be preventing as much suffering as we can without sacrificing something else of comparable moral importance. This conclusion is one which we may be reluctant to face. I cannot see, though, why it should be regarded as a criticism of the position for which I have argued, rather than a criticism of our ordinary standards of behavior. Since most people are self-interested to some degree, very few of us are likely to do everything that we ought to do. It would, however, hardly be honest to take this as evidence that it is not the case that we ought to do it. . . .

The conclusion reached earlier [raises] the question of just how much we all ought to be giving away. One possibility, which has already been mentioned, is that we ought to give until we reach the level of marginal utility—that is, the level at which, by giving more, I would cause as much suffering to myself or my dependents as I would relieve by my gift. This would mean, of course, that one would reduce onself to very near the material circumstances of a Bengali refugee. It will be recalled that earlier I put forward both a strong and a moderate version of the principle of preventing bad occurrences. The strong version, which required us to prevent bad things from happening unless in doing so we would be sacrificing something of a comparable moral significance, does seem to require reducing ourselves to the level of marginal utility. I should also say that the strong version seems to me to be the correct one. I proposed the more moderate version—that we should prevent bad occurrences unless, to do so, we had to sacrifice something morally significant—only in order to show that even on this surely un-deniable principle a great change in our way of life is required. On the more moderate principle, it may not follow that we ought to reduce ourselves to the level of marginal utility, for one might hold that to reduce oneself and one's family to this level is to cause something significantly bad to happen. Whether this is so I shall not discuss, since, as I have said, I can see no good reason for holding the moderate version of the principle rather than the strong version. Even if we accepted the principle only in its moderate form, however, it should be clear that we would have to give away enough to ensure that the consumer society, dependent as it is on people spending on trivia rather than giving to famine relief, would slow down and perhaps disappear entirely. There are several reasons why this would be desirable in itself. The value and necessity of economic growth are now being questioned not only by conservationists, but by economists as well.[2] There is no doubt, too, that the consumer society has had a distorting effect on the goals and purposes of its members. Yet looking at the matter purely from the point of view of overseas aid, there must be a limit to the extent to which we should deliberately slow down our economy; for it might be the case that if we gave away, say, forty percent of our Gross National Product, we would slow down the economy so much that in absolute terms we would be giving less than if we gave twenty-five percent of the much larger GNP that we would have if we limited our con-tribution to this smaller percentage.

I mention this only as an indication of the sort of factor that one would have to take into account in working out an ideal. Since Western societies generally

---

[2] See, for instance, John Kenneth Galbraith, *The New Industrial State* (Boston, 1967); and E. J. Mishan, *The Costs of Economic Growth* (London, 1967).

consider one percent of the GNP an acceptable level for overseas aid, the matter is entirely academic. Nor does it affect the question of how much an individual should give in a society in which very few are giving substantial amounts.

It is sometimes said, though less often now than it used to be, that philosophers have no special role to play in public affairs, since most public issues depend primarily on an assessment of facts. On questions of fact, it is said, philosophers as such have no special expertise, and so it has been possible to engage in philosophy without committing oneself to any position on major public issues. No doubt there are some issues of social policy and foreign policy about which it can truly be said that a really expert assessment of the facts is required before taking sides or acting, but the issue of famine is surely not one of these. The facts about the existence of suffering are beyond dispute. Nor, I think, is it disputed that we can do something about it, either through orthodox methods of famine relief or through population control or both. This is therefore an issue on which philosophers are competent to take a position. The issue is one which faces everyone who has more money than he needs to support himself and his dependents, or who is in a position to take some sort of political action. These categories must include practically every teacher and student of philosophy in the universities of the Western world. If philosophy is to deal with matters that are relevant to both teachers and students, this is an issue that philosophers should discuss.

Discussion, though, is not enough. What is the point of relating philosophy to public (and personal) affairs if we do not take our conclusions seriously? In this instance, taking our conclusion seriously means acting upon it. The philosopher will not find it any easier than anyone else to alter his attitudes and way of life to the extent that, if I am right, is involved in doing everything that we ought to be doing. At the very least, though, one can make a start. The philosopher who does so will have to sacrifice some of the benefits of the consumer society, but he can find compensation in the satisfaction of a way of life in which theory and practice, if not yet in harmony, are at least coming together.

QUESTIONS

1. In opposition to Singer try to defend the following argument: Contributing to famine relief is not a moral obligation which we must perform if we are to act in a morally correct way, but an act of charity which we may or may not perform.

2. Singer says, "We ought to be preventing as much suffering as we can without sacrificing something else of comparable moral importance." What moral considerations would outweigh the obligation Singer claims we have to aid famine victims?

Garrett Hardin

LIVING ON A LIFEBOAT

Biographical Information. *Garrett Hardin (b. 1915) is professor of human ecology at the Department of Biological Sciences, University of Califor-*

nia at Santa Barbara. He is the author of many books, including Nature and Man's Fate; Population, Evolution, and Birth Control; Exploring New Ethics for Survival; *and* Stalking the Wild Taboo. *He has also published numerous articles.*

Argument in the Selection. *Hardin uses the metaphor of a lifeboat to argue that the time may have come to refuse aid in the form of food to those needy countries which do not accept the responsibility for limiting their population growth. He argues that adherence to the principle "From each according to his ability; to each according to his need" will have strong adverse effects. Bolstered by our aid, needy countries will continue their irresponsible policies in regard to food production and population growth. Furthermore, he argues, the food we supply will enable these populations to continue to increase. This in the long run will jeopardize the survival of the human species.*

No generation has viewed the problem of the survival of the human species as seriously as we have. Inevitably, we have entered this world of concern through the door of metaphor. Environmentalists have emphasized the image of the earth as a spaceship—Spaceship Earth. Kenneth Boulding (1966) is the principal architect of this metaphor. It is time, he says, that we replace the wasteful "cowboy economy" of the past with the frugal "spaceship economy" required for continued survival in the limited world we now see ours to be. The metaphor is notably useful in justifying pollution control measures.

Unfortunately, the image of a spaceship is also used to promote measures that are suicidal. One of these is a generous immigration policy, which is only a particular instance of a class of policies that are in error because they lead to the tragedy of the commons (Hardin 1968). These suicidal policies are attractive because they mesh with what we unthinkingly take to be the ideals of "the best people." What is missing in the idealistic view is an insistence that rights and responsibilities must go together. The "generous" attitude of all too many people results in asserting inalienable rights while ignoring or denying matching responsibilities.

For the metaphor of a spaceship to be correct the aggregate of people on board would have to be under unitary sovereign control (Ophuls 1974). A true ship always has a captain. It is conceivable that a ship could be run by a committee. But it could not possibly survive if its course were determined by bickering tribes that claimed rights without responsibilities.

What about Spaceship Earth? It certainly has no captain, and no executive committee. The United Nations is a toothless tiger, because the signatories of its charter wanted it that way. The spaceship metaphor is used only to justify spaceship demands on common resources without acknowledging corresponding spaceship responsibilities.

An understandable fear of decisive action leads people to embrace "incrementalism"—moving toward reform in tiny stages. As we shall see, this strategy is counterproductive in the area discussed here if it means accepting rights before responsibilities. Where human survival is at stake, the acceptance of responsibilities is a precondition to the acceptance of rights, if the two cannot be introduced simultaneously.

LIFEBOAT ETHICS

Before taking up certain substantive issues let us look at an alternative metaphor, that of a lifeboat. In developing some relevant examples the following numerical values are assumed. Approximately two-thirds of the world is desperately poor, and only one-third is comparatively rich. The people in poor countries have an average per capita GNP (Gross National Product) of about $200 per year; the rich, of about $3,000. (For the United States it is nearly $5,000 per year.) Metaphorically, each rich nation amounts to a lifeboat full of comparatively rich people. The poor of the world are in other, much more crowded lifeboats. Continuously, so to speak, the poor fall out of their lifeboats and swim for a while in the water outside, hoping to be admitted to a rich lifeboat, or in some other way to benefit from the "goodies" on board. What should the passengers on a rich lifeboat do? This is the central problem of "the ethics of a lifeboat."

First we must acknowledge that each lifeboat is effectively limited in capacity. The land of every nation has a limited carrying capacity. The exact limit is a matter for argument, but the energy crunch is convincing more people every day that we have already exceeded the carrying capacity of the land. We have been living on "capital"—stored petroleum and coal—and soon we must live on income alone.

Let us look at only one lifeboat—ours. The ethical problem is the same for all, and is as follows. Here we sit, say 50 people in a lifeboat. To be generous, let us assume our boat has a capacity of 10 more, making 60. (This, however, is to violate the engineering principle of the "safety factor." A new plant disease or a bad change in the weather may decimate our population if we don't preserve some excess capacity as a safety factor.)

The 50 of us in the lifeboat see 100 others swimming in the water outside, asking for admission to the boat, or for handouts. How shall we respond to their calls? There are several possibilities.

One. We may be tempted to try to live by the Christian ideal of being "our brother's keeper," or by the Marxian ideal (Marx 1875) of "from each according to his abilities, to each according to his needs." Since the needs of all are the same, we take all the needy into our boat, making a total of 150 in a boat with a capacity of 60. The boat is swamped, and everyone drowns. Complete justice, complete catastrophe.

Two. Since the boat has an unused excess capacity of 10, we admit just 10 more to it. This has the disadvantage of getting rid of the safety factor, for which action we will sooner or later pay dearly. Moreover, *which* 10 do we let in? "First come, first served?" The best 10? The neediest 10? How do we *discriminate*? And what do we say to the 90 who are excluded?

Three. Admit no more to the boat and preserve the small safety factor. Survival of the people in the lifeboat is then possible (though we shall have to be on our guard against boarding parties).

324

The last solution is abhorrent to many people. It is unjust, they say. Let us grant that it is.

"I feel guilty about my good luck," say some. The reply to this is simple: *Get out and yield your place to others.* Such a selfless action might satisfy the conscience of those who are addicted to guilt but it would not change the ethics of the lifeboat. The needy person to whom a guilt-addict yields his place will not himself feel guilty about his sudden good luck. (If he did he would not climb aboard.) The net result of conscience-stricken people relinquishing their unjustly held positions is the elimination of their kind of conscience from the lifeboat. The lifeboat, as it were, purifies itself of guilt. The ethics of the lifeboat persist, unchanged by such momentary aberrations.

This then is the basic metaphor within which we must work out our solutions. Let us enrich the image step by step with substantive additions from the real world.

REPRODUCTION

The harsh characteristics of lifeboat ethics are heightened by reproduction, particularly by reproductive differences. The people inside the lifeboats of the wealthy nations are doubling in numbers every 87 years; those outside are doubling every 35 years, on the average. And the relative difference in prosperity is becoming greater.

Let us, for a while, think primarily of the U.S. lifeboat. As of 1973 the United States had a population of 210 billion people, who were increasing by 0.8% per year, that is, doubling in number every 87 years.

Although the citizens of rich nations are outnumbered two to one by the poor, let us imagine an equal number of poor people outside our lifeboat—a mere 210 million poor people reproducing at a quite different rate. If we imagine these to be the combined populations of Colombia, Venezuela, Ecuador, Morocco, Thailand, Pakistan, and the Philippines, the average rate of increase of the people "outside" is 3.3% per year. The doubling time of this population is 21 years.

Suppose that all these countries, and the United States, agreed to live by the Marxian ideal, "to each according to his needs," the ideal of most Christians as well. Needs, of course, are determined by population size, which is affected by reproduction. Every nation regards its rate of reproduction as a sovereign right. If our lifeboat were big enough in the beginning it might be possible to live *for a while* by Christian-Marxian ideals. *Might.*

Initially, in the model given, the ratio of non-Americans to Americans would be one to one. But consider what the ratio would be 87 years later. By this time Americans would have doubled to a population of 420 million. The other group (doubling every 21 years) would now have swollen to 3,540 million. Each American would have more than eight people to share with. How could the lifeboat possibly keep afloat?

All this involves extrapolation of current trends into the future, and is consequently suspect. Trends may change. Granted: but the change will not necessarily be favorable. If—as seems likely—the rate of population increase falls faster in the ethnic group presently inside the lifeboat than it does among those now outside, the future will turn out to be even worse than mathematics predicts, and sharing will be even more suicidal.

RUIN IN THE COMMONS

The fundamental error of the sharing ethics is that it leads to the tragedy of the commons. Under a system of private property the man (or group of men) who own property recognize their responsibility to care for it, for if they don't they will eventually suffer. A farmer, for instance, if he is intelligent, will allow no more cattle in a pasture than its carrying capacity justifies. If he overloads the pasture, weeds take over, erosion sets in, and the owner loses in the long run.

But if a pasture is run as a commons open to all, the right of each to use it is not matched by an operational responsibility to take care of it. It is no use asking independent herdsmen in a commons to act responsibly, for they dare not. The considerate herdsman who refrains from overloading the commons suffers more than a selfish one who says his needs are greater. (As Leo Durocher says, "Nice guys finish last.") Christian-Marxian idealism is counterproductive. That it *sounds* nice is no excuse. With distribution systems, as with individual morality, good intentions are no substitute for good performance.

A social system is stable only if it is insensitive to errors. To the Christian-Marxian idealist a selfish person is a sort of "error." Prosperity in the system of the commons cannot survive errors. If *everyone* would only restrain himself, all would be well; but it takes *only one less than everyone* to ruin a system of voluntary restraint. In a crowded world of less than perfect human beings—and we will never know any other—mutual ruin is inevitable in the commons. This is the core of the tragedy of the commons. . . .

WORLD FOOD BANKS

In the international arena we have recently heard a proposal to create a new commons, namely an international depository of food reserves to which nations will contribute according to their abilities, and from which nations may draw according to their needs. Nobel laureate Norman Borlaug has lent the prestige of his name to this proposal.

A world food bank appeals powerfully to our humanitarian impulses. We remember John Donne's celebrated line, "Any man's death diminishes me." But before we rush out to see for whom the bell tolls let us recognize where the greatest political push for international granaries comes from, lest we be disillusioned later. Our experience with Public Law 480 clearly reveals the answer. This was the law that moved billions of dollars worth of U.S. grain to food-short, population-long countries during the past two decades. When P.L. 480 first came into being, a headline in the business magazine *Forbes* (Paddock and Paddock 1970) revealed the power behind it: "Feeding the World's Hungry Millions: How it will mean billions for U.S. business."

And indeed it did. In the years 1960 to 1970 a total of $7.9 billion was spent on the "Food for Peace" program, as P.L. 480 was called. During the years 1948 to 1970 an additional $49.9 billion were extracted from American taxpayers to pay for other economic aid programs, some of which went for food and food-producing machinery. (This figure does *not* include military aid.) That P.L. 480 was a give-away program was concealed. Recipient countries went through the motions of paying for P.L. 480 food—with IOU's. In December 1973 the charade was brought to an end as far as India was concerned when the United States "forgave" India's $3.2 billion debt (Anonymous 1974). Public announcement of the cancellation of the debt was delayed for two months: one wonders why. . . .

What happens if some organizations budget for emergencies and others do not? If each organization is solely responsible for its own well-being, poorly managed ones will suffer. But they should be able to learn from experience. They have a chance to mend their ways and learn to budget for infrequent but certain emergencies. The weather, for instance, always varies and periodic crop failures are certain. A wise and competent government saves out of the production of the good years in anticipation of bad years that are sure to come. This is not a new idea. The Bible tells us that Joseph taught this policy to Pharaoh in Egypt more than 2,000 years ago. Yet it is literally true that the vast majority of the governments of the world today have no such policy. They lack either the wisdom or the competence, or both. Far more difficult than the transfer of wealth from one country to another is the transfer of wisdom between sovereign powers or between generations.

"But it isn't their fault! How can we blame the poor people who are caught in an emergency? Why must we punish them?" The concepts of blame and punishment are irrelevant. The question is, what are the operational consequences of establishing a world food bank? If it is open to every country every time a need develops, slovenly rulers will not be motivated to take Joseph's advice. Why should they? Others will bail them out whenever they are in trouble.

Some countries will make deposits in the world food bank and others will withdraw from it: there will be almost no overlap. Calling such a depository-transfer unit a "bank" is stretching the metaphor of *bank* beyond its elastic limits. The proposers, of course, never call attention to the metaphorical nature of the word they use.

THE RATCHET EFFECT

An "international food bank" is really, then, not a true bank but a disguised one-way transfer device for moving wealth from rich countries to poor. In the absence of such a bank, in a world inhabited by individually responsible sovereign nations, the population of each nation would repeatedly go through a cycle of the sort shown in Figure 1. P_2 is greater than P_1, either in absolute numbers or because a deterioration of the food supply has removed the safety factor and produced a dangerously low ratio of resources to population. P_2 may be said to represent a state of overpopulation, which becomes obvious upon the appearance of an "accident," e.g., a crop failure. If the "emergency" is not met by outside help, the population drops back to the "normal" level—the "carrying capacity" of the environment—or even below. In the absence of population control by a sovereign,

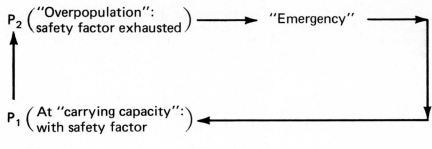

Fig. 1

sooner or later the population grows to P_2 again and the cycle repeats. The long-term population curve (Hardin 1966) is an irregularly fluctuating one, equilibrating more or less about the carrying capacity.

A demographic cycle of this sort obviously involves great suffering in the restrictive phase, but such a cycle is normal to any independent country with inadequate population control. The third century theologian Tertullian (Hardin 1969) expressed what must have been the recognition of many wise men when he wrote: "The scourges of pestilence, famine, wars, and earthquakes have come to be regarded as a blessing to overcrowded nations, since they serve to prune away the luxuriant growth of the human race."

Only under a strong and farsighted sovereign—which theoretically could be the people themselves, democratically organized—can a population equilibrate at some set point below the carrying capacity, thus avoiding the pains normally caused by periodic and unavoidable disasters. For this happy state to be achieved it is necessary that those in power be able to contemplate with equanimity the "waste" of surplus food in times of bountiful harvests. It is essential that those in power resist the temptation to convert extra food into extra babies. On the public relations level it is necessary that the phrase "surplus food" be replaced by "safety factor."

But wise sovereigns seem not to exist in the poor world today. The most anguishing problems are created by poor countries that are governed by rulers insufficiently wise and powerful. If such countries can draw on a world food bank in times of "emergency," the population *cycle* of Figure 1 will be replaced by the population *escalator* of Figure 2. The input of food from a food bank acts as the pawl of a ratchet, preventing the population from retracing its steps to a lower level. Reproduction pushes the population upward, inputs from the world bank prevent its moving downward. Population size escalates, as does the absolute magnitude of "accidents" and "emergencies." The process is brought to an end only by the total collapse of the whole system, producing a catastrophe of scarcely imaginable proportions.

Such are the implications of the well-meant sharing of food in a world of irresponsible reproduction. . . .

To be generous with one's own possessions is one thing; to be generous with posterity's is quite another. This, I think, is the point that must be gotten across to

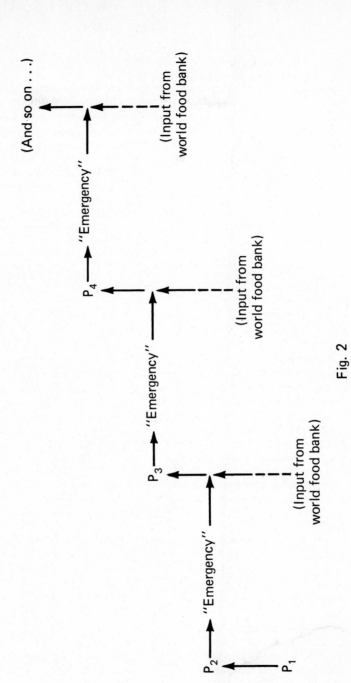

Fig. 2

those who would, from a commendable love of distributive justice, institute a ruinous system of the commons. . . .

If the argument of this essay is correct, so long as there is no true world government to control reproduction everywhere it is impossible to survive in dignity if we are to be guided by Spaceship ethics. Without a world government that is sovereign in reproductive matters mankind lives, in fact, on a number of sovereign lifeboats. For the foreseeable future survival demands that we govern our actions by the ethics of a lifeboat. Posterity will be ill served if we do not.

REFERENCES

Anonymous. 1974. *Wall Street Journal* 19 Feb.

Boulding, K. 1966. The economics of the coming spaceship earth. *In* H. Jarrett, ed. Environmental Quality in a Growing Economy. Johns Hopkins Press, Baltimore.

Hardin, G. 1966. Chap. 9 *in* Biology: Its Principles and Implications, 2nd ed. Freeman, San Francisco.

————. 1968. The tragedy of the commons. *Science* 162: 1243–1248.

————. 1969. Page 18 *in* Population, Evolution, and Birth Control, 2nd ed. Freeman, San Francisco.

Marx, K. 1875. Critique of the Gotha program. Page 388 *in* R. C. Tucker, ed. The Marx-Engels Reader. Norton, N.Y., 1972.

Ophuls, W. 1974. The scarcity society. *Harpers* 248 (1487): 47–52.

Paddock, W. C. 1970. How green is the green revolution? *Bioscience* 20: 897–902.

QUESTIONS

1. What kind of evidence would prove that the resources of the world will not be able to save all the poor countries? If it cannot be conclusively proved that all the poor countries cannot be saved, can a moral justification be given for refusing to aid famine victims in all those countries?

2. Suppose that it is highly unlikely that all the nations in the world can be saved. Which would be the better moral choice:
    (a) to deliberately cut off aid to those least likely to survive in order to ensure the survival of the others or
    (b) to continue our aid despite our awareness of the consequences which will probably follow?

SUGGESTED ADDITIONAL READINGS

Callahan, Daniel. "Doing Well by Doing Good." *The Hastings Center Report*, vol. 4, no. 6, December 1974. Callahan criticizes Garrett Hardin's "Lifeboat Ethic." Callahan's article is in turn criticized in a group of letters published in *The Hastings Center Report*, vol. 5, no. 2, April 1975. The writers of these letters do not defend Hardin, but criticize weaknesses in Callahan's arguments and suggest further arguments against Hardin's position.

Nozick, Robert. "Distributive Justice." *Philosophy and Public Affairs*, vol. 3, pp. 45–126, Fall 1973. Nozick argues that any form of socialism is unjust since it deprives people of the right to property.

Rawls, John. "Justice as Fairness." *The Philosophical Review*, vol. LXVII, April 1958. In this article, Rawls offers a definition of justice in terms of two principles which he maintains all rational, self-interested persons would agree are in the equal interests of all. He argues (1) that everyone has the right to equal liberty and (2) that differences of wealth and privilege are justified only if everyone is free to compete for them and if everyone benefits from them.

———. *A Theory of Justice.* Cambridge, Mass.: Harvard University Press, 1959. This is a more developed discussion of the position Rawls presents in the above article. It is a seminal work which has stimulated a great deal of discussion among philosophers.

Rescher, Nicholas. *Distributive Justice.* Indianapolis: The Bobbs-Merrill Company, Inc., 1966. Rescher discusses and critiques the utilitarian approach to distributive justice. Although difficult in parts, the book offers a useful discussion of the problems of distributive justice (chap. 1) and the principles of distributive justice (chap. 4). It also includes an extensive bibliography devoted solely to the problems of distributive justice (pp. 153–155).

Sterba, James. "Justice as Desert." *Social Theory and Practice*, vol. 3, no. 1, Spring 1974. This is one of the articles written in answer to some of Rawls's claims. Sterba argues that once minimal needs are met, desert should be the criterion according to which the rest of the economic goods of a society should be distributed.

TEN

Environmental and Population Control

Both environmental decay and population expansion pose serious problems for contemporary society—problems which did not arise for our ancestors. To them it seemed unthinkable that human population growth would need to be controlled. Before the advent of modern medicine, human population growth was thought to be more than adequately "controlled" by nature. Before the advent of industrial technology and its mixed blessings, drinkable water and breathable air were thought to be virtually limitless. Before the world population had grown to its present size and before the consumption habits underlying our standard of living had taken root, such natural resources as coal and oil were thought to be virtually inexhaustible. It is now widely accepted that such beliefs, however defensible in their own time, are no longer defensible in the contemporary world. As a result, we find ourselves confronted with ethical questions in regard to environmental and population control.

The central ethical question in regard to population control is easy to specify: Given the desirability (or perhaps the necessity) of population control, what methods of control are ethically acceptable? With regard to environmental control, the central ethical question might be phrased as follows: To what extent, if at all, are we morally obliged to end present practices which in effect serve to pollute the environment and/or to decimate its resources? In attempting to answer this question, we will have to take note not only of the needs and interests of the presently existing human community but also of the needs and interests of future generations. It is sometimes thought that we have also to take note of the "rights" of nonhuman forms of life.

ENVIRONMENTAL CONTROL AND THE EXISTING HUMAN COMMUNITY

It seems clear that we have a prima facie duty not to pollute the environment, that is, we are morally obligated, in the absence of over-riding moral considerations, not to pollute. This prima facie duty may be understood as being based on the needs and interests of the *existing human community,* though one may wish to argue that it is based on the needs and interests of future generations as well. Human welfare, in fact human life, crucially depends on such necessities as breathable air, drinkable water, and eatable food. Thus, in the absence of overriding moral considerations, pollution is morally unacceptable precisely because it is damaging to the public welfare. On an alternative con-strual, the prima facie duty not to pollute may be understood as being based upon a basic human right, the right to a livable environment. This view is extensively developed by William T. Blackstone in one of this chapter's readings.

Suppose it be granted that every existing human being has a right to a livable environment. It yet does not follow that *every* act of environ-mental pollution is morally unacceptable. In some cases, there may be overriding moral considerations. For example, consider the case of a city's sole power plant. Suppose that its operation does in fact generate some small measure of air and water pollution. Are we to think that the continued operation of this plant is morally unacceptable? Hardly. Here it seems clear that the public need for a continued energy supply is sufficient to warrant the continued operation of this plant.

Many concrete cases of environmental pollution confront us with grave difficulties of weighing conflicting rights and interests. Consider the following possibilities: A (small, large, massive) industrial plant, producing a product that is (unessential, very desirable, essential) to society, and providing a (small, large, enormous) number of jobs, pol-lutes the environment in a (minor, substantial, major) way. In which of these several cases is the continued operation of the plant morally unacceptable? In which of these cases does the right to a livable environ-ment demand the closing of the plant? Certainly the general public interest in the quality of the environment always demands to be recog-nized. But what of the interests of the owner, the interests of the employ-ees whose economic stability hangs in the balance, and the interests of potential consumers? In sum, how are these various interests to be equitably weighed? One plausible suggestion is that the morally correct action is that action which on balance results in the least harm. On this view, each case would have to be decided by detailed consideration of the consequences of alternative courses of action.

ENVIRONMENTAL CONTROL AND FUTURE GENERATIONS

We have seen that the well-being of the *existing* human community, or, alternatively, every existing person's right to a livable environment, may be considered the grounds of a prima facie moral obligation not to pollute the environment. Let us now widen our ethical frame of reference and pose the question: To what extent, if at all, do the needs and interests of future generations give rise to further moral obligations? Here the conservation of natural resources may be taken as the central concern. Thus the question becomes: To what extent, if at all, do we have a duty to future generations to conserve natural resources?

Broadly speaking, two approaches to this important question may be distinguished: (1) *Approaches minimizing the duty to future generations.* Here the optimistic argument is made that science and technology will develop to the point that future generations will easily find substitutes for natural resources that we find essential. At any rate, the needs of future generations are so uncertain and unforeseeable that we ought not to bother about conservation at all. (2) *Approaches maximizing the duty to future generations.* Here it is contended that, despite inevitable uncertainties about the needs of future generations, we are relatively certain of some of these needs. At any rate, we must act responsibly on the facts as we see them. Thus it is our duty to future generations to conserve the planet's natural resources, to cut excess consumption, and to recycle as effectively as possible.

In speaking of a duty *to* future generations, we imply that future generations have rights which we are morally obligated to respect. Yet some philosophers contend that it does not even make sense to speak of future generations as having rights: How can something that does not even exist have rights? Joel Feinberg, in one of this chapter's readings, defends the view that it does make sense to speak of future generations as having rights. In providing such a defense, he enters upon a difficult but enlightening analysis of the concept of a right. Along the way, he draws conclusions as to whether or not individual animals, individual plants, and whole species (of plants and animals) may be said to have rights. Such conclusions are relevant in assessing whether or not, in matters of environmental control, we have moral obligations to nonhuman forms of life.

POPULATION CONTROL

Individual freedom in matters of human reproduction is a widely appreciated human value. Because family planning programs accord maximum honor to individual freedom, they are commonly thought to be the most ethically acceptable way of dealing with the dangers of excess population. Family planning programs are dedicated to providing such medical, educational, and social services as are necessary to enable individuals to attain the number of children (and the spacing) *that they desire.* Though family planning programs have an independent justification in terms of family health and welfare, it is far from clear that in themselves they provide an adequate response to the dangers of population growth. They do enable many unwanted births to be avoided. But family planning programs are designed to help people attain the number of children they desire, and if people go on desiring large families, then population may continue to expand. It thus becomes conceivable that measures "beyond family planning" will have to be employed in order to control population growth more effectively.

Among the measures that have been suggested to achieve population control are the following:

1. *Involuntary Fertility Controls*—e.g., the compulsory sterilization of individuals after they have had a certain number of children, compulsory abortion in the case of mothers who already have had a certain number of children, or even the wide-scale control of fertility through the addition of a fertility-control agent to the water supply.
2. *Positive Incentives*—providing financial rewards for the practice of contraception, for not having children, etc.
3. *Negative Incentives*—inflicting financial penalties on those who have children or on those who have more than a certain number of children.
4. *Social Structure Adjustments*—e.g., encouraging women to find employment outside the home or raising the minimum legal age for marriage, thus remotely affecting reproductive choices by affecting the context in which reproductive choices are made.

Each of these categories of measures "beyond family planning" confronts us with ethical difficulties. Involuntary fertility controls seem to sacrifice entirely the value of individual reproductive freedom. Positive and negative incentives allow for individual freedom but raise questions of discrimination against the poor who may find "incentives" virtually coercive. If you have no money at all, and you receive $100 for not having a child, is your decision not to produce a child freely made? As for adjustments to the social structure, we must contend with the possibility that any such adjustment might occasion certain undesirable

consequences as well as the desired consequence. For example, if the
minimum legal age for marriage were raised, in an effort to lower the
birthrate, the effect might well be a lower birthrate but also more
children born out of wedlock. Daniel Callahan, in this chapter's final
reading, thoroughly analyzes all these various measures "beyond family
planning" for the sake of assessing their ethical acceptability.

T. A. M.

Judge Francis Bergan

OPINION IN *BOOMER v. ATLANTIC CEMENT COMPANY*

*Biographical Data. Francis Bergan (b. 1902), now retired, was admitted to
the New York State bar in 1924. He has served as justice of the New York
State Supreme Court (1935–1963) and as associate judge of the New York
Court of Appeals (1963–1972).*

*Argument in the Selection. This case, as brought before the New York
Court of Appeals, illustrates the legal difficulties raised by the environmental side effects of industrial operations. A group of private landown-
ers (including Boomer) brought action against a neighboring cement
company, alleging injury to private property owing to effects of air
pollution. They sought not only to be compensated for property damage
but also to have the operations of the cement plant halted.*

*Judge Bergan calls attention to the fact that the private controversy in
this case is transcended by a generalized public interest in maintaining
the quality of the air. He argues, however, that it is appropriate for the
court to take account only of the interests of the private parties involved,
not to extend its consideration to the public interest. Assessing the
private interests involved, Judge Bergan contends that the controversy
can be most equitably solved by awarding permanent property damages
but refusing to grant an injunction against the continued operation of the
cement company.*

Defendant operates a large cement plant near Albany. These are actions for
injunction and damages by neighboring land owners alleging injury to property

336

from dirt, smoke and vibration emanating from the plant. A nuisance has been found after trial, temporary damages have been allowed; but an injunction has been denied.

The public concern with air pollution arising from many sources in industry and in transportation is currently accorded ever wider recognition accompanied by a growing sense of responsibility in State and Federal Governments to control it. Cement plants are obvious sources of air pollution in the neighborhoods where they operate.

But there is now before the court private litigation in which individual property owners have sought specific relief from a single plant operation. The threshold question raised by the division of view on this appeal is whether the court should resolve the litigation between the parties now before it as equitably as seems possible; or whether, seeking promotion of the general public welfare, it should channel private litigation into broad public objectives.

A court performs its essential function when it decides the rights of parties before it. Its decision of private controversies may sometimes greatly affect public issues. Large questions of law are often resolved by the manner in which private litigation is decided. But this is normally an incident to the court's main function to settle controversy. It is a rare exercise of judicial power to use a decision in private litigation as a purposeful mechanism to achieve direct public objectives greatly beyond the rights and interests before the court.

Effective control of air pollution is a problem presently far from solution even with the full public and financial powers of government. In large measure adequate technical procedures are yet to be developed and some that appear possible may be economically impracticable.

It seems apparent that the amelioration of air pollution will depend on technical research in great depth; on a carefully balanced consideration of the economic impact of close regulation; and of the actual effect on public health. It is likely to require massive public expenditure and to demand more than any local community can accomplish and to depend on regional and interstate controls.

A court should not try to do this on its own as a by-product of private litigation and it seems manifest that the judicial establishment is neither equipped in the limited nature of any judgment it can pronounce nor prepared to lay down and implement an effective policy for the elimination of air pollution. This is an area beyond the circumference of one private lawsuit. It is a direct responsibility for government and should not thus be undertaken as an incident to solving a dispute between property owners and a single cement plant—one of many—in the Hudson River valley.

The cement making operations of defendant have been found by the court at Special Term to have damaged the nearby properties of plaintiffs in these two actions. That court, as it has been noted, accordingly found defendant maintained a nuisance and this has been affirmed at the Appellate Division. The total damage to plaintiffs' properties is, however, relatively small in comparison with the value of defendant's operation and with the consequences of the injunction which plaintiffs seek.

The ground for the denial of injunction, notwithstanding the finding both that there is a nuisance and that plaintiffs have been damaged substantially, is the large disparity in economic consequences of the nuisance and of the injunction.

This theory cannot, however, be sustained without overruling a doctrine which has been consistently reaffirmed in several leading cases in this court and which has never been disavowed here, namely that where a nuisance has been found and where there has been any substantial damage shown by the party complaining an injunction will be granted.

The rule in New York has been that such a nuisance will be enjoined although marked disparity be shown in economic consequence between the effect of the injunction and the effect of the nuisance.

The problem of disparity in economic consequence was sharply in focus in Whalen v. Union Bag & Paper Co. A pulp mill entailing an investment of more than a million dollars polluted a stream in which plaintiff, who owned a farm, was "a lower riparian owner". The economic loss to plaintiff from this pollution was small. This court, reversing the Appellate Division, reinstated the injunction granted by the Special Term against the argument of the mill owner that in view of "the slight advantage to plaintiff and the great loss that will be inflicted on defendant" an injunction should not be granted. "Such a balancing of injuries cannot be justified by the circumstances of this case", Judge Werner noted. He continued: "Although the damage to the plaintiff may be slight as compared with the defendant's expense of abating the condition, that is not a good reason for refusing an injunction".

Thus the unconditional injunction granted at Special Term was reinstated. The rule laid down in that case, then, is that whenever the damage resulting from a nuisance is found not "unsubstantial", viz., $100 a year, injunction would follow. This states a rule that had been followed in this court with marked consistency.

There are cases where injunction has been denied. McCann v. Chasm Power Co. is one of them. There, however, the damage shown by plaintiffs was not only unsubstantial, it was non-existent. Plaintiffs owned a rocky bank of the stream in which defendant had raised the level of the water. This had no economic or other adverse consequence to plaintiffs, and thus injunctive relief was denied. Similar is the basis for denial of injunction in Forstmann v. Joray Holding Co. where no benefit to plaintiffs could be seen from the injunction sought. Thus if, within Whalen v. Union Bag & Paper Co., which authoritatively states the rule in New York, the damage to plaintiffs in these present cases from defendant's cement plant is "not unsubstantial", an injunction should follow.

Although the court at Special Term and the Appellate Division held that injunction should be denied, it was found that plaintiffs had been damaged in various specific amounts up to the time of the trial and damages to the respective plaintiffs were awarded for those amounts. The effect of this was, injunction having been denied, plaintiffs could maintain successive actions at law for damages thereafter as further damage was incurred.

The court at Special Term also found the amount of permanent damage attributable to each plaintiff, for the guidance of the parties in the event both sides stipulated to the payment and acceptance of such permanent damage as a settlement of all the controversies among the parties. The total of permanent damages to all plaintiffs thus found was $185,000. This basis of adjustment has not resulted in any stipulation by the parties.

This result at Special Term and at the Appellate Division is a departure from a rule that has become settled; but to follow the rule literally in these cases would be to close down the plant at once. This court is fully agreed to avoid that immediately drastic remedy; the difference in view is how best to avoid it.[1]

One alternative is to grant the injunction but postpone its effect to a specified future date to give opportunity for technical advances to permit defendant to eliminate the nuisance; another is to grant the injunction conditioned on the payment of permanent damages to plaintiffs which would compensate them for the total economic loss to their property present and future caused by defendant's operations. For reasons which will be developed the court chooses the latter alternative.

If the injunction were to be granted unless within a short period—e.g., 18 months—the nuisance be abated by improved methods, there would be no assurance that any significant technical improvement would occur.

The parties could settle this private litigation at any time if defendant paid enough money and the imminent threat of closing the plant would build up the pressure on defendant. If there were no improved techniques found, there would inevitably be applications to the court at Special Term for extensions of time to perform on showing of good faith efforts to find such techniques.

Moreover, techniques to eliminate dust and other annoying by-products of cement making are unlikely to be developed by any research the defendant can undertake within any short period, but will depend on the total resources of the cement industry nationwide and throughout the world. The problem is universal wherever cement is made.

For obvious reasons the rate of the research is beyond control of defendant. If at the end of 18 months the whole industry has not found a technical solution a court would be hard put to close down this one cement plant if due regard be given to equitable principles.

On the other hand, to grant the injunction unless defendant pays plaintiffs such permanent damages as may be fixed by the court seems to do justice between the contending parties. All of the attributions of economic loss to the properties on which plaintiffs' complaints are based will have been redressed.

The nuisance complained of by these plaintiffs may have other public or private consequences, but these particular parties are the only ones who have sought remedies and the judgment proposed will fully redress them. The limitation of relief granted is a limitation only within the four corners of these actions and does not foreclose public health or other public agencies from seeking proper relief in a proper court.

It seems reasonable to think that the risk of being required to pay permanent damages to injured property owners by cement plant owners would itself be a reasonable effective spur to research for improved techniques to minimize nuisance. . . .

Thus it seems fair to both sides to grant permanent damages to plaintiffs which will terminate this private litigation. . . .

---

[1] Respondent's investment in the plant is in excess of $45,000,000. There are over 300 people employed there.

QUESTIONS

1. On what grounds does Judge Bergan base his contention that considerations of public interest are inappropriate to the deliberations of the court in this case?
2. Suppose in this case that the public interest in preserving the quality of the air were to be weighed together with the relevant private interests; what general line of resolution would you consider most equitable?

William T. Blackstone

ECOLOGY AND RIGHTS

Biographical Information. William T. Blackstone is professor of philosophy and chairman of the Division of Social Sciences at the University of Georgia. He is the editor of a recent anthology, Philosophy and Environmental Crisis, *from which this selection is excerpted. Also among his numerous published works are* The Concept of Equality *and* Political Philosophy.

Argument in the Selection. Blackstone poses the question: Is a livable environment merely a desirable state of affairs, or does every person have a right to a livable environment? Referring to a general theory of human rights, he argues that every person does have a right to a livable environment, precisely because a livable environment is a necessary condition of fulfilling human capacities. Blackstone also argues that the right to a livable environment ought to be granted a formal legal status. On his view, the magnitude of the present environmental crisis warrants the recognition of such a legal right. The recognition of the right to a livable environment, he further argues, is nowise incompatible with a continued recognition of property rights, but the former will necessarily qualify or restrict the latter.

Much has been said about the right to a decent or livable environment. In his 22 January 1970 state of the union address, President Nixon stated: "The great question of the seventies is, shall we surrender to our surroundings, or shall we make our peace with Nature and begin to make the reparations for the damage we have done to our air, our land, and our water? . . . Clean air, clean water, open spaces—these would once again be the birthright of every American; if we act now, they can be." It seems, though, that the use of the term *right* by President Nixon, under the rubric of a "birthright" to a decent environment, is not a strict sense of the term. That is, he does not use this term to indicate that one has or

340

should have either a legal right or a moral right to a decent environment. Rather he is pointing to the fact that in the past our environmental resources have been so abundant that all Americans did in fact inherit a livable environment, and it would be *desirable* that this state of affairs again be the case. Pollution and the exploitation of our environment is precluding this kind of inheritance.

Few would challenge the desirability of such a state of affairs or of such a "birthright." What we want to ask is whether the right to a decent environment can or ought to be considered a right in a stricter sense, either in a legal or moral sense. In contrast to a merely desirable state of affairs, a right entails a correlative duty or obligation on the part of someone or some group to accord one a certain mode of treatment or to act in a certain way.[1] Desirable states of affairs do not entail such correlative duties or obligations.

THE RIGHT TO A LIVABLE ENVIRONMENT AS A HUMAN RIGHT

Let us first ask whether the right to a livable environment can properly be considered to be a human right. For the purposes of this paper, however, I want to avoid raising the more general question of whether there are any human rights at all. Some philosophers do deny that any human rights exist.[2] In two recent papers I have argued that human rights do exist (even though such rights may properly be overridden on occasion by other morally relevant reasons) and that they are universal and inalienable (although the actual exercise of such rights on a given occasion is alienable).[3] My argument for the existence of universal human rights rests, in the final analysis, on a theory of what it means to be human, which specifies the capacities for rationality and freedom as essential, and on the fact that there are no relevant grounds for excluding any human from the opportunity to develop and fulfill his capacities (rationality and freedom) as a human. This is not to deny that there are criteria which justify according human rights in quite different ways or with quite different modes of treatment for different persons, depending upon the nature and degree of such capacities and the existing historical and environmental circumstances.

If the right to a livable environment were seen as a basic and inalienable human right, this could be a valuable tool (both inside and outside of legalistic frameworks) for solving some of our environmental problems, both on a national and on an international basis. Are there any philosophical and conceptual difficulties in treating this right as an inalienable human right? Traditionally we have not looked upon the right to a decent environment as a human right or as an

---

[1] This is a dogmatic assertion in this context. I am aware that some philosophers deny that rights and duties are correlative. Strictly interpreted this correlativity thesis is false, I believe. There are duties for which there are no correlative rights. But space does not permit discussion of this question here.

[2] See Kai Nielsen's "Scepticism and Human Rights," *Monist* 52, no. 4 (1968): 571–594.

[3] See my "Equality and Human Rights," *Monist* 52, no. 4 (1968): 616–639 and my "Human Rights and Human Dignity," in Laszlo and Gotesky, eds., *Human Dignity*.

inalienable right. Rather, inalienable human or natural rights have been conceived in somewhat different terms; equality, liberty, happiness, life, and property. However, might it not be possible to view the right to a livable environment as being entailed by, or as constitutive of, these basic human or natural rights recognized in our political tradition? If human rights, in other words, are those rights which each human possesses in virtue of the fact that he is human and in virtue of the fact that those rights are essential in permitting him to live a human life (that is, in permitting him to fulfill his capacities as a rational and free being), then might not the right to a decent environment be properly categorized as such a human right? Might it not be conceived as a right which has emerged as a result of changing environmental conditions and the impact of those conditions on the very possibility of human life and on the possibility of the realization of other rights such as liberty and equality?[4] Let us explore how this might be the case.

Given man's great and increasing ability to manipulate the environment, and the devastating effect this is having, it is plain that new social institutions and new regulative agencies and procedures must be initiated on both national and international levels to make sure that the manipulation is in the public interest. It will be necessary, in other words, to restrict or stop some practices and the freedom to engage in those practices. Some look upon such additional state planning, whether national or international, as unnecessary further intrusion on man's freedom. Freedom is, of course, one of our basic values, and few would deny that excessive state control of human action is to be avoided. But such restrictions on individual freedom now appear to be necessary in the interest of overall human welfare and the rights and freedoms of *all* men. Even John Locke with his stress on freedom as an inalienable right recognized that this right must be construed so that it is consistent with the equal right to freedom of others. The whole point of the state is to restrict unlicensed freedom and to provide the conditions for equality of rights for all. Thus it seems to be perfectly consistent with Locke's view and, in general, with the views of the founding fathers of this country to restrict certain rights or freedoms when it can be shown that such restriction is necessary to insure the equal rights of others. If this is so, it has very important implications for the rights to freedom and to property. These rights, perhaps properly seen as inalienable (though this is a controversial philosophical question), are not properly seen as unlimited or unrestricted. When values which we hold dear conflict (for example, individual or group freedom and the freedom of all, individual or group rights and the rights of all, and individual or group welfare and the welfare of the general public) something has to give; some priority must be established. In the case of the abuse and waste of environmental resources, less individual freedom and fewer individual rights for the sake of greater public welfare and equality of rights seem justified. What in the past had been properly regarded as

----

[4] Almost forty years ago, Aldo Leopold stated that "there is as yet no ethic dealing with man's relationship to land and to the non-human animals and plants which grow upon it. Land, like Odysseus' slave girls, is still property. The land relation is still strictly economic entailing privileges but not obligations." (See Leopold's "The Conservation Ethic," *Journal of Forestry* 31, no. 6 (October 1933): 634–643. Although some important changes have occurred since he wrote this, no systematic ethic or legal structure has been developed to socialize or institutionalize the obligation to use land properly.

freedoms and rights (given what seemed to be unlimited natural resources and no serious pollution problems) can no longer be so construed, at least not without additional restrictions. We must recognize both the need for such restrictions and the fact that none of our rights can be realized without a livable environment. Both public welfare and equality of rights now require that natural resources not be used simply according to the whim and caprice of individuals or simply for personal profit. This is not to say that all property rights must be denied and that the state must own all productive property, as the Marxist argues. It is to insist that those rights be qualified or restricted in the light of new ecological data and in the interest of the freedom, rights, and welfare of all.

The answer then to the question, Is the right to a livable environment a human right? is yes. Each person has this right qua being human and because a livable environment is essential for one to fulfill his human capacities. And given the danger to our environment today and hence the danger to the very possibility of human existence, access to a livable environment must be conceived as a right which imposes upon everyone a correlative moral obligation to respect.[5]

THE RIGHT TO A LIVABLE ENVIRONMENT AS A LEGAL RIGHT

If the right to a decent environment is to be treated as a legal right, then obviously what is required is some sort of legal framework which gives this right a legal status. Such legal frameworks have been proposed. Sen. Gaylord Nelson, originator of Earth Day, recently proposed a Constitutional Amendment guaranteeing every American an inalienable right to a decent environment.[6] Others want to formulate an entire "environmental bill of rights" to assist in solving our pollution problems. Such a bill of rights or a constitutional revision would provide a legal framework for the enforcement of certain policies bearing on environmental issues. It would also involve the concept of "legal responsibility" for acts which violate those rights. Such legal responsibility is beginning to be enforced in the United States. President Nixon on 23 December 1970 signed an executive order requiring industries to obtain federal permits before dumping pollutants. He issued the order not under the authority of new legislation but under the Refuse Act of 1899, which was originally designed to control discharges in connection with dredging and water construction operations but now has been broadened by Supreme Court decisions to cover pollution resulting from industrial operations. (The extension of this act is similar to my suggestion above, namely, the extension of the constitutional rights to equality, liberty, and property to include the right to a livable environment.)

Others propose that the right to a decent environment also be a cardinal tenet

---

[5] The right to a livable environment might itself entail other rights, for example, the right to population control. Population control is obviously essential for quality human existence. This issue is complex and deserves a separate essay, but I believe that the moral framework explicated above provides the grounds for treating population control both as beneficial and as moral.

[6] *Newsweek,* 4 May 1970, p. 26.

of international law. Pollution is not merely a national problem but an international one. The population of the entire world is affected by it, and a body of international law, which includes the right to a decent environment and the accompanying policies to save and preserve our environmental resources, would be an even more effective tool than such a framework at the national level. Of course, one does not have to be reminded of the problems involved in establishing international law and in eliciting obedience to it. Conflicts between nations are still settled more by force than by law or persuasion. The record of the United Nations attests to this fact. In the case of international conflict over environmental interests and the use of the environment, the possibility of international legal resolution, at least at this stage of history, is somewhat remote; for the body of enforceable international law on this topic is meager indeed. This is not to deny that this is the direction in which we should (and must) move.

A good case can be made for the view that not all moral or human rights should be legal rights and that not all moral rules should be legal rules. It may be argued that any society which covers the whole spectrum of man's activities with legally enforceable rules minimizes his freedom and approaches totalitarianism. There is this danger. But just as we argued that certain traditional rights and freedoms are properly restricted in order to insure the equal rights and welfare of all, so also it can plausibly be argued that the human right to a livable environment should become a legal one in order to assure that it is properly respected. Given the magnitude of the present dangers to the environment and to the welfare of all humans, and the ingrained habits and rules, or lack of rules, which permit continued waste, pollution, and destruction of our environmental resources, the legalized status of the right to a livable environment seems both desirable and necessary.

Such a legal right would provide a tool for pressing environmental transgressions in the courts. At the present the right to a livable environment, even if recognized as a human right, is not generally recognized as a legal one. One cannot sue individuals or corporations for polluting the environment, if the pollution harms equally every member of a community. One can sue such individuals or corporations if they damage one's private property but not if they damage the public environment. It is true that public officials have a legal standing in cases of generalized pollution, but unfortunately they have done little to exercise that standing.

Since public officials are failing to take steps to protect the environment, Joseph Sax, professor of law at the University of Michigan, argues that the right to take environmental disputes to court must be obtained as a right of private citizens: "The No. 1 legal priority of those concerned with governmental protection now is that the old restraints of the public nuisance doctrine and other archaic rules be rooted out of the law and be replaced with the recognition of every citizen's opportunity to enforce at law the right to a decent environment."[7] Sax himself drafted a model environmental law which was presented to the

[7] Joseph Sax, "Environment in The Courtroom," *Saturday Review*, 3 October 1970, p. 56.

Michigan legislature, which "empowered any person or organization to sue any private or public body and to obtain a court order restraining conduct that is likely to pollute, impair, or destroy the air, water, or other material resources or the public trust therein."[8] This bill has now become law, and a similar bill is pending in the U.S. Congress, having been introduced by Senators McGovern and Hart and Representative Udall. I concur with Sax that this law, which provides an enforceable right to a decent environment and which places the burden of proof on a polluter or would-be polluter to show that his action affecting the environment is consistent with public health and welfare, "offers the promise of a dramatic legal break-through in the effort to protect environmental quality."[9] Although it may add to the clogged conditions of the courts, it should also have the effect of encouraging careful planning of activities which affect the environment.

The history of government, in this country and elsewhere, has been that of the gradual demise of a laissez-faire philosophy of government. Few deny that there are areas of our lives where government should not and must not intrude. In fact, what we mean by a totalitarian government is one which exceeds its proper bounds and attempts to control nearly all human activities. But in some areas of human life, it has been seen that the "keep-government-out-of-it" attitude just will not work. The entire quality of life in a society is determined by the availability and distribution of goods and services in such vital areas as education, housing, medical treatment, legal treatment, and so on. In the field of education, for example, we have seen the need for compulsory education and, more recently, for unitary school systems in order to provide equality of educational opportunity. In the area of medical treatment it is plain that we need "new systems of health service delivery that stress better distribution, accessibility, cost containment and increased quality without sacrificing quality."[10] Dr. John Knowles, former president of the American Medical Association argues that we cannot expect this from a system in which the free market economy sets the fees of physicians. Nor can we expect it from the AMA which some characterize as an "ogre in the form of a vast and powerful trade union interested only in economic advancement of its members."[11] Government must step in to provide these vital health services.

In the same way, it is essential that government step in to prevent the potentially dire consequences of industrial pollution and the waste of environmental resources. Such government regulations need not mean the death of the free enterprise system. The right to private property can be made compatible with the right to a livable environment, for if uniform antipollution laws were applied to all industries, then both competition and private ownership could surely continue. But they would continue within a quite different set of rules and attitudes toward the environment. This extension of government would not be equivalent to totalitarianism. In fact it is necessary to insure equality of rights and freedom, which is essential to a democracy.

[8] Ibid.
[9] Ibid.
[10] John Knowles, "Where Doctors Fail," *Saturday Review*, 27 August 1970, p. 63.
[11] Ibid.

ECOLOGY AND ECONOMIC RIGHTS

We suggested above that it is necessary to qualify or restrict economic or property rights in the light of new ecological data and in the interest of the freedom, rights, and welfare of all. In part, this suggested restriction is predicated on the assumption that we cannot expect private business to provide solutions to the multiple pollution problems for which they themselves are responsible. Some companies have taken measures to limit the polluting effect of their operations, and this is an important move. But we are deluding ourselves if we think that private business can function as its own pollution police. This is so for several reasons: the primary objective of private business is economic profit. Stockholders do not ask of a company, "Have you polluted the environment and lowered the quality of the environment for the general public and for future generations?" Rather they ask, "How high is the annual dividend and how much higher is it than the year before?" One can hardly expect organizations whose basic norm is economic profit to be concerned in any great depth with the long-range effects of their operations upon society and future generations or concerned with the hidden cost of their operations in terms of environmental quality to society as a whole. Second, within a free enterprise system companies compete to produce what the public wants at the lowest possible cost. Such competition would preclude the spending of adequate funds to prevent environmental pollution, since this would add tremendously to the cost of the product—unless all other companies would also conform to such antipollution policies. But in a free enterprise economy such policies are not likely to be self-imposed by businessmen. Third, the basic response of the free enterprise system to our economic problems is that we must have greater economic growth or an increase in gross national product. But such growth many ecologists look upon with great alarm, for it can have devastating long-range effects upon our environment. Many of the products of uncontrolled growth are based on artificial needs and actually detract from, rather than contribute to, the quality of our lives. A stationary economy, some economists and ecologists suggest, may well be best for the quality of man's environment and of his life in the long run. Higher GNP does not automatically result in an increase in social well-being, and it should not be used as a measuring rod for assessing economic welfare. This becomes clear when one realizes that the GNP

> aggregates the dollar value of all goods and services produced—the cigarettes as well as the medical treatment of lung cancer, the petroleum from offshore wells as well as the detergents required to clean up after oil spills, the electrical energy produced and the medical and cleaning bills resulting from the air-pollution fuel used for generating the electricity. The GNP allows no deduction for negative production, such as lives lost from unsafe cars or environmental destruction perpetrated by telephone, electric and gas utilities, lumber companies, and speculative builders.[12]

To many persons, of course, this kind of talk is not only blasphemy but subversive. This is especially true when it is extended in the direction of addi-

[12] See Melville J. Ulmer, "More Than Marxist," *New Republic*, 26 December 1970, p. 14.

tional controls over corporate capitalism. (Some ecologists and economists go further and challenge whether corporate capitalism can accommodate a stationary state and still retain its major features.)[13] The fact of the matter is that the ecological attitude forces one to reconsider a host of values which have been held dear in the past, and it forces one to reconsider the appropriateness of the social and economic systems which embodied and implemented those values. Given the crisis of our environment, there must be certain fundamental changes in attitudes toward nature, man's use of nature, and man himself. Such changes in attitudes undoubtedly will have far-reaching implications for the institutions of private property and private enterprise and the values embodied in these institutions. Given that crisis we can no longer look upon water and air as free commodities to be exploited at will. Nor can the private ownership of land be seen as a lease to use that land in any way which conforms merely to the personal desires of the owner. In other words, the environmental crisis is forcing us to challenge what had in the past been taken to be certain basic rights of man or at least to restrict those rights. And it is forcing us to challenge institutions which embodied those rights. . . .

QUESTIONS

1. Blackstone mentions a movement to formulate an "environmental bill of rights." Draft and defend such a bill of rights.

2. Explain how Blackstone would answer the following claim: The recognition of a right to a livable environment is incompatible with the recognition of property rights.

3. Blackstone contends that we cannot expect private business to provide solutions for the pollution problems it has largely generated. Critically analyze the arguments Blackstone advances in support of this contention.

John Passmore

CONSERVATION AND POSTERITY

Biographical Information. *John Passmore is presently professor of philosophy at the Australian National University (Canberra, Australia). His published works include* Hume's Intentions *(1952),* A Hundred Years of Philosophy *(1957), and* Philosophical Reasoning *(1961).* Man's Responsibility for Nature *(1974), from which this selection is excerpted, is a book dedicated entirely to ecological themes.*

Argument in the Selection. *Passmore reviews the question of the extent to which we can be certain that our successors will need certain natural*

[13]See Murdock and Connell, "All about Ecology," *Center Magazine* 3, no. 1 (January–February 1970): p. 63.

resources. He concludes that uncertainties in this regard are difficult to eradicate. Yet, he argues, to the extent that there is a reasonable certainty that our successors will need certain resources, we are obliged not to waste them. On Passmore's view, we ought to be prepared to sacrifice certain forms of enjoyment for the sake of conservation, but we ought not to sacrifice the continued development of our cultural heritage. To allow human "loves" (art, science, friendship, etc.) to languish in the name of conservation, he argues, is not in the true interest of posterity.

The conservationist programme confronts us with a fundamental moral issue: ought we to pay any attention to the needs of posterity? To answer this question affirmatively is to make two assumptions: first, that posterity will suffer unless we do so; secondly that if it will suffer, it is our duty so to act as to prevent or mitigate its sufferings. Both assumptions can be, and have been, denied. To accept them does not, of course, do anything to solve the problem of conservation, but to reject them is to deny that there is any such problem, to deny that our society would be a better one—morally better—if it were to halt the rate at which it is at present exhausting its resources. Or it is to deny this, at least, in so far as the arguments in favour of slowing-down are purely conservationist in character—ignoring for the moment, that is, such facts as that the lowering of the consumption-rate is one way of reducing the incidence of pollution and that a high rate of consumption of metals and fossil fuels makes it impossible to preserve untouched the wildernesses in which they are so often located.

To begin with the assumption that posterity will suffer unless we alter our ways, it is still often suggested that, on the contrary, posterity can safely be left to look after itself, provided only that science and technology continue to flourish. This optimistic interpretation of the situation comes especially from economists and from nuclear physicists. . . . If these scientists, these economists, are right, there simply is no 'problem of conservation'.

Very many scientists, of course, take the opposite view, especially if they are biologists. Expert committees set up by such scientific bodies as the American National Academy of Sciences have, in fact, been prepared to commit themselves to definite estimates of the dates at which this resource or that will be exhausted. This is always, however, on certain assumptions. It makes a considerable difference whether one supposes or denies that rates of consumption will continue to increase exponentially as they have done since 1960; it makes a very great—in many cases an overwhelming—difference whether one supposes or denies that substitutes will be discovered for our major resources. The Academy's extrapolations are best read as a *reductio ad absurdum* of the supposition that our present patterns of resource consumption can continue even over the next century.

The possibility that substitutes will be discovered introduces a note of uncertainty into the whole discussion, an uncertainty which cannot be simply set aside as irrelevant to our moral and political decisions about conservation, which it inevitably and properly influences. At the moment, for example, the prospect of developing a fuel-cell to serve as a substitute for petrol is anything but bright; confident predictions that by 1972 nuclear fusion would be available as an energy

itself.) With regard to unborn generations, he contends, it is clear that they will have interests when they eventually come to exist. Feinberg argues that the rights of unborn generations are contingent; he denies that they have a right to be born, but given the fact that some persons will in fact be born, they have the right to be born into a world which is not "a used up garbage heap."

Every philosophical paper must begin with an unproved assumption. Mine is the assumption that there will still be a world five hundred years from now, and that it will contain human beings who are very much like us. We have it within our power now, clearly, to affect the lives of these creatures for better or worse by contributing to the conservation or corruption of the environment in which they must live. I shall assume furthermore that it is psychologically possible for us to care about our remote descendants, that many of us in fact do care, and indeed that we ought to care. My main concern then will be to show that it makes sense to speak of the rights of unborn generations against us, and that given the moral judgment that we ought to conserve our environmental inheritance for them, and its grounds, we might well say that future generations *do* have rights correlative to our present duties toward them. Protecting our environment now is also a matter of elementary prudence, and insofar as we do it for the next generation already here in the persons of our children, it is a matter of love. But from the perspective of our remote descendants it is basically a matter of justice, of respect for their rights. My main concern here will be to examine the concept of a right to better understand how that can be.

THE PROBLEM

To have a right is to have a claim[1] to something and *against* someone, the recognition of which is called for by legal rules or, in the case of moral rights, by the principles of an enlightened conscience. In the familiar cases of rights, the claimant is a competent adult human being, and the claimee is an officeholder in an institution or else a private individual, in either case, another competent adult human being. Normal adult human beings, then, are obviously the sorts of beings of whom rights can meaningfully be predicated. Everyone would agree to that, even extreme misanthropes who deny that anyone in fact has rights. On the other hand, it is absurd to say that rocks can have rights, not because rocks are morally inferior things unworthy of rights (that statement makes no sense either), but because rocks belong to a category of entities of whom rights cannot be meaningfully predicated. That is not to say that there are no circumstances in which we ought to treat rocks carefully, but only that the rocks themselves cannot validly

---

[1] I shall leave the concept of a claim unanalyzed here, but for a detailed discussion, see my "The Nature and Value of Rights," *Journal of Value Inquiry* 4 (Winter 1971): 263–277.

claim good treatment from us. In between the clear cases of rocks and normal human beings, however, is a spectrum of less obvious cases, including some bewildering borderline ones. Is it meaningful or conceptually possible to ascribe rights to our dead ancestors? to individual animals? to whole species of animals? to plants? to idiots and madmen? to fetuses? to generations yet unborn? Until we know how to settle these puzzling cases, we cannot claim fully to grasp the concept of a right, or to know the shape of its logical boundaries.

One way to approach these riddles is to turn one's attention first to the most familiar and unproblematic instances of rights, note their most salient characteristics, and then compare the borderline cases with them, measuring as closely as possible the points of similarity and difference. In the end, the way we classify the borderline cases may depend on whether we are more impressed with the similarities or the differences between them and the cases in which we have the most confidence.

It will be useful to consider the problem of individual animals first because their case is the one that has already been debated with the most thoroughness by philosophers so that the dialectic of claim and rejoinder has now unfolded to the point where disputants can get to the end game quickly and isolate the crucial point at issue. When we understand precisely what *is* at issue in the debate over animal rights, I think we will have the key to the solution of all the other riddles about rights.

INDIVIDUAL ANIMALS

Almost all modern writers agree that we ought to be kind to animals, but that is quite another thing from holding that animals can claim kind treatment from us as their due. Statutes making cruelty to animals a crime are now very common, and these, of course, impose legal duties on people not to mistreat animals; but that still leaves open the question whether the animals, as beneficiaries of those duties, possess rights correlative to them. We may very well have duties *regarding* animals that are not at the same time duties *to* animals, just as we may have duties regarding rocks, or buildings, or lawns, that are not duties *to* the rocks, buildings, or lawns. Some legal writers have taken the still more extreme position that animals themselves are not even the directly intended beneficiaries of statutes prohibiting cruelty to animals. During the nineteenth century, for example, it was commonly said that such statutes were designed to protect human beings by preventing the growth of cruel habits that could later threaten human beings with harm too. Prof. Louis B. Schwartz finds the rationale of the cruelty-to-animals prohibition in its protection of animal lovers from affronts to their sensibilities. "It is not the mistreated dog who is the ultimate object of concern," he writes. "Our concern is for the feelings of other human beings, a large proportion of whom, although accustomed to the slaughter of animals for food, readily identify themselves with a tortured dog or horse and respond with great sensitivity to its sufferings."[2] This seems to me to be factitious. How much more natural it is to say

---

[2] Louis B. Schwartz, "Morals, Offenses and the Model Penal Code," *Columbia Law Review* 63 (1963): 673.

with John Chipman Gray that the true purpose of cruelty-to-animals statutes is "to preserve the dumb brutes from suffering."[3] The very people whose sensibilities are invoked in the alternative explanation, a group that no doubt now includes most of us, are precisely those who would insist that the protection belongs primarily to the animals themselves, not merely to their own tender feelings. Indeed, it would be difficult even to account for the existence of such feelings in the absence of a belief that the animals deserve the protection in their own right and for their own sakes.

Even if we allow, as I think we must, that animals are the intended direct beneficiaries of legislation forbidding cruelty to animals, it does not follow directly that animals have legal rights, and Gray himself, for one,[4] refused to draw this further inference. Animals cannot have rights, he thought, for the same reason they cannot have duties, namely, that they are not genuine "moral agents." Now, it is relatively easy to see why animals cannot have duties, and this matter is largely beyond controversy. Animals cannot be "reasoned with" or instructed in their responsibilities; they are inflexible and unadaptable to future contingencies; they are subject to fits of instinctive passion which they are incapable of repressing or controlling, postponing or sublimating. Hence, they cannot enter into contractual agreements, or make promises; they cannot be trusted; and they cannot (except within very narrow limits and for purposes of conditioning) be blamed for what would be called "moral failures" in a human being. They are therefore incapable of being moral subjects, of acting rightly or wrongly in the moral sense, of having, discharging, or breeching duties and obligations.

But what is there about the intellectual incompetence of animals (which admittedly disqualifies them for duties) that makes them logically unsuitable for rights? The most common reply to this question is that animals are incapable of *claiming* rights on their own. They cannot make motion, on their own, to courts to have their claims recognized or enforced; they cannot initiate, on their own, any kind of legal proceedings; nor are they capable of even understanding when their rights are being violated, of distinguishing harm from wrongful injury, and responding with indignation and an outraged sense of justice instead of mere anger or fear.

No one can deny any of these allegations, but to the claim that they are the grounds for disqualification of rights of animals, philosophers on the other side of this controversy have made convincing rejoinders. It is simply not true, says W. D. Lamont,[5] that the ability to understand what a right is and the ability to set legal machinery in motion by one's own initiative are necessary for the possession of rights. If that were the case, then neither human idiots nor wee babies would have any legal rights at all. Yet it is manifest that both of these classes of intellectual incompetents have legal rights recognized and easily enforced by the courts. Children and idiots start legal proceedings, not on their own direct initiative, but

---

[3] John Chipman Gray, *The Nature and Sources of the Law,* 2d ed. (Boston: Beacon Press, 1963), p. 43.

[4] And W. D. Ross for another. See *The Right and the Good* (Oxford: Clarendon Press, 1930), app. 1, pp. 48–56.

[5] W. D. Lamont, *Principles of Moral Judgment* (Oxford: Clarendon Press, 1946), pp. 83–85.

rather through the actions of proxies or attorneys who are empowered to speak in their names. If there is no conceptual absurdity in this situation, why should there be in the case where a proxy makes a claim on behalf of an animal? People commonly enough make wills leaving money to trustees for the care of animals. Is it not natural to speak of the animal's right to his inheritance in cases of this kind? If a trustee embezzles money from the animal's account,[6] and a proxy speaking in the dumb brute's behalf presses the animal's claim, can he not be described as asserting the animal's *rights*? More exactly, the animal itself claims its rights through the vicarious actions of a human proxy speaking in its name and in its behalf. There appears to be no reason why we should require the animal to understand what is going on (so the argument concludes) as a condition for regarding it as a possessor of rights.

Some writers protest at this point that the legal relation between a principal and an agent cannot hold between animals and human beings. Between humans, the relation of agency can take two very different forms, depending upon the degree of discretion granted to the agent, and there is a continuum of combinations between the extremes. On the one hand, there is the agent who is the mere "mouthpiece" of his principal. He is a "tool" in much the same sense as is a typewriter or telephone; he simply transmits the instructions of his principal. Human beings could hardly be the agents or representatives of animals in this sense, since the dumb brutes could no more use human "tools" than mechanical ones. On the other hand, an agent may be some sort of expert hired to exercise his professional judgment on behalf of, and in the name of, the principal. He may be given, within some limited area of expertise, complete independence to act as he deems best, binding his principal to all the beneficial or detrimental consequences. This is the role played by trustees, lawyers, and ghost-writers. This type of representation requires that the agent have great skill, but makes little or no demand upon the principal, who may leave everything to the judgment of his agent. Hence, there appears, at first, to be no reason why an animal cannot be a totally passive principal in this second kind of agency relationship.

There are still some important dissimilarities, however. In the typical instance of representation by an agent, even of the second, highly discretionary kind, the agent is hired by a principal who enters into an agreement or contract with him; the principal tells his agent that within certain carefully specified boundaries "You may speak for me," subject always to the principal's approval, his right to give new directions, or to cancel the whole arrangement. No dog or cat could possibly do any of those things. Moreover, if it is the assigned task of the agent to defend the principal's rights, the principal may often decide to release his claimee, or to waive his own rights, and instruct his agent accordingly. Again, no mute cow or horse can do that. But although the possibility of hiring, agreeing, contracting, approving, directing, canceling, releasing, waiving, and instructing is present in the typical (all-human) case of agency representation, there appears to be no reason of a logical or conceptual kind why that *must* be so, and indeed there are some special examples involving human principals where it is not in fact so. I have in mind legal rules, for example, that require that a defendant be represented at his trial by an attorney, and impose a state-appointed attorney upon

---

[6] Cf. H. J. McCloskey, "Rights," *Philosophical Quarterly* 15 (1965): 121, 124.

reluctant defendants, or upon those tried *in absentia,* whether they like it or not. Moreover, small children and mentally deficient and deranged adults are commonly represented by trustees and attorneys, even though they are incapable of granting their own consent to the representation, or of entering into contracts, of giving directions, or waiving their rights. It may be that it is unwise to permit agents to represent principals without the latters' knowledge or consent. If so, then no one should ever be permitted to speak for an animal, at least in a legally binding way. But that is quite another thing than saying that such representation is logically incoherent or conceptually incongruous—the contention that is at issue.

H. J. McCloskey,[7] I believe, accepts the argument up to this point, but he presents a new and different reason for denying that animals can have legal rights. The ability to make claims, whether directly or through a representative, he implies, is essential to the possession of rights. Animals obviously cannot press their claims on their own, and so if they have rights, these rights must be assertable by agents. Animals, however, cannot be represented, McCloskey contends, and not for any of the reasons already discussed, but rather because representation, in the requisite sense, is always of interests, and animals (he says) are incapable of having interests.

Now, there is a very important insight expressed in the requirement that a being have interests if he is to be a logically proper subject of rights. This can be appreciated if we consider just why it is that mere things cannot have rights. Consider a very precious "mere thing"—a beautiful natural wilderness, or a complex and ornamental artifact, like the Taj Mahal. Such things ought to be cared for, because they would sink into decay if neglected, depriving some human beings, or perhaps even all human beings, of something of great value. Certain persons may even have as their own special job the care and protection of these valuable objects. But we are not tempted in these cases to speak of "thing-rights" correlative to custodial duties, because, try as we might, we cannot think of mere things as possessing interests of their own. Some people may have a duty to preserve, maintain, or improve the Taj Mahal, but they can hardly have a duty to help or hurt it, benefit or aid it, succor or relieve it. Custodians may protect it for the sake of a nation's pride and art lovers' fancy; but they don't keep it in good repair for "its own sake," or for "its own true welfare," or "well-being." A mere thing, however valuable to others, has no good of its own. The explanation of that fact, I suspect, consists in the fact that mere things have no conative life: no conscious wishes, desires, and hopes; or urges and impulses; or unconscious drives, aims, and goals; or latent tendencies, direction of growth, and natural fulfillments. Interests must be compounded somehow out of conations; hence mere things have no interests. *A fortiori,* they have no interests to be protected by legal or moral rules. Without interests a creature can have no "good" of its own, the achievement of which can be its due. Mere things are not loci of value in their own right, but rather their value consists entirely in their being objects of other beings' interests.

So far McCloskey is on solid ground, but one can quarrel with his denial that any animals but humans have interests. I should think that the trustee of funds

---

[7] Ibid.

willed to a dog or cat is more than a mere custodian of the animal he protects. Rather his job is to look out for the interests of the animal and make sure no one denies it its due. The animal itself is the beneficiary of his dutiful services. Many of the higher animals at least have appetites, conative urges, and rudimentary purposes, the integrated satisfaction of which constitutes their welfare or good. We can, of course, with consistency treat animals as mere pests and deny that they have any rights; for most animals, especially those of the lower orders, we have no choice but to do so. But it seems to me, nevertheless, that in general, animals *are* among the sorts of beings of whom rights can meaningfully be predicated and denied.

Now, if a person agrees with the conclusion of the argument thus far, that animals are the sorts of beings that *can* have rights, and further, if he accepts the moral judgment that we ought to be kind to animals, only one further premise is needed to yield the conclusion that some animals do in fact have rights. We must now ask ourselves for whose sake ought we to treat (some) animals with consideration and humaneness? If we conceive our duty to be one of obedience to authority, or to one's own conscience merely, or one of consideration for tender human sensibilities only, then we might still deny that animals have rights, even though we admit that they are the kinds of beings that *can* have rights. But if we hold not only that we ought to treat animals humanely but also that we should do so for the animals' own sake, that such treatment is something we owe animals as their due, something that can be claimed for them, something the withholding of which would be an injustice and a wrong, and not merely a harm, then it follows that we do ascribe rights to animals. I suspect that the moral judgments most of us make about animals do pass these phenomenological tests, so that most of us do believe that animals have rights, but are reluctant to say so because of the conceptual confusions about the notion of a right that I have attempted to dispel above.

Now we can extract from our discussion of animal rights a crucial principle for tentative use in the resolution of the other riddles about the applicability of the concept of a right, namely, that the sorts of beings who *can* have rights are precisely those who have (or can have) interests. I have come to this tentative conclusion for two reasons: (1) because a right holder must be capable of being represented and it is impossible to represent a being that has no interests, and (2) because a right holder must be capable of being a beneficiary in his own person, and a being without interests is a being that is incapable of being harmed or benefitted, having no good or "sake" of its own. Thus, a being without interests has no "behalf" to act in, and no "sake" to act for. My strategy now will be to apply the "interest principle," as we can call it, to the other puzzles about rights, while being prepared to modify it where necessary (but as little as possible), in the hope of separating in a consistent and intuitively satisfactory fashion the beings who can have rights from those which cannot.

VEGETABLES

It is clear that we ought not to mistreat certain plants, and indeed there are rules and regulations imposing duties on persons not to misbehave in respect to certain members of the vegetable kingdom. It is forbidden, for example, to pick wildflowers in the mountainous tundra areas of national parks, or to endanger trees by starting fires in dry forest areas. Members of Congress introduce bills designed, as they say, to "protect" rare redwood trees from commercial pillage. Given this background, it is surprising that no one[8] speaks of plants as having rights. Plants, after all, are not "mere things"; they are vital objects with inherited biological propensities determining their natural growth. Moreover, we do say that certain conditions are "good" or "bad" for plants, thereby suggesting that plants, unlike rocks, are capable of having a "good." (This is a case, however, where "what we say" should not be taken seriously: we also say that certain kinds of paint are good or bad for the internal walls of a house, and this does not commit us to a conception of walls as beings possessed of a good or welfare of their own.) Finally, we are capable of feeling a kind of affection for particular plants, though we rarely personalize them, as we do in the case of animals, by giving them proper names.

Still, all are agreed that plants are not the kinds of beings that can have rights. Plants are never plausibly understood to be the direct intended beneficiaries of rules designed to "protect" them. We wish to keep redwood groves in existence for the sake of human beings who can enjoy their serene beauty, and for the sake of generations of human beings yet unborn. Trees are not the sorts of beings who have their "own sakes," despite the fact that they have biological propensities. Having no conscious wants or goals of their own, trees cannot know satisfaction or frustration, pleasure or pain. Hence, there is no possibility of kind or cruel treatment of trees. In these morally crucial respects, trees differ from the higher species of animals.

Yet trees are not mere things like rocks. They grow and develop according to the laws of their own nature. Aristotle and Aquinas both took trees to have their own "natural ends." Why then do I deny them the status of beings with interests of their own? The reason is that an interest, however the concept is finally to be analyzed, presupposes at least rudimentary cognitive equipment. Interests are compounded out of *desires* and *aims*, both of which presuppose something like *belief*, or cognitive awareness. . . .

WHOLE SPECIES

The topic of whole species, whether of plants or animals, can be treated in much the same way as that of individual plants. A whole collection, as such, cannot have beliefs, expectations, wants, or desires, and can flourish or languish only in the human interest-related sense in which individual plants thrive and decay. Individual elephants can have interests, but the species elephant cannot. Even where individual elephants are not granted rights, human beings may have an interest—economic, scientific or sentimental—in keeping the species from dying out, and *that* interest may be protected in various ways by law. But that is quite another matter from recognizing a right to survival belonging to the species itself.

---

[8] Outside of Samuel Butler's *Erewhon*.

Still, the preservation of a whole species may quite properly seem to be a morally more important matter than the preservation of an individual animal. Individual animals can have rights but it is implausible to ascribe to them a right to life on the human model. Nor do we normally have duties to keep individual animals alive or even to abstain from killing them provided we do it humanely and nonwantonly in the promotion of legitimate human interests. On the other hand, we do have duties to protect threatened species, not duties to the species themselves as such, but rather duties to future human beings, duties derived from our housekeeping role as temporary inhabitants of this planet. . . .

FUTURE GENERATIONS

We have it in our power now to make the world a much less pleasant place for our descendants than the world we inherited from our ancestors. We can continue to proliferate in ever greater numbers, using up fertile soil at an even greater rate, dumping our wastes into rivers, lakes, and oceans, cutting down our forests, and polluting the atmosphere with noxious gases. All thoughtful people agree that we ought not to do these things. Most would say that we have a duty not to do these things, meaning not merely that conservation is morally required (as opposed to merely desirable) but also that it is something due our descendants, something to be done for their sakes. Surely we owe it to future generations to pass on a world that is not a used up garbage heap. Our remote descendants are not yet present to claim a livable world as their right, but there are plenty of proxies to speak now in their behalf. These spokesmen, far from being mere custodians, are genuine representatives of future interests.

Why then deny that the human beings of the future have rights which can be claimed against us now in their behalf? Some are inclined to deny them present rights out of a fear of falling into obscure metaphysics, by granting rights to remote and unidentifiable beings who are not yet even in existence. Our unborn great-great-grandchildren are in some sense "potential" persons, but they are far more remotely potential, it may seem, than fetuses. This, however, is not the real difficulty. Unborn generations are more remotely potential than fetuses in one sense, but not in another. A much greater period of time with a far greater number of causally necessary and important events must pass before their potentiality can be actualized, it is true; but our collective posterity is just as certain to come into existence "in the normal course of events" as is any given fetus now in its mother's womb. In that sense the existence of the distant human future is no more remotely potential than that of a particular child already on its way.

The real difficulty is not that we doubt whether our descendants will ever be actual, but rather that we don't know who they will be. It is not their temporal remoteness that troubles us so much as their indeterminacy—their present face-lessness and namelessness. Five centuries from now men and women will be living where we live now. Any given one of them will have an interest in living space, fertile soil, fresh air, and the like, but that arbitrarily selected one has no other qualities we can presently envision very clearly. We don't even know who his parents, grandparents, or great-grandparents are, or even whether he is related to us. Still, whoever these human beings may turn out to be, and whatever they might reasonably be expected to be like, they will have interests that we can affect, for better or worse, right now. That much we can and do know about them. The identity of the owners of these interests is now necessarily obscure, but the fact of their interest-ownership is crystal clear, and that is all that is necessary to certify the coherence of present talk about their rights. We can tell, sometimes, that shadowy forms in the spatial distance belong to human beings, though we know not who or how many they are; and this imposes a duty on us not to throw bombs, for example, in their direction. In like manner, the vagueness of the human future does not weaken its claim on us in light of the nearly certain knowledge that it will, after all, be human.

Doubts about the existence of a right to be born transfer neatly to the question of a similar right to come into existence ascribed to future generations. The rights that future generations certainly have against us are contingent rights: the interests they are sure to have when they come into being (assuming of course that they will come into being) cry out for protection from invasions that can take place now. Yet there are no actual interests, presently existent, that future generations, presently nonexistent, have now. Hence, there is no actual interest that they have in simply coming into being, and I am at a loss to think of any other reason for claiming that they have a right to come into existence (though there may well be such a reason). Suppose then that all human beings at a given time voluntarily form a compact never again to produce children, thus leading within a few decades to the end of our species. This of course is a wildly improbable hypothetical example but a rather crucial one for the position I have been tentatively considering. And we can imagine, say, that the whole world is converted to a strange ascetic religion which absolutely requires sexual abstinence for everyone. Would this arrangement violate the rights of anyone? No one can complain on behalf of presently nonexistent future generations that their future interests which give them a contingent right of protection have been violated since they will never come into existence to be wronged. My inclination then is to conclude that the suicide of our species would be deplorable, lamentable, and a deeply moving tragedy, but that it would violate no one's rights. Indeed if, contrary to fact, all human beings could ever agree to such a thing, that very agreement would be a symptom of our species' biological unsuitability for survival anyway.

CONCLUSION

For several centuries now human beings have run roughshod over the lands of our planet, just as if the animals who do live there and the generations of humans who will live there had no claims on them whatever. Philosophers have not helped matters by arguing that animals and future generations are not the kinds of beings who can have rights now, that they don't presently qualify for membership, even "auxiliary membership," in our moral community. I have tried in this essay to dispel the conceptual confusions that make such conclusions possible. To acknowledge their rights is the very least we can do for members of endangered species (including our own). But that is something.

QUESTIONS

1. Argue for or against the following claim: We have a moral obligation to preserve all endangered plant and animal species.
2. Argue for or against the following claim: Future generations have a right to exist.
3. It seems clear that we regard euthanasia for animals and euthanasia for human beings in different lights. To what extent is this difference in attitude the result of our conception of the moral status of animals?

Daniel Callahan

ETHICS AND POPULATION LIMITATION

A biographical sketch of Daniel Callahan is found on page 24.

Argument in the Selection. Appealing to the grave dangers of excessive population, Callahan contends that the traditional acceptance of an unlimited right of procreation is no longer a defensible view. On his analysis, ethical dilemmas surround the population problem because three ultimate human values—individual freedom, justice, and security-survival—compete for recognition. Callahan accepts the view that individual freedom occupies a position of primacy, but he holds that it is possible for considerations of personal freedom to be overridden by considerations of justice and/or considerations of security-survival. Thus, under certain conditions, he finds governmental policies "beyond family planning" to be ethically acceptable. Callahan considers several types of proposed governmental programs, evaluating them in terms of the three ultimate human values referred to above. He concludes by formulating some general ethical guidelines.

Throughout its history, the human species has been preoccupied with the conquest of nature and the control of death. Human beings have struggled to survive, as individuals, families, tribes, communities, and nations. Procreation has been an essential part of survival. Food could not have been grown, families sustained, individuals supported, or industry developed without an unceasing supply of new human beings. The result was the assigning of a high value to fertility. It was thought good to have children: good for the children themselves, for the parents, for the society, and for the species. While it may always have been granted that extenuating circumstances could create temporary contraindications to childbearing, the premise on which the value was based endured intact. There remained a presumptive right of individual procreation, a right thought to sustain the high value ascribed to the outcome: more human beings.

That the premise may now have to be changed, the value shifted, can only seem confounding. As Erik Erikson has emphasized, it is a risky venture to play with the "fire of creation," especially when the playing has implications for almost every aspect of individual and collective life [1]*. The reasons for doing so would have to be grave. Yet excessive population growth presents such reasons— it poses critical dangers to the future of the species, the ecosystem, individual liberty and welfare, and the structure of social life. These hazards are serious enough to warrant a reexamination and, ultimately, a revision of the traditional value of unrestricted procreation and increase in population.

The main question is the way in which the revision is to proceed. If the old premise—the unlimited right of and need for procreation—is to be rejected or amended, what alternative premises are available? By what morally legitimate social and political processes, and in light of what values, are the possible alternatives to be evaluated and action taken? These are ethical questions, bearing on what is taken to constitute the good life, the range and source of human rights and obligations, the requirements of human justice and welfare. If the ethical problems of population limitation could be reduced to one overriding issue, matters would be simplified. They cannot. Procreation is so fundamental a human activity, so wide-ranging in its personal and social impact, that controlling it poses a wide range of ethical issues. My aim here is primarily to see what some of the different ethical issues are, to determine how an approach to them might be structured, and to propose some solutions.

With a subject so ill-defined as "ethics and population limitation," very little by way of common agreement can be taken for granted. One needs to start at the "beginning," with some basic assertions.

FACTS AND VALUES

There would be no concern about population limitation if there did not exist evidence that excessive population growth jeopardizes present and future welfare. Yet the way the evidence is evaluated will be the result of the values and interests brought to bear on the data. Every definition of the "population problem" or of "excessive population growth" will be value-laden, expressive of the ethical orientations of those who do the defining. While everyone might agree that widespread starvation and malnutrition are bad, not everyone will agree that crowding, widespread urbanization, and a loss of primitive forest areas are equally bad. Human beings differ in their assessments of relative good and evil. To

*Ed. note—Footnotes and references appear at the end of this article, p. 370, for ease of cross-reference.

say that excessive population growth is bad is to imply that some other state of population growth would be good or better—for example, an "optimum level of population." But as the demographic discussion of an optimum has made clear, so many variables come into play that it may be possible to do no more than specify a direction: "the desirability of a lower *rate* [italics added] of growth" [2].

If the ways in which the population problem is defined will reflect value orientations, these same definitions will have direct implications for the ways in which the ethical issues are posed. An apocalyptic reading of the demographic data and projections can, not surprisingly, lead to coercive proposals. Desperate problems are seen to require desperate and otherwise distasteful solutions [3]. Moreover, how the problem is defined, and how the different values perceived to be at stake are weighted, will have direct implications for the priority given to population problems in relation to other social problems. People might well agree that population growth is a serious issue, but they might (and often do) say that other issues are comparatively more serious [4]. If low priority is given to population problems, this is likely to affect the perception of the ethical issues at stake.

WHY ETHICAL QUESTIONS ARISE

Excessive population growth raises ethical questions because it threatens existing or desired human values and ideas of what is good. In addition, all or some of the possible solutions to the problem have the potential for creating difficult ethical dilemmas. The decision to act or not to act in the face of the threats is an ethical decision. It is a way of affirming where the human good lies and the kinds of obligations individuals and societies have toward themselves and others. A choice in favor of action will, however, mean the weighing of different options, and most of the available options present ethical dilemmas.

In making ethical choices, decisions will need to be made on (i) the human good and values that need to be served or promoted—the ends; (ii) the range of methods and actions consistent and coherent with those ends—the means; and (iii) the procedure and rationale to be used in trying to decide both upon ends and means and upon their relation to each other in specific situations—the ethical criteria for decision-making. A failure to determine the ends, both ultimate and proximate, can make it difficult or impossible to choose the appropriate means. A failure to determine the range of possible means can make it difficult to serve the ends. A failure to specify or articulate the ethical criteria for decision-making can lead to capricious or self-serving choices, as well as to the placing of obstacles in the way of rational resolution of ethical conflicts.

In the case of ethics and the population problem, both the possibilities and the limitations of ethics become apparent. In the face of a variety of proposals to solve the population problem, some of them highly coercive, a sensitivity to the ethical issues and some greater rigor in dealing with them is imperative. The most fundamental matters of human life and welfare are at stake. Yet because of the complexity of the problem, including its variability from one nation or geographical region to the next, few hard and fast rules can be laid down about what to do in a given place at a given time. . . .

362

GENERAL ETHICAL ISSUES

Philosophically, solving the population problem can be viewed as determining at the outset what final values should be pursued. The reason, presumably, that a reduction in illiteracy rates is sought is that it is thought valuable for human beings to possess the means of achieving knowledge. The elimination of starvation and malnutrition is sought because of the self-evident fact that human beings must eat to survive. The preservation of nonrenewable resources is necessary in order that human life may continue through future generations. There is little argument about the validity of these propositions, because they all presuppose some important human values: knowledge, life, and survival of the species, for instance. Historically, philosophers have attempted to specify what, in the sense of "the good," human beings essentially seek. What do they, in the end, finally value? The historical list of values is long: life, pleasure, happiness, knowledge, freedom, justice, and self-expression, among others.

This is not the place to enter into a discussion of all of these values and the philosophical history of attempts to specify and rank them. Suffice it to say that three values have had a predominant role, at least in the West: freedom, justice, and security-survival. Many of the major ethical dilemmas posed by the need for population limitation can be reduced to ranking and interpreting these three values. Freedom is prized because it is a condition for self-determination and the achievement of knowledge. Justice, particularly distributive justice, is prized because it entails equality of treatment and opportunity and an equitable access to those resources and opportunities necessary for human development. Security-survival is prized because it constitutes a fundamental ground for all human activities.

Excessive population growth poses ethical dilemmas because it forces us to weight and rank these values in trying to find solutions. How much procreative freedom, if any, should be given up in order to insure the security-survival of a nation or a community? How much security-survival can be risked in order to promote distributive justice? How much procreative freedom can be tolerated if it jeopardizes distributive justice?

Ethical dilemmas might be minimized if there were a fixed agreement on the way the three values ought to be ranked. One could say that freedom is so supreme a value that both justice and security-survival should be sacrificed to maintain it. But there are inherent difficulties in taking such a position. It is easily possible to imagine situations in which a failure to give due weight to the other values could result in an undermining of the possibility of freedom itself. If people cannot survive at the physical level, it becomes impossible for them to exercise freedom of choice, procreative or otherwise. If the freedom of some is unjustly achieved at the expense of the freedom of others, then the overall benefits of freedom are not maximized. If security-survival were given the place of supremacy, situations could arise in which this value was used to justify the suppression of freedom or the perpetuation of social injustice. In that case, those suppressed might well ask, "Why live if one cannot have freedom and justice?"

For all of these reasons it is difficult and perhaps unwise to specify a fixed and abstract rank order of preference among the three values. In some circumstances, each can enter a valid claim against the others. In the end, at the level of abstractions, one is forced to say that all three values are critical: none can permanently be set aside.

THE PRIMACY OF FREEDOM

In the area of family planning and population limitation, a number of national and international declarations have given primacy to individual freedom. The Declaration of the 1968 United Nations International Conference on Human Rights is representative [5, 6]: ". . . couples have a basic human right to decide freely and responsibly on the number and spacing of their children and a right to adequate education and information in this respect." While this primacy of individual freedom has been challenged [7], it retains its position, serving as the ethical and political foundation of both domestic and foreign family planning and population policies. Accordingly, it will be argued here that (i) the burden of proof for proposals to limit freedom of choice (whether on the grounds of justice or security-survival) rests with those who make the proposals, but that (ii) this burden can, under specified conditions, be discharged if it can be shown that a limitation of freedom of choice in the name of justice or security-survival would tend to maximize human welfare and human values. This is only to say that, while the present international rank order of preference gives individual freedom primacy, it is possible to imagine circumstances that would require a revision of the ranking.

One way of approaching the normative issues of ranking preferences in population limitation programs and proposals is by locating the key ethical actors, those who can be said to have obligations. Three groups of actors can be identified: individuals (persons, couples, families), the officers and agents of voluntary (private-external) organizations, and the government officials responsible for population and family planning programs. I will limit my discussion here to individuals and governments. What are the ethical obligations of each of the actors? What is the right or correct course of conduct for them? I will approach these questions by first trying to define some general rights and obligations for each set of actors and then by offering some suggested resolutions of a number of specific issues.

I begin with individuals (persons, couples, families) because, in the ranking of values, individual freedom of choice has been accorded primacy by some international forums—and it is individuals who procreate. What are the rights and obligations of individuals with regard to procreation?

Individuals have the right voluntarily to control their own fertility in accordance with their personal preferences and convictions [5]. This right logically extends to a choice of methods to achieve the desired control and the right to the fullest possible knowledge of available methods and their consequences (medical, social, economic, and demographic, among others).

Individuals are obligated to care for the needs and respect the rights of their existing children (intellectual, emotional, and physical); in their decision to have a child (or another child), they must determine if they will be able to care for the needs and respect the rights of the child-to-be. Since individuals are obliged to respect the rights of others, they are obliged to act in such a way that these rights are not jeopardized. In determining family size, this means that they must exercise their own freedom of choice in such a way that they do not curtail the freedom of others. They are obliged, in short, to respect the requirements of the common good in their exercise of free choice [8]. The source of these obligations is the rights of others.

The role of governments in promoting the welfare of their citizens has long been recognized. It is only fairly recently, however, that governments have taken a leading role in an antinatalist control of fertility [9]. This has come about by the establishment, in a number of countries, of national family planning programs and national population policies. While many countries still do not have such policies, few international objections have been raised against the right of nations to develop them. So far, most government population policies have rested upon and been justified in terms of an extension of freedom of choice. Increasingly, though, it is being recognized that, since demographic trends can significantly affect national welfare, it is within the right of nations to adopt policies designed to reduce birthrates and slow population growth. . . .

In any case, the premise of my discussion will be that governments have as much right to intervene in procreation-related behavior as in other areas of behavior affecting the general welfare. This right extends to the control of fertility in general and to the control of individual fertility in particular. The critical issue is the way in which this right is to be exercised—its conditions and limits—and that issue can only be approached by first noting some general issues bearing on the restriction of individual freedom of choice by governments.

Governments have the right to take those steps necessary to insure the preservation and promotion of the common good—the protection and advancement of the right to life, liberty, and property. The maintenance of an orderly and just political and legal system, the maintenance of internal and external security, and an equitable distribution of goods and resources are also encompassed within its rights. Its obligations are to act in the interests of the people, to observe human rights, to respect national values and traditions, and to guarantee justice and equality. Since excessive population growth can touch upon all of these elements of national life, responses to population problems will encompass both the rights and the obligations of governments. However, governmental acts should represent collective national decisions and be subject to a number of stipulations. . . .

SOME SPECIFIC ETHICAL ISSUES

Since it has already been contended that individual freedom of choice has primacy, the ethical issues to be specified here will concentrate on those posed for governments. This focus will, in any event, serve to test the limits of individual freedom.

Faced with an excessive population growth, a variety of courses are open to governments. They can do nothing at all. They can institute, develop, or expand voluntary family planning programs. They can attempt to implement proposals that go "beyond family planning" [10].

Would it be right for governments to go beyond family planning if excessive population growth could be shown to be a grave problem? This question conceals a great range of issues. Who would decide if governments have this right? Of all

365

the possible ways of going beyond family planning, which could be most easily justified and which would be the hardest to justify? To what extent would the problem have to be shown to be grave? As a general proposition, it is possible ethically to say that governments would have the right to go beyond family planning. The obligation of governments to protect fundamental values could require that they set aside the primacy of individual freedom in order to protect justice and security-survival. But everything would depend on the way they proposed to do so.

Would it be right for governments to establish involuntary fertility controls? These might include (if technically feasible) the use of a mass "fertility control agent," the licensing of the right to have children, compulsory temporary or permanent sterilization, or compulsory abortion [10]. Proposals of this kind have been put forth primarily as "last resort" methods, often in the context that human survival may be at stake. "Compulsory control of family size is an unpalatable idea to many," the Ehrlichs have written, "but the alternatives may be much more horrifying . . . human survival seems certain to require population control programs. . . ." [3, p. 256]. Their own suggestion is manifestly coercive: "If . . . relatively uncoercive laws should fail to bring the birthrate under control, laws could be written that would make the bearing of a third child illegal and that would require an abortion to terminate all such pregnancies" [3, p. 274].

That last suggestion requires examination. Let us assume for the moment that the scientific case has been made that survival itself is at stake and that the administrative and enforcement problems admit of a solution. Even so, some basic ethical issues would remain. "No one," the United Nations has declared, "shall be subjected to torture or to cruel, inhuman, or degrading treatment or punishment" [11, Article 5]. It is hard to see how compulsory abortion, requiring governmental invasion of a woman's body, could fail to qualify as inhuman or degrading punishment. Moreover, it is difficult to see how this kind of suggestion can be said to respect in any way the values of freedom and justice. It removes free choice altogether, and in its provision for an abortion of the third child makes no room for distributive justice at all; its burden would probably fall upon the poorest and least educated. It makes security-survival the prime value, but to such an extent and in such a way that the other values are ignored altogether. But could not one say, when survival itself is at stake, that this method would increase the balance of good over evil? The case would not be easy to make (i) because survival is not the only human value at stake; (ii) because the social consequences of such a law could be highly destructive (for example, the inevitably massive fear and anxiety about third pregnancies that would result from such a law); and (iii) because it would be almost impossible to show that this is the *only* method that would or could work to achieve the desired reduction in birthrates.

Would it be right for governments to develop "positive" incentive programs, designed to provide people with money or goods in return for a regulation of their fertility? These programs might include financial rewards for sterilization, for the use of contraceptives, for periods of nonpregnancy or nonbirth, and for family planning bonds or "responsibility prizes" [10, p. 2]. In principle, incentive schemes are noncoercive; that is, people are not forced to take advantage of the incentive. Instead, the point of an incentive is to give them a choice they did not previously have.

Yet there are a number of ethical questions about incentive plans. To whom would they appeal most? Presumably, their greatest appeal would be to the poor, those who want or need the money or goods offered by an incentive program; they would hold little appeal for the affluent, who already have these things. Yet if the poor desperately need the money or goods offered by the incentive plan, it is questionable whether, in any real sense, they have a free choice. Their material needs may make the incentive seem coercive to them. Thus, if it is only or mainly the poor who would find the inducements of an incentive plan attractive, a question of distributive justice is raised. Because of their needs, the poor have less choice than the rich about accepting or rejecting the incentive; this could be seen as a form of exploitation of poverty. In sum, one can ask whether incentive schemes are or could be covertly coercive, and whether they are or could be unjust [12]. If so, then while they may serve the need for security-survival, they may do so at the expense of freedom and justice.

At least three responses seem possible. First, if the need for security-survival is desperate, incentive schemes might well appear to be the lesser evil, compared with more overtly coercive alternatives. Second, the possible objections to incentive schemes could be reduced if, in addition to reducing births, they provided other benefits as well. For instance, a "family planning bond" program would provide the additional benefit of old-age security [13]. Any one of the programs might be defended on the grounds that those who take advantage of it actually want to control births in any case (if this can be shown). Third, much could depend upon the size of the incentive benefits. At present, most incentive programs offer comparatively small rewards; one may doubt that they offer great dilemmas for individuals or put them in psychological straits. The objection to such programs on the grounds of coercion would become most pertinent if it can be shown that the recipients of an incentive benefit believe they have no real choice in the matter (because of their desperate poverty or the size of the benefit); so far, this does not appear to have been the case [14].

While ethical objections have been leveled at incentive programs because of some experienced corrupt practices in their implementation, this seems to raise less serious theoretical issues. Every program run by governments is subject to corruption; but there are usually ways of minimizing it (by laws and review procedures, for instance). Corruption, I would suggest, becomes a serious theoretical issue only when and if it can be shown that a government program is *inherently* likely to create a serious, inescapable, and socially damaging system of corruption. This does not appear to be the case with those incentive programs so far employed or proposed.

Would it be right for governments to institute "negative" incentive programs? These could take the form of a withdrawal of child or family allowances after a given number of children, a withdrawal of maternity benefits after a given number, or a reversal of tax benefits, to favor those with small families [10, p. 2]. A number of objections to such programs have been raised. They are directly coercive in that they deprive people of free choice about how many children they will have by imposing a penalty on excess procreation; thus they do not attach primary importance to freedom of choice. They can also violate the demands of justice, especially in those cases where the burden of the penalties would fall upon those children who would lose benefits available to their siblings. And the penalties would probably be more onerous to the poor than to the rich, further increasing the injustice. Finally, from quite a different perspective, the social consequences of such programs could be most undesirable. They could, for instance, worsen the health and welfare of those mothers, families, and children who would lose needed social and welfare benefits. Moreover, such programs could be patently unjust in those places where effective contraceptives do not exist (most places at present). In such cases, people would be penalized for having children whom they could not prevent with the available birth control methods.

It is possible to imagine ways of reducing the force of these objections. If the penalties were quite mild, more symbolic than actual [as Garrett Hardin has proposed (15)], the objection from the viewpoint of free choice would be less; the same would apply to the objection from the viewpoint of justice. Moreover, if the penalty system were devised in such a way that the welfare of children and families would not be harmed, the dangerous social consequences would be mitigated. Much would depend, in short, upon the actual provisions of the penalty plan and the extent to which it could minimize injustice and harmful social consequences. Nonetheless, penalty schemes raise serious ethical problems. It seems that they would be justifiable only if it could be shown that security-survival was at stake and that, in their application, they would give due respect to freedom and justice. Finally, it would have to be shown that, despite their disadvantages, they promised to increase the balance of good over evil— which would include a calculation of the harm done to freedom and justice and a weighing of other, possibly harmful, social consequences.

An additional problem should be noted. Any penalty or benefit scheme would require some method of governmental surveillance and enforcement. Penalty plans, in particular, would invite evasion—for example, hiding the birth of children to avoid the sanctions of the scheme. This likelihood would be enhanced among those who objected to the plan on moral or other grounds, or who believed that the extra children were necessary for their own welfare. One does not have to be an ideological opponent of "big government" to imagine the difficulties of trying to ferret out violators or the lengths to which some couples might go to conceal pregnancies and births. Major invasions of privacy, implemented by a system of undercover agents, informants, and the like, would probably be required to make the scheme work. To be sure, there are precedents for activities of this kind (as in the enforcement of income tax laws), but the introduction of further governmental interventions of this kind would raise serious ethical problems, creating additional strains on the relationship between the government and the people. The ethical cost of an effective penalty system would have to be a key consideration in the development of any penalty program.

Would it be right for governments to introduce antinatalist shifts in social and economic institutions? Among such shifts might be a raising of marriage ages, manipulation of the family structure away from nuclear families, and bonuses for delayed marriage [10, pp. 2–3]. The premise of these proposals is that fertility patterns are influenced by the context in which choices are made and that some contexts (for example, higher female employment) are anti- rather than pronatalist. Thus instead of intervening directly into the choices women make, these proposals would alter the environment of choice; freedom of individual choice would remain. The attractiveness of these proposals lies in their noninterference with choice; they do not seem to involve coercion. But they are not without their ethical problems, at least in some circumstances. A too-heavy weighting of the environment of choice in an antinatalist direction would be tantamount to an interference with freedom of choice—even if, technically, a woman could make a free choice. In some situations, a manipulation of the institution of marriage (for example, raising the marriage age) could be unjust, especially if there exist no other social options for women.

The most serious problems, however, lie in the potential social consequences of changes in basic social institutions. What would be the long-term consequences of a radical manipulation of family structure for male-female relationships, for the welfare of children, for the family? One might say that the consequences would be good or bad, but the important point is that they would have to be weighed. Should some of them appear bad, they would then have to be justified as entailing a lesser evil than the continuation of high birthrates. If some of the changes promised to be all but irreversible once introduced, the justification would have to be all the greater. However, if the introduction of shifts in social institutions had some advantages in addition to antinatalism—for instance, greater freedom for women, a value in its own right—these could be taken as offsetting some other, possibly harmful, consequences. . . .

A RANKING OF PREFERENCES

Ethical analysis can rarely ever say exactly what ought to be done in x place at y time by z people. It can suggest general guidelines only. I want now to propose some general ethical guidelines for governmental action, ranking from the most preferable to the least preferable.

1) Given the primacy accorded freedom of choice, governments have an obligation to do everything within their power to protect, enhance, and implement freedom of choice in family planning. This means the establishment, as the first order of business, of effective voluntary family planning programs.

2) If it turns out that voluntary programs are not effective in reducing excessive population growth, then governments have the right, as the next step, to introduce programs that go beyond family planning. However, in order to justify the introduction of such programs, it must be shown that voluntary methods have been adequately and fairly tried, and have nonetheless failed and promise to continue to fail. It is highly doubtful that, at present, such programs have "failed"; they have not been tried in any massive and systematic way [16].

3) In choosing among possible programs that go beyond family planning, governments must first try those which, comparatively, most respect freedom of choice (that is, are least coercive). For instance, they should try "positive" incentive programs and manipulation of social structures before resorting to "negative" incentive programs and involuntary fertility controls.

4) Further, if circumstances force a government to choose programs that are quasi- or wholly coercive, they can justify such programs if, and only if, a number of prior conditions have been met: (i) if, in the light of the primacy of free choice, a government has discharged the burden of proof necessary to justify a limitation of free choice—and the burden of proof is on the government (this burden may be discharged by a demonstration that continued unrestricted liberty poses a direct

threat to distributive justice or security-survival); and (ii) if, in light of the right of citizens to take part in the government of their country, the proposed limitations on freedom promise, in the long run, to increase the options of free choice, decisions to limit freedom are collective decisions, the limitations on freedom are legally regulated and the burden falls upon all equally, and the chosen means of limitations respect human dignity, which will here be defined as respecting those rights specified in the United Nations' "Universal Declaration of Human Rights" [11]. The end—even security-survival—does not justify the means when the means violate human dignity and logically contradict the end.

As a general rule, the more coercive the proposed plan, the more stringent should be the conditions necessary to justify and regulate the coercion. In addition, one must take account of the possible social consequences of different programs, consequences over and above their impact on freedom, justice, and security-survival. Thus, if it appears that some degree of coercion is required, that policy or program should be chosen which (i) entails the least amount of coercion, (ii) limits the coercion to the fewest possible cases, (iii) is most problem-specific, (iv) allows the most room for dissent of conscience, (v) limits the coercion to the narrowest possible range of human rights, (vi) threatens human dignity least, (vii) establishes the fewest precedents for other forms of coercion, and (viii) is most quickly reversible if conditions change.

While it is true to say that social, cultural, and political life requires, and has always required, some degree of limitation of individual liberty—and thus some coercion—that precedent does not, in itself, automatically justify the introduction of new limitations [17]. Every proposal for a new limitation must be justified in its own terms—the specific form of the proposed limitation must be specifically justified. It must be proved that it represents the least possible coercion, that it minimizes injustice to the greatest extent possible, that it gives the greatest promise of enhancing security-survival, and that it has the fewest possible harmful consequences (both short- and long-term). . . .

REFERENCES AND NOTES

¹ E. H. Erikson, *Insight and Responsibility* (Norton, New York, 1964), p. 132.

² B. Berelson, in *Is There an Optimum Level of Population?*, S. F. Singer, Ed. (McGraw-Hill, New York, 1971), p. 305.

³ See, for instance, P. R. Ehrlich and A. H. Ehrlich, *Population, Resources, Environment Issues in Human Ecology* (Freeman, San Francisco, 1970), pp. 321–324.

⁴ A 1967 Gallup Poll, for example, revealed that, while 54 percent of those surveyed felt that the rate of American population growth posed a serious problem, crime, racial discrimination, and poverty were thought to be comparatively more serious social problems. J. F. Kanther, *Stud. Fam. Plann.* No. 30 (May 1968), p. 6.

⁵ *Final Act of the International Conference on Human Rights* (United Nations, New York, 1968), p. 15.

⁶ "Declaration on Population: The World Leaders Statement," *Stud. Fam. Plann.* No. 26 (January 1968), p. 1.

⁷ For instance, not only has Garrett Hardin, in response to the "The World Leaders' Statement" (6), denied the right of the family to choose family size, he has also said that "If

we love the truth we must openly deny the validity of the Universal Declaration of Human Rights, even though it is promoted by the United Nations" [*Science 162*, 1246 (1968)]. How literally is one to take this statement? The declaration, after all, affirms such rights as life, liberty, dignity, equality, education, privacy, and freedom of thought. Are none of these rights valid? Or, if those rights are to remain valid, why is only the freedom to control family size to be removed from the list?

[8] See A. S. Parkes, in *Biology and Ethics*, F. J. Ebling, Ed. (Academic Press, New York, 1969), pp. 109–116.

[9] In general, "antinatalist" means "attitudes or policies directed toward a reduction of births," and "pronatalist" means "attitudes or policies directed toward an increase in births."

[10] See B. Berelson, *Stud. Fam. Plann.* No. 38 (February 1969), p. 1.

[11] "Universal Declaration of Human Rights," in *Human Rights: A Compilation of International Instruments of the United Nations* (United Nations, New York, 1967).

[12] See E. Pohlman and K. G. Rao, *Licentiate 17*, 236 (1967).

[13] See, for instance, R. G. Ridker, *Stud. Fam. Plann.* No. 43 (June 1969), p. 11.

[14] The payments made in six different family planning programs are listed in *Incentive Payments in Family Planning Programmes* (International Planned Parenthood Federation, London, 1969), pp. 8–9.

[15] G. Hardin, *Fam. Plann. Perspect. 2*, 26 (June 1970).

[16] See D. Nortman, in *Reports on Population/Family Planning* (Population Council, New York, December 1969), pp. 1–48. Judith Blake is pessimistic about the possibilities of family planning programs [*J. Chronic Dis. 18*, 1181 (1965)]. See also J. Blake [*Science 164*, 522 (1969)] and the reply of O. Harkavy, F. S. Jaffe, S. M. Wishik [*Ibid.* 165, 367 (1969)].

[17] See E. Pohlman, *Eugen. Quart. 13*, 122 (June 1966): "The spectre of 'experts' monkeying around with such private matters as family size desires frightens many people as being too 'Big Brotherish.' But those involved in eugenics, or psychotherapy, or child psychology, or almost any aspect of family planning are constantly open to the charge of interfering in private lives, so that the charge would not be new. . . . Of course, many injustices have been done with the rationale of being 'for their own good.' But the population avalanche may be used to justify—perhaps rationalize—contemplation of large-scale attempts to manipulate family size desires, even rather stealthily." This mode of reasoning may explain how some people will think and act, but it does not constitute anything approaching an ethical justification.

QUESTIONS

1. Callahan rejects the contention that we have an *unlimited* right of procreation. Can any argument be made in support of such a right?

2. Callahan alludes briefly to the responsibility of individuals in making procreative choices: "They are obliged, in short, to respect the requirements of the common good in their exercise of free choice. The source of these obligations is the rights of others." What concrete obligations are entailed by this general view?

3. Callahan contends that every government is morally obligated to establish family planning programs before having recourse to any other measures of population control. Is this requirement well grounded?

4. Construct your own assessment of the ethical acceptability of the various measures "beyond family planning."

SUGGESTED ADDITIONAL READINGS

Berelson, Bernard. "Beyond Family Planning." *Science,* vol. 163, pp. 533–543 (Feb. 7, 1969). Berelson wrote this article while he was president of the Population Council. He provides an exhaustive categorization of proposals that go "beyond family planning" for the sake of "solving" the population problem. He then appraises these proposals in terms of technological readiness, political viability, administrative feasibility, economic capability, *ethical acceptability,* and presumed effectiveness.

Blackstone, William T., ed. *Philosophy and Environmental Crisis.* Athens: University of Georgia Press, 1974. This excellent anthology provides a collection of articles representing diverse philosophical reactions to a demand for the development of an "environmental ethic."

Passmore, John. *Man's Responsibility for Nature.* New York: Charles Scribner's Sons, 1974. In this book, entirely devoted to ecological themes, Passmore provides chapters on what he sees as the four major areas of ecological concern: pollution, conservation, preservation, multiplication (population). He also discusses those Western traditions which have given rise to various contemporary attitudes toward the environment.

Wogaman, J. Philip, ed. *The Population Crisis and Moral Responsibility.* Washington, D.C.: Public Affairs Press, 1973. This anthology emphasizes theological perspectives but contains articles by ethicists and population experts as well. The various articles are collected in four separate sections: (1) the moral basis of policy objectives; (2) the moral responsibility of government; (3) moral analysis of policy proposals; (4) moral responsibility of religious communities.

Acknowledgments

Chapter 1—Abortion

Roe v. Wade, 410 U.S. 113, 93 S.Ct. 705 (1973).

John T. Noonan, Jr., from *The Morality of Abortion: Legal and Historical Perspectives,* Harvard University Press, 1970, pp. 51–59. Reprinted by permission.

Mary Anne Warren, from "On the Moral and Legal Status of Abortion," *The Monist,* January 1973, Vol. 57, No. 1. Reprinted by permission of The Open Court Publishing Company and the author.

Daniel Callahan, from *Abortion: Law, Choice and Morality* by Daniel Callahan. Copyright © 1970 by Daniel Callahan. Reprinted with permission of Macmillan Publishing Co., Inc.

Chapter 2—Euthanasia

In the Matter of Karen Quinlan, An Alleged Incompetent; Docket No. C-201-75, Superior Court of New Jersey, Chancery Division, Morris County (November 10, 1975).

An Act Relating to the Right to Die with Dignity, Florida Legislature, HB 2614 (1971).

Yale Kamisar, "Euthanasia Legislation: Some non-Religious Objections," 1958. Reprinted by permission of the *Minnesota Law Review* and the author.

Glanville Williams, "Euthanasia Legislation: Rejoinder to non-Religious Objections," 1958. Reprinted by permission of the *Minnesota Law Review* and the author.

James Rachels, "Active and Passive Euthanasia." Reprinted with permission from *The New England Journal of Medicine,* Vol. 292, pp. 78–80, January 9, 1975.

Tom L. Beauchamp, "A Reply to Rachels on Active and Passive Euthanasia," © 1976 by Tom L. Beauchamp. Excerpted from a longer article and reprinted by permission of the author.

Chapter 3—The Death Penalty

Furman v. Georgia, 408 U.S. 238, 92 S.Ct. 2726 (1972).

Jacques Barzun, "In Favor of Capital Punishment," *The American Scholar,* Vol. 31, no. 2, Spring 1962. Reprinted by permission.

Sidney Hook, "The Death Sentence," from *The Death Penalty in America* (New York, 1967). Reprinted by permission of the author.

Hugo Adam Bedau, "Death as a Punishment," from *The Death Penalty in America* by Hugo Adam Bedau. Copyright © 1964, 1967 by Hugo Adam Bedau. Reprinted by permission of Doubleday & Company, Inc.

374

G. L. Simons, from *Pornography without Prejudice*, Copyright © 1972 by G. L. Simons. Reprinted by permission of Abelard-Schuman, Ltd., publisher.

E. J. Mishan, "Making the World Safe for Pornography," *Encounter*, March 1972. Reprinted by permission.

Joel Feinberg, "Harmless Immoralities and Offensive Nuisances," from *Issues In Law and Morality*, ed. by N. Care and T. Trelogan, Case Western Reserve University Press, 1973. Reprinted by permission.

Chapter 8—Violence

Dennis v. United States, 341 U.S. 494, 71 S.Ct. 857 (1951).

Maurice Cranston, "Ethics and Politics," *Encounter*, Vol. 38, 1972. Reprinted by permission of the author.

Newton Garver, "What Violence Is," *The Nation*, 1968. Revised version. Reprinted by permission.

Robert Audi, "Violence, Legal Sanctions, and Law Enforcement," from *Reason and Violence*, ed. by Sherman M. Stanage, published 1974 by Littlefield, Adams, and Company. Reprinted by permission.

Sidney Hook, "The Ideology of Violence," *Encounter*, vol. 34, 1970. Reprinted by permission.

Arnold S. Kaufman, "Democracy and Disorder," from *Society: Revolution and Reform*, ed. by Robert H. Grimm and Alfred M. McKay, 1971. Reprinted by permission of The Press of Case Western Reserve University.

Chapter 9—Economic Injustice

Goldberg v. Kelly, 397 U.S. 254, 90 S.Ct. 1011 (1970).

Joel Feinberg, from *Social Philosophy*, © 1973, pp. 107–117. Reprinted by permission of Prentice-Hall, Inc., New Jersey.

Peter Singer, "Famine, Affluence, and Morality," from *Philosophy and Public Affairs*, Vol. 1, no. 3, copyright © 1972 by Princeton University Press. Reprinted by permission.

Garrett Hardin, "Living on a Lifeboat," reprinted with permission from *BioScience*, October, 1974, published by the American Institute of Biological Sciences.

Chapter 10—Environmental and Population Control

Boomer v. Atlantic Cement Company, 26 N.Y. 2d 219, 257 N.E. 2d 870, 309 N.Y.S. 2d 312 (1970).

William T. Blackstone, "Ethics and Ecology," from *Philosophy and Environmental Crisis*, University of Georgia Press, 1974. Reprinted by permission.

John Passmore, "Conservation and Posterity," reprinted by permission of Charles Scribner's Sons from *Man's Responsibility for Nature* by John Passmore. Copyright © 1974 by John Passmore.

Joel Feinberg, "The Rights of Animals and Unborn Generations," from *Philosophy and Environmental Crisis*, University of Georgia Press, 1974. Reprinted by permission.

Daniel Callahan, "Ethics and Population Limitation," *Science*, Vol. 175, No. 4, February 1972. Reprinted by permission.

WALT FREEMAN
(213) 924- 8570
        v 8767

        5th floor corner lab
           (left front)